TO THE STORM

China, 1985

TO THE STORM

The Odyssey of a
Revolutionary Chinese Woman

RECOUNTED BY YUE DAIYUN

WRITTEN BY CAROLYN WAKEMAN

UNIVERSITY OF CALIFORNIA PRESS

BERKELEY   LOS ANGELES   LONDON

University of California Press
Berkeley and Los Angeles, California
University of California Press, Ltd.
London, England
© 1985 by
The Regents of the University of California
Printed in the United States of America
1 2 3 4 5 6 7 8 9

Library of Congress Cataloging in Publication Data

Yüeh, Tai-yün.
  To the storm.

  Includes index.
  1. Yüeh, Tai-yün. 2. College teachers—China—
Biography. I. Wakeman, Carolyn. II. Title.
LA2383.C52Y849 1985   378′.12′0924   85-8482
ISBN 0-520-05580-2 (alk. paper)

I have walked through these twenty-one years one step at a time, and I am convinced that not a single step was taken in vain. My only wish is that we firmly remember this lesson paid for in blood, tears, hardship, and unimaginable suffering so that the actual situation can recover its true features and be recorded in the annals of history.

WANG MENG
Bolshevik Salute

CONTENTS

FOREWORD

A great part of China's recent history, back to the end of the Qing dynasty and through the two republics, has revolved around the nation's intellectuals. They founded the Communist Party and provided much of its leadership. The revolution was not finally consolidated until, as a group, they turned away from the Guomindang and gave the Communists their support. Yet the seeds of dissension were always present, not far below the surface.

The intellectuals in China have always been a class apart, a true elite. They were the self-proclaimed and socially recognized guardians of civic truth and moral rectitude. Their high status was earned by merit, through mastering the Confucian Classics and competing in national examinations. It could not be passed on by inheritance: each generation had to win it anew. The scholar son honored his scholar father by rearing his son as a scholar. Thus proud family traditions were built. In theory, one's life was devoted to governance and service to the country. That service, though, was never physical: the intellectual's long fingernails were a badge of privilege.

Of course, much of this changed with the twentieth century. Intellectuals were early rebels against the bonds of Confucianism. They led in exploring new ideas: constitutional monarchy, federal republicanism, anarchism, socialism, liberal democracy. They were an ever-ready activist force in the May Fourth Movement of 1919, and every other progressive movement of the passing years. Their self-image continued to demand selfless patriotism and a rightful voice in the nation's affairs. They shed the long fingernails, and after liberation considered themselves as one with the people. But some old habits and assumptions were not easily put aside. Many of

their compatriots saw them as elite, urban, and tied to the bourgeoisie. Who else, after all, could send their children to university?

After 1920, a powerful new doctrine found growing acceptance.
Marxism rivaled the discredited Confucianism in positive authority
and all-encompassing scope: that may have been part of its attraction. Like the Confucian monopoly of truth, it conceded no legitimacy to an opposition. It started, as usual, among intellectuals. To
assist and guide the young Party's development, watchful Russian
mentors selected the brightest and sent them to the fountainhead
to be crammed with Marxist dogma. But China, 80 percent rural
peasantry and lacking a sizable proletariat, did not fit the blue-
print. Mao Zedong, nativist and vigorous populist, had a different
design: peasant communism supported by people's war. This hung
on precariously until the Japanese attack in 1937 made it possible to
add peasant nationalism. After Japan's defeat, the combination was
more than the faltering Guomindang could match.

The intellectuals' share in this process was limited. Mao himself
was a self-made intellectual but not a typical one. As an indigent
young scholar he had met a cold shoulder at Peking University,
proud citadel of the intellectual establishment. His leadership of
the Party was won by twenty years of bitter struggle against those
Russian-trained intellectuals. Moreover, the Communist victory in
1949 required twenty-two years of continuous war—in the countryside, isolated from the cities. Thus, the overwhelming majority of
the Party and its cadres, the fighting men of the vast guerrilla ar-
mies, the rank and file of the liberated area governments, were all
from the countryside. Tough, spartan, self-confident, they often
had little book learning, and scant awe of city intellectuals who had
not joined in the long, hard fight.

In 1949 the countryside engulfed the cities. However, the guerrillas lacked the personnel and know-how to administer an urban,
industrializing society. Party and intellectuals found themselves
partners, but it was not an enthusiastic union of free choice. Each
side had doubts and reservations; each was ambivalent about the
other.[1] Power, though, resided firmly with the Party: thus its reservations were vital. Mao Zedong had stated some of them:

1. This situation of mutual reservations is cogently discussed by Suzanne Pep-

The revolutionary forces cannot be successfully organized and revolutionary work cannot be successfully conducted without the participation of revolutionary intellectuals. But the intellectuals often tend to be subjective and individualistic, impractical in their thinking and irresolute in action until they have thrown themselves heart and soul into mass revolutionary struggles, or made up their minds to serve the interests of the masses and become one with them. Hence although the mass of revolutionary intellectuals in China can play a vanguard role or serve as a link with the masses, not all of them will remain revolutionaries to the end. Some will drop out of the revolutionary ranks at critical moments and become passive, while a few may even become enemies of the revolution. The intellectuals can overcome their shortcomings only in mass struggles over a long period.[2]

Yue Daiyun's odyssey vividly documents the appalling costs of this mutual ambivalence: the tragic human cost in senseless suffering, and also the immeasurable cost to a developing country in the blind waste of the talents of its best-trained citizens. Yue Daiyun's observation point could not have been closer: she was in the vortex.

The third generation in an intellectual family, she won admission to prestigious Peking University, known as Beida, and journeyed north from her native Guizhou province. Despite the risks during the civil war, she committed herself by joining the Party. The class representative in her graduation ceremonies and a proven leader, she received the high accolade of a faculty position at Beida. Soon she married a young philosophy teacher, the son of a former president of the university and scion of a prominent intellectual family. As an intellectual, these qualifications were hard to match. There was also no flaw in her political credentials: she became secretary of the Party branch in her academic department.

The early years of the People's Republic were both a stimulating and a nervous time. At intervals, several well-known older intellectuals were targeted for criticism. In the spring of 1957, Yue Daiyun

---

per in *Civil War in China: The Political Struggle, 1945–1949* (Berkeley and Los Angeles: University of California Press, 1973); see especially chapter 6.

2. Mao Tse-tung, *Selected Works* (Peking: Foreign Languages Press, 1965), 2:322.

had a premonition of more turmoil to come. She expressed her thoughts in a poem entitled "To the Storm." It was not a cry of alarm or fear, for she had nothing to fear. Instead she explains, "However strong, however violent, I welcomed the approaching tempest because it would rouse people . . . and raise them to a new level of awareness; it would cleanse and renew everything, even my own heart, my soul, my will." Not Yue Daiyun, nor anyone else, could have imagined the future.

Yue Daiyun's poem has given us the title of her book. But, alas, she cannot provide us with the exact words. The reason why is a part of the story:

> The specific lines of this and other poems I wrote over the years have all been lost. Shortly after the onset of the Cultural Revolution in 1966, I burned my only copies, fearful that my verses would be seized by search parties of militant students and used as evidence somehow to incriminate me.

Her caution was prudent. "To the Storm" had already been appropriated by her critics and cited against her at the very outset of her troubles. The missing poems are thus part of her story, which, the reader should bear in mind, is wrested from her memory, without the help of diaries, letters, or other aids that we might wish had been available.

Yue Daiyun's premonition of upheaval was timely: it came within a few months. The catalyst was the Hundred Flowers campaign. Seeking more wholehearted cooperation, Mao Zedong—with Zhou Enlai certainly prominent in the background—urged the intellectuals to speak their minds. After much hesitation, they finally did— and critically, as Chinese intellectuals could be expected to. But not for long. There was an immediate and violent reaction from the massive anti-intellectual forces: the guerrillas of the long years in the countryside, the cadres and *apparatchiks* of the Party, reinforced perhaps in those days by close ties with the Party in Russia. This was the Anti-rightist Campaign. There would be lulls and then new campaigns, but for most intellectuals the travail and harassment seemed endless. For Yue Daiyun it lasted more than twenty-two years, until the autumn of 1979.

Some features of the roller coaster seemed unchanging. Once accused, the unfortunate individual was always at the head of the list for the next go-around. Even what may have been meant as a moderating admonition from on high ("Most of them are good, perhaps only 5 percent are bad") automatically became a quota for competitive compliance by the *apparatchiks* (it is much better to exceed than not meet one's quota). Guilt by association was elevated to new extremes, especially in requiring that "lines be drawn" even within nuclear families. Perhaps cruelest of all forms of guilt by association was to refuse the children of intellectuals any chance for higher education, thus denying them their intellectuals' heritage. And the changing political kaleidoscope (such as the rise and fall of Lin Biao and the Gang of Four) meant that the faithful orthodoxy of one day could become the treasonable heterodoxy of the next.

Yue Daiyun focuses, naturally, on the tribulations of the intellectuals. We tend to forget that they were not the only ones in China to suffer. Clearly in the Anti-rightist Campaign they *were* the principal victims. But each new major campaign expanded the target list. The Socialist Education Movement included many of the grassroot cadres. Then came the greatest convulsion of all, the Cultural Revolution, which began in 1966 and had not been fully resolved by 1979. Mao's original objective was political. He saw the Party abandoning his goal of continuing revolution and class struggle by following the Russian revisionist path and creating a new elite class separated from the people. His primary targets were the leaders of his own Party— Liu Shaoqi, Deng Xiaoping, and most of the others. But it was the universities that were producing the new elite. So the university heads were attacked, and then all who had served under them to carry out the policies of the time. Thus the intellectuals were singled out once again. But there was still another group of individuals who proportionately seem to have suffered more than any. These—surprisingly because it seems so illogical—were the senior military commanders, who had more than amply proved their loyalty in the Long March and Civil War.

As an informed, intimate history of those years, this book has much value. What makes it great is that it is far more than an account of human suffering. Yue Daiyun tells her story honestly and perceptively: the faults are not all on one side. We see an intellectual of immense courage, strength, and fortitude, a woman never cowed who, against incredible trials, struggles to preserve her family and to assure her children's future. In the end, after her long walk "one step at a time," she can still assert "that not a single step was taken in vain." [3] Her love of country, loyalty to the Party, and dedication to her country's future have survived. When she is finally rehabilitated and offered reinstatement in the Party, she accepts.

Yue Daiyun's story relates to a particular time and place, China during the past four decades. But out of her terrifying experience, she has given us an example and a testament of the indomitable human spirit that has meaning beyond time and place. Many of us tend to think, perhaps, that these events were somehow peculiarly Chinese or Communist. Strict comparisons are impossible, but what country is without some major historic episode of violent intolerance. Millions died in the Holocaust, for example. No one knows how many thousands were burned during the Inquisition. On a far more limited scale and without the crude violence, we had our own recent period of infamy that is commonly referred to as McCarthyism.

Is it possible that this kind of nightmare could return in China? Will there be another Cultural Revolution? As I understand Yue Daiyun, she thinks not. I agree. The experience affected the whole country and will not be forgotten. Practically all of the present leadership, from Deng Xiaoping and Hu Yaobang down, were themselves victims of the Cultural Revolution (fortunately, one can enjoy rehabilitation in China, if one survives). The old guard of guerrilla cadres has passed on or is being retired. Utopian Maoism has been set aside; and no future leader will forget that Mao's name in history would have been far greater were it not for the Cultural Revolution. The country is resolutely set on modernization and economic development. Far more than ever before, the intellectuals are needed; and this fact is recognized by Party and country. Fi-

---

3. From Wang Meng's *Bolshevik Salute,* quoted as the epigraph.

nally, the very appearance of this book itself is a hopeful sign. If it accurately reflects the continuing loyalty and commitment of the intellectuals, China's future is bright.

To Yue Daiyun, who has shared with us these painful but inspiring confidences of her heart and life, our gratitude is great. But we could not have had them without the painstaking, perceptive reconstruction by Carolyn Wakeman. They both deserve deep thanks.

John S. Service

PREFACE

One wintry Peking afternoon early in 1981, after I returned to the Friendship Hotel from the university where I taught English literature, a woman bundled in the ubiquitous padded greatcoat came to call, eager to discuss her plans for study in the United States the following year. She hoped to leave at the start of the summer, she explained, so that she could spend two months improving her English before beginning a year of research at Harvard University. As she talked with my husband in Chinese, I could understand enough of the conversation to notice that she spoke more openly about her life than many of our Chinese acquaintances. I was struck by the earnestness of her tone, the quiet animation of her voice, but most of all by her uncommonly expressive eyes. Later we went to her home to sample the cooking for which she is justly famous, after which she walked beside me to the bus stop, her arm linked through mine, venturing a number of sentences in her newly acquired English. Listening to her good-natured attempts to express herself in this unfamiliar tongue, I sensed a warmth, a generosity of spirit, that made me sorry her departure for Cambridge would put an end to our contact.

In the fall of 1982, I met Yue Daiyun at a small sidewalk restaurant near the Berkeley campus of the University of California. She had arrived some six weeks before to assume her post as research linguist at the university's Center for Chinese Studies and still felt quite out of place, repelled by the informality and spontaneity for which Berkeley is renowned. Several weeks later, her culture shock somewhat abated, we met for tea one afternoon to discuss our shared interest in recent Chinese literature, after which she told me something of her life as a schoolgirl in Guiyang. For the second time I realized that she spoke about her experiences with a candor I had never before encountered. Busy with our own lives, we met only occasionally that fall, but each time I found that I had learned something of unusual interest and value, and that a vast cultural distance had been bridged with surprising ease.

Early in 1983, as we worked together on a review article about women in recent Chinese fiction, I offered to write down some of her personal reminiscences, certain that they would benefit others besides myself. I could sense that in addition to completing her research on the fictional representation of Chinese intellectuals, she wanted to use her stay in the United States to write a second book, one that would tell her own story. Troubled that the experiences, the motivations, the responses of intellectuals during the thirty years after Liberation were not always accurately perceived abroad, she hoped to contribute to a fuller understanding of China in the West. At the same time, she believed that the life of a Chinese intellectual needed to be documented outside the realm of fiction, to be made part of the historical record, so that future generations at home could know, and consequently judge, the events of those three tumultuous decades. With our mutual goal the illumination of China's recent past, we decided, hesitantly at first, to proceed.

At the outset we met irregularly, enjoying the chance to talk together, but soon our meetings became a regular weekly occurrence, her accounts more systematic and also more intimate. By the end of her two-year stay in Berkeley, our homes just a five-minute walk apart, we saw each other almost daily. Often, quite incongruously, we would snatch the peaceful moments while my baby slept to detail the chaos and brutality of some phase of the Cultural Revolution. As she recounted her hopes, her frustrations, her sorrows, our friendship steadily deepened.

Over the months her English improved considerably, as did my familiarity with her patterns of speech. But her vocabulary was still limited, her explanations sometimes confused. After our talks I would spend hours at the typewriter, trying first to capture the range of her experiences, the nuances of her perceptions, and then to order and arrange her remembered time into something approximating an historical progression. Thus while the experiences, the sentiments, the insights, insofar as I could reproduce them accurately, are always Yue Daiyun's, the words, the sequence, and often the synthesis are necessarily mine. Indeed, the final rewriting of her story took place after Yue Daiyun had returned to China.

The present book has gone through many drafts, the first essentially a transcript of my notes of our conversations. Able to read English with relative ease, Yue Daiyun then supplied extensive revisions, answering my queries and probing her own memory to make her account of the past as precise and detailed as possible. The second draft incorporated those additions, while the third and fourth drafts further refined, organized, and focused the narrative. At each of these stages, she read and criticized the chapters with sensitivity and care. The book that has resulted from our countless meetings and discussions is thus truly a collaborative effort to chronicle the life of one woman against the turbulent backdrop of contemporary Chinese history.

Many friends and colleagues have generously contributed their time and support to this endeavor. In addition to the Center for Chinese Studies at Berkeley, we wish specifically to express appreciation to James H. Clark of the University of California Press, and to Margaret Carpenter, Betsey Cobb, Lowell Dittmer, Tom Engelhardt, Joyce K. Kallgren, David N. Keightley, Vannie Keightley, Phyllis Killen, Craig Mackay, Mel Mackay, Betsey Scheiner, Irwin Scheiner, Vera Schwarcz, Caroline Service, Tang Shuang, Frederic Wakeman, Sr., and James D. Wilkinson for their often extensive and always useful criticisms. We also wish to thank Frances Wilcox for her enthusiastic typing of the manuscript. Above all we want to convey our gratitude to John Stewart Service for his skillful editing and his wise counsel, and to Frederic Wakeman, Jr., for his patience as a husband, his encouragement as a friend, and his guidance as a scholar.

In the chapters that follow, the names of all prominent public figures, of family members, and of the deceased have been retained, the identities of others changed to accord them some anonymity.

Carolyn Wakeman

Berkeley
January 1985

CHRONOLOGY

1931	January 31	*Yue Daiyun (YDY) born in Guiyang, Guizhou.*
	September 18	Mukden Incident; start of Japanese aggression.
1937	July 7	Lugouqiao Incident; start of Anti-Japanese War.
1938	October	Capital moved to Chongqing; Guiyang a major war base.
1942		*Family moves to Huaxi, outside Guiyang.*
1945	August	Japan surrenders; end of WWII.
1946	March	General Marshall's mediation fails; civil war becomes general.
1948		*Enters Beijing University (Beida); active underground in CP Democratic Youth League.*
1949	February	PLA liberates Beijing.
	July 1	*Joins Communist Party.*
	October 1	People's Republic established in Beijing.
1950	May 4	*Leads students in May 4 celebrations.*
	Summer	*Delegate to 2nd World Student Congress, Prague.*
1951	Fall	*To Jiangxi with land reform team (to spring 1952).*
1952	Summer	*Graduates from Beida, selected as graduating class representative, joins Beida faculty as teacher in Chinese literature.*
	September	*Marries Tang Yijie (Lao Tang); lives with his family on Beida campus.*
1953	July	*Daughter, Tang Dan, born.*
1955	Summer	Campaign against counter-revolutionaries begins.
	September	*Reprimanded for taking leave to visit family in Guizhou; suspended from teaching and as Party branch secretary; becomes campus newspaper editor.*

Italic type records events in the life of Yue Daiyun and her family; roman type records the chronology of China's history during these years.

1956	May	Mao Zedong decrees: "Let a hundred flowers bloom."
	September	*Restored to teaching, and as Party branch secretary.*
1957	February	Mao's speech on internal contradictions within the people.
	May	*Organizes a new literary magazine; plan soon abandoned.*
	June	Beginning of Anti-rightist Campaign.
	December 24	*Son, Tang Shuang, born.*
1958	January 24	*Criticized as rightist.*
	February	*Declared a rightist; Party membership revoked; sentenced to labor.*
	Spring	Great Leap Forward commences.
	September	*Starts work in countryside at Zhaitang.*
1959	February	*Lives with old peasant family.*
	Autumn	Poor harvest and economic mismanagement cause famine.
1960	February	*Allowed 3-week visit to family in Beijing.*
	Summer	*Rightist cap removed.*
	Autumn	*Works on village history at Lingyuesi.*
	November	*Sent back to Beida.*
1961	February	*Denied teaching; assigned to write commentary on Tang poetry.*
1962	August	Beidaiho conference; Mao warns: "Never forget class struggle."
	Autumn	*Allowed to resume teaching, but of composition, not literature.*
1963		Socialist Education Movement.
	October 1	*Accompanies husband's family to be received by Mao Zedong at Tiananmen celebration.*
1964	Spring	Central Committee work team comes to Beida.
	Winter	*Summarily suspended from teaching.*
1965	February	*Selected for attack by Beida work team as example; target of 3 meetings.*
	June	*Assigned to gather material for movement to criticize bourgeois literary viewpoints.*
	July	International Hotel conference on education in Beijing; *Lao Tang important participant.*
	September	*Sent to Xiaohongmen in countryside to implement Four Clean-ups.*
	November 11	Yao Wenyuan article attacks Wu Han and commences Cultural Revolution.

Chronology

1966	February	Jiang Qing gives keynote speech at PLA conference on art and literature.
	May 25	Nie Yuanzi poster at Beida acclaimed by Mao Zedong.
	June	New work team sent to Beida.
	June 10	*YDY returns to Beida from Xiaohongmen.*
	June 18	Beginning of violence on Beida campus; *Lao Tang becomes a target; YDY assigned to physical labor on campus.*
	July 22	Mass meeting at Beida addressed by Jiang Qing; *YDY burns all her poems.*
	August	Period of anarchy and terror begins on campus; *Red Guards vandalize Tang family books and records; family forced to give up most of house.*
	August 18	First mass Red Guard parade in Tiananmen Square.
	September	*YDY's mother dies.*
1967		Campus torn by Red Guard factional warfare.
1968	January	*YDY moves to separate house with husband and children.*
	July	Workers' Mao Zedong Thought Propaganda Team takes control of campus.
	Autumn	Clean the Ranks movement commences. *Families divided and put in dormitories.*
1969	February	*YDY again attacked as rightist.*
	April	9th Party Congress; Lin Biao named Mao's successor.
	Autumn	*Tang Dan sent to Heilongjiang.*
	October	Alarm over threat of Soviet attack; *YDY sent to cadre school at Liyuzhou, Jiangxi.*
1970		Chi Qun given responsibility at Beida.
	Summer	Liyuzhou cadre school becomes branch campus of Beida; *YDY resumes teaching literature.*
	November	*Accident on abortive school trip to Jinggangshan.*
	December	*YDY on successful field trip to Anyuan and Jinggangshan.*
1971	May	Liyuzhou cadre school discontinued; *YDY returns to Beida.*
	September 12	Lin Biao flight and crash in Mongolia.
	Winter	Beida Big Criticism Group established to criticize Lin Biao.
1972		*YDY participates in physical labor and teaches about literary policy.*

Chronology

1978	Spring	*Tang Shuang enlistment rejected by PLA.*
	March	5th National People's Congress.
	July	*Tang Dan released from work assignment in Heilongjiang.*
	Summer	*Tang Dan and Tang Shuang again pass entrance exams but are denied university admission.*
	September	*Tang Shuang admitted to Science and Technology University at Hofei; Lao Tang released from detention.*
	Winter	Democracy Wall.
	December	3rd Plenum of 11th Central Committee confirms Deng Xiaoping and new policies.
1979	Spring	*Tang Dan admitted to branch of Beida.*
	Autumn	*Lao Tang resumes teaching philosophy at Beida.*
		YDY rehabilitated; Party membership restored.

The Goddess Departs

ACCORDING TO Chinese folklore a special goddess, named Songzi Niangniang, "the princess who sends children," is responsible for delivering babies into the world and for safeguarding them during the first perilous weeks after birth. Having remained beside them on earth for one month, this kind guardian returns to heaven, and that morning the baby smiles to bid farewell. Always we watch eagerly for that special smile, relieved that the goddess has departed and left the child safely behind.

Until recently, newborns were greatly at risk in China, and modern medicine has not totally quelled the apprehensions reinforced by centuries of parental loss and grief. Even today a baby's one-month birthday is considered an auspicious event, announced by sending out the red-dyed eggs that for generations have symbolized happiness and prosperity. It is an occasion for celebration and feasting when friends and relatives, confident that the child's continued presence in the family is now assured, drop by to offer gifts and congratulations and to enjoy the traditional snack of eggs poached in homemade sweet rice wine.

During this first month the mother must stay at home, her activities strictly curtailed to protect her health as she recovers from the birth. She must not venture outside, eat cold foods, wash her hair, or read books for fear that such actions might expose her to a chill or strain her eyes. Some people believe that she must not even brush her hair, close a door, or pour tea because of the danger of damaging her already weakened joints. And because she is still considered unclean, she may not touch anyone except members of her immediate family. Thus the one-month celebration commemorates the mother's freedom from confinement as well as the infant's safe entry into the world.

Our son was the first male grandchild in the family of Lao Tang's* parents, then in their sixties. It was only natural that they doted on this grandson, even though I had given them a granddaughter four years earlier. Each morning as they passed our bedroom door, they would pause to admire the new baby. Concerned about my health, Lao Tang's mother would look in from the corridor many times during the day, stopping to draw the pink satin quilt more tightly about my shoulders or to close the pale yellow curtains, certain that exposure to bright sunlight would injure my eyes. A beautiful woman with white hair and refined features, she always dressed in jackets and pants of blue or brown silk, her tiny bound feet clad in specially made black satin shoes. Admiring her kind and gentle disposition and realizing that she desired only to hasten my recovery, I never minded the many restrictions she imposed.

Shortly after my marriage in 1952 I had moved with my husband's family to this large, comfortable house on the campus of Beijing University, known as Beida, where my father-in-law, Tang Yongtong, was then a vice-president. In the area known as Yanjing South Courtyard were the former residences of faculty and administrators at the American-funded Yanjing (Yenching) University, whose site had been turned over to Beida after Liberation in 1949. Ours was a semidetached house, the other half of which was home to the family of Feng Youlan, one of Beida's most eminent philosophy professors. Built of gray brick with window frames painted a deep red, its dark tiled roof sloping down to meet gracefully upturned eaves, our house combined Chinese decor with Western

---

*"Lao," meaning "old," is a form of address commonly used in China instead of a given name to signal respect or familiarity. Yue Daiyun referred to her husband, her friends, and many of her colleagues in this way, with Lao as a prefix to the surname. Thus she called her husband, not Tang Yijie, but Lao Tang.

convenience. The bedroom I shared with Lao Tang had an adjoining bathroom, for example, and there was a large brick fireplace in the living room, a telephone in the hallway, and an oven in the spacious kitchen. Roses bloomed beside the bamboos in our front garden, and a strawberry bed had been planted in back. In these surroundings, unimaginably luxurious by Chinese standards, I had spent five happy years, far from my native Guizhou province.

On the day of our son's one-month celebration, I awakened very early to watch for the smile of the baby. Propped against the bed pillows, their white cases embroidered with blue chrysanthemum blossoms, I waited impatiently for Lao Tang to return. As I gazed at the tiny face smiling sweetly in my arms, I called to his father to come and see. Hearing no reply, I assumed Lao Tang must have gone out to help prepare for the day's festivities. Then through the door I heard him speaking in a muffled voice to Daolan, the kind and capable young woman who for ten years had helped Lao Tang's mother with the housework and meals.

"You must be careful; don't let her see it."

"I won't, you needn't worry."

"And my father is not to know either."

Cradling the baby contentedly and wishing that Lao Tang would hurry back, I wondered idly what they were talking about. I had no thought about politics or about my work, nor had I any idea my husband had hidden something from me. Because of lingering high blood pressure, I had been allotted two extra weeks of maternity leave, and the political issues of the day were far from my mind. I was surprised only that no one was talking about the one-month birthday or the banquet that was to be given for Lao Tang's relatives that evening.

The baby had been two weeks overdue, amazing everyone with his eight and a half pounds and with the abundance of his thick, black hair. Lao Tang's mother, intensely proud of this first grandson, had talked ever since the birth about giving a big party to celebrate his arrival. Several times we had discussed what the baby should wear, wanting to show him to advantage when the guests arrived. My mother had already sent us the customary gift of the maternal grandmother, a complete layette for the infant's first year, including ten pairs of embroidered satin shoes in graduated sizes. I had initially planned to wrap Tang Shuang in the quilt she had made of red and blue flowered satin, but had deferred to my mother-in-law, who thought her own gift of a crimson quilt more appropriate on such a happy occasion. After all this anticipation, it seemed strange that no one spoke of the celebration now that the day had arrived, that Lao Tang's mother had not come to see her grandson, and that Daolan had not gone out to buy food for the guests.

As the door opened, I saw immediately from Lao Tang's face that something was wrong. Standing beside the bed, he looked only at me, ignoring his son's endearing smile. Eager that nothing disrupt the peace and contentment of the moment, I continued humming the Brahms lullaby that had always been our favorite when our daughter was small. Still Lao Tang's expression did not soften. Something must have happened, I realized with a sinking feeling, something involving me. Clinging to the warm feelings of motherhood, I tried to perpetuate the illusion of well-being as long as possible. Lao Tang hesitated also, unable to begin, neither of us willing to break the awkward silence.

Outside the window the snow fell silently, coating the branches of the crabapple trees with white powder. In the pale light of early morning, I stared fixedly at the photograph that hung on the wall across from our bed. Taken a few days after our marriage, it captured the revolutionary spirit and the tender affection of those youthful days. When Lao Tang cleared his throat to speak, I saw tears in his eyes.

"Listen, we must talk about something very serious."

Despite his distress, I spoke lightly, struggling to preserve the special joy of that morning, determined not to be apprehensive. "What is it? Don't I have two more weeks of maternity leave? We will talk of work and politics later."

Lao Tang spoke urgently, "We cannot wait."

"Why?" I asked. "Can it be so pressing? Today is the one-month birthday of our son. Can't these other matters be put off?"

"No, we must talk about it now." He paused, then continued softly: "At ten o'clock you must attend a meeting to be criticized."

4

"But I'm on maternity leave," I protested.

"You still must go," he told me sadly. "They wanted you to appear ten days ago, and I pleaded with them to wait until this first month had passed. I told them you could not leave the house and finally they relented, but now you cannot delay, Xiao Dai.* You don't know how difficult it was to get them to postpone the meeting this long."

"Why should I be criticized?" I asked.

"They claim you are a rightist," he replied, his words low and tense with emotion.

"But," I objected, aghast, "I have never said anything against our Party or against Chairman Mao. I have never done anything to harm our country. In my heart I am completely loyal, you know that."

"I know, and I have been to your department and to mine, I have appealed and protested, but they just instruct me to draw a line separating myself from my wife."

Only later did I learn that Lao Tang had known for perhaps a month that I would be criticized, that he was disciplined for his defense of me, that he had received a serious warning from the Party. In a moment he remarked, his voice breaking, "As a husband I cannot even protect my wife." Then his tears of anger and frustration, so long suppressed, spilled out. Holding me tightly, he said with bitterness, "Sometimes people act just like wolves towards each other," echoing a line from *Jean Christophe*. He wept sadly, but at that time I had no tears.

My composure stemmed partly from disbelief. Surely such a serious accusation could not apply to me, I reasoned; surely the error would be quickly corrected. And partly it resulted from my greater familiarity with adversity. Lao Tang's life had always progressed smoothly. His father, a famous scholar of Buddhism and professor of philosophy, had received a master's degree from Harvard in 1921. Lao Tang's family had always been comfortable and affluent, his childhood sheltered from hardship and pain. During the war against Japan, when my own father's career as a middle-school

* "Xiao," meaning "small," is a diminuitive commonly used to convey familiarity and often affection. Thus Yue Daiyun's husband referred to her as Xiao Dai.

5

teacher had been interrupted and my family had fled frequently from enemy bombs, I had grown accustomed to danger, disruption, and scarcity, becoming resilient and adept at surviving. Now instead of thinking about my own situation I automatically began to comfort Lao Tang, trying to ease his distress.

"We must trust the Party," I assured him. "Even if in the short run something about my actions is seen to be wrong, the problem will be resolved quickly." I couldn't imagine that the situation was so serious, but neither could I block out a flood of painful memories.

It was January 24, 1958, just one month after the Christmas Eve birthday of our son. My two-month maternity leave had begun at the end of November, when Lao Tang's parents had persuaded me to stop work, knowing that I was exhausted and needed a rest. It had been a relief to leave the world of politics behind and to pass the days reading stories to my daughter, with whom I had spent little time in the preceding months, and rereading two French novels, Stendhal's *The Red and the Black* and Romain Rolland's *Jean Christophe*, both of which had long been translated into Chinese and were very popular.

Alleged to be important sources of support for reactionary students, these novels had come under sharp attack in the early summer. We were continually exhorted in those days to emulate the strength and selflessness of a simple screw, fitting in contentedly wherever the Party needed us, yet these two novels were said to encourage dissatisfaction with such self-effacing ideals and to stress instead the idea that creative individual effort makes life worthwhile. The novels were further accused of portraying individual rather than class struggle and of influencing the younger generation to chase after fame and fortune, thereby undermining the collective goal of serving the people. Having heard all of these allegations, I read the novels carefully, but never could I see any harm in enjoying such literary works, nor imagine that readers in China would actually take these foreign protagonists as models.

During those weeks of late pregnancy, I had made many trips downtown to the hospital so that my elevated blood pressure could be monitored. Worried about my health and that of our unborn child, Lao Tang had purposely kept me uninformed about the accelerating pace of the current political campaign. He had wanted the weeks before our baby's birth to be peaceful, restful ones for me, knowing how exhausted I had become by the beginning of November. The previous summer had been entirely occupied with political meetings, ever since June 8 when the official Party newspaper, *People's Daily*, had warned that counter-revolutionaries were trying to seize state power. This had marked the start of the Anti-rightist Campaign, and I, as head of the Party branch for teachers in the Chinese literature department, had been assigned many duties.

How quickly the atmosphere had changed. That spring had been a time of "blooming and contending" in response to Chairman Mao's call in May 1956 to "Let a hundred flowers bloom, let a hundred schools of thought contend." Intellectuals, still cautious after the attacks they had suffered in the campaign against counter-revolutionaries in 1955, had initially been slow to respond to the invitation to criticize the weaknesses of the Communist Party. But after Chairman Mao delivered his famous speech "On the Correct Handling of Contradictions among the People" in February 1957, many people were persuaded that their criticisms of the Party were genuinely welcomed, that the country would now move forward to a new era of openness, harmony, and progress. We held frequent meetings during which the teachers and students in our department were urged to speak out, to voice their opinions about the Party's shortcomings, and I wrote down everyone's comments, certain that many of these candid observations would help the Party improve.

When a rectification campaign was launched in April 1957 to strengthen the Party's work by eliminating the "triple evils" of subjectivism, sectarianism, and bureaucratism, I had shared excitedly in the spirit of confidence and optimism. Big character posters written on bright sheets of pink, yellow, and green paper had appeared on the notice boards outside the central dining hall, later on the walls of the building itself. Many of these were lengthy essays presenting thoughtful and searching analyses of such stirring questions as the role of democracy in a socialist system or the acceptability of official privilege in a society predicated on equality.

7

Some of the posters, written by people dissatisfied with the Party's accomplishments, contained bitter complaints that I thought departed too sharply from the official policies. At that time I could not condone the call for a complete reversal of Hu Feng's * verdict, for example, because I trusted the Party's allegations that he was a traitor and an agent of the Guomindang. I could not agree with the many posters that criticized the 1955 movement to eliminate counter-revolutionaries, even though this campaign had become excessive, because I thought it was necessary in a class struggle to kill those who were guilty. Above all I could not accept the posters attacking Chairman Mao personally, some of them comparing him to the Pope, and his writings to the Bible, for I believed without reservation in his greatness as the person who alone had been able to unify China and get rid of the foreign powers.

While disapproving of the most strident attacks, I nevertheless thought this opportunity to discuss such previously forbidden topics and express opinions freely about the Party's practices was the best way for the promise of Liberation to be fulfilled. I especially admired the probing essays written by the students of physics, who seemed the most sensitive, capable, and broad-minded of that generation. The students in my department had written many evocative poems appealing for a better future. One, entitled "Now Is the Time," became especially famous for it captured the prevailing sentiments of that exhilarating moment. The time was right, the student wrote, to examine the deficiencies of the society and the Party in order to make necessary improvements, to stand up and speak out in order to influence the leaders, to express individual opinions rather than obeying blindly in order to usher the country into a new epoch. All of these were goals that I fervently shared.

Yet despite my sympathy with those who were speaking out, some sense of inner caution prevented me from joining this chorus of critical voices. I felt it prudent to wait and see what would happen before commenting openly myself, and decided to participate in another way. Inspired by the open and permissive atmosphere

*Hu Feng, a prominent Marxist literary critic and follower of Lu Xun, was denounced for his bourgeois viewpoints in 1954 and made the target of a nationwide vilification campaign.

and believing that creativity could now be promoted to a new level, I joined together with seven other young teachers and graduate students in the Chinese literature department to discuss the formation of a new literary magazine. Even though unofficial journals were forbidden in China, we felt that the climate was right to undertake something new.

What we envisioned was an alternative to the established *Beida Journal*, a publication staffed by senior scholars that accepted only highly academic articles about literature, philosophy, and history. We wanted to provide a forum where younger intellectuals could explore contemporary problems, and called the proposed magazine *Contemporary Heroes*, borrowing the title of Lermontov's novel, to signify the role that we saw for ourselves as pathbreakers in this new era. Our purpose was to follow Chairman Mao's call and encourage everyone to develop his own talents for the building of the new China. Even though at twenty-six I was the eldest of this founding group, I was too busy with political responsibilities to accept the leadership of the new magazine, and suggested that Lao Lu, another young teacher and a close friend, take charge.

At our first meeting on May 16, believing the future to be bright and promising, we talked enthusiastically about providing some new perspectives on Chinese literary theory and practice. After a second meeting on May 20, however, we decided to suspend our discussions. Not only had we been unsuccessful at raising enough money to cover publication costs, but also we sensed a change in the political atmosphere. Perhaps the rectification movement was not as straightforward as we had imagined, in which case continued meetings would be ill-advised. Knowing that some of the small student groups had become increasingly radical, their attacks upon the Party more daring and drastic, we decided to wait and perhaps try to publish our journal later.

Suddenly, on June 8 the official editorial in *People's Daily* changed everything. The Party's line had reversed; a movement to rid the country of counter-revolutionary elements had begun in earnest. At a secret meeting for Party members, we listened to a Central Committee document that ominously declared the situation to be very serious. Some people, we were told, wanted to attack the

Party in order to gain control of the government. We must increase our vigilance, we must protect the class struggle, we must defend against class enemies. Everyone could interpret this as a warning to adopt from then on a completely different viewpoint toward the earlier posters and to criticize anyone who had expressed anti-socialist, or rightist, views.

Posters continued to appear, but after June 8 their content was utterly transformed as another group of spokesmen emerged to trumpet the new political line. In subsequent weeks I would read that critics who had attacked official privilege were really opposed to the Party, that people who had encouraged the expression of private opinions really thought some organization within the Party was oppressing the people, that those who had claimed democracy should be a goal for our country really desired to overthrow socialism, that any who had attacked the feudal remnants in the Party were really attacking Chairman Mao as a patriarch and thus were themselves counter-revolutionaries. Such an abrupt and total reversal left me confused and depressed.

The students who had spoken out in the spring I knew to be the most sensitive and intelligent members of their classes, the most thoughtful and far-sighted. But obviously another group, some of them simply obedient followers of the changing policy, others eager to become distinctive through displays of loyalty, had waited to see which way the wind would blow. Alert to the Party's signal that the criticisms had gotten out of hand, this second group had jumped to the attack, isolating those who had expressed opinions in the spirit of rectification. I had agreed with many in that first group, finding their contributions valuable and instructive, but suddenly those same people were being accused of opposing the Communist Party.

At a flurry of meetings, we Party leaders were told to separate the first group of dissident students out from the majority, to criticize them and expose the real faces that lurked behind their masks, to make clear the fact that inwardly those critics were opposed to Chairman Mao, to the Communist Party, to socialism itself. Each department had to select some people to be condemned as "bourgeois rightists," and the task of the four-person teachers' branch committee that I headed was to provide evidence and make suggestions, even though the final decisions about who would be labeled rightists would be made at a higher level by the Beida Party Committee.

I spent many hours that summer poring over the records of the rectification meetings held the previous spring, trying to decide who among the department's teachers should now be construed as enemies of the Party. We had been provided with examples, with the profiles of "standard persons," and we assiduously compared the cases of likely suspects with those prototypes. By November when I went on maternity leave, our Party branch had identified five people as possible rightists.

The first, a teacher in his early fifties, was not difficult to select, because his complicated past had already triggered the Party's suspicions. Skilled at reading classical texts, this Lao Yang had previously been a secretary to the warlord Feng Yuxiang, then had worked at a publishing house, and only recently had achieved his lifelong goal of becoming a teacher at Beida. Shortly after being appointed to this post, he had married, and his subsequent mood of confidence and optimism had prompted him to speak out all his thoughts after Chairman Mao's call in February. Quoting Mencius, he had asserted: "If you have morality, then you can oppose a person in power." Later, we interpreted this to mean that intellectuals were justified by their integrity to oppose Party officials. Lao Yang had also suggested that the Party had moved too fast in its campaigns, that movements like the collectivization of agriculture had sometimes made the peasants' situation worse. This indication that he preferred the old capitalist system to socialism led us to pronounce another of his crimes to be the belief that "today is not as good as yesterday." I had taken careful notes of Lao Yang's remarks, all of which had been offered in an effort to help the Party correct its mistakes. Later our branch committee read the transcript from a different perspective, singling out incriminating sentences and arranging them in a new way. This is how guilt was established at that time.

The second person to be accused was the vice-secretary of our branch committee, a young man from a middle peasant family who like me was a recent graduate of Beida. This Lao Xie had been so concerned to find ways to improve the work of the Party and had responded so earnestly when the critical posters had appeared, trying to understand how such weaknesses could have come about, that he had finally decided there must be something wrong with the system itself to have fostered the "triple evils." When we analyzed the record of his comments, we concluded that he wanted to overthrow socialism and promote democracy if he believed weaknesses were inherent in the socialist system. It was clear, given the criteria used at that time, that these first two could not escape the label of rightist.

The third, a young teaching assistant from Shanghai, open-minded, cheerful, and optimistic, an expert at English, was particularly concerned about international affairs. He had expressed the opinion that Khrushchev was correct in criticizing the blind belief in leaders and in opposing the blind worship of individuals. Like all of us, he had been deeply affected by a secret report in 1956 that named Stalin a dictator and urged the Russian people to guard against blindly worshipping a leader or clinging to superstitions about an individual ruler. The translated report had appeared in a lengthy wall poster on our campus, producing shock, dismay, and disillusionment in those of us who for years had revered Stalin. When we reviewed this young man's remarks, several people concluded that he must actually be attacking Chairman Mao if he opposed the worship of a leader.

Moreover, this Lao Wan had praised the Hungarian incident of 1956, an event that Mao Zedong had read as a warning about a leader's inability to control his people. Having learned of the Hungarian people's opposition to Stalin, Mao ultimately changed his mind about allowing the free expression of opinions in China, apparently fearful that he too might lose control of his populace. Because Lao Wan had stated that the Hungarian people were right to protest the Soviet Union's control of their country, he was also accused of opposing the Communist system. Disagreeing, I argued that he had just misunderstood the Hungarian situation, but my objections were overruled by the newly appointed branch vice-secretary, whose father was a dock worker and whose proletarian background made his influence with the department Party secretary far greater than mine.

The fourth suspect, Lao Pan, was a young teacher who had been a member of our magazine group. Having observed his repeated attempts to win the approval of anyone in a position of power, I had originally opposed his joining, but Lao Lu had accepted him, saying the group was open to all. This young man, whose academic record was excellent, wanted desperately to continue his study of literary theory in the Soviet Union, but his father was a landlord. Angry that his class background had denied him the chance to study abroad, he had spoken out bitterly when called upon to voice criticism, claiming that in the socialist system an individual's fortune was decided by his ancestors' tombstones. He had also complained that everyone's destiny was controlled by his file, referring to the brown paper folder in the university's central personnel office that contained reports about each person's political reliability.

This dossier was indeed influential. In those years an annual meeting was held for all the teachers in the department at which criticisms and self-criticisms were offered, written down by a recording secretary, and given to the branch leader for signature and comments. Those annotated transcripts were then sent to the Beida Party Committee to be placed in the person's dossier, along with the statements of friends and associates who had been asked to verify the individual's own account of his past history. The contents of the personnel files were secret and could be read only by the branch secretaries and higher Party cadres.

A person's future, this young teacher had alleged, is determined by his dossier; the leaders don't trust the people, but the files they trust absolutely. I argued that Lao Pan's remarks revealed not his opposition to the Party but his personal disappointment. On this case I was also overruled; although I could initiate discussion, I must finally bow to the will of the majority. After these two decisions, I felt discouraged and weary of such political debates.

The fifth person we proposed as a rightist, a recent graduate and just twenty-three, was talkative, broad-minded, well liked by his teachers and classmates, an active member of the Youth League, and the conductor of the department's student chorus. This Lao Shi had been alerted by a close friend who worked as assistant to the secretary of the Youth League's central committee about a major rift between Chairman Mao and Liu Shaoqi,* a division said to be of such consequence that it would influence everyone's life. Lao Shi, greatly concerned, had mentioned this split in the highest leadership to someone else, who had reported his comment. He was subsequently accused of spreading a rumor in an effort to divide the Central Committee of the Communist Party. This accusation was so serious that I dared not argue for him. On such an issue, no one would want to get involved.

As I reviewed the details of those cases, all thoughts of my baby's smile were chased from my mind, but still I could detect no reason for anyone to criticize me. I had never spoken out about the Party's failings during those months when frankness was encouraged. Moreover, the two meetings to plan our magazine had happened months ago. Ever since June it had remained only a conception. My thoughts raced to find some other action that might now make me vulnerable. I had gone to ask several professors to contribute financial support to the journal after informing the Beida Party Committee of our publication plans. Later that Party secretary had suggested I refrain from soliciting money in such a way, especially since I was a Party leader, but he had expressed no disapproval of the magazine itself. Before my maternity leave the journal plans had never been mentioned, and I saw no reason why they should suddenly make me a target of attack.

Nursing my baby one last time, I felt remarkably calm, confident that the problem would be cleared up. Mechanically I began to dress, pulling on the two dark-green sweaters that I wore each day, knowing I would not need my new wine-colored jacket or the baby's crimson quilt. There would be no guests, no festivities in the hours ahead. Lao Tang asked if he should walk to the meeting with me, but I dismissed his concern, concealing whatever apprehen-

---

*Liu Shaoqi, a member of the Politburo's standing committee and Mao Zedong's unofficial successor, formally became Chairman of the People's Republic in April, 1959.

sion and awkwardness I felt in this unfamiliar role. As a student and teacher, after all, I had always been one to criticize others, not to be criticized myself.

At the door I handed my baby to Daolan and pulled the fleece collar of my thickly padded overcoat higher around my neck. Above the white cotton square of the face mask I often wore in winter as a shield against the wind and dust, only my eyes could be seen. Today I needed protection not only from the cold but from the inquisitive, accusing stares I would soon have to face. Nonetheless, I felt strong and not easily intimidated.

I set off at a quick pace, knowing there was time for a walk around No-Name Lake, the most scenic part of the campus, and eager for a chance to compose my thoughts. In the distance I could see on the walls of the literature and history building a riot of posters, their edges tattered and flapping in the wind. I would have liked to walk closer, hoping for some clue to the accusations being leveled against me, but concern about meeting someone I knew held me back. Across the lake the graceful gray-tiled pagoda that I had so often admired seemed almost intentionally to deny me a glimpse of the shimmering reflection it cast on brighter days, and to loom menacingly against the wintry sky.

Nagging thoughts about the proposed magazine stubbornly resisted every effort to put my mind at ease. *Contemporary Heroes* had never been published, I kept reminding myself, trying to recall exactly what we had discussed in those two meetings held some seven months before. Reviewing the four feature articles planned for the first two issues, I tried to assess whether any could now be construed as anti-Communist, but I was out of touch with the antirightist movement and unfamiliar with the kinds of evidence currently being used to establish guilt.

One article, adapted from a young teacher's master's thesis, would have presented a new interpretation of Chairman Mao's "Yan'an Talks on Art and Literature" at Yan'an, urging that this influential address be used to encourage rather than restrict the development of Chinese literature. Lao Lu was to have provided an article challenging the official literary policies dictated by Zhou

15

Yang, the chief Party spokesman on cultural affairs, while I would contribute an essay promoting romanticism in modern Chinese literature. I intended to use the poems of Guo Moruo to stress the importance of individual liberation, of everyone's using and developing his talents to assist in the construction of socialism, but I had not yet found time to write my essay. In addition, we had planned to publish a novel, titled *The Degeneration of a General*, written by a journalist from *People's Daily*, a member of our group sent to Beida to improve his knowledge of literature. The plot reflected his boyhood experience in Yan'an as the aide-de-camp to a general in its account of a high military officer's transformation from hero to villain. Like every other piece to be included in *Contemporary Heroes*, it had been conceived in the spirit of openness and honesty that the Party leaders had encouraged.

Forcing my thoughts away from the magazine, I probed my earlier history, wondering what actions might have provided grounds for such a serious accusation. My commitment to the revolution and the Party had developed naturally out of the experiences of my middle-school years in Guizhou province, where I had seen abundant evidence of the Guomindang government's failings. I had observed the poverty of the people in Guiyang, the provincial capital, especially in the areas immediately outside the city. A family in those outlying districts might own just one pair of pants, so that only one person could leave the house at a time, the others remaining on the bed under a worn quilt until the pants could be passed to another wearer. Salt was so expensive, since Guizhou had neither seacoast nor salt mines, that a peasant family would often hang a small block of salt over the table for each person to lick after a bite of food. Such conditions made me long for fundamental changes.

Not only was the people's life hard, but evidence of Guomindang oppression was everywhere. Even students from my middle school had been arrested because of alleged Communist activities. The boy who sat behind me, a quiet, studious fellow, was met outside of class one day by two plainclothes policemen who escorted him roughly to a car and then gagged him so he couldn't cry out. It was all done quickly and quietly, and no one would have known about his disappearance had four of us not been on our way to the dining hall and seen what happened. We didn't dare report the abduction to the authorities, as anyone who complained about oppression would be accused of secret Communist Party connections. I knew my mother worried about my safety, aware that I often spoke critically of the Guomindang.

During those impressionable years I observed the behavior not only of Guomindang officials but also of their American allies, those foreign soldiers who seemed to me unbearably offensive as they waved beer bottles and shouted, "Yield!" when their jeeps drove through our city streets. How can they act that way, I often thought; this is my country. Sometimes they would pick up local girls and take them for rides in their jeeps just for fun. Once when I was swimming with my cousin in the river that ran in front of our house in the country, some American soldiers came along while we were lying on a bridge, drying off in the sun. One soldier put his arm around my cousin, then eighteen, and kissed her; I was frightened, angry, and deeply offended. Her brother knew English, having studied aeronautical engineering in the United States for two years, and went to the commanding officer to accuse the soldier, who then offered us an apology. Still, I could not forget the incident, and from the age of thirteen I always hated Americans.

Events such as the dance party in 1946, when someone turned off the lights and the G.I.'s all embraced and kissed their partners, reinforced my prejudice. Not liking to dress up or to dance with Americans, I had stayed at home, but from my middle-school classmates I heard vivid accounts of the incident. The details of the American soldiers' behavior may well have been exaggerated, but I was young and filled with outrage at the insult to my friends. Already in those years I had begun to believe that the hope for our future lay in the north with the Communist Party.

In 1948 when I graduated from middle school, I wanted to take the national examinations for university entrance, but they were not given in Guizhou province. Traveling to Chongqing to sit for the tests was a dangerous and expensive undertaking, and bus tickets were scarce. From attending Sunday English services held for American soldiers at the Guiyang Episcopal Church where I sang in the choir, I had come to know some of the missionaries. I respected these foreigners, so different from the offensive G.I.'s I had seen in the streets, and welcomed the chance to improve my English and at the same time enjoy the beautiful choral music. When the missionaries offered me transportation in their weekly truck to Chongqing, I accepted gratefully.

For ten days I sweltered in the heat of summertime Sichuan. With the other examinees I moved into a vacant dormitory at Chongqing University, choosing a bed platform at random and spreading out my mat and lightweight quilt. Not until the next morning when I awoke covered with bites did I notice the tiny red insects that lurked in the cracks between the bed boards. I had enough money for only two simple meals a day, and had to summon all of my energy for the first session of tests. For the next several days I strolled through the city streets, reviewing my notes to prepare for the final day of testing.

Through a family friend I was offered return passage in the back of an open truck carrying sacks of salt from Chongqing over the mountains to Guiyang. Grateful to be able again to travel free of charge, I ignored the hazards of this mode of transportation. The road was famous for its seventy-two curves, however, and as the truck lurched along I worried constantly that the weight of the load might shift, leaving me crushed beneath the heavy bags of salt.

When the examination scores were announced, I learned I was accepted at three universities, two in Nanjing, then the nation's capital, and one in Beijing. The first two would provide my educational expenses, and the college that trained Guomindang officials offered a generous monthly stipend in addition. But having seen the corruption of the Guomindang administration in Guizhou, I refused even to consider going to such a school. I was determined to study at Beida, the country's most prestigious, most progressive institution, even though no financial assistance would be provided.

My father strongly disapproved of my plan, uncertain how I would survive and aware that fighting had already broken out in North China. He tried to persuade me to stay at home, attend Guizhou University, then settle down and raise a family. Even in 1948 any young woman who left home and ventured forth on her own was assumed to be courting unhappiness, but I didn't want

18

the kind of peaceful life my father had chosen. My mother's encouragement that I pursue a more ambitious and independent path, despite its risks, fired my determination. I knew I would be plunging into a whirlpool of war, but I wanted to go north and join the struggle.

Some people said the dangerous journey to Beijing was an impossible undertaking for an eighteen-year-old girl. My mother had given me ten silver dollars and a gold ring; that was all I had. In those days there was no railway in Guizhou, and I had no money to buy a passenger bus ticket, so I traveled cheaply by cargo bus, arranged through a family friend. On this bus carrying tea and other merchandise to supply the owner's shops, I rode south for three days to Liuzhou in Guangxi province, the end of the rail line, sleeping at shabby roadside hostels along the way. Always the only woman in those dingy inns, I would struggle to close my ill-fitting door tightly, hoping to protect myself from the unsavory lodgers, most of whom were drivers and transport workers. Such men were notorious for having women at three or four homes on their route, and the thin walls, made only of rushes covered with lime, hardly muted their vulgar talk as they drank wine and played finger gambling games late into the night. Alarmed by their reputations and repelled by their language, I would try to calm my fears, block out the noise, and fall asleep.

At Liuzhou, dubbed the world's largest toilet because people waiting for trains north had no facilities to relieve themselves and just used the streets, I bought a rail ticket to Wuhan. From there I went by steamboat down the Yangzi River to Shanghai, and finally by ship from Shanghai to Tianjin. Those last two days and a night in the hold of a cargo vessel, the only passage I could afford, were a nightmare of continuous seasickness. At Wuhan, however, I had joined a group of more than twenty young people traveling to Beijing to study, having been notified in advance of a rendezvous point by the Beida Student Union, an organization with connections to the Communist underground. Our leader was a young physicist from Wuhan University who was going to Beida to study history, believing that a knowledge of the past would best equip him to serve society in the future. Warm, helpful, dedicated, this

19

Lao Chen immediately won our respect, and we joined him enthusiastically in singing folk ballads and revolutionary songs on the bus from Tianjin to Beijing.

By the time I arrived, I had three dollars left, having sold my gold ring for food. Because my father's salary was too high for me to qualify for a regular scholarship, a cousin, the son of my father's eldest brother and the magistrate of a county in Guizhou province, had certified that I belonged to the Miao minority, exaggerating my ancestry a bit. Thus I was able to receive the special financial support awarded minority students to pay for my food. I even received some warm clothing as well, donated by an American relief organization after the war, as protection against the bitter northern winters.

At Beida it was only natural for me to become involved with the underground student movement because of my hatred of the Guomindang. All of my work in this Democratic Youth League was conducted in the greatest secrecy, as discovery meant certain arrest. I never knew anyone in the organization except Lao Gu, my immediate leader. Together we would check the leaflets that were printed clandestinely by workers in the university print shop, looking for errors in the typescript. Enclosed between covers identical to those of well-known novels, these pamphlets described life in the Liberated Areas, and I felt very adventurous slipping out of my dormitory at night to proofread such materials, using a flashlight when the moon was not full. Even though Beijing was then under siege, such secret work seemed very romantic, as we students in the underground all felt deeply committed to the Communist cause. Lao Gu, who was six years older than I and from a Hunan peasant family, was very pragmatic about the Communist Party and what needed to be done to defeat the Guomindang, and sometimes criticized me for my romantic ideas.

After the proofreading work was completed, I helped prepare maps of important diplomatic and historic sites in Beijing to show the exact location of the embassies in the Legation Quarter and of such places as the Imperial Palace and the Temple of Heaven so that these monuments would not be damaged by the Communist artillery that was shelling the city. This was a particularly dangerous assignment as the streets were regularly patrolled by Guomindang soldiers. To prevent suspicion, Lao Gu and I would pretend to be a couple out for an evening stroll as we measured the distances between buildings.

I admired my leader greatly, aware of how much he knew about the Communist Party and about life in the Liberated Areas. From our talks I could envision a new society based on complete equality, free of corruption, so different from what I had known in the Guomindang-controlled areas of South China. When he suggested that we make emergency plans to escape to the Communist-controlled areas outside of the city and start a new life together, I agreed and even had my photograph taken to be used on a secret identification card in case such a flight should be necessary. A few months later, however, the general in charge of Beijing surrendered and the People's Liberation Army (PLA) entered the city. Soon the Party asked Lao Gu to go to work as a journalist at the *Workers' Daily*, and he urged me to go with him, saying that later on we would get married. I had always thought him a model Communist, strong, intelligent, and courteous, but I found his suggestion unwelcome, as I was not in love with him. After that our relationship became strained; he never concealed his anger at being rejected, and I felt great regret that our friendship, our bond of commitment to the same cause, had been destroyed. A year later he returned to Beida to ask me to reconsider his proposal, but by then I had met Lao Tang.

My life had been filled with promise in my student years, I thought, reviewing my political accomplishments in an effort to quell my mounting anxiety. My pace quickened; the time for my criticism meeting was approaching. Any of my colleagues could attest to my political loyalty, I reasoned. They knew that I was one of twenty students active in underground work to be admitted into the Party in 1949. The bright blue skies of that summer morning, the solemn ceremony, the heartfelt oath sworn before the Party flag, flashed before my mind. I had remained politically active throughout my years at Beida; I had always felt trusted, respected, useful. My classmates had even selected me to represent them in 1952, when all nine hundred seniors had pledged five *mao* from their first salary as a donation for a class gift, a flagpole surrounded by a handsome marble bench. I was the one to make the presentation at our graduation ceremony, offering a replica to the university president, who at that time was Lao Tang's father.* Tang Yongtong had looked at me with pride and happiness, knowing that soon I would marry his son. The students all knew as well, and when they clapped their hands so hard, I felt they were conveying to me an extra meaning. I was embarrassed, but also very happy.

So eager had I been to commit all my energy to the new China that after my daughter was born the next year I fell ill, requiring a lengthy operation to correct a thyroid problem and causing Lao Tang and his mother great anxiety during the eight hours I was under anesthesia. I had felt pulled in so many directions in the years after my graduation. Teaching, writing articles about literature, serving first as administrative secretary of the Chinese literature department, then as head of the teachers' Party branch when it was formed in 1956—all had been completely absorbing. My only regret was that I had little time to spend with my family.

Everyone was so optimistic about the future in 1956 that such personal sacrifice had seemed worthwhile. We had just completed a fundamental transformation of our economic system, reconstructing industry and collectivizing agriculture. Those who had previously expressed counter-revolutionary viewpoints had been exposed the previous year, some criticized, some jailed, in accordance with Mayor Peng Zhen's exhortation to make our capital as clean and sparkling as a crystal, free of criminals and political enemies. We believed that the groundwork had been completed; a new life lay ahead. In the universities we began studying in earnest, confident that we needed only knowledge to be able to construct a new country.

After Zhou Enlai's speech in January 1956, urging that intellectuals be given more authority and their contributions accorded more respect, our salaries were raised, our living and working conditions improved. Even our small needs were considered. On our campus, for example, there had previously been just one barber-

---

*Tang Yongtong was president of Beida from 1949 to 1952, and vice-president from 1952 until his death in 1964.

shop for the whole community of some eight thousand people, but now another was provided for the teachers. For people like me who had short hair, this one minor change saved much time. In addition, a special bus was provided twice a day for any teachers who needed to make the hour-long trip downtown, and this too was a great convenience, freeing us from waiting in long lines. Special restaurants were set up for teachers, and while these facilities were still crowded, they greatly reduced the length of time we had to wait for a meal.

By 1956 I had published perhaps a dozen articles, the most prominent being a survey of the development of modern Chinese fiction that was serialized in four issues of *Literary Studies*. Thus when the movement to "go forward with science" began, a campaign to raise the educational level of the teachers, I was selected, along with three people from the sciences, to give a talk at a meeting for the whole faculty. Viewed as a model Party member, I was asked to describe my experiences for the benefit of the others, and I spoke earnestly about how to accomplish useful work for society on the one hand, and how to pursue research, teach well, and be appreciated by the students on the other.

Everybody was excited in 1956; we thought the fight had finished and that we could concentrate finally on building our country. There was to be no more class struggle, no more antagonism; instead, the Party's policy was that people should develop themselves and thus contribute to the socialist future. I had even taken this opportunity to learn how to ice skate at night when finally the tasks of the day were finished. For several years I had wanted to try this sport, thinking how wonderful it would be just to glide across the frozen lake, an experience totally unknown to anyone from South China. Sometimes when I walked to an evening meeting at our department chairman's house, following the path around the lake, I would wedge my ice skates in between two large rocks and then on my way home stop for an hour to practice under the moonlight.

Now, passing the same familiar rocks in a far more somber mood, I recalled the atmosphere of that period and remembered those happy moments on the ice, unthinkable when everyone was preoccupied with political issues and such frivolous pastimes were frowned upon. Looking out across the lake, I could see that the area once used as a skating rink lay unswept, its surface brown with dust, littered with papers and twigs. In just one year so much had changed.

It was nearly ten o'clock. My history was irreproachable, my commitment to the Party obvious to everyone, I reminded myself one final time. Like the secretaries of the graduate students' branch and the visiting teachers' branch who had also joined the magazine group, I was a representative of the Party leadership; I couldn't possibly be accused of anti-Party intentions. Nevertheless, the confidence I had mustered for Lao Tang was ebbing. Feeling increasingly apprehensive, I thought of those sacks of salt towering above me as the truck wound its way up the steep road from Chongqing to Guiyang. Once again I seemed about to be crushed beneath some huge weight. Surely my innocence would be quickly established; surely I would not become a victim of the campaign I had so recently helped to wage.

A Chain of Judgment

OUTSIDE THE classroom building, wall posters attacking our magazine greeted me. Some proclaimed that Lao Lu and I advocated individual heroism and opposed Chairman Mao's thought; others announced, "The Traitor Yue Daiyun must be expelled," or urged people to "See the true face of *Contemporary Heroes*." Inside the door a poster declared this a "Meeting to denounce the reactionary gang of *Contemporary Heroes*," while an even more threatening banner warned: "If the rightists don't surrender we will smash them." In 1956 I had walked happily and confidently into this same lecture hall many times to deliver my course on the history of modern Chinese literature to perhaps a hundred eager students. Now I saw twice that many expectant faces, almost all of the teachers in the department and many students, but this time they looked at me suspiciously, condemningly, as I slid into an empty seat in the second row, feeling like a criminal about to be sentenced.

Recalling a scene from my childhood, I saw again the crowd that had gathered one summer's day in a small Guizhou town to watch a water buffalo being killed. The farmer, unable to feed his draft animal once it was too old to work in the fields, had no choice but to sell its hide for leather. We had all heard that when a buffalo was about to be slaughtered tears welled up in its eyes, as if in anticipation of its fate, and I had joined the group of onlookers waiting curiously to learn whether this rumor was true. Watching the buffalo kneel down, its eyes indeed brimming with tears, its expression suggesting that somehow it knew its destiny, I had felt enormous pity. Now as I glanced around the lecture room and saw the look of cold curiosity on the faces of those assembled to watch my own fate decided, I remembered that distant scene. Nobody spoke to me; some even seemed to wear looks of distinct satisfaction, perhaps thinking that now I would be judged, I who had been responsible for the condemnation of five other department members. The crowd seemed to be saying accusingly that now it was my turn.

Outside the window the snow kept falling, but everyone's attention was directed toward the drama about to be enacted inside those walls. Some eyes had sympathy, I could feel it, while others were merely detached, grateful that the proceedings would not concern them personally. Some were simply curious to see what would happen to such a woman, a person who had been sent to the Soviet Union and to Czechoslovakia as a representative of Beijing's students, a person who had been asked to report on her studies as a model for others, a person who had progressed so smoothly to be a high-ranking Party cadre, a person who had fallen so low.

My mind continued to race in the moments remaining before the meeting began. Again I remembered those five people I had helped to judge. Even when I had not understood the Party's decisions, even when I had disagreed, I had felt obligated to carry out official policy. A person in my position should always act with confidence to convince others, be worthy of the Party's trust, stifle any doubts or confusion, remembering always that the Party has greater wisdom than any individual, that it liberated all of China, that its judgment was therefore above question. Obedience to higher authority was pledged by everyone who joined the Party, and I had accepted this strict discipline willingly. Trusting in Chairman Mao and the Beida Party Committee, believing that they knew more than I, that their decisions must be necessary and correct, I had collected material that would be used to accuse five of my colleagues. Now I questioned those judgments.

Perhaps the others were just like me, never intending to do or say anything to harm the Party. Throughout my maternity leave, I had tried not to think about my role in that process, but now I saw a chain of involvement and accusation, with people meting out judgment and then being judged in turn. As I sat in the lecture hall, I too thought that now it was my turn.

The weekly campus newspaper that Lao Tang had concealed from me that morning, and that I read in the library out of curiosity only in 1979, had appeared with a single story occupying its entire second page, the headlines urging everyone in bold characters to "See the True Face of the Big Traitor Yue Daiyun." During the Anti-rightist Campaign there were many labels for those being attacked, "alien class element" for someone whose parents were deemed capitalists or landlords, or "counter-revolutionary" for someone thought to have opposed the Party. I was being termed a traitor, one of five types of counter-revolutionaries, and alleged to have betrayed the Communist cause. With Lao Lu I was accused of promoting individualism and undermining the socialist collective spirit, of insulting the PLA, and of attacking the leader of the literary field in China, all of which were anti-Communist acts. Even though I was not the head of the magazine group, I was being treated as the person responsible for its formation because of my Party position. The newspaper ran four articles about us, the central piece written by the Party secretary in my department.

Transferred to his position as a political cadre the previous summer, this man had formerly worked in a newspaper office and knew nothing about literature. In fact, before joining the Revolution he had been a primary-school principal, though himself only a middle-school graduate. His hostility toward intellectuals, whom he often accused of wanting to usurp the authority of the Party, was well known, perhaps a consequence of his own limited education. In this newspaper article he accused me of being an individualist, of setting myself apart from others, of acting according to my private convictions, and of organizing an anti-Party clique. New to the department, he wanted to show his revolutionary fervor.

One of the secondary articles offered further testimony about my individualist attitudes, claiming that I always liked to be the center of attention and that I favored doing things with a small group, practices that destroyed the unity of the collective. A third article attested that my attitudes were clearly individualistic, but ignored the question of whether I was a counter-revolutionary. A much less serious accusation, this opinion had been written by the department's Party vice-secretary, a man with whom I had often argued because of his formal, cautious manner and excessive concern with mechanical details, but whose viewpoint nevertheless was the least condemning. Later I learned that because he had insisted in the Party meetings that my individualist tendencies did not warrant labeling me a rightist, he was attacked and criticized in the Cultural Revolution.

All of these accusations were reiterated in the criticism meeting, when perhaps eight or nine people spoke out against me. Some of the speeches were just short admonishments, with people standing up to demand, "Why do you oppose the Party? What has it done to hurt you? The Party has helped you so much, yet you are ungrateful. You must confess what you have done; you must speak out what you really think." Other people argued in greater detail that the projected magazine was clearly anti-Communist, or that I was a member of an anti-Mao Zedong thought group that was attempting to tarnish the image of the PLA. Throughout those attacks I remained calm. But three people made statements that undermined my composure.

The first was a young man who had been criticized in 1955 for attacking the Communist Party during his student days at Yanjing University. The campaign against counter-revolutionaries was very intense at Beida that spring, and each department had to investigate whether it harbored any enemies in its midst. In the Chinese literature department no one could be found who clearly opposed the revolution, but still we had to carry out the Party's instructions, so we singled out several people whose past actions were open to question. One was this Lao Song, whom we claimed had written a reactionary article depicting the Communist Party as a dictatorship that oppressed the people. When we ordered him to reveal why he had written such things, to confess his purpose, and to identify who had asked him to make such statements, he replied evasively that he had written the piece for a Guomindang newspaper as a way of earning money, but that was a common excuse and we weren't satisfied. We pressed him to scrutinize his thoughts more closely and confess the real reason he had written such a piece.

Always the meetings in 1955 were like this, dragging on and on, and after several months I had become impatient, unable to discover anyone in our department who truly opposed the Party. Finally I asked permission to return to Guiyang to see my parents during the summer vacation. Without waiting for approval, I left Beijing with my brother, traveling by train to Guangxi province and then by bus for two additional days to Guiyang, singing folk songs all the way. It was a happy occasion to be reunited with my family after seven years and to see the many improvements that had occurred during my absence.

When I returned in September, I was criticized for having broken Party discipline and as a reprimand was removed from my academic work and my departmental Party position, and transferred to the university's weekly newspaper. My new assignment as editor was an interesting one, however, and I didn't mind such consequences, especially since in my absence the campaign against counter-revolutionaries had essentially been completed. After one year I was reassigned to my department at the urging of the chairman, and in the fall of 1956 was even allowed to teach a course to senior students on my own, rather than continuing to function as a teaching assistant. At the same time I was given the position of Party branch secretary.

Always afraid of the punishment that might someday befall him because of his "historical problem," and no doubt still bearing a grudge for my role in his criticism two years before, this Lao Song spoke out in the meeting to investigate me. Many times in the past months he had tried to consult me about his situation, he claimed, since as branch secretary I was responsible for the attitudes of all one hundred teachers in the department. Because I was a "bureaucratic person," too arrogant to concern myself with ordinary people's affairs, he continued, I had never been willing to meet with him despite his efforts. Once he had even gone to my home, only to find me still sleeping at eight o'clock in the morning and to be sent away by the *ayi**** at my instructions. These charges frightened me, for I was hearing what seemed a total fabrication. Then I realized that such an incident could have happened without my knowledge, that Daolan could have sent Lao Song away to protect me, eager for me to sleep late occasionally if I had been up past midnight attending a meeting. Although I did not feel responsible for the actions being criticized, Lao Song's comments made me suddenly aware that my behavior was not above reproach.

Next, one of my favorite students, a young man who had sought me out frequently after class, spoke up. We would sometimes spend an entire evening discussing literature, sharing our appreciation of poets like Xu Zhimou who could not be mentioned in class because of their allegedly bourgeois thoughts. I had even shown this Lao Lin one of my own poems, titled "To the Storm." In the spring of 1957, Lao Tang and I had been caught in a fierce downpour one day walking home from the Fragrant Hills. We had pressed on, thoroughly drenched, through the thunder and lightning, and the next morning I had written a poem to express premonitions about another oncoming storm. However strong, however violent, I welcomed the approaching tempest, I wrote, because it would rouse people from their routines and raise them to a new level of awareness; it would cleanse and renew everything, even my own heart, my soul, my will.

The specific lines of this and the other poems I wrote over the years have all been lost. Shortly after the onset of the Cultural Revolution in 1966, I burned my only copies, fearful that my verses would be seized by search parties of militant students and used as evidence somehow to incriminate me. Most of my poems, like this invocation to the storm, were lyrics, but my most famous one, written during the Korean War, had a political theme. I was in my third year of university in 1951, and we students were intensely angry at the United States, thinking that the Americans wanted to invade our country and subject us again to imperialist control. No one could bear to contemplate a return to that kind of subjugation and

---

**An *ayi*, or "auntie," is a person who helps with domestic work and child care.

humiliation, and we felt we must defend our motherland at all costs and keep the war outside our boundaries.

My poem urged that we protect the fruits of our revolution, which had been won with so much hardship and suffering. Addressed to Chairman Mao, it was titled, "If Only You Call Us." If only you call us, I had written, we will give up everything, our warm clothes, our comfortable homes, our secure jobs, and follow you. The poem became very popular, and many people wanted a copy. It was displayed on a wall poster on the campus, and every day young people from the neighborhood and students from middle schools would come to write down its words. Later it even won four prizes, from Beida, from the Beijing student union, from the Communist Youth League, and from the Canton Association of Literature. I was amazed that my poem was known so far away, but for years afterward when people were introduced to me they would recall those lines. It was not my best poem, but it captured a shared sentiment and expressed what people wanted to hear. Everyone felt proud that China had thrown off the imperialist powers and wanted to prevent that domination from recurring. Patriotic feelings were intense, though no one knew anything about the war really.

When Lao Lin stood up in the criticism meeting and claimed that I had used poetry like opium to harm the younger generation, I felt a stab of pain that my trust and confidence could be so betrayed. In a cold voice this young man asserted that while my poem "To the Storm" had spoken of renewing my soul, it was obvious that a person with a soul would not have tried to harm the youth of China. Then he became irate, shouting, "Stand up, stand up; you must take responsibility for poisoning so many students!" In Lao Lin's words, facts had become totally distorted, meaning falsified, intentions belied.

This student had just graduated. He hoped to stay at the university as a teacher, and knew that the competition for those coveted positions was keen. Future teachers would be chosen partly because of their academic achievements, but more importantly, because of their political reliability. I understood why he was speaking against me. After I was rehabilitated, Lao Lin told me he regretted having been so obedient to the leaders, but I knew that precisely because of our former closeness, he had felt compelled to draw a line between himself and me after I was declared an enemy.

The third person whose words stung me was Lao Pan, the young teacher whose membership in the magazine group I had initially opposed. Already a rightist himself, he was eager for a chance to lessen his own guilt, and his allegations were the most extreme. After Lao Lu had invited him to join the magazine, he declared, he had been uncertain, but since I, the branch secretary, was an active member, he had assumed that he should not hesitate. In those two meetings, he continued, the group members had attacked Zhou Yang because of their own ambitions for power; moreover, Yue Daiyun, not content just to be branch secretary, clearly aspired to the position of department chairman. When I heard such preposterous allegations, I grew amazed at the way the truth had become distorted, but because this man had been part of the group and present at its discussions, his testimony carried great weight.

The audience grew aroused, thinking all of us greedy for power. After those last charges everyone began to shout, "Stand up, you must stand up!" Finally I stood, but just for a short time, as the vice-secretary soon said, "Let her sit down and listen to the judgment of the people."

The accusations reverberated in my head. Since the facts are nothing like what I have heard, how can I know what is right or what my future will be, I thought despairingly. Before my maternity leave the anti-rightist meetings had been conducted differently; a person would be criticized, but no one shouted or demanded that the accused stand up. Now it was 1958 and the movement had grown more intense, dedicated to the eradication of the most elusive enemies who were said to be posing as loyal Party members to evade detection. The Party had instructed that the Anti-rightist Campaign must be conducted thoroughly, that no rightists could be allowed to escape, that a place like Beida should uncover even more rightists than the 5 percent expected of other work units. Accordingly, each department had searched again, going through lists of its members to see if anyone had been missed. It was at this point that our magazine group was reconsidered, the digging out of these enemies who pretended to be revolutionaries hailed suddenly as a great achievement of the movement. We were the last group of rightists to be so labeled at Beida.

My mind struggled to absorb my new circumstances, but I couldn't believe what had taken place. After the lecture hall emptied, I remained behind, plagued by self-doubts. Was I really a counter-revolutionary, I queried, recalling how deeply committed I had been to revolutionary ideals.

I thought back to my wedding day, to my efforts to make that a revolutionary occasion. My mother had sent me one hundred *yuan*, nearly three months' salary for a middle-school teacher, but all I had bought were the simple clothes I would wear that day and a dressing table with a large mirror. Lao Tang's mother had made all the bedding for us, colorful pillow covers and quilts, but I wanted none of the expensive suits, watches, jewelry, or radios that were typical betrothal gifts in those days, even though Lao Tang's mother gave me a gold watch, a gold bracelet, and a fur coat. Nor did I want to be transported in a rented car decorated with satin streamers and rosettes. Ignoring the tradition that a bride must be carried to her husband's home to show she is truly welcomed, I walked with my closest friend, Zhu Jiayu, from my dormitory along the canal to Lao Tang's house, where a tea party would be held for us after dinner. We two wore matching white blouses and similar skirts made of flowered cloth from the Soviet Union.

Lao Tang's home, then near Beihai Park in central Beijing, was built around a large courtyard where we had set out three tables with bowls of fruit and candy, peanuts and sunflower seeds, and a piece of pink silk on which the guests would write their names with brush and ink. I still keep that piece of silk as a memento, for some of the guests are now important leaders, and others have died in the Cultural Revolution. The courtyard was crowded with our classmates and friends. It was the day after our graduation ceremony, a date we had picked because soon the students would disperse, returning to their homes or setting out for new jobs.

First I gave a short speech about why we had decided to marry and what we planned for the years ahead. Now that I had become part of a bourgeois intellectual family, I announced, I would draw a line to keep from being wrongly influenced. I would keep our life revolutionary; our marriage would only increase and not detract from our contribution to the revolution. Because Tang Yijie and I were completely equal and shared the same political viewpoint, I concluded, we had decided to join our lives together. Next Lao Tang's father spoke, welcoming me to their family and pledging that they would treat me like the daughter they had never had. He was very kind, and though I feared he would be offended by my strong words, his face revealed no displeasure. He was famous for his tolerance and his ability to conceal personal feelings.

Finally, one of Lao Tang's closest friends from middle school spoke, the son of Wen Yiduo.* Determined to lighten the serious tone of this celebration, he made several joking remarks about the relationship between a man and a woman, implying that even in a revolutionary marriage newlyweds act like any other couple. Quoting Chairman Mao's principles for guerrilla warfare, he quipped: when the enemy approaches, you withdraw; when the enemy is tired, you attack; when the enemy protects itself, you advance. The blatant sexual innuendoes, clear to everyone, left me embarrassed and offended, for I idolized Chairman Mao and could not tolerate hearing his speech used so irreverently. The crude jokes about the married couple's behavior on their wedding night, though utterly conventional, seemed most inappropriate and distasteful given the serious atmosphere we had tried to create. That evening we returned to Lao Tang's small room at the school for local Beijing cadres where he taught theoretical philosophy, refusing to stay at his family's home as a further assertion of our independence. We were determined to renounce the values and practices of the old society and to set an example as revolutionaries.

As I recalled the intensity of my commitment to the ideals of the Party, I heard footsteps approaching from the back of the deserted lecture hall. My brother, then twenty-one and a student of physics at Qinghua University, had been sitting somewhere behind me all

*Wen Yiduo became famous as a romantic poet in the 1920s, and was assassinated by the Guomindang in Kunming in 1946 for his criticism of the Nationalist regime.

this time. Since I was now an enemy, he dared not speak and instead slipped a sheet of paper onto my knee as he walked past. All I saw was his back as he headed toward the door. On the paper was written one verse of the Stephen Foster folk song, "My Old Kentucky Home."

> Weep no more, my lady,
> Oh, weep no more today!
> We will sing one song for the old Kentucky home,
> For the old Kentucky home, far away.

We had always been very close, especially after 1940 when I would carry my brother on my back as we sought refuge from the Japanese air raids. Guiyang was only bombed six or seven times, but nearly every day the tall signal pole in the center of the city, just visible from our house, would raise one yellow ball of woven bamboo, meaning enemy planes were near and we must prepare for an attack. When two red balls appeared, we knew the planes were very close and we must immediately take shelter. Many times we sought refuge in a village outside the old city walls, fearing that we might be buried alive in the crowded bomb shelters. We never knew if our home would be destroyed while we were gone, so my mother would carry a bag containing food, money, and valuables, and my baby sister as well. I was nine and strong enough to hoist my brother onto my back for the half hour walk to the village. My father, then an English teacher in a Guiyang middle school that had moved outside of the city to Wudang because of the danger of enemy bombs, came home only on weekends and missed most of those hurried treks.

Sometimes we climbed a little way up the steep mountainside, seeking protection under the dense cover of bamboos and palm trees. Sometimes we stopped at a friendly peasant's house where we would be given food and hot water for a modest fee. Then in the late afternoon we would return home, knowing that the planes flew over only during daylight hours. Often I would pass the time amusing my brother with small sailboats made from bamboo leaves folded over at the ends.

I had also taken care of him when we lived in Huaxi, a village appropriately named the "brook of flowers," ten miles outside of Guiyang, where my father in 1939 had designed a rustic wooden cabin in a beautiful natural setting as a retreat from the city. In those years Huaxi was still a Miao area undiscovered by other Guiyang residents, and my father used his inheritance, his share of the gold, houses, and land left by my grandfather, to buy a piece of land on a hillside where honeysuckle and other wildflowers grew in profusion among the rocks. Sitting in bamboo chairs on the stone porch that extended the length of the cabin, we would look out across the clear green waters of the Huaxi River, its rocky bottom glistening in the sunlight, to the lush rice fields and irrigation ponds beyond. From 1942 to 1945, we lived in this five-room house year round, as Guizhou University, where my father was then teaching English literature, had moved to Huaxi to escape the Japanese air raids.

Greatly interested in Western culture, my father subscribed to *Life* and several other American magazines, and often would go by bus with my mother into Guiyang to see an American movie at one of the many commercial theaters, leaving me alone overnight to care for my brother and sister. After dinner we children would chase away our fear of the darkness by singing the Western folk songs I had learned in my middle school. I taught my brother one about San Francisco and one about hibiscus flowers in Hawaii, but our favorite was "My Old Kentucky Home." Sitting on the porch overlooking the river, we would sing this simple two-part harmony. Thus the folded paper my brother dropped into my lap evoked all the memories of our childhood together, and the closeness we had shared in that peaceful time now so far away. I understood that he hoped to ease my present pain by reminding me of our country home, reassuring me that such good times would come again.

I was still sitting there when Lao Tang appeared, worried about what had happened. I walked slowly home beside him, but hesitated at the door, unable to face his family. Then I heard the sound of crying and forgot everything except my baby's hunger. I opened the door, scooped Tang Shuang into my arms, and began to nurse. Finally my tears fell down, wetting his thick, black hair.

Although it was after one o'clock, the family had delayed lunch for me. Reluctantly, I left the seclusion of my bedroom, fighting against tears, certain I could not eat. Then I saw Lao Tang's brother's face, and my resolve stiffened. During the Korean War when the government had urged everyone to make a contribution for weapons, we had persuaded Lao Tang's mother to offer her gold jewelry to buy airplanes, and she had given us almost every piece. His father agreed with our request, but not his younger brother, who always resented me for helping dispose of his family's wealth. I, in turn, had little respect for him.

In high school he had found a very nice girl friend, and we had sometimes talked together or gone to movies. When she was accepted by a college in Baoding, he found it inconvenient to continue seeing her and broke off their relationship. She was heartbroken, but could not change his mind. While away at school she contracted a lung infection and, unable to get good medicine, became seriously ill. She sent for him to come and see her but he refused, and soon she died. Later he went to say farewell to her body, but still I could not forgive him for his heartlessness, thinking him cruel and selfish, and we quarreled. After that we spoke only when necessary. That day at the lunch table, seeing in his eyes some satisfaction at my shame, I grew determined not to reveal any weakness. I choked back tears and even managed to eat one bowl of rice, reminding myself sternly that as I faced my future I would have to be strong.

Back in our room, Lao Tang said nothing, knowing that no words could ease my distress. I pretended to read a novel, but my thoughts were far away. Uppermost in my mind was my mother and the pain that my condemnation as a rightist would bring her. I knew she had always looked to me to achieve what her own life had never allowed. When I went to the Soviet Union as a representative to the World Student Congress and when my brother was accepted at Qinghua with the highest grade on the entrance exam in all of Southwest China, she had been so proud and happy.

Her own father, a district magistrate, had died when she was twelve, her mother a year later, after which she had withdrawn from school to care for her younger sister. Capable and ambitious, she always dreamed of traveling to Beijing or Shanghai to continue her education, but having no money she married at seventeen, giving birth to me a year later in 1931. When I was three, frustrated at how little she had achieved in her life, she went with my father and me to Hangzhou to enroll in a one-year training course at an art institute, returning to Guiyang to teach painting at a middle school. Still feeling unchallenged, she decided after Liberation to study Russian by radio. Then in her forties, an age when women in China rarely break out of their established routines, she earned a high score on the exam and received her diploma. Since every middle school then wanted to offer a course in Russian, she had no difficulty finding a job and after two years of successful teaching was transferred to the Guizhou Agricultural Institute, where my father had become the head librarian. She remained there as an instructor of Russian until her retirement.

My father had been far more content with his life, having graduated from Beida in 1927 with a degree in English literature. Unlike his two best friends, he never became interested in politics, even in that year of great hope, and disappointment, for China's revolution, and refused to support either the Communists or the Guomindang. His goal was to return to Guiyang and lead a peaceful life of Wordsworthian simplicity and retirement. On his way back to his native city, his resolve was confirmed. Having stopped in Wuhan so that he might visit the nearby Lushan mountains, he again met his two closest classmates and listened unmoved to their separate entreaties that he join in their bitterly opposed political struggles. His tour of the scenic mountain area completed, he returned to Jiujiang to find one friend's head hanging from the city wall, a Guomindang warning about the fate that would befall Communist sympathizers. More than ever repelled by political activities, my father returned, appalled and grief stricken, to Guiyang to begin life as a middle-school teacher.

I knew that my mother had never been happy in her marriage, even though my father loved her deeply, for his was a smothering, controlling love that denied her any independence. She always resented his domination, believing that her own lack of education as well as his family's greater wealth would keep her forever subordinate to his authority. My paternal great-grandfather had been a prosperous merchant, originally from Jiangxi province, whose business in opium, sugar, and textiles had nine branches in cities like Wuhan, Hangzhou, and Shanghai. As a young child I loved to see the poppy fields in rural Guizhou ablaze with pink blossoms. My great-grandfather's success enabled him to select a different path for his two sons, whom he educated to be scholars and officials. My grandfather, the child of a Miao concubine, became well known in Guiyang as a poet and calligrapher, and his brother, a prominent architect in Beijing, became recognized both for his participation in the 1911 Revolution and for having written the first book on the history of Chinese architecture.

Like his father before him, my grandfather was very concerned about the proper education of his children. His first son went abroad to study chemistry at Harvard, where he became friends with Lao Tang's father; the second son studied business and became manager of the family enterprises; the third son was educated at Hamburg and became chairman of the geology department at Beida; the fourth son studied medicine in Shanghai and became a respected Guiyang physician; and my father, the youngest, who was expected to study economics and not English literature, became a teacher.

My mother was by temperament far more aggressive. An attractive woman, called the flower of her middle school, she was slightly taller than my father, a short man of undistinguished appearance. She always wished for a more successful and ambitious husband, and she longed for a career of her own.

My parents argued often during my childhood, usually because my father would impose his opinions and values on my mother, and I was painfully aware of her unhappiness. During the anti-Japanese war, after my father had quit his teaching job in Wudang to be with the family in Huaxi, we had very little money, but my mother wanted a new coat. One month when my father had some extra cash, he offered to buy one for her, or at least to help her shop, but she insisted on making her purchase alone and chose a coat of artificial fur that she found very beautiful. Disapproving of her choice, my father lost his temper and chided her for her lack of taste. A bitter argument ensued. My mother wept angrily, anguished that because she had no job she could exercise no choice of her own and utterly depressed at always having to submit to my father's will.

Then she left the house abruptly, disappearing down the path beside the river. After several hours my father began to worry and sent me out to search for her. It was after sunset, and I finally found her perched on a rock beside the river in the dusk, still weeping. She hugged me sadly and confessed her wish to jump into that clear water and end her suffering forever. We wept together; then I took her hand and led her home.

When I heard my parents' argument continuing, I felt so helpless, so frustrated, that my own life seemed unbearable. In my room I impulsively gulped down a whole bottle of liniment intended for massaging inflamed joints, knowing that the mixture contained alcohol and that the label warned the contents were poisonous. With the empty bottle in my hand, I ran to their room to ask if now they would finally stop arguing. Uncertain how dangerous the medicine was, they rushed me to a hospital, where my stomach was washed out with soapy water, my throat tickled with a brush to make me vomit. The treatment was vile, but I never regretted my rashness, for my parents didn't argue again for a long time.

As I recalled those vivid scenes, I realized that my father would be distressed as well to learn of my disgrace. He had read Marxist theory at my urging, and had agreed that this was indeed the world's most enlightened system of thought. His letters to me in Beijing said that I had chosen the right path and expressed his confidence that I would make an important contribution to our country. Both of my parents had been proud of my achievements; I knew how much sadness they would feel to learn of my fate. Without telling me, my brother left for Guiyang the following week to carry the news that I had been declared a rightist, thus relieving me of that burden.

Time stood still as I lay on my bed, staring vacantly at the novel in my hands. Thoughts of past and present tumbled together; my world had suddenly turned upside down. I was now an outcast, an enemy of the Party and the people. My new identity was publicly confirmed, unalterable. It was only mid-afternoon, but the red-dyed eggs seemed a distant memory.

A telephone call jolted me back to the present with instructions to attend a meeting on February 7, just two weeks away, at which time my membership in the Communist Party would be revoked. I should think about my crimes, I was told, and prepare a self-criticism. I would be dismissed regardless of my response, but my situation would be worse if I did not prepare some comment. That evening I began to consider how I would act in my last Party meeting. I could hardly remember the morning's happiness or my baby's smile to the goddess.

February 7 is an important date in modern Chinese history, the anniversary of the first large-scale mass movement guided by the Communist Party. When I awoke that morning, I thought of the two leaders of the railway workers who, in 1923, had refused to end their strike and had been shot by the warlords. I had always felt deep respect for such selflessness, such devotion to the welfare of the proletarian class. Now on the same date that they were killed, I was to be condemned to a political death, cast out forever from the ranks of the people. Because I had always considered politics so important, this fate seemed almost harder to face than the warlords' bullets. I had no idea how to stand before my fellow Party members at that final meeting, or what to say.

Those five people whom I had helped to judge as rightists had not yet been dismissed from the Party. Punishments always are reserved for the final stage of a movement, and no such meetings had as yet been held, no precedent set. I was worried, not knowing whether to speak the truth, object that I was not a rightist, that it was wrong to dismiss me, or whether to remain silent and swallow all the protestations of innocence surging within me. I would have greatly preferred to speak out, but Lao Tang counseled me to accept the judgment of the Party. Maybe later things will be clarified, he argued; to oppose the Party's decision will only make your situation worse. He urged me to be obedient for the sake of the Party's authority and submit to the opinion that I was a rightist. Perhaps he was right, I decided, remembering that individual injustice must always be considered far less important than maintaining the authority of the Party. I decided to be obedient.

Although this meeting for dismissal had caused me much anticipatory anxiety, when it took place it was surprisingly easy. All the Party members from our branch, perhaps twenty, had assembled before I arrived, and the vice-secretary, his face grave, read the decision. Yue Daiyun is a traitor who has organized an anti-Communist group with the aim of making her own power take the place of the department chairman's, he began. In literary thought Yue Daiyun has followed a bourgeois approach; all her academic viewpoints are influenced by bourgeois literature, and she has repeatedly spread those ideas, poisoning the minds of her students. Yue Daiyun organized a magazine intending to publish anti-Party ideas. Because of her crimes the Party branch of the Chinese literature department has decided to dismiss her from membership.

With the judgment solemnly pronounced, he asked if I wished to express an opinion. It would be useless to deny the charges, I realized; my objecting would do no good either for me or the Party, whose authority I still believed should be absolute. I remained silent. When the vice-secretary repeated his question, I didn't answer. Then he called for a vote to approve the decision. Not daring to look up to see if anyone had failed to raise his hand, I put my own hand in the air. The vote was said to be unanimous. Next I was asked to sign my name to the decision, having been informed that I would be dismissed whether I signed or not. I didn't speak, just took the paper, signed it, and gave it back. I could sense the others in the room relaxing, the tension beginning to subside. The meeting had lasted only half an hour.

Back at home, I felt overcome by a depression far more intense than after my criticism meeting, for this was a final verdict. Now I was cut off from the central meaning of my life, from my guiding purpose, and I felt utterly lost, a stranger in my own land. But even in the dismissal meeting, another voice had spoken inside me. How could they really disconnect me from the Party, since ultimately my membership was not theirs to revoke? Even if I was no longer an official member, in my mind, my heart, my thoughts, I vowed, no one can separate me from what I believe. A person's lifelong ideals cannot so easily be dismissed; in my heart I would remain a Party member, and nobody could change that.

The next day I wrote a poem to Lao Tang describing a tall, sturdy tree, its trunk entwined with a wisteria vine that bore fragrant, cascading blossoms. Supported by the tree, the vine prospered, flowering abundantly every year. Then one day the wisteria died. Not realizing this, the tree still hugged the vine tightly and stretched out its strong arms, waiting for the purple flowers to reappear, but the vine never blossomed again. It was a brief poem, just seventeen lines, and it never became famous, but it was my best one.

After three days had passed, I was told to attend another meeting at which the leadership would announce the punishments for all the rightists in our department. Everyone had been summoned to hear the sentences pronounced. The proceedings were brief, the leaders anxious to dispense with anti-rightist matters, for it was the spring of 1958 and the Great Leap Forward had already begun. The secretary of the department read the decisions. Six different kinds of punishment were being imposed, depending on the seriousness of the crimes: the first was an indefinite jail sentence; the second, dismissal from employment to work under the supervision of the laboring people at the monthly salary of sixteen *yuan*; the third, suspension of employment and reduction of salary during labor in the countryside; the fourth, reduction of salary and demotion one or two grades in rank; the fifth, labor on campus during one-year probation, after which some other punisment could be administered if warranted; the sixth, label of rightist with no other punishment. To my relief no one in our department received the harshest of these, a jail sentence, but three received the second-degree punishment: Lao Xie, who had said the socialist system was responsible for the "triple evils," Lao Lu, and myself.

My own fate did not surprise me, for I had assumed that anyone considered the leader of an anti-Party group would necessarily receive severe treatment, but I had hoped to take sole responsibility for the magazine. Lao Lu had two children exactly the same ages as mine, his wife was a worker in a childcare center and earned only thirty *yuan* a month, and he was the sole supporter of his seventy-year-old mother. Without his income I could not imagine how his family would survive, and I felt great regret for having encouraged him to take on the magazine work. The cancellation of my salary was unimportant, for Lao Tang and I often spent my sixty *yuan* a month on books, not having to pay for either housing or food; but for Lao Lu that monthly salary was essential.

The other members of the magazine group received lighter sentences. Lao Pan, the young teacher who had spoken against me, received no punishment at all and even retained a position as a research assistant in the department. Undoubtedly, his testimony about my guilt had helped. The journalist author of *The Degeneration of a General* was sent back to *People's Daily* to be sentenced by his own unit, but there he was viewed as a committed revolutionary and given no punishment. The young man who had written his master's thesis on Chairman Mao's "Yan'an Talks" was not sentenced immediately, because he was a graduate student, but later received the fourth-degree and was sent to the countryside, having no job or salary to cancel. Ultimately he became an assistant professor at People's University, but his wife, a promising student of mine, suffered more permanently. The strain of resisting her parents' pressure that she demand a divorce left her mentally unbalanced, unable to work for many years, and later capable only of copying data cards for *Red Flag* magazine.

All the others condemned as rightists in our department, like Lao Yang, the older man with the questionable history who had quoted Mencius, received the fourth-degree punishment. None of this was unexpected, but what shocked me utterly was the third reason that determined I would receive the second-degree sentence. Not only had I been the virtual head of a counter-revolutionary group, not only had I organized an illegal magazine with the intention of opposing the Party's literary policy, but I had disclosed Party secrets and caused someone's death.

Zhu Jiayu was my dearest friend, and I had sponsored her application to join the Party. The daughter of a wealthy Shanghai merchant with many connections abroad, she had been offered a chance to study in the United States in 1948 and had refused, at least in part because I had urged her to stay and work for the future of the new China. A student of folklore and folk literature at Beida, she was sent in the spring of 1957 to the Association of Chinese Folklore to do research on local people's songs and poems and thus was away from our campus during the months when people were voicing criticisms of the Party. At rectification meetings in her host organization, she spoke out frequently about ways to improve the study of folklore and the Party's policy toward minorities. Convinced that their music and literature were a national treasure soon to be lost if money was not allocated for preservation, she criticized the leader of the association and the policy of the Party. After her return we worked together in the branch committee from May through July preparing the material that would be used to condemn those five rightists in our department. While we worked, she told me about her desire to bring reforms to the field of folklore.

That August she joined a tour to the coastal city of Dalian organized for teachers by the university trade union. I was surprised that she brought me a baby gift before she left, since the birth was still four months away, but I greatly appreciated the large package of old, soft sheets and bedspreads that make the best kind of diapers. Expressing concern about my health, she urged me not to work so hard and then said good-bye. On the overnight boat trip from Dalian to Tianjin, the last night of the tour, she had played bridge with a group of teachers, had gone to bed at eleven o'clock, and had never been seen again. Everyone said she committed suicide, but I was not convinced. I did know that she was secretly in love with a married man, who was ignorant of her affections, and that she desired to marry no one else; I wondered if she could somehow have guessed that she would soon be labeled a rightist, a possibility I had not even considered. But these reasons seemed insufficient, and I suspected some unseen accident, even foul play. Her death has always remained a mystery.

Now the secretary had declared that Zhu Jiayu's suicide resulted from my warning that she might be declared an enemy. Suicide, always considered a crime, a way of disconnecting yourself from the people and of threatening the Party with your life, is assumed to be committed because you are unable to face your guilt. Zhu Jiayu's death was viewed in this light. After my criticism meeting, I

45

had been ordered to turn over the letter she wrote me from Dalian, and was told that this was a very serious matter, that I would be held responsible if I didn't cooperate. I searched everywhere, but I never saved letters if they seemed unimportant, and this one surely had been routinely tossed away. She had written me only about her safe arrival, about the beautiful landscape, about the gifts she had brought me, sweater buttons made in the Soviet Union and a can of sea conch, a delicacy unavailable in Beijing. The authorities were wrong in assuming that her letter gave some hint about her decision to end her life, but since I couldn't produce evidence to the contrary, the Party held me responsible for her death.

Zhu Jiayu was posthumously declared a rightist because of her criticisms of the folklore association leader and the Party's policy, and because of her contention at one of our branch meetings that democracy was not just a means to an end but the goal of our life, our work, our Party. Another teacher had asserted that democracy was only a means, not an end, that it could be used to achieve a larger purpose but should then be put aside. I had countered that democracy could indeed be a tool but could also be a goal in itself. However, because Chairman Mao had stated that democracy was a means of achieving communism, Zhu Jiayu's disagreement was judged as evidence of her opposition to Mao Zedong thought. Her name was the last on the list of rightists when the sentences were announced; clearly she could be given no further punishment.

In 1979 when rightists were being rehabilitated, I went to the department secretary to inquire about Zhu's case and was told that no one had asked about reversing her verdict. Her father had died in the Cultural Revolution, her mother was an illiterate housewife in Shanghai, and her only sister had left for the United States in 1948. One day her uncle somehow found me and together we requested that her name be cleared. Her posthumous rehabilitation was important for the future of a young half-brother, the son of a concubine, who had been sent to do labor in Guizhou after her condemnation. The procedure was straightforward; we were simply given a notice bearing the red stamp of the Chinese literature department's Party branch committee. "After an investigation we find that Zhu Jiayu is not a rightist. We hereby correct the mistake and return to her all her rights."

When I met her sister in Princeton in 1981, shortly after arriving in the United States to study at Harvard University, I was struck by their physical resemblance, even though the sister, a technician in a chemical company, was in her sixties. I had mailed the rehabilitation decision to her two years before, and immediately she brought it out. "This is so brief, so cruel," she cried; "how can these few words make amends?" I could offer no answer to her bitter query, no solace for her grief. I said only that I felt responsible for Zhu Jiayu's decision to stay in China, which I had encouraged, and that I stood guilty before her older sister. It was not I who was guilty but the whole system, she replied sadly, for even when she herself had come abroad, she had believed in the new China and planned to return someday. We talked and wept together until midnight.

Zhu Jiayu's posthumous accusation brought the meeting to pronounce punishments to an end. Everyone sentenced to labor in the countryside would leave in two days, we were told; all baggage should be delivered to the department office at nine o'clock in preparation for departure at ten. I could not bear to think of such an immediate departure, certain that my milk was essential to the health of my baby, who had grown chubby and strong. To deprive him of my milk, to leave him so soon, seemed unendurable. Trying to control my emotions, I repeated time and again a silent injunction: "Don't be frightened, be strong, no one can save you but yourself."

Too upset to think, I realized that perhaps it was better to leave before this numbness wore away. Later I would feel the pain much more intensely. Lao Tang's mother hastily hired another *ayi* to care for the baby, as Daolan was busy with household chores. Yang Dama, as we called her, was a peasant woman in her fifties who became devoted to my son. In those two days there was little to occupy my time; I just arranged my few belongings and nursed my baby, feeling dazed, my mind blank.

Lao Tang was kept busy with meetings in his own department to finish up the business of the Anti-rightist Campaign, being very obedient so as not to offend anyone. As no teaching took place during that semester, his days were filled with meetings for organization, for criticism, and for discussions with the students about what was correct, about how to draw lines separating themselves from those who had been accused, and about how to criticize themselves for being influenced by rightists. Education had come to a halt; the two overlapping movements occupied everyone's time.

On the morning that I was to leave, I was suddenly notified that I could remain at home for an additional seven months. Lao Tang's father, I later learned, had gone to Lu Ping, another vice-president and the Party secretary of Beida, and had said he would be grateful if they could delay my departure. He explained that he was old, that he could not bear to have anything happen to his only grandson, who was still so small and in need of its mother. Because of his request, my department was instructed to let me stay. Still, I must deliver my baggage at the appointed time, as there would be no truck to carry my heavy bedroll seven months later.

Just before nine o'clock that morning I set out, pushing a bicycle on which I had loaded two quilts, a pillow, and a few clothes tied neatly together, and for the first time I felt what it was like to be considered an enemy of the people. Others besides the rightists were going to the countryside to be reeducated by the laboring people and to help organize communes and work for the Great Leap Forward. They too had gathered outside the department office. These people had been my friends and fellow workers for years, but now they pretended not to see me and turned away as I approached. I realized with a shock that I was truly an outcast. From a position of great respect I had ceased to exist in the eyes of others. Feeling hurt and angry, I wondered how people could change so quickly. Maybe I have fallen this time, I thought defiantly, but I will stand up again and then you will see my real face; I am not so weak. But I said nothing, just deposited my bedroll and pedaled quickly home.

Shortly after this my daughter returned from nursery school one afternoon to recite a new poem in the hallway for her grandmother.

> Down with the rightists, down with the rightists,
> We will all follow Chairman Mao, who tells us the right
>   way to go;
> When the rightists have all perished,
> Then we will have a bright future.

From my room I could hear her happy, innocent voice. Lao Tang's mother spoke sharply, telling her not to say such things, and immediately offered her candy. "Why," I heard Tang Dan ask, "do you like rightists? My teacher says they are the worst people in our country." Her questions pierced my heart. I could think of no response and sat there speechless, thinking about the difficulties my children would encounter in the future.

Tang Dan was already accomplished at singing and dancing and had been chosen at the age of three to perform before Zhou Enlai as a representative of her nursery school. Such distinctions would quickly end, and my children would grow up being ostracized and scorned by others. When they reached middle school, they would have many forms to fill out, each one requiring a declaration of their parents' political status. Tang Dan would have to state that her mother had been dismissed from the Party, had lost her job, and was being supervised to do labor in the countryside. If she denied or obscured my status, she would be accused of trying to deceive the Party. As she stood there asking so innocently about her grandmother's disapproval, a great sadness swept over me. Now she knows nothing, I thought, but before long she will realize, it will hurt her so deeply, and I can do nothing to prevent it. This was the second time I learned what it meant to be a rightist. For the next seven months I rarely crossed my threshold, and no one came to see me.

Now a member of the Beida philosophy department, Lao Tang was among those cadres sent down to the countryside for reeducation, and he soon left for the village of Huangcun, some two hours away by bus, to investigate the effects of the people's commune movement and participate in the production of backyard steel and the reform of agriculture. Every Saturday his group returned to report its findings and have some rest, and I would eagerly await his arrival. Then on Monday very early I would board the bus with him, staring out at the flat fields of wheat and corn as we bumped along the dusty dirt road together before I made the return trip alone.

On the weekends we had long talks about the situation in the countryside and about the commune movement. Lao Tang, believing this to be the beginning of a wonderful new period, advised me that the months we would each spend in the rural areas would provide an important chance for children of intellectual families to learn about the peasants. Encouraging me to adopt a positive outlook, he brought me books on vegetable growing, pig raising, and popular forms of entertainment. While the baby slept, Yang Dama taught me folk songs and a form of local opera called drum songs. I read eagerly about the Great Leap Forward, about the people's communes, about agricultural methods, and even learned to play the harmonica, thinking that because there was so little to enliven the peasants' routine, they might enjoy hearing some music.

During this spring my greatest worry was my baby's deteriorating health. His digestion was constantly upset, his bowel movements very frequent. Gradually he grew thinner. One day after his diarrhea had been especially severe, his eyes began to look sunken, a symptom of dehydration, and I rushed him to the Hospital for Traditional Medicine. The doctors wanted him to remain for several weeks, so Yang Dama and I took turns at his bedside, sleeping on the cot provided for the parent. Following the prescribed treatment, I made him drink a full cup of bitter herbal medicine several times a day, pinching his nose to force down the necessary dosage. Sometimes he even vomited the medicine back up, and I suffered to watch his distress.

One day another baby afflicted with a similar kind of intestinal illness was moved into the second crib in this hospital room. That child's mother, a teacher in Beida's Russian literature department, had in 1956 sung with me in the teachers' chorus once a week. Because I was fond of Russian literature, we would occasionally talk together. Not herself a Party member, she had once remarked that she looked up to me as an example. Unlike most Party members who were stiff and cold, she had commented admiringly, I liked to sing, was sensitive to literature, and still did my political work.

Yet when she moved into this room, she pretended not to know me, refusing to speak. I felt hurt, but pride made me resolve that if she didn't want to acknowledge me, I wouldn't speak either. I was fortunate to have Yang Dama to help with my son's care so that I could occasionally go out to eat or buy something, but the other mother could not leave her baby's bedside. I told Yang Dama to ask if she needed anything, and if so to buy it for her. Later as I approached the room I heard her say accusingly, "Don't you know she is a rightist, an enemy of the people? Don't be so nice to her; you must draw a line to separate yourself. These rightists want to overturn our government and make the peasants suffer again." This was my third lesson in what it meant to be a rightist.

Yang Dama replied firmly, "I don't know a rightist from a leftist, I don't care about such things, and besides, she asked me to help you, don't you realize that?" Quietly I slipped outside to the garden that adjoined the hospital and sat on a stone by a small pond, weeping. Peasants, I had grown convinced, were far more humane than intellectuals.

My baby's health did not improve, even after he had drunk quantities of that vile medicine, and finally Lao Tang's mother, who came every day, asked the doctor why there had been no improvement. She was told that my milk might be harming the baby, that if a mother was upset, her emotions in turmoil, her milk often would be bad. At this suggestion, my fury burst forth. How could they try to take away even my right to nurse my own child, I thought. In a fiery temper, I spoke sharply to my mother-in-law, saying I wanted no one to interfere and that I would certainly continue nursing. My milk was plentiful, it was white and pure, it could not possibly be the cause of my son's illness. At my insistence, we left immediately and took the baby to Beijing's best children's hospital, where the doctors were Western-trained. Lao Tang's mother tried to persuade me just to experiment with cow's milk, but I was adamant. Even a rightist, I thought angrily, does not poison her own baby.

My son grew steadily worse. His diarrhea continued, and he began to turn blue around the mouth and dark around the eyes. The doctor said it was essential to give him fluids intravenously, but the baby was so small that the staff could not find a blood vessel in his wrist or arm. Once they managed to attach the drip briefly to his ankle, but the vein was too small to be effective. All this time the nurses were holding him down while he screamed in pain and fear. Next the doctor tried to find a vein in his temple. On the third attempt I was so frantic that I berated the young doctor, saying, "You can't even insert a needle; how can you be so stupid; why are you a doctor anyway?" My outburst only made him more nervous; it was hot, and he began to sweat profusely. Finally the needle was successfully inserted in Tang Shuang's temple, but for three days his condition did not improve, and even the Western doctor suggested that I should stop nursing. This time I had no choice but to agree. After three more days, Tang Shuang had nearly recovered; I could see the difference as soon as he switched to cow's milk.

Just after I had been forced to concede that my milk was harmful to my baby, I developed a serious breast infection and a fever from engorgement. The pain in my breast seemed to come from my very heart. My baby was able to return home, but I had to be hospitalized so that the infection could be treated surgically. Since this was a simple procedure, I was told just to go to the local Beida clinic. The medical care there was not of the highest quality, however, and the inexperienced doctor lanced the infected area in the wrong place, necessitating a second incision. I still carry those scars.

To prevent further infection, I had to remain in the hospital for a week, intensely unhappy days during which I could not think, could not do anything. I missed my baby terribly, but knew it would be unhealthy for him to visit me in those surroundings. With Lao Tang away, I felt totally bereft. After recuperating for two months at home, I received instructions to leave for the countryside the following day. Maybe the authorities knew I had stopped nursing. A little over seven months had passed, and my reprieve was over. I wanted to say good-bye to Lao Tang when he returned home that weekend, but I could not ask for another delay. Since you must leave, I told myself strictly, earlier or later doesn't matter, just let it be done. I kept repeating the proverbial saying that at such moments a person must turn his heart over, make it numb, empty it of all feelings.

Early the next morning I held my baby one last time and said good-bye to my daughter and to Lao Tang's parents. His mother cried sadly, and Yang Dama tearfully held the baby up to the window as I closed the door behind me. Daolan carried my small duffel bag of clothing and walked in silence beside me for a long distance; we had developed a deep feeling for each other. As the bus carried me to the train station, a layer of fog, unusual in Beijing, made the cityscape indistinct. My vision blurred; I could not begin to imagine what the future held in store.

Cast Out from the People

STEPPING ONTO the platform at Yanchi, I sensed that I had reached the end of more than just the rail line. Located at the notch between two mountain chains, a setting that had earned it the name "geese in flight," this small town some forty miles west of Beijing appeared cheerless and utterly uninviting. Above its gray rooftops jutted treeless mountain peaks, their rocky slopes covered at the base with patches of dark brown moss. The landscape was barren, gloomy, oppressive, and the rapidly gathering clouds warned of an approaching storm. In this inhospitable place I bought a bus ticket, then a steamed bun in a tiny restaurant, waiting for the hour to pass before I would embark on the last stage of my journey. An overwhelming sense of isolation made me fight against tears, but the few others near the bus stop were oblivious to my pain.

The bus followed the rocky river bed out of Yanchi, arriving two hours later in Zhaitang, the commune headquarters that would become my home for the indefinite future. Prepared for an equally desolate setting, I peered out of the window with relief at gentler mountains covered with walnut and apricot trees. My first sight after being deposited in the center of this apparently deserted village was of a neatly whitewashed wall covered with paintings and poems. Bold and colorful strokes depicted a towering haystack on top of which sat an old peasant, his outstretched arm holding up a long-stemmed pipe to touch the sun. The Promethean message radiated optimism: the peasants will reap such plentiful harvests that they can climb to the very heavens and light their fires from the sun itself. A couplet continued this theme, promising that the heaven of communism could be reached via the bridge of the people's commune. Another poem warned the mountains to make way for the peasants, who would remove even the tallest obstacles to achieve their goals. The Great Leap Forward policy of covering all available surfaces with inspiring messages was obviously being implemented here. My despondency began to lift, for I could see that the people sent down to the countryside from the university had already made a contribution in this village. Feeling slightly cheered, I thought that perhaps I would after all be able to find a new life here among the peasants.

Nestled at the foot of a mountain beside the appropriately named Qingshui (Clear Water) River, Zhaitang seemed a beautiful place. I could see a narrow strip of fertile soil on either bank of the river where the peasants were growing some vegetables and wheat, but I guessed that the many small terraced plots I had noticed along the mountainsides, probably suitable only for raising millet, provided most of the arable land. The commune's income, I would soon learn, came primarily from the sale of apricot seeds, a valuable source of oil, and walnuts, both crops that were raised exclusively for export. Two cooperative stores and an outlet where the peasants could sell their produce to the government made Zhaitang, with its population of about one thousand, the economic center for the surrounding area.

Initially, I knew only that Zhaitang was the commune administrative headquarters and thus a political center, its bus and telephone connection to Beijing making it a suitable location for the control of serious political enemies. The less important rightists from my department had been sent to more remote places in the mountains, to Damo, for example, but Zhaitang had received a group of less serious rightists from the history and math departments as well as four others with the second-degree sentence, two from the Chinese literature department and two from history. I was the fifth and the only woman.

From Lao Tang's experience, I knew that the sent-down cadres who supervised the rightists were themselves a mixed group, not all of them considered politically reliable. By then only the most trusted teachers and cadres remained on campus to organize, educate, and criticize the students, and to criticize as well the work of those professors being attacked for their "bourgeois academic viewpoints." Everyone not needed to conduct the ongoing campaigns or lead discussions about how to avoid following the "white and expert way"* had simply been sent to the countryside. It was never said that the sent-down cadres were being relocated primarily to get them out of the way; it was said that in the countryside they would receive education and at the same time organize the peasants, while others would stay behind to organize the students on campus. Supposedly the two tasks were equally important, but few believed the official explanation. The desire among the sent-down cadres to prove their political reliability and demonstrate their dedication to the Party's policies would, I anticipated, make them inevitably adopt a severe posture toward the rightists whom they were allowed to supervise.

Not knowing what to do next, I had started hesitantly along the single cobblestoned street when a figure approached, no doubt notified in advance of my arrival. To my surprise it was Deng Minghua, a member of the Beida economics department and apparently the person responsible for the rightists assigned to Zhaitang. We had worked together in the same Party branch before 1955 and he had been a guest at my wedding, but I had no idea how to act toward him now that I was classed as an enemy. Ignoring my wariness, he greeted me warmly and reached out to carry my duffel bag. Recalling how I had been spurned in Beijing, I wondered whether here in the countryside people had been less affected by the recent political movements. Deng accompanied me to the place where my bedroll had been stored since January, a room empty except for a large cistern of water and a *kang*† on which five quilts lay neatly folded.

---

*A person following the "white and expert way" disregards political goals and cares only for academic or technical expertise, as opposed to a person who is both "red and expert."

†A *kang* is a heated earthen or brick platform used in North China for sleeping and sitting.

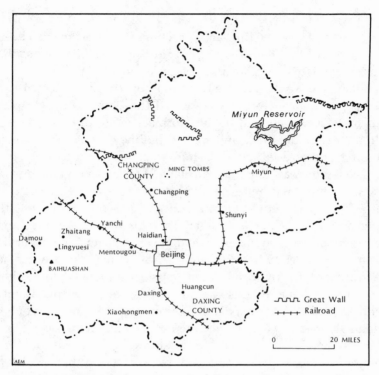

Beijing Municipality

Here I was told to rest until the sent-down cadres returned from their labor and gave me further instructions. My welcome had been warmer than I had dared hope, but my apprehensions about the future remained strong. I could not guess what lay ahead.

After I had waited anxiously on the *kang* for what seemed like hours, the five women cadres returned from their labor. Hearing their footsteps, I stepped outside to meet them, offering to help with their shoulder poles and spades, but they coldly rebuffed my overtures and refused to speak, their faces stern and condescending. Feeling increasingly uncomfortable, I again sat on the edge of the *kang* while they proceeded routinely to wash their faces and feet. When Deng returned to announce that I would move in with this group of women, their leader, Yang Li, a Party member from the library department whom I had never met, remarked sharply that the *kang* already had five quilts. Clearly they didn't welcome the intrusion of a rightist in their midst, but there was no other place in the village to house me, and Deng told them placatingly that he would perhaps make other arrangements later. Yang Li begrudgingly made a very small space for my quilt on the *kang*.

It was nearly seven o'clock and almost dark when I followed them out to dinner, carrying along the wash basin that had been rudely thrust at me. In accordance with the commune movement, the peasants had constructed a collective kitchen in the former village temple, and three stoves with enormous cooking pots now filled the space in front of the largest Buddha. The kitchen was large and dark; the lack of ventilation made the air so smoky that at first I could hardly see the food. Yang Li instructed me to fill my basin with the steamed buns made of coarse corn flour and water, while they filled two other basins with a thin corn-flour porridge. This meager fare was the staple diet in the village.

As there was no collective dining hall, the women led me without speaking to one of the four rooms allocated to the sent-down men. The cadres all sat cross-legged on the *kang* beside a small table, while I took a stool on the floor, following the example of Lao Shi, the young man from my department who had been accused of starting the rumor about a rift between Chairman Mao and Liu Shaoqi. He pretended not to see me, but just took a bun and a bowl of porridge and began to eat. I sat with him in silence while the others on the *kang* talked animatedly about their labor or about the peasants in the village. Yang Li had cooked a dish of carrots, soybeans, and dried beancurd, vegetables she had purchased from the peasants, and she rather contemptuously thrust a small spoonful in each of our bowls, acting as if it were a special favor to toss us small scraps of food. Not only did I feel hurt and insulted, but it was physically difficult to swallow the coarse grains. Especially if you were a rightist, however, you could not appear ungrateful or wasteful, so I forced down every bite.

Back in our room, Yang Li noticed immediately that I had placed my duffel bag in a small square opening beneath the *kang*. "Don't you know that hole was not made for your bag," she snapped sarcastically. I had never lived in a North China village before and knew nothing about the operation of a *kang*. I soon learned, however, that the nights in Zhaitang were so damp that even in August the stove would be lit. Though that region is rich in coal, the black powder cannot be burned in the *kang* until it is mixed with the local yellow clay and water, three shovels of coal, two of clay, and one dipper of water, laboriously blended. When the mixture is the consistency of porridge, it can be put into the stove.

After I had hastily removed my belongings, Yang Li next ordered me curtly to fetch some clay. Outside a dog began barking loudly. Despite my fear of this unknown animal, I could not return empty-handed, so I cowered beside the door, silently willing the cur to get used to me. The barking made me think of a time when I was seven and a student in the Guiyang primary school run by Catholic missionaries. My mother had wanted me to learn to play the piano, as she and my father both admired Western culture, and the Italian nuns gave lessons to the local children on the convent piano. The lessons were expensive, but I liked music and agreed to go three times a week. Each day when I arrived at the churchyard the convent dog barked so ferociously that I didn't dare to enter and always ran away. Now in this dark courtyard, the fierce barking seemed like a distant reverberation of my childhood.

When Yang Li shouted impatiently for me to hurry up as they were all waiting to go to sleep, I realized that I had more to fear from her than from any dog and walked nervously past the growling animal to carry out my orders. Never in my whole life had I been treated with such contempt, such hostility. I had not changed, I thought angrily; I still felt just as committed to the ideals of the Party as before.

They all slept soundly, but this was my first night on a *kang*. It was so hard I could not get comfortable; the fire felt so hot that I tossed and turned, baking like a sweet potato first on one side and then another. During that sleepless night I reviewed again the choices I had made since leaving Guiyang a decade earlier, trying to determine where I had gone wrong. Could I have chosen to live my life again, I would not have changed my decision to become a Party leader, despite my present predicament. But as I lay there restlessly, still smarting from Yang Li's abuse, my future looked bleak, far different from what I had envisaged during those months of studying books about agriculture.

Rising before any of the others, I resolved to start the new day by doing something useful. The morning air smelled much fresher than in Beijing, and on the mountainsides the walnut leaves shimmered in the early light. I could hear cocks crowing and see oxen being led to water. Following the peasants' example, I picked up a shoulder pole, having learned that skill during the land reform in Jiangxi, and started off toward the communal well. Because of its height above the river bed, the well had been dug very deep, and despite my eagerness I quickly realized that filling an empty metal bucket was no easy task. Behind me other peasants were waiting in line, and I grew increasingly embarrassed at my ineptitude. Perhaps five or six minutes passed as I repeatedly lowered my pail, but still it floated stubbornly on the surface. Finally an old peasant began to laugh and stepped over to show me how to swing the bucket first and then drop it suddenly. His manner was warm and helpful, and I felt very grateful, especially after having had to endure the hostility of the women who were now my supervisors. He urged me to fill my pails just halfway so as not to strain my back on this first trip, and I smiled my appreciation. Finally, I returned with the water and poured it into the cistern that stood just inside the door.

Without any acknowledgment, the other women began to wash,

apparently assuming it was my function to serve them. They offered no word of thanks, just ordered me to set out for the mountains to bring back clay for the next night's fuel. Carrying a heavy wicker shoulder basket, I followed them up the steep and difficult path, the discomfort of the task greatly alleviated by my first panoramic glimpse of the landscape. In this beautiful setting, I mused, the clean river water could be brought up to the mountain slopes and fruit trees planted everywhere. I felt ready to dedicate myself to the goals announced by Chairman Mao, who had said that in the countryside, where so much needs to be done, one can happily perform many kinds of useful and satisfying tasks. The trip down put an end to such idealistic thoughts, for the descent was even more precarious with a basket full of clay; negotiating the narrow, slippery mud steps took all my attention. Unwilling to appear weaker than the others, I had taken an equal load, even though they had grown accustomed to this work after seven months in the village. By the time we had walked the half hour back to our courtyard and deposited the clay, it was not yet eight o'clock.

In the cooperative kitchen I again took a bowl of porridge for breakfast and a steamed cornflour bun. An old peasant woman, realizing I was a newcomer, urged me to take two more buns. I did not know this was all I would have for lunch. The rightists, I soon learned, did heavy labor each day, while the cadres undertook less burdensome tasks, like building carts to help modernize the village, making pig food out of leaves mixed with yeast, or refining tannic acid from walnuts for export. With a group of peasants, we twelve set out for the mountains in search of fairly flat rocks for the construction of a dam that would block the course of a mountain stream. Our goal was to create a small reservoir to provide water for the terraced fields high above the Qingshui River. After we had climbed for about twenty minutes on another steep footpath, the daily routine began. Two peasants filled the bottom of my shoulder basket with straw, then positioned a rock on top and sent me back to the village. I soon found that the sand and loose stones on the path made it easy to slip, especially with my weight thrown forward under the heavy load. The ropes dug into my shoulders, and the rock pressed painfully against the back of my neck. The peasants do this work for their whole lives, I reminded myself grimly, picking my way down the slope, so why shouldn't I share their labor for a day or two, even a year or two.

In a few days I too would be carrying the eighty-five pounds of rocks expected of a woman, a heavy burden but nothing compared with the hundred-and-forty-pound loads that Lao Shi carried. For my first trip, though, the peasants had selected a relatively small stone, warning me to take care when removing the heavy pack from my shoulders. Despite their advice, I found the unloading nearly impossible. Another rightist from the history department came over, smiling, and showed me how to jerk one shoulder sharply to dislodge the stone and drop it to the ground. Since no sent-down cadres were near, we could talk together for awhile.

Lao Wei, who until recently had taught Communist Party history at Beida, had been the secretary of the Party branch that until 1955 included all the faculty Party members from the philosophy, history, and literature departments. We were old friends. He had joined the revolution early, in 1945, and had been active in the underground student movement. Now he was a rightist, having complained that the prejudice of the university leaders had denied him deserved promotions. His career had suffered because of a continuing struggle between two groups within the Party's youth movement. Since before Liberation, one had operated in the Northeast, behind Japanese lines, and one in the Southwest, in areas controlled by the Guomindang. Each had its own youth organization, one called the League of Youth, the other the Democratic Youth League that I had joined, and Lao Wei was the leader of those at Beida who belonged to the less influential Northeast faction. Because members of the dominant group protected the interests of their own constituency, Lao Wei was never promoted to the high position that his notable revolutionary history warranted. Later he was condemned as a rightist, his complaint about prejudice judged an attempt to destroy the unity of the Party.

When we stopped for lunch, Lao Wei sat on a rock beside me and offered some advice based on his experiences in Zhaitang during the past seven months. He told me to be careful, to adapt

quickly to the new circumstances, and above all not to offend anyone. His words introduced me to a whole new way of thinking.
"Now we are enemies of the Party," he counseled me, "even though
for years we have devoted ourselves to the revolution. At present
we must admit we are guilty and acknowledge that we really are
criminals, for only in this way can we resume our normal lives and
at the same time help the Party by confirming the correctness of its
policy. You must acknowledge that you have done something to oppose the Party and concede your guilt."

"But," I protested, astonished, "that would be a denial of the
truth."

"There can be no absolute standard for truth and falsehood," he
replied firmly, "for what is true depends always on necessity and
circumstance. If you can prove you have a deep consciousness of
your mistake, you can return to the side of the people, and that is
what matters most. Above all, you must never offend the sent-
down cadres, for they control your destiny. Even if they do something you know is wrong, you must pretend not to notice it."

Such an expedient, dishonest approach to life was totally re-
pugnant to me, but I could see how this philosophy had served Lao
Wei well. He was a practical person, very capable, and everyone
liked him, even the cadres, who would sometimes give him a break
from carrying rocks to write some calligraphy for them. Having
learned how to function as a rightist, he sincerely wanted to help
me adjust.

At sunset I felt so exhausted after this first day of strenuous labor that I could hardly move my legs after the final trip down the
mountain. Having eaten a quick dinner, I wanted to do nothing but
collapse on the *kang,* but just then the gong sounded, signaling the
start of a compulsory meeting in the primary school. The purpose
of the gathering was to read newspapers to the peasants, who
seemed utterly indifferent to this effort to educate them. They just
smoked, sewed padded shoe soles, or chatted together, taking advantage of the chance for a good gossip. Some even dozed when
the newspaper reading droned on for more than an hour, as everyone was tired by the end of the day. Finally, the reading ended, but

before the meeting adjourned, the cadres issued a warning to the "five black types" in the village to be "attentive to regulations and obedient to the supervision of the masses."

Though such warnings quickly became routine, I initially found it humiliating to be ostracized as a rightist and publicly classed with the landlords, rich peasants, counter-revolutionaries, and bad elements, those offenders who were set apart from the rest of the villagers in a back corner of the schoolroom. Dirty and shabbily dressed, their faces worn and deeply lined, those ten people truly looked like criminals. The two former landlords had been removing nightsoil and cleaning latrines for seven years, ever since the land reform, which had come to this village in 1950. Now in their fifties and considered too old to do heavy labor, these men were so humbled and dejected that they no longer bothered to wash their faces. The others had been low-level Guomindang officials or soldiers in the Nationalist army who had made anti-Communist remarks and thus had been labeled counter-revolutionaries. This group was always assigned the dirtiest, most fatiguing tasks, like ladling manure into the irrigation canals to fertilize the fields, or going off to work on road construction crews far from home where the living conditions were harsh. Now, like them, I was a public enemy.

Seven years had passed since my six-month stay in Jiangxi as the head of a land reform team, an experience that now returned vividly to my mind. Wan'an county had for years been a Guomindang-controlled area, and because Lutian village where I worked was near the main road through the province, many of the local men had joined the Nationalist army before Liberation to earn money, and had then come back home to settle down. After the Beida work team arrived, the local Party committee announced the decision to kill all the landlords in that village, claiming they had seriously harmed the peasants and owed a "blood debt," as well as those who had connections with the Guomindang; but first the villagers wanted to learn where these enemies had buried their money. They were harangued, even beaten, until they revealed their hiding places. Some of the ones so punished were leaders of the household responsibility teams (*baojia*), some were low-ranking Nationalist officers, and some were landlords who had beaten the peasants, forced them to pay exorbitant rents, or jailed them for debt.

At the time I thought it necessary to kill those people because they had caused the peasants such extreme suffering. Often the father of a family would have died in prison, for example, causing great pain and hardship to his dependents. We were instructed that the harsh treatment of such criminals was also necessary to raise the peasants' consciousness and remove their fear. The process of land reform, we were told, could not be peaceful; it must be a class struggle to give the peasants confidence in the new system. Otherwise, they would fear that once the work team left, the landlords would exact their revenge. Often, in fact, the peasants didn't want to accept the land given to them and turned back their property deeds secretly at night, fearful that the system of exploitation would reassert itself. After being told to consider all these factors, I became convinced that there was no way to avoid violence. I too thought it necessary to condemn the landlords in order to make the peasants feel masters of the village and to convince them that the changes instituted by the Party were permanent.

But one of the condemned men, a tailor from Shanghai, was a widower who had always worked hard, lived very simply, and invested all of his savings to buy land in his native village in Jiangxi. Little by little he had accumulated quite a bit of property, more than 300 *mou*,* and had rented out his land, taking half of the produce from each tenant family as rent while he made clothing in the city. According to the land reform code, if a person owned enough land before 1945 to hire laborers, he was by definition an exploiter, and if his land holdings were greater than anyone else's, he was a "number one landlord" who must be condemned to death. This tailor was about seventy, and I thought that even though he owned the most land, even though he had hired someone else to till the soil for him, still he had been working hard all those years doing another kind of

*A *mou* is approximately one-sixth of an acre.

65

labor in Shanghai. Because of such extenuating circumstances, I believed he should be allowed to offer his land voluntarily and then be left in peace.

The leader of the six work teams in this area, a member of the local Jiangxi government, said I was wrong to have sympathy for a landlord, that this was an opportunity to train myself to get used to class struggle and to learn the correct attitude toward an enemy. He held a meeting to discuss how we students should teach ourselves to have a class struggle viewpoint about everything, arguing that I should not consider whether this tailor had been a laborer himself but only see that he had exploited the peasants, taking their sweat and blood. Once, I was told, the person hired to collect rents for the tailor had abused a sick peasant, the father of several children, so cruelly that the man had died, leaving the tailor with a blood debt. I didn't know whether the tailor was truly at fault, especially since the rent collector, also a poor peasant, received no punishment, but I was told sternly that under no circumstances should I have compassion for a class enemy.

This leader was himself a member of a peasant family and had previously been a member of the Red Army. When the Guomindang had captured Jiangxi, the Red Army had been forced to march north, and the Guomindang had burned all the houses and killed everyone they met in the former Red area. Their policy was known as the "three destructions": kill all the people, burn all the houses, and loot all the valuables. At first I couldn't understand the reasons for such inhumane actions, but after we were taken to one of those areas to learn a lesson from the ruins, I understood. Had the Nationalists not pursued such a policy, they would have feared that the Red Army would remain behind and attack them from the rear. The struggle was very cruel, and they believed this policy to be essential for their safety. The leader took us to see what remained after the looting and burning, to educate us and help us understand the nature of class struggle. Because of his years of experience, we looked up to him as a model.

Even though I could accept the necessity of condemning to death most of the landlords and Guomindang officers in our village, I still could not in my heart agree with this tailor's sentence.

After our discussion meeting the others criticized me, saying that to have compassion in a class struggle was very dangerous, and that the peasants deserved revenge. We were often reminded of Chairman Mao's story about the peasant who, finding a snake lying on the ground cold and stiff, put it to his breast to warm it. As soon as the snake revived, it bit the peasant, wounding him fatally, illustrating the danger of showing sympathy to an enemy who will only attack you once he has regained his strength. Always in China, when someone is placed in another category and classified as an enemy, he is moved outside the range of pity. Even the most extreme treatment is then justified.

One of the men condemned in this village was indeed a cruel landlord who had sent many people to jail for failure to pay rents. This man's land holdings were smaller than the tailor's, but his offenses were much greater. As the leader of a local administrative unit of thirty households, he had worked closely with the Guomindang. One of his duties was to oversee conscription for its army; if the conscripts tried to hide or escape, he would have them beaten, then sent back to the army, where often they would be shot as deserters. He had also hired a gang of toughs to beat up a peasant who, in a drought year, had been unable to pay his rent. The peasant had died from his injuries.

At the big meeting held in the town square to sentence this landlord, several village families sat on the platform and wept as they related the sufferings he had caused. Clearly many wanted revenge, but he was the only condemned man who provoked this desire for retribution. When the tailor was shot, some of the villagers' eyes were wet with tears. He was old, lonely, hardworking, and had done many good things for the village, once providing funds for the rebuilding of a washed-out bridge, another time paying for the construction of a road. But there was no way to save him.

As I sat in the schoolroom in Zhaitang listening with half an ear to the newspaper reading, I recalled my sorrow at what had seemed to me that tailor's undeserved punishment. Now I couldn't help wondering as well about the fairness of the sentences leveled against the landlords and other enemies with whom I was suddenly grouped. Again I seriously questioned this system of condemnation. Since I knew that Lao Wei and I did not deserve to be treated as enemies, having never opposed the revolution or the Party, perhaps the others had been accused unjustly as well. By preventing such people from contributing to the construction of the country, by denying them not only social status but even a shared humanity, the Party seemed to be making a terrible mistake.

My mind strayed farther from the newspaper articles as I tried to decide how landlords and others who had been pronounced enemies should be treated. Such confusing questions called into doubt all that I had been taught to believe, just as Lao Wei's advice about how I should behave conflicted with my own values. Finally, I decided it was better not to think about such unanswerable questions but rather to concentrate on the immediate problem of getting myself out of this village and back home as quickly as possible.

During that first week, I tried to accustom myself to life as a rightist, but I found the attitudes of the sent-down cadres difficult to bear. One day I returned from carrying rocks down the mountainside to hear two of the women cadres talking about me. "How could he call her 'comrade' now," one was asking angrily, and another indignantly replied, "We must immediately write a letter to his department. He must draw a line; we must insist that he never use that form of address again." I soon found out what had aroused their ire. A letter had arrived from Lao Tang addressed in the customary way to "Comrade Yue Daiyun," outraging those women who believed I should be denied the privilege of such a title now that I was no longer one of the people. I could hardly contain my anger at their insulting remarks, shouting out in my heart that I was more truly a Communist than any of them. Some of those women didn't even belong to the Party, and only two were teachers, while the others worked in the library or prepared teaching materials. Stifling my resentment, I took the envelope and walked outside to the foot of the mountain. Even though it was almost dark, I wanted to read my first letter alone.

Lao Tang's words conveyed his sadness at my unexpected departure. When he had returned from the countryside and found me gone, he had not known what else to do and had spent most of the weekend walking back and forth in the empty bedroom, humming the Brahms lullaby to our baby. On Sunday he had taken Tang Dan to the zoo and to the nearby Exhibition Hall restaurant, then the most expensive in Beijing, thinking that he must try somehow to compensate for her mother's unfair absence. I was moved by his words and wrote back immediately, urging him not to address me as "comrade" anymore. He ignored my concern, and every week after that an identical envelope arrived.

In 1966 at the outset of the Cultural Revolution we buried all of those letters, precious mementos from this and our other periods of separation, fearing they would be discovered by the Red Guards and seized. The doubts I had occasionally expressed in writing about official policy would surely have brought serious reprisals if our correspondence had been read by those over-zealous young revolutionaries. We selected a spot beneath the grape arbor of my parents' simple retirement house near the campus, assuming that their sturdy grapevine would serve in later years for a landmark. After wrapping the letters carefully in plastic, we prepared a deep hole. But in 1976 when we dug the package up again, nothing was left of our correspondence but a soggy mass. Our idea had been disastrous, for the vine had been watered continually over the years, and our wrapping had quickly deteriorated. Every letter was ruined.

In the subsequent weeks at Zhaitang, I was so busy with the labor and so physically exhausted after my endless treks down the steep path to the village each day that I had little time or inclination to think. I grew accustomed to the *kang* and slept soundly every night; I also got used to the coarse diet. Just as my body gradually adjusted to the physical strains of the work, so also I became inured to the rebuffs of the cadres. Time passed imperceptibly with little change in the routine. As autumn merged into winter, everyone began to anticipate the festivities of the Spring Festival holidays.

Late one night loud noises awakened me from a deep sleep. Outside I saw the other women unloading shoulder baskets brimming with walnuts. In preparation for their return to Beijing, where walnuts were unavailable, they had walked a long distance after work that day to buy a large supply illegally from peasants who had picked them in secret. Later they burned the shells in the stove so no one would discover their purchase. The sharp sound of cracking shells had awakened me. Listening enviously to their happy chatter about what to take back to their children now that their stay in the countryside was nearly over, I pretended to sleep and tried to stifle the longings their comments aroused.

We rightists had been led to hope that we might also return home for that Spring Festival in early 1959 if we worked very conscientiously and revealed a clear understanding of our guilt. With that goal in sight, I did many extra jobs each day, providing the women cadres with water, always carrying back more clay than the others, taking responsibility for cleaning not only our room but the whole courtyard. I wanted desperately to see Lao Tang and my children. Everyone longed for a chance to go home, so the last days of that year were filled with hope, but soon it was announced that only Lao Wei would be permitted to return to the city. During the absence of the sent-down cadres, the other rightists "must remain under the supervision of the local people's militia, be completely obedient, and not break the law."

A special meeting was then called by the people's militia for all the five black types to stress that we must respect their authority. Demoralized at having to attend a separate meeting just for enemies of the people, disappointed and angry about the decision to keep the rest of us in Zhaitang over the holidays, I felt drained of every shred of optimism. Bitterly I recalled my efforts to learn the harmonica and the drum songs, my plan to teach new agricultural techniques to the peasants, all of which seemed utterly wasted.

Returning dejectedly from the meeting, I heard someone in my room mention my name. "After we leave, who will supervise this rightist," one cadre was asking. Deng Minghua then suggested that I be sent to live in a peasant family and another woman agreed, warning that if I stayed alone in this room I might even burn down the building sometime, that there was no way to predict what such a serious enemy was capable of. Deng just laughed, and as I entered told me to pack my things, since the next day the cadres and Lao Wei would return to Beijing, and I would move. With their departure, the first stage of my term in the countryside came to an end.

My new house had belonged to the biggest landlord in the village, and when his property was divided, one room was given to an elderly couple, whom I called Old Aunt and Old Uncle. Old Aunt, now sixty-one, had married twice before and had twice been widowed. Old Uncle, three years younger, had never married before the land reform, as he had been a shepherd and sometimes a courier, transporting merchandise on horseback from one village to another. He had led an itinerant life, never having enough money to marry. When he was given a room at the time of the land reform, he had finally been able to find a wife and settle down.

The landlords' houses in that village were always built as four separate rooms around a courtyard. Previously the best room in the richest landlord's house, my new quarters faced south and caught the warmth of the afternoon sun. Against one wall stood a *kang*, around the others, pieces of furniture inherited from the landlord, a beautifully carved antique table of red peach wood, flanked by two red lacquered chests, one for food storage and one for clothing, and a simple cupboard for bowls. In the middle of the tamped earth floor was a cooking fire; a cistern for water and a kerosene lamp completed the furnishings and satisfied all of our daily needs. Against one of the outside walls was the latrine, open to the sky, where every day we dumped the ashes from the fire on the hard earth floor. With the urine absorbed by the ashes and the excrement consumed eagerly by the pigs, the toilet was always very clean.

The *kang* in my new home was not hot like the one I had gotten used to, but always pleasantly warm, as the old couple knew just how to regulate the fire. With only three sleeping together instead of six, I was much more comfortable. At first I felt offended when Old Uncle would get up in the night and urinate into a wooden bucket beside the door, but I soon got used to the sound. From the day I arrived, Old Aunt treated me just like a daughter, saying that all her life she had never had children and that heaven had sent me to her. That first night after we had washed the supper dishes by the fire, I told stories from the books Lao Tang had brought me, then sang some drum songs I had learned from my baby's nurse. I felt cheerful and relaxed in my new surroundings, and very relieved that the cadres had left.

The labor was also less demanding now because Spring Festival

71

was near and the whole village bustled with preparations. Every day I helped Old Aunt to clean and mend, readying the house for the coming year by dusting the windows and sweeping the corners free of cobwebs. Sometimes we would soak soy beans, then grind them and wrap the paste in a cloth, finally pressing it with a heavy stone to produce dried bean curd. Sometimes we would fry almonds, grind them to a paste, and boil the fragrant mixture until the oil could be spooned from the surface. Sometimes we would grind millet and sweet rice, making the New Year's cakes to fry in the almond oil.

Some days I would go out instead with Old Uncle to care for the sheep, listening with interest to his reminiscences. Once when I asked why he had married so late, he admitted that not only had he lacked money, but he had always been afraid of women, feeling unable to speak easily around them and preferring the freedom of a single man. I admired his honesty and directness, and found my estimation of intellectuals diminishing during those peaceful days. I even began to think maybe I would like to spend my life in just such a small village and not in a university at all.

When the other chores were finished, I would go out alone to gather grass for pig food on the far mountain slopes, admiring the beauty of the landscape near Baihuashan, "One Hundred Flowers Mountain." The many varieties of trees and shrubs, the clear waters of the river far below, the crisp blue skies of the North China winter made me recall classical poems that celebrated a return to nature. It cheered me to recite lyrics extolling just such a life of simplicity, of rising like a bird with the sun to go out to work, then returning to rest when the light had disappeared from the sky. As I grew accustomed to the uncomplicated routine of my days, and the love of the two old peasants, I thought that I had found something very precious indeed. To be far from politics, from the competition for power, from the struggle for better living conditions, seemed daily more desirable.

Even after the holidays, life was much happier than before. Work on the dam had stopped because of the freezing weather, and I was carrying smaller rocks for a collective piggery now that pigs were no longer allowed to remain in individual households. But far more important, after months without feeling any human warmth I had become part of a family again. Each evening I looked with pleasure at the new curtains I had made from cheerful peach-flowered cotton bought with my small monthly wages, and at the red paper scrolls I had hung beside the windows and doors to bring prosperity in the new year.

The old peasants spoke very little, but I needed no words to sense their love and concern. When Old Uncle and I returned from our work, Old Aunt would always have prepared something special to supplement the daily portions of steamed buns and porridge from the communal kitchen. One day she would stew some soy beans or fry some peanuts, another day she would simmer some beans with hot sauce, and once she even cooked eight eggs together, a feast fit for a festival. I never learned where she got such delicacies, perhaps from the village store or from the supplies she kept carefully hidden away in her chest. She may have found the peanuts on the walks she took when we went out to our labor each day, and the eggs she must have carefully saved from her two chickens, since most of what they laid had to be sold to the state at a low price. We ate with great relish whatever she prepared, sitting beside a low table on the *kang*, but she always refused to join us, saying that we were doing the heavy work and she didn't need the extra food. The warmth of this couple made me think differently even about my labor, seeing it no longer as a hardship and a punishment but simply as participation in the tasks of the village.

During the two months of the cadres' absence, I also made two other close friends among the villagers. One was a woman my age who had never been to school and could neither read, write, nor count above ten. She was eager to learn, and I met with her every night. After two months she was able to write down such practical information as the number of days she had done labor.

The second young woman would never accept my help. Given to another family as a child bride, she was twenty-four and long considered a widow, her future husband having died before she had reached marriageable age. As she walked with me in the mountains gathering grass, she taught me folksongs from the Zhaitang area in her clear, lilting voice. Gradually I learned of the oppression

73

she suffered from her mother-in-law, for whom she cleaned the house, sewed clothing, prepared meals, all the while enduring constant abuse and being told she was the cause of her intended husband's death. I urged her not to weep at her situation, but to begin a new life, go away, marry again. Always she replied woodenly that she had no parents and no place to go, that remarriage was unthinkable, that she would just endure her bitter fate. None of my urging could convince her to seek some alternative to such passive submission. Nor would she let me teach her to read, insisting that she was too stupid to learn. I greatly admired the diligence with which she performed her burdensome tasks, but lamented her acquiescence. She had just given up hope.

Also during the cadres' absence I was able to spend more time with Lao Shi. At first we had pretended scarcely to know each other, even though we had been close friends for several years. In Zhaitang he had become the favorite of all the peasants because of his strong physique and sunny personality. He could carry as much as two hundred and twenty pounds on his back, walk very fast, and climb the highest trees to pick walnuts. Handsome, tall, broad shouldered, and always helpful, he carried water for any family that had no strong male to perform such tasks.

During the early weeks of 1959, we often worked together carrying rocks for the piggery, and he would help me with the heaviest ones, at the same time telling amusing stories to lift my spirits. He knew I was pondering many unanswerable questions, wondering what had gone wrong in my life, trying to understand how I had become an enemy. He always urged me not to think so much, but to be more like the peasants. When he was declared a rightist, his girl friend had left him for another man, but he always said he didn't mind; maybe he would someday find a simple peasant girl to be his wife.

One day when we had finished our labor, this time carrying manure from the piggery to the fields, I sat on a rock beside a small stream to wash my feet, and he came to sit nearby. It was still very cold, but we couldn't waste wood to heat water for washing, and this fast-moving stream never froze. Even the highest official, Lao Shi reflected, cannot see a more beautiful sunset than a peasant sees, so why be melancholy at such a change of fortune. Perhaps in the future we will be viewed as genuine patriots, no one can tell. Then his tone lightened and he entertained me with the latest village gossip, recounting details about current love affairs, all the while making these petty intrigues sound lively and humorous. Theirs is a natural life, he commented admiringly; they have their own way, concentrate on their own needs, and have no interest in political affairs. Through such conversations we grew closer.

When in March the second group of sent-down cadres arrived from Beida, Lao Wei returned to Zhaitang with them. Accompanying the cadres from the Chinese literature department was Lao Chen, who had been the leader of that group of eager new university students I joined in Wuhan for the journey to Beijing in 1948. During the land reform he had been the head of the Beida students assigned to Jiangxi province, and we had remained good friends. Now he was Party secretary of my department. After settling the others in a nearby village, he returned to Zhaitang to find me.

Drawing me aside for a talk, Lao Chen urged me to remember that even though things sometimes go wrong, they will before long be turned right again. Such trying times as these, he counseled, were a test for a true revolutionary, a precious test of a person's character and loyalty to the Party. In such adverse circumstances, in the face of such harsh treatment, the revolutionary could reveal his true morality. Advising me to adopt a long-range view and not think only about the present, he reminded me that my whole future stretched ahead, then said he felt confident that one day I would return to my department and make an important contribution to the field of Chinese literature.

To hear such encouragement from a friend in authority gave me renewed strength during that period when my whole life seemed in doubt. At least one person understands I am not as bad as people have testified, I thought gratefully. In his warmth and confidence I found the courage to persevere, do my best, and retain some faith in the capacity of intellectuals for human feeling.

The new cadres, members of the math department, spent their first five days in the village attending meetings to learn about the class struggle situation in Zhaitang. Only the rightists went out for labor with the peasants that week, so I had several opportunities to talk with Lao Wei about what was happening in Beijing. One piece of news was deeply distressing: Lao Lu had been caught stealing someone's purse on a crowded bus. Such petty theft ordinarily would have been considered a minor offense, but since Lao Lu had already been condemned as a rightist, he was sent immediately to Chadian prison farm. A bleeding ulcer had kept him from being sent to the countryside along with the other rightists, and he had stayed at home, agonizing over his inability to feed his family. Together he and his wife earned each month only forty-eight *yuan*, about twenty-four dollars, hardly enough to feed his older child, his new baby, and his elderly mother. The authorities may have had the right to make him endure hunger, since they had cast him out from the people, he told me later, but they had no right to impose this suffering on his two small children. Desperate for money and outraged at the injustice to his family, he decided to steal from some high official's child in return.

Much later I learned the details of his ordeal on that prison farm during the three years of famine from 1959 to 1961. The prisoners, regardless of the scarcity of food, were assigned to do heavy labor, constructing new buildings on the prison grounds. They became so hungry that they would search for frogs in the fields, skin them, and eat them raw. Four people shared Lao Lu's cell, one of whom was too sick to work. In this cell the prisoners kept a cricket, just to hear its song, as they had no other source of amusement. Every day they would give it small bits of food, and every night listen to its music, but one day they had returned to find the cricket missing. The sick cellmate admitted he had been so hungry he had eaten their tiny pet.

Lao Lu labored on the prison farm as a bricklayer for three years, surviving somehow despite his illness. Then for twenty-four years after his release, he worked as a skilled mason, popular among his fellow laborers and admired by his apprentices, continuing to read and write at home in the evenings. Finally, he was assigned a job teaching ancient Chinese poetry once again at another university in Beijing.

Lao Wei's account of my friend's arrest and imprisonment revived my earlier questioning, and I pondered with renewed distress issues of philosophy and morality. Although Lao Lu's petty theft was clearly wrong, it had been motivated by the intolerable conditions under which he had been forced to live, not by some flaw in his character. He had always been a gentle, thoughtful, dedicated man who would never have turned to crime had he been given a way to survive within the system. Again I thought sadly that the policy of casting people as enemies and forcing them outside the circle of society did far greater harm than good.

A Handful of Walnuts

DURING THE autumn of 1959, our situation in Zhaitang grew increasingly difficult. The porridge became thinner daily until the peasants remarked laconically that a watery bowlful was just like a mirror, useful only for reflecting your face. We were told that the harvest had been very bad in our village, but I knew that the climate was not the cause of our deprivation. That spring the peasants had been instructed to plow up all the fields they had just planted, for the unnecessary distance between seedlings was reducing production. The fields were subsequently replanted according to the new guidelines, but by then the time for sowing had passed, and the cold weather arrived before the new crops could mature.

The peasants were also ordered to renew the soil by digging deeper than ever before, but beneath the fertile topsoil lay the sand from the river bed in which nothing could grow. The cadres implementing the new policies usually knew little about agriculture, but they insisted that the peasants dig down three feet, and even walked through the fields to measure the depth of the furrows. As a result, the only harvest that year came either from the few fields that had escaped the plow, saved by recalcitrant village leaders or truculent old peasants skeptical about the new orders, or from the small terraced plots deep in the mountains where the cadres had not bothered to check.

The harvest time brought personal disaster as well. One day Lao Shi was picking walnuts from the very top of a tall tree when he slipped, fell to the ground, and was knocked unconscious. Realizing that he was injured seriously, the old man with whom he lived walked more than ten miles, a whole day's journey, to find a local doctor who made his living as a hunter in the mountains, occasionally practicing the folk remedies passed on by his father. If Lao Shi had been a cadre, a car would have been ordered from Beida to take him back for medical treatment, but since he was a rightist, he was not entitled to such consideration.

Lao Shi soon regained consciousness but remained paralyzed from the waist down, unable to control his bladder functions. The local doctor massaged his back, which caused great pain, then began a kind of surgical procedure, inserting a long needle at one-inch intervals along his spine to draw out some thread-like matter that the peasants called "white wool." After removing what must have been part of the nerve sheath, he left some herbs to be boiled and drunk. Somehow the treatment worked, and gradually Lao Shi recovered. In one week he could move his lower limbs again, and after an additional week's rest, he was sufficiently cured to return to labor, although he never undertook such strenuous tasks as before. In the damp weather he continued to feel pains in his back, but otherwise he was cured.

Throughout his recuperation I visited the peasants' house where he lived to assist three times a day with his care, even changing his soiled bedding, a routine that led to a familiarity unthinkable under normal circumstances. Every day I would take him some special food purchased surreptitiously, since rightists were not allowed to buy from the village store. Knowing that the peasants would never report my breach of regulations, I would wait until the cadres were busy elsewhere, then slip inside to buy a few small biscuits with the food coupons I had saved. Hard and stale as those cookies were, their slight sweetness tasted delicious to someone very hungry. Lao Shi at first could only lie on the *kang* looking intently at me, unable even to smile. The old peasants took special care of him as well, grateful for the many household chores he performed. Wanting to rebuild his strength, the old woman, herself unable to leave the *kang* because of paralyzed legs, somehow prepared eggs for Lao Shi and buns made from white flour, a great luxury when the peasants ate only millet.

After our rightist labels were removed in 1961, Lao Shi returned to Beida for one year, but then was transferred to Yunnan, his father's birthplace, to be a middle-school teacher, his virtual exile a consequence of having earned the leaders' disfavor with his ironic and sometimes disrespectful remarks. After that he would send me a poem every year on my birthday, but he never included his return address. Then in the Cultural Revolution the letters stopped altogether. Worried by his silence, I tried unsuccessfully to find out what had happened. Not until 1976 did a secretary in our department inform me that Lao Shi had been beaten to death by Red Guards for trying to escape to Burma. Such a story seemed preposterous. I could imagine no extremity that would have driven him to such a desperate effort to escape, and felt certain that the official story was merely an excuse. Undoubtedly, the Red Guards had needed some justification for administering a fatal beating and had claimed self-righteously that they were punishing a traitor. Since his father was also dead, a cousin came to the university in 1979 to request posthumous rehabilitation. Lao Shi received the same terse letter reversing his verdict as had Zhu Jiayu.

I had relied heavily on his cheerful resilience during the months of severe famine in Zhaitang, which lasted from the autumn harvest of 1959 until the following June when the first winter wheat ripened. For more than half a year, sheer survival became everyone's overriding concern. Like the other villagers, Lao Shi and I would go daily to the mountains to collect pits from the fallen apricots, discarding the bitter fruit, edible only in times of extreme hunger, but saving the seeds to be pressed for oil or boiled for porridge. The sent-down cadres organized a group to investigate other ways of obtaining nourishment, by crushing corncobs into powder, for example, and mixing this with a little corn flour to make buns. Such rough, unpalatable fare was given the elegant name of "plant protein." An even cruder kind of bun was made by mixing crushed rice husks and corncobs together with a small amount of ground corn. We also gathered apricot leaves, dried them in the sun, and ground them into flour, sometimes mixing this with powdered elm tree bark to make a porridge. It was a desperate time.

Lao Tang's weekly letters were a source of great comfort, even though my heart would ache to read the simple notes from Tang Dan talking about her favorite foods and remarking, "I miss eating fish," or seeing the scribbles in Tang Shuang's baby hand that were his only means of communication. Lao Tang always wrote about the children's development and about how much he missed me. Week after week he encouraged me to find some way to surmount whatever difficulties I was encountering and reassured me that my personality, my talents, and my strength of will would enable me to perform successfully whatever was demanded. His confidence in my ability to endure gave me courage.

In those weeks of scarcity, the village pigs were starving in the collective piggery that we had labored day after day to build. Finally, the pen was abandoned, and the pigs were sent back to individual households to forage in the latrines. The new cadres who had arrived the previous March had purchased four small pigs of their own, intending them to provide meat by the time of the next Spring Festival. Tired of struggling to find ways to feed their animals, the new leader of the women cadres in the early autumn of 1959 assigned me that job. She was less abusive and rigid than Yang Li, and seemed to want to give me a respite from the harsher kinds of labor. However, she warned me sternly that if I was unable to raise the pigs successfully, I would bear full responsibility. After giving me a little precious rice-husk powder to mix with whatever else I could find, she told me just to manage somehow to make the pigs fatten. I took my new responsibilities very seriously, and from that day on began a new life with those pigs, growing deeply attached to my charges and wanting them with all my heart to survive.

Every day I got up early and took the pigs either to the mountain terraces to search for a few soy beans or a sweet potato that might have been overlooked, or else to the foot of the mountains where some corn might have fallen among the leaves or some nuts or apricots been buried in the underbrush. I also gathered a bitter weed that grew on the hillsides and wrote to ask Lao Tang to send me some yeast so that I could prepare a kind of fermented fodder. The mixture exuded a rich fragrance, and the pigs consumed it avidly. Now that I was applying some of the information I had gained from those books in Beijing, I too felt happy and useful.

That year the walnut and apricot harvest had been plentiful, and many pits still remained in the distant mountains where the fruit could not be easily harvested for export. Often I would just head off for a new part of the hills with a stick and the four pigs, letting them forage while I filled a shoulder basket with edible weeds to carry back and mix with small amounts of rice-husk flour. Sometimes while watching the pigs feeding so eagerly I would even forget my own hunger. Despite my efforts, the cadres in December sold their animals to the government outlet store, having decided that the pigs would never be fat enough to slaughter by Spring Festival. I actually felt bereft when my companions were taken away.

Pigs were also the source of my greatest travail during those months, for our food was so coarse that everyone was seriously constipated. The mothers would even have to dig the feces out of their children's rectums with sticks. When I met my brother in 1982 in Reno, Nevada, where we shared a room in the luxurious MGM Hotel, he recalled a particularly vivid letter I had written him during this period of famine. I had longed to tell someone about the difficulties of those days, but had not wanted to alarm Lao Tang and instead had written my brother about the terrible problem of going to the latrine that winter, when the ground was frozen hard and it was so painful to move the bowels. I always had to take with me a long, stout stick to keep away the desperately hungry pigs, who would follow me and try frantically to snatch the fresh excrement right from my body as I squatted. They were large animals and dangerous because of their extreme hunger, making me dread the daily ordeal of having to strain to move the bowels and at the same time fight off the starving pigs.

In those bitter months of winter, there had been no food for the sheep, so Old Uncle would take them far away to search for scarce grass and fallen apricots. Always he brought me back something from those trips, sometimes two or three walnuts, sometimes four or five peanuts salvaged from nests where the squirrels had hidden them the previous summer. Old Uncle never ate any of this bounty, saying that he had been hungry many times before, while the famine must be very difficult for me. Never had I experienced such generosity. When everyone is rich, a handful of walnuts means nothing, but in those conditions such a gift is unspeakably precious, the gift of life itself. I could not imagine being treated with such selflessness by an intellectual. Old Uncle, saying only that it made him happy to see me eat, always refused to share the nuts, ostensibly because his teeth were bad and he could not chew very well.

During those months nearly everyone in Zhaitang became swollen from malnutrition. After some of the sent-down cadres returned to Beida with alarming reports about the severity of the famine, a team of doctors was dispatched to examine us, but neither my legs nor my face had grown puffy from dropsy. I always felt certain that those walnuts and peanuts had helped sustain my health.

My weeks of wandering alone in the mountains gave me endless hours to think, and sometimes I felt almost lighthearted, so pleasant was it to enjoy this unaccustomed sense of freedom and closeness to nature. But always my mind returned to the same unsettling questions. What had happened to the bright future I had so fervently envisioned for myself and my country? I would sometimes recite a poem by the Russian poet Pushkin, titled "When You Discover Life Has Cheated You," which captured my own feelings quite aptly. A more cheerful diversion was to recall the songs I had sung during a particular period of my life, and then, by association, to remember everything that had happened to me in those days. Revolutionary ballads, and Protestant hymns, Guizhou folk tunes and Stephen Foster lyrics would spill from my lips in the clear mountain air, unleashing a cascade of memories.

My favorite song was a Russian movie tune that I had learned in Moscow that summer of 1950 when I was nineteen, en route to Prague as a delegate from Beijing to attend the second World Student Congress. The chairman of our group of twenty-four had been a formal and orthodox man, a high official of the Youth League, but the vice-chairman was far less rigid. A young man who had previously been chairman of the Beida Student Union and who had led all the student movements to oppose the Guomindang in 1947, this Lao Hong had been placed at the top of the Guomindang's black list and had fled to the Liberated Areas to escape being killed. It was he who taught me this song.

In those years the Soviet people considered China a member of the "big socialist family," and all across Siberia we received an enthusiastic welcome. At every stop the people waved banners with slogans expressing their warm wishes and gave us flowers, sometimes even carrying us on their shoulders when we stepped from the train. Enjoying this hospitality, we rested after our long trip on the trans-Siberian railroad at the elegant International Hotel in Moscow before continuing on to Prague.

In those luxurious surroundings I never felt at ease. I would gaze in awe at the lobby's magnificent carpets and chandeliers, at the gleaming silver in the dining room, at the waiters in cutaway jackets and bow ties. Those waiters particularly troubled me, and I wondered why in a socialist country some people should remain so servile. I had assumed that here everyone would be treated equally. Everything around me seemed strange, and our leader's instructions did nothing to lessen my discomfort. We students should not go out alone, he ordered, as we might lose our way and never be able to get back to the hotel, or we might be kidnapped, something that often happened in foreign countries, for either political or economic reasons. The Soviet Union was not turning out to be at all as I had imagined.

Despite those warnings and my fatigue after the eight-day journey, I was so eager to see Lenin's tomb that I could scarcely conceal my disappointment. To my surprise there was a knock on my door just after ten o'clock that evening, and Lao Hong, who had been to Moscow several times before, offered to accompany me to Red Square. Astonished, I replied that we were forbidden to leave our rooms, but he waved away my concern, assuring me that everyone was asleep. The Kremlin wall and the group of church domes outlined against the night sky filled me with awe. We walked around the square, pausing at Lenin's tomb, then sat on the steps to rest. It was there that Lao Hong taught me this haunting revolutionary love song, "My Heart Is Singing." The lyrics describe a man who is sent to the revolutionary wars but who always remains in the heart of the woman he has left behind.

We developed a warm relationship during those weeks, and in Prague Lao Hong asked me to marry him. He wanted me to stay there at the student headquarters as his secretary, assuring me that later I could study at Moscow University or in Leningrad. I was fond of Lao Hong, and the opportunity to study in the Soviet Union was very tempting, but still I felt reluctant to become totally dependent on someone else, even this man I considered a revolutionary hero. Besides, I wanted to finish my studies at Beida, where that spring I had come to know Lao Tang. After some hesitation, I returned home with the rest of the delegation. When Lao Hong came to Beijing the next year, he urged me to reconsider his proposal, but I had already fallen in love.

Lao Tang was then secretary of the Youth League branch for all the social science departments, while I was in charge of propaganda. As we worked together, I noticed how different he seemed from other students, more thoughtful, more interesting, more knowledgeable. When we visited a temple together, he could tell its date just by observing the architectural details; he could date the Bodhisattvas by their sculptural lines and entertain me with their stories. The short essays he had published in the newspaper at sixteen, philosophical reflections on beauty, truth, and death, impressed me with their sensitivity. Death should be approached not as something frightening and repellent, he had written, but rather as an everlasting rest, a visit to an unknown realm, a transformation comparable to that of an ugly black pupa after eight long years into a winged cicada.

Lao Tang was also fond of music and had managed to buy a number of records from people hastily selling their belongings before fleeing to Taiwan. Sometimes he would carry his phonograph to the Youth League office and after the others had left, I would stay to listen to scratchy renditions of Mozart and Tchaikovsky. One weekend evening in the spring of 1950, we went with two friends to the lotus-filled pond beside the Natural Sciences Institute on our campus, then still located in the center of Beijing. Taking along the phonograph, we listened to records under a full moon. Annoyed that the frogs were disturbing the music, Lao Tang jumped up, pulled off his shoes and socks, and waded into the pond. He never caught the frogs but managed to scare them momentarily into silence. I found this young man more than ever interesting, his enthusiasm and spontaneity very appealing. We four sat on the grass beside that pond all night, relating stories from our childhood and talking about the future until five o'clock in the morning, when we climbed to the top of Coal Hill behind the Imperial Palace to watch the sunrise. As the first golden rays reached the yellow roofs of the palace buildings, we spoke of our visions of the bright future that awaited us.

My admiration for Lao Tang grew after the annual Beida Youth League Congress held in April for some three hundred delegates. During the time for criticisms to be aired, someone stood up to attack him sharply as a typical bourgeois person who lacked a proletarian consciousness. Rather than sleeping, the critic accused, Lao Tang would spend the whole night beside a pond talking with girls; such a person was not fit to be a Youth League branch leader. I was criticized as well for not having a sufficiently strong political consciousness, since on the one day a month set aside as Youth League Day, rather than organizing a political discussion or session of newspaper reading, I had taken a picnic with Lao Tang to the Fragrant Hills. Despite the strong objections raised against us, we both received a majority of the votes and thus retained our Youth League positions. Having weathered the storm of criticism together, we grew closer.

On May 4, 1950, Beida planned a big celebration to commemorate the student protests on that date in 1919, and I was given responsibility for the whole affair. That night we lit a huge bonfire in Democracy Square where the demonstrators had gathered more than thirty years before, after which a professional troupe led us in the steps to a collective dance. More than a thousand of us danced together in the firelight, our voices joined in the revolutionary song, "United Together We Have Great Strength." Having spent hours making arrangements for the music, the dance troupe, the loudspeakers, the firewood, I was quite exhausted by the end of the evening when Lao Tang came up to offer his congratulations on my successful organization of the celebration.

The day before I left for Moscow, he asked me to meet him in our office in the Red Building that evening for a talk. Munching peanuts and sipping the bottles of soda he had provided, we stood beside the second floor window looking out across the beautiful yellow-tiled palace. It was then that he declared his feelings, saying that he admired my personal qualities, that we shared the same political viewpoints, and that he wanted to spend the rest of his life with me. Although I remained silent, he could sense my response. I asked if he wasn't fearful of criticism for staying so long in the evening alone with a girl, but he insisted he didn't care, reinforcing my respect for his courage and determination, his disdain for rumor and scandal. In addition, I knew he was trusted by the Party and admired as a political leader, all of which enhanced my attraction to his romantic personality. All of these unspoken reasons contributed to my refusal of Lao Hong's proposal in Prague.

How different my life would have been had I stayed in Prague, I reflected, or even had I studied foreign languages at Beida and pursued my interest in Western culture as I had originally intended. But Shen Congwen, an eminent novelist and a teacher in the Chinese literature department, had urged me on the basis of my entrance examination essay to become his student. Otherwise I would no doubt have become a translator or interpreter after graduation with no thoughts about a new magazine, no visions of a new beginning for Chinese literature. Had I not chosen to study with Shen Congwen, I realized, I might never have become a rightist. I pondered the ironies of fate. In 1949, as part of my Democratic Youth League activities, I had, in turn, urged Shen Congwen not to be frightened of the Communist victory, not to take advantage of the free airplane tickets to Taiwan being given to the country's most prestigious intellectuals, but to stay and work for the future of the new China. Had he made a different decision, he would have avoided being attacked in 1952 for his bourgeois viewpoints, dismissed from Beida, and condemned to a tedious and isolated position as an archivist in the Palace Museum.

Others were also dismissed from Beida in 1952, like Fei Ming, also a teacher in my department and a poet famous for merging the techniques of Western modernism and Chinese lyricism. I had come to know Fei Ming in 1951 when he was assigned to my production team in Jiangxi province to reform his thoughts. He was not expected to aid with the land reform; he was just to observe the transformation of the countryside so that he would come to appreciate the contributions of the people's government. The other young people were too impatient to listen to him speak in his strong Hubei accent, but I would sit until late into the night in the small administration building where we both stayed, learning his views of life.

Often he would speak of his teacher Zhou Zuoren, the brother of China's most famous modern writer, Lu Xun. Head of the Ministry of Education under the Japanese puppet government, Zhou had been condemned as a collaborator and a traitor. Fei Ming always insisted, however, that Zhou's actions were motivated by a desire to protect Chinese education and preserve Chinese culture, even when that goal necessitated cooperation with the enemy. Human dilemmas are never clear-cut, Fei would argue passionately, and they can never be judged simply.

During the daytime when the rest of us were away in the mountains, Fei often bought meat in the village and stewed it secretly on the coal stove to supplement the evening meals we were obliged to eat with the peasants. Always he would leave some for me at night. Such trivial infractions seemed to me insignificant; I never objected when people in my group bought small cakes to augment the peasants' diet. At the annual meeting to draw conclusions about the teachers' political thought, however, I was criticized for having petit bourgeois inclinations, for being too liberal, and for not strictly enforcing Party discipline.

In 1952 Fei Ming was attacked as a bourgeois writer, dismissed, and sent to Changchun University far away in the northeast. Periodically, he wrote me letters recalling the time we had spent together during the land reform, referring to me as the sunshine from the proletariat appearing on the horizon, and saying that I had made his acceptance of the new society much easier. Both he and Shen Congwen had believed that I would make some important contribution to the new China. Both would be shocked and dismayed to learn what my future had become, I thought, as I followed my pigs. No one could have foreseen the changes that would occur in a decade, nor predict that the promise of so many lives would disappear, along with the promise of the land reform period.

The part of Jiangxi province to which Fei Ming and I had been sent in 1951 was very prosperous, the mountainsides covered with large bamboo trees, their thick trunks prized for building houses or furniture, carts or baskets, and a valuable source of income. Every day I had gone with work teams of eager peasants into those high mountains to measure the land previously owned by landlords. We would walk long distances and climb steep slopes to determine the acreage and distribute it equitably, usually in plots of ten *mou* per family, allotting smaller parcels if the land was particularly fertile. Each morning we would take along only some sweet potatoes and a *wok*, then at mid-day gather as many wild bamboo shoots as we could eat, collect some wood, and cook a tasty dish. At night with the peasants we had eaten sweet potatoes, beans, rice, and sometimes even small fish from the river. Now the peasants no longer owned their land; there was no eagerness, no optimism, not even simple food.

As I thought about the vastness of China and the official explanation that the famine in 1959 was the result of natural conditions, of inadequate rainfall, I had many doubts. I knew that nearly every year China faced some climatic problems, but that often a good harvest in the South would compensate for a drought in the North. This year the famine had struck across the land. The whole country was afflicted and people everywhere were desperately hungry.

A letter from my father had described the severe dearth in Guiyang, where the bark had been stripped from the trees for food. When you walk in the mountains, he wrote, an eerie landscape confronts you, especially at night in the moonlight when you can see nothing but white, naked trunks, shorn of their bark and leaves. Some of the peasants had left to seek other places where the famine was less severe, others had gone to the mountains in search of anything edible. Many had died.

The rest of the letter was cheerful, describing how my parents had walked six miles to a spot deep in the mountains to gather seeds from the tea oil bushes. The wheat they had grown in their courtyards had just yielded a good harvest, and they had returned from their trek via a small country mill, carrying back nearly a quart of oil and a bag of flour. With strict rationing in effect for oil and each person allowed only three ounces per month, and with no one in South China able to eat wheat flour, such bounty was extremely precious. The taste of the fried pancakes they had cooked, even though my father was allotted a special ration of corn as a high-ranking intellectual, had never before been so delicious, he wrote, as when such simple pleasures were unobtainable. His letter concluded with an observation that I shared: perhaps a simple existence, just working for one's daily bread, actually afforded life's greatest fulfillment.

When I read my father's letter and thought about the conditions around me, I found the outcome of the past decade to be quite unimaginable. Many more people had died in Zhaitang that year than usual, especially the older ones who often gave away their food and thus grew steadily weaker. I had seen that human error had caused the disastrous harvest; I knew that the climate had been favorable; I had picked fruit from the trees in the mountains, observing their plentiful yield. Never before had I been directly skeptical about official policy, but now I could not avoid recognizing that the Party itself was to blame.

Even when I had been condemned as a rightist and my own fate had seemed so unjust, I had been able to believe that maybe the leaders were right, maybe some people were truly trying to destroy the Communist Party, maybe strong measures were necessary to eliminate this threat. I always consoled myself with the thought that in such a big movement there would inevitably be innocent victims, that to cut out a cancerous growth, some healthy tissue must also be sacrificed. If my country wanted me to be such a victim, I would simply bear that burden. But when the famine came, my trust was shaken. I knew that the Party's goal was to improve the standard of living in the countryside, yet what had happened was precisely the opposite. This time I could find no justification. Unlike me, the peasants never seemed to attribute their sufferings to the Party's policies; they just found what they could to eat, concentrating all their attention on the daily struggle to survive.

As the winter of 1959 dragged on and the famine continued, the Party began to relax its policies in compensation for the extreme economic depression. The cadres' attitudes toward us became less severe. We were even advised of the possibility of removing our "rightist caps" if we truly understood and acknowledged our mistakes. We all knew that the most important criterion for the restitution of our rights as citizens was a confession of guilt. Arguing that it was not important what one said in such a situation, since mere words didn't constitute actual guilt, Lao Wei wrote a long confession, after which he was carefully observed and evaluated. Taking off a rightist's cap was a very serious political act then, and his personality and attitude toward labor were thoroughly discussed among the cadres, all of whom had to express an opinion. Many meetings were held to solicit the views of the peasants as well, for if just one peasant had dissented, Lao Wei would have remained a rightist. However, the peasants all testified that he had worked conscientiously, and the cadres agreed that his attitude toward his crime was sufficiently penitent. The decision to remove his cap was unanimous. Because we had been friends for many years, he talked with me at length about what he had written in his confession, urging me to follow his example.

Complying with the demand that rightists acknowledge their guilt fully, he had admitted an ambitious desire to attain a position of leadership in the League of Youth. Knowing him to be selflessly devoted to the goals of the Party, I voiced my disbelief in his self-criticism and told him I could never similarly falsify my own motivations. He advised me to learn from the ancient sage Zhuangzi that nothing in life is absolute. He didn't mind admitting whatever the cadres wanted, he said, for such an action was useful for the Party and advantageous for him as well.

A fierce struggle waged within me, for I wanted to go home, and the possibility that Lao Wei held out to me was very tempting. But in the end, I could not write something dishonest. I confessed that I had wanted to do something to distinguish myself and had not been sufficiently obedient to authority, but I just could not allege that I had intended to take over the power of the department or that I had wanted to harm the Party. Predictably, the cadres were not satisfied with my confession, so Lao Wei alone had his cap taken off.

Some of the others did confess to all of the crimes they had been accused of, unaware that only a few exemplary rightists in the whole country were in fact to be allowed to remove their caps at that time. When Lao Wei left for Beijing as Spring Festival approached, the others of us felt greatly discouraged. Lao Wei had known how to flatter the cadres and maintain good relations with everyone in the village. Sensing my regret, Lao Shi said to me firmly: "We will simply tell the truth."

Our situation in Zhaitang became increasingly relaxed, and on that second Spring Festival Eve, in February 1960, we rightists were even allowed to hold a party. Pooling the monthly coupons for the three ounces of refreshments allotted each of us, we purchased a few coarse cakes and biscuits from the village store. Even such a simple gathering had been unimaginable in the first year, when we were not permitted to speak together. At the party everyone carefully avoided political talk and spent the evening singing. Lao Shi had a beautiful voice and sang a famous Russian folk song about a revolutionary who had been exiled by the czar. Lake Baikal is our mother, he sang, and she always warms the hearts of exiles; as I wander around the lake, I know our cause is just, even though we suffer for the cause of freedom. The melody was haunting, the lyrics moving; but afterward the mood of the party changed and people seemed disconsolate. When my turn came, hoping to revive the cheerful atmosphere, I chose a rousing piece that we had sung often in the university chorus and during the land reform in Jiangxi when the work teams gave performances for the peasants. My mother country, I began, I sing for your tomorrow, a tomorrow that will be bright and clear, with no hardship, hunger, or cold, a time when everyone can share in your abundant blessings.

The next day the cadres declared that the atmosphere of our gathering had been unhealthy. They criticized us sharply. Why had Lao Shi sung of suffering for freedom when we were suffering only for our crimes, they asked. I was attacked even more strongly; in my soul, they said, I was still opposed to the Party's policies. If I wanted a tomorrow that was different from today, then apparently I was dissatisfied with the current situation. Their accusation stung me, for I had sung with all my heart, my voice filled with hope, only to be told that it was forbidden even to imagine a better future.

A few days later we were abruptly informed that our whole group of cadres and rightists would return in two days to Beijing for the Spring Festival holidays. Old Uncle gave me ten walnuts, saved from his trips to the mountains, and Old Aunt presented me with ten eggs. I knew how precious those gifts were during times of such scarcity. Our group took the bus to Yanchi, then the train to Beijing, retracing the steps of so many months before. Since the mail took four days, I had not informed Lao Tang of my arrival, and just walked into our house, totally unannounced.

The homecoming was not at all what I had hoped. Lao Tang was away, and my baby cried when I held him. Yang Dama tried to make him understand that I was his mother, but he didn't know me. Now he was two and running around on sturdy little legs, so changed that I could hardly recognize him. My daughter still remembered me, but I immediately felt the distance between us. She greeted me politely, then stood silently, watching.

Lao Tang's mother welcomed me warmly, but quickly busied herself with practical considerations. My clothing must all be boiled so that the children would not catch my lice, she insisted, and I realized with a start that I must look like an exile or a long-term prisoner in my shabby padded clothing. I had not yet seen a mirror, but of course my skin was not as white as before, due to constant exposure to the sun, and my hair must appear unusually short and crudely cut. When Lao Tang's father commented tactfully that I looked very healthy now, the awkwardness was palpable. I had no idea how to continue the conversation and murmured simply that I was fine, that everything was all right. All the time my daughter stood apart. Finally, Lao Tang's mother broke the silence, saying that I should have something to eat and a bath, and that Daolan would see to boiling my clothing. My obvious distance from everyone was painful, my elation quite dispelled. I sensed that I had lost something forever, that my worlds had split apart, that life among the peasants had unalterably changed me.

When Lao Tang arrived for supper, overjoyed at my return, I concealed my distress and asked brightly about the work he was doing to criticize Feng Youlan, still our neighbor, and to educate students about the distance separating a bourgeois from a proletarian viewpoint. In the Big Criticism Movement that had begun in 1958, an effort to establish definitively a new political system, every professor had been investigated to determine which ones still possessed a bourgeois outlook as a residue of their education under the capitalist system. The goal of the movement was to eradicate such reactionary views and replace them with a proletarian consciousness. Each department had one or two main targets, and the philosophy department was attacking Feng Youlan. All the time that Lao Tang talked about his work, I was thinking sadly that instead of developing a close relationship with my children, I had been developing a close relationship with those four pigs. Sharp pangs of regret and loss mingled in my heart.

The days of the Spring Festival were especially busy in our household that year because of the family's economic situation. Lao Tang's father earned a high salary and had special rations that provided small amounts of butter, sugar, and meat each week and a quart of milk each day, unheard-of luxuries in those hard times. Tang Yongtong was then not only vice-president of Beida but also a vice-president of the People's Political Consultative Conference, which had its own shop and a cafeteria for high officials. Knowing that we had access to special foods, many guests came to call, but they kept a distance from me.

At the time of my marriage when Lao Tang's mother had reserved three tables in the best restaurant for a wedding banquet, I had refused to attend, alienating the family friends who thought me an arrogant revolutionary, not the same kind of person as they. Now that I was a counter-revolutionary, they were curious about how I would act. Sensing their coldness, I didn't know how to behave or even whether to go forward to greet them as courtesy demanded. I could see the questions in every eye, but I could not just shut myself in my room. Throughout those days my baby was indifferent to me, my daughter stayed away and refused to speak, and Lao Tang spent long hours at his department organizing the students. No one from my department came to call, although many students had remained on campus to criticize reactionary professors. The students were also busy compiling a revised literary history, one that excluded any writers thought to express reactionary views, such as the classical poets who described the beauty of nature without reference to the burdensome life of the peasants. Those were the lyrics that had given me such comfort in recent months. I felt utterly estranged and even thought about returning to Zhaitang early. There at least, in a curious way, I belonged.

My home leave, so long awaited, was thus profoundly depressing. My colleagues ignored me and my children were distant; I was a stranger on the campus and in my family. Professors whom I had admired and respected were being subjected to criticism, while people around me talked endlessly about food, particularly about the mixture of soybeans with several kinds of ground leaves called "protein in chlorophyl" that was supposed to serve as a substitute for meat. With ordinary people allotted just three ounces of oil and nine ounces of meat per month during the famine, subsisting otherwise on grains, I was acutely aware of how privileged I was to live with Lao Tang's family and be spared such daily concerns. But despite my good fortune, I could not forget the discrepancy between my present circumstances and those I had grown accustomed to in Zhaitang. I thought with sadness of the precious nuts and eggs I had brought back, now meaningless amid this relative abundance. Moreover, I had never been able to reestablish the easy familiarity I had always enjoyed with Lao Tang's parents, or my former closeness to my husband. A certain bond had been irreparably broken. Thus it was with a heavy heart that I returned with the new group of sent-down cadres to the countryside after the three-week holiday.

Treating politics even less seriously than the last group, these new cadres sometimes even talked and joked with us. There was no need now to continue constructing the communal piggery, as most of the animals were dead; even the sheep had been sold to the government as meat for the cities. Nobody spoke of the reservoir that had been under construction. All interest in such collective projects was lost, our months of strenuous labor totally wasted.

Throughout that spring of 1960, we just worked with the peasants in the fields, and Old Uncle chose me to help him plant millet seeds on the small terraced plots that covered the mountainsides. We used an ancient method, unchanged for two thousand years, that was ingeniously effective. With a single heavy spade-shaped wooden tool, we could plow the furrows, plant the seeds, and cover them with dirt, all in the same process. Manipulating this cumbersome device required a skilled hand, and only the old peasants knew the technique of jolting the handle to dislodge the seeds individually at the proper intervals. Since the plots were too small for a donkey to turn around in, I would harness myself into a shoulder strap to perform the draft animal's work, sometimes walking fifteen miles in a single day. This routine labor was exhausting but at the same time satisfying. In addition, we were far less hungry than before. Not only had the spring apricot leaves provided a new source of food, but we had been able to harvest some winter wheat and our village had been given some Canadian grain in exchange for the walnuts sent out for export. Occasionally, we even could eat dumplings made with a filling of eggs and vegetables. From my father's letters I knew that in other parts of the country, like Guizhou and Sichuan, the famine had not yet abated, and we considered ourselves fortunate.

In that summer of 1960, many rightists were being permitted to take off their caps, a relatively easy procedure then, as a current slogan announced that people must look to the future and not to the past. The kind of thorough confession that Lao Wei had written was no longer required; we merely had to state that we would never do anything to harm the Party and would be obedient and loyal when we returned to the people. Neither Lao Shi nor I hesitated about signing such a pledge, after which both of us were "uncapped." Because this policy stated that a few people had to retain their caps to educate others about what a rightist was, two in our village were still unable to change their political status, allegedly because their labor had not been as diligent or their confessions had been less sincere.

The difference between them and us was not appreciable, however, for the whole process of restoring political rights was by then imbued with little significance. We felt none of the special accomplishment or dramatic change that Lao Wei had experienced. Even as an "uncapped rightist" there were village meetings I could not attend, but at least I no longer had to make monthly reports on my thoughts or sit with the five or six landlords and bad elements who had survived the famine.

That same summer a heated debate broke out in the Party over the success of the "Three Red Banners," as the Great Leap Forward, the people's commune movement, and the general line for socialist construction were called. Not everyone believed these innovations to be effective, but Party leaders in the Beijing municipality were determined to prove the policies correct. To muster evidence, they sent university students to the countryside to write about the history of the people's communes, confident that such investigations would confirm the Party's judgment.

In the autumn of 1960, now formally reinstated among the people, I was assigned to write the history of one village in the Zhaitang commune. All the cadres participated in similar projects, and I was sent to Lingyuesi, named the Temple of Spiritual Peaks after its famous Buddhist temple, a four-hour walk from Zhaitang. Perched on the top of a mountain, Lingyuesi had been an important pilgrimage site where every Buddhist wanted to burn incense to show his devotion. I took only a small shoulder bag and set out along the footpath in the direction the peasants indicated.

In the distance I could already see the temple surrounded by pine trees. As I drew closer, the tinkling of bells made my destination seem almost ethereal, as if I were walking toward heaven, and I stopped to admire the beautiful fish-shaped copper wind chimes hanging from the temple's gracefully curved rooftops. But I was puzzled by the nearly deserted village street; such a magnificent temple surely testified to a prosperous past. Curious, I presented my letter of introduction, found the production team headquarters, and soon was assigned lodgings. I would move in with a widow whose reputation was above suspicion, her husband having been killed in the Anti-Japanese War, a tragedy assumed to guarantee her loyalty to the Communist cause.

Before Liberation, I learned from the few peasants I met, Lingyuesi had been a bandit hideout. From there marauders would swoop down on the more affluent surroundings of Zhaitang, select hostages, and then return to their mountain redoubt to await ransom. The Japanese had occupied the village because of its strategic location, and later the Guomindang had established a garrison there. The peasants without exception emphasized their sufferings in those successive occupations, explaining how the Nationalists had been relentless in searching for Communist sympathizers, and how the Communists in turn had tried to drag out former Nationalist "baojia" leaders. Many innocent people had been killed by both sides, and almost every family reported losing someone in the struggles.

Lingyuesi was a tiny village with a population of two hundred situated in a remote area far from the political center of the country, but still the recent policies had been strictly enforced there. When the people's commune movement had incorporated all the villages in that area, the cadres had ordered the iron *woks* broken and burned in the backyard furnaces to make steel. Then they had taken the peasants' wood, sometimes the courtyard doors, which were very thick, and the coffins prepared by the elderly, and out of those materials had tried to construct wheeled carts to replace the more primitive carrying baskets. In their efforts to dismantle the family structure and institute collective life, they had organized the adults to live together in the ancestral hall, normally used for meetings, and had sent the young children to a nursery. But the peasants hated the new system, and after a few months everyone went back home, though by then many of the cooking pots and wooden doors had been destroyed.

The policies had never produced their desired results. The carts, as in Zhaitang built by novices, never worked and had all been discarded, the wood simply wasted. The furnaces had produced no steel, just consumed the cooking pots; and the pigs, brought together in a communal pen, were almost all dead of sickness and starvation. A few years ago there had been five oxen in this village, but four had died from lack of food and individual care. The remaining ox was now being raised for the commune by a peasant family.

The newspapers continually heralded the advantages of the commune system, lavishing praise on the reorganization of the countryside and its accomplishments at increasing production. When I arrived in Lingyuesi, however, I found agricultural work largely halted, the plots of terraced land virtually deserted, as there was no one to farm them. All the strong young peasants had been sent away to do collective labor on construction projects for a reservoir and a new road, leaving only the old and the sick behind in the village. The new road across the mountains would eventually connect Zhaitang with the railroad line, replacing the existing road that ran along the river bed and was impassable in times of flood. Someday the fruit grown in those mountains would reach urban markets, whereas now it often fell to the ground, going to waste unless it was consumed by the foraging pigs. I knew that the new road would be useful, but I could also see that the policy of sending so many people to work on collective projects ignored the needs of agriculture.

These observations posed a serious dilemma. Should I report what I had concluded or write what the Party wanted to prove the Three Red Banners correct? I guessed that everyone engaged in similar investigations would be faced with the same question. What I had seen showed the recent policies to be largely wasteful and destructive; you cannot simply put iron into burning coal and expect steel to emerge. Ultimately, I decided to emphasize the tragic history of Lingyuesi and comment as little as possible on the present situation, although I could not fail to include some praise for the official policies.

When an order arrived instructing all of the cadres and rightists to return home before the next Spring Festival, I was filled primarily with apprehension. Aware that we rightists were no longer members of Beida, I could not guess what conditions we would face next. When a list was posted announcing that some of us, myself and Lao Shi included, should report to the university for some unspecified work, those fears were partially allayed. Other people were being sent to the government of Beijing municipality to await a job assignment, to a factory, or to another part of the countryside. At least I would not be separated again from my family. But the last painful vacation was still fresh in my mind, and I had few expectations. It was the winter of 1961; more than two years had passed. My children had grown, Lao Tang's brother had married, and I had changed in more ways than just my political status. For months I had longed to go home, but as the date of departure approached, I felt little joy.

Never Forget Class Struggle

STANDING IN the late November cold awaiting the train that would return me from Yanchi to Beijing, I gazed for a last time at the steep, brooding mountains that had so filled me with dread on my initial journey to Zhaitang. A driving wind whistled through the wires, stinging my cheeks with the pelting sand. Squinting against the dust, I saw again the faces of the two old peasants as they said farewell. Old Aunt had insisted on accompanying me to the truck, even though she coughed continually and walked with difficulty now that intestinal parasites had settled in her gall bladder. In my handbag were their parting gifts, a small packet of walnuts and a half dozen eggs. I pledged silently that I would soon bring this old couple to my home so that they could enjoy the sights of Beijing, but because of Old Aunt's illness and all that was soon to unfold at Beida, my plan was never realized.

Seeking refuge from the bitter weather, I sat inside the small station building looking out through open doors at the impassive mountains beyond. Sadness, anxiety, and anticipation surged together in a tangle of emotions. Behind me lay a life that had grown comfortable and familiar despite its hardships; before me stretched an unknown future. The simple routine of a peasant home, the welcome sight of Old Aunt preparing some hot food at the end of each day, would soon fade into memory. Without question, I decided, the positive aspects of those two years outweighed the negative. I actually felt grateful to have learned about peasant life at firsthand, to have witnessed the way the peasants suffer adversity without complaint, and to have experienced a kind of warmth and kinship that my life as an urban intellectual would probably never provide.

Near me on the station floor sat a young teacher from the math department who had spent nearly three years in another village of the Zhaitang commune. His eyes, so bright and alert when I had known him at Beida, showed only depression and fatigue, and he looked thin and weakened from ill health. Since his academic work had always before been highly praised by his professors, he confided quietly, he hoped to be allowed to remain at the university to finish his research. Even if he succeeded, however, he could never aspire to a position higher than that of a middle-school teacher after having been condemned as a rightist.

This young man should be part of the group leading China into the future, I thought, after he had lapsed back into silence, but along with so many of the most gifted students of his generation, he would probably disappear into obscurity. The student rightists, I knew, were faring worse than the teachers. Many of them, without jobs to return to, were being sent back to their native towns and cities, often to be assigned permanent work on a commune or in a factory. Sadly, I recalled the essays written by the physics students during that spring of 1957, testimonials to their commitment and their capability, their talents now simply wasted.

One night in 1958, before my departure for Zhaitang, the chairman of the physics department, who was a neighbor, had called on Tang Yongtong to discuss the fate of his favorite graduate student. Wanting to save this very promising young man from being exiled to the countryside as a rightist, the professor had appealed to the head of the Beida Party Committee, but had been unable to alter the student's fate. Tang Yongtong characteristically had remained silent, but I could feel his sympathy. "If this is how our future scientists are treated," the distraught professor had remarked fervently, "then all of our work has been in vain." I did not yet know that five hundred students and one hundred faculty members, more than seven percent of the university community, had been declared rightists, but as the train drew nearer to Beijing, I tried to comprehend how the Anti-rightist Campaign would affect the future of my country.

A big open truck met us at the Beijing railroad to transport our group of cadres and rightists back to the campus. Inside the gate all the teachers in my department had assembled to meet their returning colleagues. I stood nearby with the members of the math department who had been with me in Zhaitang, but my former comrades all passed me by. Now that I had taken off my cap and rejoined the people, I had hoped to be treated as before, but some pretended not to see me, while others merely said coldly, "So, you are back."

A crowd of family members had also gathered to meet the truck and help with the unloading of baggage. As more and more people left with their relatives, wheeling their heavy bedrolls on bicycles, I watched eagerly, then nervously, for Lao Tang to arrive. Only after everyone else had left did I see him walking toward me. He said apologetically that he had been unable to leave a meeting, but I still felt hurt, not knowing whether his delay had really been unavoidable. Maybe even he felt insulted to associate with me in front of others and thus had waited for the crowd to disperse to avoid embarrassment. How proud of me he had always been before, I recalled sadly, wondering whether I would ever again feel that same admiration.

At our door his father greeted me with warm words, saying dismissingly that no matter what had happened, at least I was safely back home. He had often been ill after I left, and some months earlier had suffered a stroke. Now half of his body was paralyzed, but even with this handicap, his gentle manner and peace of mind remained unaltered. Lao Tang's mother had prepared a special dinner, serving foods that were still difficult to obtain, and my children had been carefully coached for my arrival. My son called me "Mama," as Yang Dama had taught him; my daughter greeted me politely, then helped me take my things to my room.

Summoned to a meeting the next morning in my department to receive my job assignment, I met a far less cordial reception. Instead of joining the returned cadres, we rightists were directed to a separate room. I had expected to be considered a regular depart-

103

ment member once again, not to remain indefinitely isolated, but we were being signaled from the moment of our return that taking off the rightist's cap did not mean resuming automatically our previous lives.

The department's literary history group had previously numbered thirty-seven members. Before the anti-rightist movement, eleven of those were young teachers who had graduated after Liberation, like me, and ten of those young teachers had received some punishment in 1958, eight of them receiving rightist caps. Some had been sent to the countryside; others had been dismissed from their jobs and reassigned as proofreaders in a publishing house, positions that denied them any contact with students. The single young teacher in our group who had escaped punishment was a person totally uninterested in politics who spent his time reading and studying Tang poetry. This Lao Ding had been criticized for following the "white and expert path," but had ignored the attacks and persevered with his scholarly work. During the spring of 1957, he had tried to remain silent, participating as little as possible. Now many people said that his way was perhaps best, since those who had been concerned with the course of the revolution and had tried to help the country had been punished. Such narrow academic specialists, people said, would invariably be criticized at times, but in the long run that was safer than being involved in political affairs.

If I had not been so involved, I reflected as I waited for the meeting to begin, I could have spent the last two years studying rather than letting my mind essentially lie dormant. Now that I was once again part of the academic world, I couldn't help envying those who had continued to expand their knowledge. Eager to make up for the time I had lost, I even began to lose sight of what I had gained in the countryside. Realizing that I am by nature too direct and unsophisticated about politics to escape censure, and that it is easy for a politically naive person to become a victim, I resolved that in the future I would ignore social issues and concentrate single-mindedly on my studies.

At this meeting, all fourteen rightists from our department, two of whom had not yet taken off their caps, were assembled in a separate room to meet our new leader. When I saw that he was the person on the department Party committee responsible for matters of security, I understood instantly that we were still to be considered enemies. He addressed us formally, instructing us to understand the crimes we had committed and to begin our lives anew. We would not be allowed to stand on a podium and address the students at this time because our thoughts could not be trusted, he declared. If we could prove that we really had returned to the socialist path, we could perhaps resume our teaching positions at some later date.

Our job assignments varied widely. Lao Pan, the person from our magazine group who had criticized me so severely, would cut the stencils for some supplementary materials designed to assist the students in understanding the new literary history. This was considered a privileged position, since it would bring him into contact with students, allowing him to solicit their support and thus return to teaching quickly. The rest of us were to be isolated from the students entirely. The two still with rightist caps were assigned to do physical labor on campus, working on the grounds and tending the flower beds. Four of us, myself and Lao Shi included, were sent to the materials library to write commentaries on classical poems so that the students compiling the new literary history could understand these ancient lyrics.

I was assigned the poetry of the Tang dynasty, and therefore was responsible for the works of Tu Fu and Li Po. My task would be to provide a gloss for every word, but rather than resenting this tedious assignment I was delighted at the chance to further my education in the classics. Every day I worked quietly in the library, removed from the rest of the department and alone with those poetic masterpieces, comparing different texts and arriving at a new and deepened appreciation of their meanings.

One rightist from my department, a student named Lin Zhao, faced a far more terrible fate. In the spring of 1957, she had written several moving poems to protest the privilege and stratification of the Party, and inevitably she had been condemned for her outspoken views. Because of ill health, she had been sent not to the countryside to do labor but to People's University in Beijing to collect materials. While there, she had secretly translated, along with two other rightists, the manifesto of the Yugoslav Communist Party, believing it superior to its Chinese counterpart because it was less dictatorial and promised the people more rights. Having access to a stencil machine in the library materials department, those three people had somehow at night printed copies of their translation as well as two leaflets elaborating their views. Before long their activities were discovered. Since they had already been labeled rightists, they were immediately condemned as "active counterrevolutionaries" and sent to jail.

The news of her imprisonment swept through my department in 1961, rekindling my admiration for Lin Zhao's courage. Even after having been declared a rightist, she had refused to submit and had done more than a non-rightist would dare. All those months that I had been leading a simple life with the peasants, trying not to think and never considering struggling again, she had been acting with extraordinary bravery. But she was to pay dearly for her defiance. One of my roommates at Beida's Jiangxi cadre school was sent to that Shanghai jail in 1971 to question Lin Zhao about another person under investigation. From my roommate I learned that Lin was crippled by arthritis, her condition aggravated by the dampness of her cell. She looked close to death in her white prison uniform, with her hair uncut, her figure gaunt, her complexion pale. In spite of her failing health, she had apparently continued to write poems on scraps of toilet paper, sometimes with her own blood.

In 1978 I was among the three hundred people who attended a memorial meeting for Lin Zhao. The youngest in her class at Beida, she had been very popular. On the platform, surrounded by banks of white chrysanthemums, stood a large photograph of Lin at eighteen, young, attractive, and smiling happily. Flanking the photograph hung a pair of enormous white scrolls contributed by her boyfriend. On one he had drawn a question mark, on the other an exclamation point, nothing more. I gazed at those arresting, provocative scrolls, listening to the boyfriend's moving account of their brief reunion in her jail cell, when he had found her body weak but her spirit unbroken. It was the last time he saw her.

In 1975 Lin Zhao was condemned to death and shot for the crime of attacking Chairman Mao. Even in jail she had maintained that ever since the Anti-rightist Campaign Chairman Mao's policies had resulted in disaster for China. "She is the truth itself," the anguished young man asserted, "and before long everyone will acknowledge the correctness of her beliefs." To conclude the meeting, someone sang the words to one of Lin Zhao's poems set to music, lyrics about how even when the autumn wind blows steadily and the autumn rain pelts down, sometimes the sun still shines bravely through.

For those of us rightists who had been more submissive than Lin Zhao and remained obedient after our sentencing, life in 1961 quickly became routine, and the days spent in the library passed quite peacefully for me. Some of the student body had remained on campus, those in our department continuing the task of revising the literary history, but the majority had been sent to the countryside, to factories, or to mines to work among the laboring people. All the Chinese literature students not needed for the revision project, for example, had been assigned to work in the coal mines in Mentougou, west of Beijing, there to unite with and learn from the workers. It was believed salutary for students of literature and history to see the most deprived strata of society and experience the most difficult, depressing, and dangerous kinds of work. Once intellectuals had shared the life of the people and the bitterness of their labor, they would presumably not become separated from the masses.

Although safety conditions were primitive, the students valiantly climbed deep into the mine shafts, wielding pick-axes, scooping the coal into baskets, and carrying it out on their shoulders along the dank and slippery paths. Many of the teachers also participated in this labor, and although the program supposedly allowed half time for study, actually everyone was too tired to be effective at academic work. Some of the Beida leaders like President Lu Ping, concerned about serious injuries, were requesting that the students be returned to the campus. Later he was criticized for opposing Chairman Mao's line. Since the workers face such dangers and hardships every day, why should the students be protected from difficult situations, argued Lu Ping's opponents. I considered myself fortunate to be peacefully ensconced in the library.

While my academic life became pleasantly routine in 1961, Lao Tang's brother's marriage introduced a new kind of strain into our previously harmonious household. The wedding, early in 1961, had necessitated preparations that I found inappropriately elaborate during that time of scarcity. The large bookcases that divided Tang Yongtong's study area from the rest of the living room had been taken down, for example, to expand the space for the festivities, and new curtains had been hung. The floor had been cleaned and rubbed with candle wax in preparation for dancing, and on the day of the wedding red and green crepe paper streamers festooned the ceiling. The tables had been spread with candy and fruit purchased from the special store that catered to the privileged elite, and the bride had worn a new suit of expensive red silk.

The festivities themselves had further offended my sense of decorum, with traditional games evoking raucous laughter from the guests. Someone would dangle an apple from a string, for example, and command the bride and groom to bite from it at the same time, jerking the string at the crucial moment to cause them to bump faces. Next, the bride would be instructed to hold a lighted cigarette in her mouth, then, without using her hands, to light the cigarette held between the groom's lips. The crowd of some thirty guests shouted and laughed uproariously at these antics, later turning their attention to dancing and singing popular songs. A greater contrast to my own wedding was hard to imagine.

During the celebration, the bride's father had been the only one who talked with me. Himself a rightist, he had reminded me of a traditional Chinese proverb: "When one contracts another's illness, he feels great sympathy." We both feel lonely here, he remarked, in the face of such frivolity. Before Liberation he had been the cultural attaché in the Guomindang's embassy in India, and then had become a professor of English at People's University in Beijing, known as Renda. As we talked together with warmth and understanding, I thought that perhaps I could develop a close relationship with his daughter. Having had a rightist for a father, I reasoned, she surely would sympathize with my situation. My hopes were quickly dashed when I learned of her hatred for her father and her belief that his political mistakes had prevented her from being admitted to a university. She never ignored a chance to reproach him. Her bitterness and resentment had led her to draw a line between them, and naturally, she also wanted to draw a line between herself and me, not wishing to be further contaminated by family ties that were politically disadvantageous. Listening to her complaints, I would think anxiously about my own daughter's future, wondering whether she would feel such antipathy toward me someday.

Two years later, in 1963, my new sister-in-law's father was arrested, accused of illicit relationships with foreigners. It was said that he had attached a transmitter-receiver, an illegal possession, to his radio, and that he could send and receive messages from foreign countries. Even though the search of his house and the investigation of his radio revealed no such illegal device, he was condemned to ten years in jail. Later it became known that he had written a letter to a friend abroad saying that life in China was intolerable, that he wanted to find some means to go abroad, and that he would like help obtaining a ticket. Somehow the letter reached the hands of the censors. It was actually for this reason that he had been given a prison sentence; the story about the radio had been just a rumor. The first time I met him after his release in 1971 I was surprised at how much more vigorous he looked. Because the Beijing jails were overcrowded, he had been sent to a prison in his native Fujian, where conditions were less harsh than in northern jails, and had worked as a ceramics painter, able daily to read the *Oxford English Dictionary*, brought to him by his wife before his sentencing. He conveyed a surprising lightheartedness born of his eight-year confinement. Having survived this ordeal after assuming he would die in prison, he said, the years remaining to him seemed an unexpected bonus.

Lao Tang's brother's wife bore little resemblance to her father. Like her husband she was uninterested in books and preferred to spend her time going to movies, attending private dance parties, and patronizing the special shops that served the elite. From the beginning of their marriage, our relationship had been strained, but still we had to eat every meal together. She was attractive and clever, but she had not been given the chance to attend a university. Instead she had been assigned to a middle school as a Russian teacher right after her own middle-school graduation. After her marriage she had asked Lao Tang's father to get her a job at Beida, and he had found work for her in the library. But she was still resentful that she had not received a higher education, and directed her anger at me.

Aware of Tang Yongtong's affection for me and offended that he had asked for my help with the articles he was writing that year, she competed with me for his attention. "I never knew paternal love before," she would tell him, "because my own father was a villain and always cruel to his children, but now at last I have found a real father." Unmoved by her flattery, Tang Yongtong would only smile in response. Frustrated in her efforts to win his affection, she often tried to better me in front of him, but I never engaged in such competition, preferring to remain silent.

When their baby was born in 1963, they refused to allow Yang Dama to care for it, even though she had spare time now that Tang Shuang was nearly six. Yang Dama loved Tang Shuang too much, they said, and could never develop a similar affection for their child. At their insistence, Lao Tang's mother hired a new nurse, a former prostitute from Tianjin, thus enlarging our household even more. Living under our roof by then were Daolan, the two nurse-maids, and the assistant for Tang Yongtong, in addition to the seven adults and three children, for Tang Yongtong's sister had joined the family as well. Every day when I returned from the library, I felt like a stranger in my own home, my sister-in-law having taken care to make all the domestic decisions while I was at work. Every meal was a burden, conversation difficult to sustain, but Lao Tang's parents had been so kind to me that I could not bring myself to suggest moving to a home of our own.

Nineteen sixty-two was a year of agricultural recovery, owing to the policy that encouraged the development of some private initiative in the countryside. At the same time, the leadership decided it was counter-productive to send the nation's best students to labor in factories and coal mines, and a new educational policy was formulated, a kind of back-to-basics movement that stressed three essential capabilities: the basic knowledge of some field, the basic ability to analyze, and the basic techniques of writing and of conducting experiments.

That fall I was told to return to teaching, but my former course on modern literature was considered too politically sensitive for a rightist. Instead, I was assigned to the politics department to teach a composition course on the techniques of writing political essays. It seemed ironic that since modern literature was too political, I would be assigned the task of teaching political writing, but I realized that the assignment was partly punitive. This new two-year course was assumed to be especially difficult to teach since no one had as yet developed a methodology or a set of teaching materials. Soon after the assignments were made, Lao Chen, the Party secretary who had offered me such encouragement in Zhaitang, came to see me. "This is a new course," he said, "and no one knows how to teach it, but surely you can manage this difficult assignment." He urged me to accept the assignment as a challenge and to devote myself wholeheartedly to such an important task. For two years that was what I did, committing all my time and energy to my new work, reading widely and practicing the various writing techniques myself. The new students found the course interesting, and I enjoyed the challenge.

To celebrate the economic recovery, the National Day Celebration was to be especially lavish in 1963. Lao Tang's father, who by then had recovered his health enough to work regularly, received an invitation to sit in the reviewing stand at Tiananmen Square, where there was to be an elaborate fireworks display attended by Chairman Mao and all of the country's top leaders. Tang Yongtong was permitted to invite five family members, and naturally everyone wanted to go, eager for the coveted opportunity to see Chairman Mao in person, perhaps even shake his hand. Finally my father-in-law announced that he would take me, Lao Tang, and our children, as well as his wife. We were overjoyed, considering this a rare and precious honor, and were thrilled at the prospect of being driven to Tiananmen in a car.

We arrived to find the atmosphere charged with excitement, the huge square filled with groups of performers singing and dancing.

Watching the festivities, I thought back to the earlier time I had been invited to Tiananmen Square in 1950 when I was a student. To celebrate the Festival of Youth on this first May Fourth after the nation's Liberation, two young women had been selected to present a huge bouquet of flowers to Liu Shaoqi. I represented the nation's students; another young woman, China's workers. As I stood excitedly on the platform in my crimson shirt and blue overalls, I thought how bright the future of our country looked, filled with hope and promise.

Having assumed that such an honor would never again be mine after the Anti-rightist Campaign, here I was, thanks to Tang Yongtong's kindness, in the middle row of the reviewing stand amid a distinguished audience. Suddenly the band began to play the stirring notes of "The East Is Red," and through the crowd walked Chairman Mao flanked by his top officials. Passing among the rows of guests, he came up to our family as we waited breathlessly, shaking all of our hands, even the children's, and telling Tang Yongtong how happy he was to see him in good health again.

I had seen Chairman Mao's picture so many times, but in real life he was taller and more imposing than I had imagined. As he drew close and I saw him face to face, I couldn't help noticing, however, that his skin glowed unnaturally from some kind of makeup. Why should so great a man pretend and wear a kind of mask, I wondered uneasily, then pushed the thoughts away. His face seemed not so expressive and kindly on this public occasion as I had grown to know it in his photographs, but still his hand felt very warm and he smiled at us his special smile. I set aside my briefly disquieting thoughts and gave myself over to the extraordinary thrill of those moments. All the suffering I had undergone seemed worth this personal encounter with the man I regarded reverently as the savior of my country. United with my countrymen in a sense of common purpose and mutual commitment, I considered that perhaps even the Anti-rightist Campaign had been worthwhile if the country was now stabilized again, its internal enemies routed, its path of socialist construction cleared. When I left Tiananmen Square, a new passion burned within me.

The euphoria of that moment renewed my sense of purpose. As

the days passed and I recalled the touch of Chairman Mao's hand clasping mine, so large and warm, I felt a compelling desire to do something for my leader and my country. Once again believing that a bright future lay ahead of us, I pledged to devote myself with fresh energy to the cause of the revolution. Lao Tang's future was to be even more directly influenced by his meeting with the Chairman. A few days later an official came to visit to report that Chairman Mao had paid a compliment to our family. We already knew that Mao Zedong's interest in Buddhism had led him in the past to read several of Tang Yongtong's books. After greeting us in Tiananmen Square, Chairman Mao had turned to this official to remark that Tang Yongtong obviously had a very capable son, whose own academic career would surely carry on the important work of his father.

In those years Lao Tang was always busy, working every day to help reassess the philosophy of Confucius and spending a great deal of time organizing the students to write critical articles and to prepare a short history of Chinese philosophy. After the anti-rightist movement, when he had been warned and I had been punished, he had felt it urgent to solidify his own position at Beida. Knowing that after the Great Leap Forward those people not highly valued at the university were being assigned elsewhere, he had worked hard to demonstrate his academic merit and his political loyalty, adhering to the line of the Central Committee and participating enthusiastically in the effort to reevaluate traditional philosophers. As a result, the articles he wrote sometimes reflected his own opinions, sometimes the position of the Party, resulting in occasional contradictions. In the early 1960s, for example, he emphasized the progressive aspects of Confucius' thought, while a few years later he would stress the reactionary aspects of the same texts, shifting his focus in accordance with the changes in official viewpoints. Especially after Chairman Mao's acknowledgement, he wanted to support the Party and prove himself worthy of such confidence.

While Lao Tang's spirits remained buoyed after his meeting with Chairman Mao, my own elation did not last, and I soon regretted ever going to the National Day festivities at all. Not two weeks had passed when my sister-in-law appeared very excited one evening at dinner. She was bursting with the news that people were speaking disapprovingly of Lao Tang's father for having invited a rightist to attend such an important celebration. Tang Yongtong's decision was said to be a serious matter, since a rightist even without a cap was still dangerous and could easily have carried a concealed weapon. People were saying that it was essential not to relax our vigilance, she continued, and that Lao Tang's father had made a mistake in allowing a former enemy of the people to get so close to Chairman Mao. I could sense the jubilation behind her show of sympathy.

After several days a cadre from the Beida Party Committee visited Tang Yongtong to say, in a polite and deferential manner, that it was wrong for Yue Daiyun to have attended the festivities even though she had taken off her rightist's cap. She might seek revenge, he suggested tactfully; you cannot know what she might be thinking. Affirming the Party's unaltered respect for Tang Yongtong's integrity, the cadre urged him to be more alert to class struggle matters and remarked that the Party committee hoped he would refrain from similar actions in the future. The rebuke was not terribly serious, but Tang Yongtong was deeply offended. He continued to treat me with his customary warmth and concern, but I knew he had been hurt by this criticism.

My father-in-law's decision to invite me must have been difficult, I realized with regret, for he would have known the risks involved. Even so, he had ignored my sister-in-law's angry protest that she was not being treated equally with me. I could only guess that he had wanted to console me, to restore my self-respect, regardless of the repercussions. The list of invited guests had been approved both by Lu Ping and by the Beida security office, so Tang Yongtong may have thought my attendance would go unnoticed. He was wrong, of course, and even after his death some posters during the Cultural Revolution referred to this incident as a way of attacking Lu Ping, who was said to so favor the intellectuals as to permit them to take rightists to Tiananmen Square to shake hands with Chairman Mao.

By the end of 1963, Tang Yongtong was again bedridden with heart disease and arteriosclerosis. During those months I always cared for him at home, but by March 1964 he had to be hospitalized. Someone had to attend him at night in the special hospital for high cadres, and as my sister-in-law was pregnant, I would spend alternate nights at his bedside, sharing the responsibility with Lao Tang's mother and observing him carefully as he slept, using the late night hours to read and to grade my student essays. Tang Yongtong treated me very warmly during those weeks, knowing that he had not much time to live. One night he spoke in unusually personal and confiding tones, with an intensity I had never before seen. "You must take care of mother," he said, "for I can trust only you. You must promise to take care of my sister as well, even though the two women are jealous of each other and have a difficult relationship."

He spoke quietly of his sister, whom we called Fourth Aunt, describing her as a kind and generous woman and recounting the hardships she had endured. Their father, a county official in Gansu province, had hired a tutor to educate his children at home, and Fourth Aunt had shown such talent, such cleverness, that the teacher considered her a woman scholar. Later she had been married to a wealthy man but, unable to provide him with sons, had been replaced in his esteem by a concubine, who soon gave birth to a boy. Before many years had passed, the husband had frittered away his money on opium and women, and the concubine, tired of his dissolute ways, had collected the remaining valuables and left, leaving Tang Yongtong's sister to care for both children. During the land reform period she had been harshly criticized and struggled against as a landlord, and had lost all of her remaining property. Only after Tang Yongtong was paralyzed following his stroke in 1960 was he allowed to send for her, hoping finally to provide an end to her years of bitterness and offer her a peaceful life, but even then her troubles had not ended. Unable to participate in their discussions, his wife, feeling excluded and resentful, had never made Fourth Aunt feel welcome.

I promised my father-in-law that I would fulfill his wishes, and when Lao Tang's mother awoke at six o'clock, I started the two-hour bus ride back home, hoping for an hour of sleep before beginning my day's work. But just at eight o'clock, Lao Tang's mother telephoned to say that Tang Yongtong had passed away. It was May 1,

1964, and he had said upon awakening, "May first, *wan sui*," * with such fervor to his wife and the nurse that they had assumed he was in no danger. Lao Tang's mother had left his side for a few minutes to go to the bathroom, but when she returned he was dead. Reproaching herself for not being beside him at the end, she cried so sadly. The funeral, a resplendent affair, was presided over by Chen Yi,† who gave a moving talk, emphasizing Tang Yongtong's kindness, his love of the country and the Party, and the example he set for all of China's intellectuals. Twenty-four musicians played with great solemnity as the mourners filed past his casket, after which he was buried in the revolutionary cemetery at Babaoshan, a very special privilege accorded only to important dignitaries.

To adorn his monument, Lao Tang's mother ordered a porcelain portrait of Tang Yongtong to be made in Jiangxi province. Later I realized that, despite her disappointment, we were fortunate that the order was never filled. During the Cultural Revolution, the Red Guards desecrated many of the graves in that part of the cemetery, smashing the monument commemorating the burial site of Long Yun,‡ for example, and even digging up the earth in an effort to remove the casket and deface the remains. Tang Yongtong's monument was spared, probably because it was so undistinctive, with an open book its only decoration. We decided to leave it like that, simple and humble.

Lao Tang's father had earned the respect of everyone at Beida. A man of unusual self-discipline, he never smoked or drank and was always loyal to his wife, even though he spent several years outside of China. A member of the first group from Qinghua University to study abroad, he returned to China in 1921 after receiving his master's degree in philosophy from Harvard. At Southwest

---

* *Wan sui*, meaning "ten thousand years," here expresses the wish that the spirit of May Day will endure forever.

†Chen Yi, a veteran marshal of the Red Army, was Foreign Minister of the People's Republic and a member of the Politburo.

‡Long Yun, a warlord from Yunnan province, was made a member of the First People's Political Consultative Conference after offering his support to the Communist government in 1949.

United University* during the Anti-Japanese War, he was a prominent professor and dean of the humanities and social sciences.
There he protected the students from arrest by the Guomindang,
and became a close friend of Wen Yiduo. His whole life was devoted to the study of Buddhism and Indian philosophy, accepting
Western scholarly approaches so that traditional Chinese materials
could be systematically researched.

Following World War II, Chen Shixiang† invited him to Berkeley
in 1947–1948 to lecture on Buddhism and on Indian and Chinese
philosophy. At the completion of this guest professorship, despite
the danger posed by the civil war and the urging of his friends that
he should bring his family to America, he returned to China in the
summer of 1948. When the siege of Beijing was over and Hu Shi‡
offered airplane tickets, so desperately sought by those wishing to
escape to Taiwan before the Communist take-over, to everyone in
Lao Tang's family, Tang Yongtong took one ticket for a niece and returned the rest. Wanting to contribute to China's future, he refused
to leave his country.

Tang Yongtong was also famous for his tolerance, a trait that I
tried to emulate. During the twelve years I knew him, I never once
saw him angry. He was always gentle with his wife, while I had a
quick temper, for which Lao Tang blamed my Miao blood. Whereas
I was hasty in my criticisms of people's failings, my father-in-law
unfailingly discovered some praiseworthy quality in everyone. For
this generosity of spirit, I greatly admired him. Tang Yongtong inspired me academically as well, teaching me about the insufficiency
of my knowledge of the Chinese classics and counseling me that
only with such a background could I understand modern literature
fully. He made me realize the inadequacy of my undergraduate

---

*Southwest United University was established in Kunming in 1938 when Beida,
Qinghua, and Nankai Universities were evacuated from Beijing and Tianjin.

†Chen Shixiang, a professor in the Department of Oriental Languages at
Berkeley and famed for his scholarly erudition, left China in 1941.

‡Hu Shi, the prominent Western-educated statesman and man of letters, returned to China from the United States in 1946 to become president of Beida, appointed by the Nationalist leadership because of his eminence and his opposition to
the Communist cause.

education, acquired during years when I was deeply involved in political work, and inspired me to work hard to deepen my knowledge.

During those years following my return from Zhaitang, my pride and pleasure in Lao Tang's growing prominence contrasted strikingly to my dejection over my own position in the university community. Gradually, I had to recognize that our family life had been ruined by politics; I was no longer my husband's equal, but was far lower than he in both political and academic status. Promoted twice in recent years and entrusted with a graduate-level course on Buddhist texts, he had become increasingly distinguished. When Lu Ping was making changes to raise the educational level at Beida, he selected Lao Tang among a small group of special faculty members who would be released from all political obligations to concentrate exclusively on academic work.

In every department in the humanities and social sciences, three or four teachers were thus excused from other duties in the fall of 1963 so that they could read, write, and raise their academic level. All of these scholars were targeted to be promoted to the rank of professor after a few years, and Lao Tang was the most distinguished of the faculty members selected from the philosophy department. He was expected, as Chairman Mao had wished, to carry on the work of his father. Although I was proud of his recognition, it coincided with a drastic decline in my own prestige. No longer did he seem proud of my accomplishments, and I felt woefully inferior. He was always busy and surrounded by people, especially by young teachers who often came to our house to talk until midnight about reassessing the writings of Confucius, Zhuangzi, or Laozi. During those sessions I would prepare tea and snacks, afraid that I would never be able to rejoin their circle or be accepted among them again as an intellectual. I was further saddened by the realization that my relationship with Lao Tang had suffered, since always before it had been based on mutual respect and equality.

Hoping to rebuild my academic reputation, I decided to act on the feelings of renewed dedication that had followed my meeting with Chairman Mao and to begin a new research project myself. In this way I could try to make some contribution to my country and at the same time to reestablish my position in my department. It was still too dangerous for me to resume work on modern literature, but the classics were less politically sensitive, so I began to study the literary thought of Mencius. By reading late into the nights, I was able to complete a book in just one year, and in September 1964 turned my manuscript over to a publishing house. The only way they would issue a contract to me as a rightist, however, was with Lao Tang's name listed as the first author and my pseudonym appearing below. Ultimately, the obscuring of my authorship was of no consequence, for during the Cultural Revolution when the publishing house was in chaos, the entire manuscript was lost.

Even while hard at work on my study of Mencius, I was unable to ignore politics as completely as I wished. By that time a new movement was in full swing, with Beida as usual the testing ground. A part of the Socialist Education Movement, the Four Clean-ups Campaign, devoted to the rectification of politics, of the economy, of organization, and of ideology, had begun to alter radically the educational environment that had briefly encouraged scholarship and allowed me to devote my energies to literary work. The primary goal of the new movement, we were told in our political study meetings, was to accomplish the unification of thought.

In the spring of 1964, the Central Committee had dispatched a work team led by Zhang Panshi to conduct an investigation of Beida, and Lu Ping soon became the focus of its attack. Appointed to the presidency in 1958 after the anti-rightist struggle, he had been widely respected for his abilities as an underground student leader at Qinghua University during the Anti-Japanese War. Such a distinguished history was now totally ignored. His efforts to raise the level of education in the previous year by promoting the three basic principles were construed as an attempt not only to prevent students from being politically active but to deny workers, peasants, and soldiers access to the university.

Claiming that it was essential to clean up political matters, the work team asserted that the university's policies were fundamentally incorrect, its president guilty of oppressing the proletarian class. This accusation stemmed from Lu Ping's decision in 1963 to bring the students back from the countryside, the factories, and the coal mines in accordance with a national policy to promote edu-

cational achievement. At that time he had also established stan-
dardized requirements and reinstituted examinations, requiring
that any student who failed exams in two subjects withdraw from
the university. In the spring semester of 1963, many did fail and
were subsequently provided with a stipend and assigned other
work, some going to the countryside, some to factories, some to
middle schools to be teachers. Perhaps ten percent of the students
enrolled in the natural science departments were disqualified in
this way, most of them members of worker-peasant families where
the educational level was typically lower than in intellectual families. As a result of these policies, Lu Ping was accused of pursuing
a bourgeois educational line and of being concerned only with educating the children of the elite.

When the work team set about cleaning up organizational matters, it made similar claims, arguing that at Beida only intellectuals
were valued and placed in high positions. Lu Ping's policies had
caused some of the worker-peasants to be demoted, another instance of his crime of oppressing the working class. The clean-up of
ideology further revealed that Lu Ping paid insufficient attention to
political instruction, for he had reduced the number of political
courses required of students in the natural sciences from four to
two, eliminated the study of political economy and of the international Communist movement, and left only Communist Party history and Marxist philosophy in the required curriculum. He had
also insisted that the remaining political courses impart some information and not just undertake the remolding of thought, thereby
demonstrating his exclusive concern with the acquisition of knowledge and his indifference to the development of the students' political consciousness.

The denunciation of Lu Ping was only the most visible manifestation of the realignment taking place among Beida's three con-
stituent groups. One group was composed of those already established as faculty members and administrators before Liberation,
people educated under the old system and therefore presumed to
have lingering bourgeois viewpoints despite their often exemplary
work for the Communist underground in the "white," or urban,
areas of the country. A second group was composed of people like

me, who were educated largely after Liberation, who often had participated enthusiastically in the underground movement, but who had been influenced by the older generation of intellectuals and shared some of their ideals. The third group was composed of workers, peasants, and soldiers, many of whom had worked in the "red," or rural, areas of the country during the revolution, people who had come to Beida after Liberation to receive an education and stayed on as teachers and Party cadres. It was this group that Chairman Mao had hoped would change the character of the universities.

During the Four Clean-ups Campaign members of the three groups became bitter adversaries in a so-called "struggle between two lines." One faction allegedly wanted to perpetuate the old ways of education and thereby undermine socialism; the other insisted upon abolishing every remnant of the country's capitalist past. While those accused of harboring bourgeois thoughts were in fact usually deeply loyal to the Party, they were nonetheless suspected of attempting to subvert the goals of the new society. Like Lu Ping, they desired to improve the level of education only to contribute to the socialist future, but they were vigorously opposed by the less well educated members of the university, who had come in from the outside and were eager to gain ascendency through political rather than academic expertise.

Termed the Occupied and Anti-occupied Struggle, this ideological opposition that became the focus of the Four Clean-ups Campaign reflected a conflict dating from the time of Liberation. Before 1949 the university's goal, the work team declared, had been to serve the bourgeois class. During those pre-Liberation years the whole campus had been infused with foreign and capitalist ideas, but even after Liberation, when the Communist Party had occupied the university, attempting to lead it in a proletarian direction, many intellectuals had resisted the new ideals and tried to perpetuate the old attitudes toward education and the old methods of teaching.

This intensifying rhetoric divided the university into two antagonistic camps, each wanting to influence the younger generation, each wanting to train successors. Fearful that the young people would be influenced by bourgeois thought and grow up to espouse the principles of democracy and challenge the notion of dictatorship, the Party was vilifying those from whom it feared poisonous ideas might spread in an effort to enforce uniformity of thought. The struggle between the so-called reactionary and progressive educational lines was thus deadly serious, a struggle for the control of China's future.

As the Party pursued its efforts to eliminate potential opponents, the older professors were termed "bourgeois academic authorities," the young teachers who had studied under them dubbed "sprouts of bourgeois authorities." Those who had returned from study in the Soviet Union when the relationship between the two countries soured were called "sprouts of revisionism," as were those, like Lao Tang, who were associated with the policies of Lu Ping. In every department, people of academic influence were being attacked with such pejorative labels, accused of siding with Lu Ping and obstructing the goals of the Communist Party at Beida.

By the winter of 1964, some six months after their arrival, the original ten work team members had been joined by enough others to establish a branch in each department. The verdict of their investigation, never publicly announced, reached us by word of mouth. Beida had been pronounced a "thoroughly bourgeois institution," a "reactionary fortress" that had for the past ten years continued to pursue its traditional ways, relying first on the model of European and American education and later on the example of the Soviet Union, but never working toward the establishment of a new and uniquely Chinese approach to education. Concerning itself only with "ancient, foreign, and high-level things" and never with proletarian ideals, Beida had totally ignored the needs of the people. Lu Ping's tenure as president, claimed Zhou Peiyuan,* who had aided the work team's investigation and thus earned its trust, had been the darkest period in the university's long history. Such vehement denunciations left those of us who had devoted our lives to Beida during the past decade, believing devoutly in the cause of socialism, utterly dumb struck.

It was not possible at that moment to understand why the fac-

*Zhou Peiyuan, a prominent American-trained physicist and vice-president of Beida, became the university's president after the Cultural Revolution.

tional lines had become so sharply drawn. I knew that positions of power and influence had until 1964 been held by people like Lu Ping, men who had been active in the white areas before Liberation and behind whom stood the authority of Liu Shaoqi, his position greatly enhanced after the debacle of the Great Leap Forward. I also knew that Chairman Mao's power, substantially reduced in the early 1960s because of the failure of his economic policies, depended largely on the support of those who had been active in the red areas. Determined to expand his influence over education in order to ensure his ability to chart the course of China's future, Chairman Mao had been trying to insert people he trusted into leadership positions at such key places as Beida and the government ministries. One part of this strategy had involved having Kang Sheng, the powerful head of the Party's public security system, send a work team to the university to overturn Liu Shaoqi's supporters.

Dismayed by the work team's verdict, I was even more shocked when Peng Zhen, mayor of Beijing and head of its Party committee, and Deng Tuo, vice-secretary of Beijing's Party Committee, rejected those seemingly definitive conclusions and asserted that Beida was truly a socialist institution. Chairman Mao, of course, endorsed the decision that Lu Ping had committed many crimes, but Peng Zhen and Deng Tuo, with the tacit support of Liu Shaoqi, refused to capitulate and asserted, so we were told, that the work team's pronouncements were incorrect, that Beida was indeed a socialist institution and Lu Ping a loyal comrade. Since the work team had been sent by the Central Committee itself, I could not imagine anyone daring to question its judgment. Always I had believed that the Central Committee was firmly united, standing as solidly as a rock. At that time I had no way of comprehending the power struggle unfolding at the highest levels of the Party. It was not until Chairman Mao in 1966 called for the masses to attack the Party headquarters, an obvious assault upon Liu Shaoqi's authority, that I could guess what had fueled the antagonisms of the Four Clean-ups Campaign.

Unknown to us in 1964, the bitter struggle between the two lines, one that contended Beida was bourgeois and reactionary, one that maintained Beida was truly a progressive, socialist university, marked the inception of the Cultural Revolution. Here in retrospect we could see the origins of that cataclysmic decade in the emergence of such irreconcilable viewpoints, one with adherents primarily from the urban areas, the other with adherents largely transplanted from the countryside, each group fiercely espousing a set of contradictory beliefs. The unrelieved antagonism would make an ultimate explosion inevitable.

But in those preliminary days we had no idea what form the struggle would take. All we knew was that the general atmosphere in the fall and winter of 1964 had grown extraordinarily strained, the relative relaxation of 1963 just a memory. Every day we were reciting Chairman Mao's famous injunction, "Never forget class struggle," a warning originally issued to Party leaders in the summer of 1962, reminding ourselves that class contradictions and class struggle must be attended to "every year, every month, and every day." The signals were clear that some as yet undefined period of strife was upon us.

Cleaning Up the Countryside

BY EARLY 1965, I could personally testify that the Four Clean-ups Campaign was gathering strength. The previous fall I had been assigned to teach a new composition course in the law department. Then, just three weeks into the semester, I was abruptly informed that a younger instructor would replace me, and that I should advise him how to proceed. Embarrassed at being so summarily relieved of my teaching duties, I nonetheless assumed initially that I was being returned to some kind of literary work, in keeping with new efforts by the Party to revolutionize literature and art. It was nearly winter vacation before a meeting was held that disabused me of such a naive notion.

Shortly after that meeting convened, I realized that the work team members attached to my department had decided to use me as an example of following the wrong line in organization and politics because of a student essay I had praised that could be seen as critical of the system. In the fall of 1963, I had asked the students to write about their families and their native towns and discuss some local political issue that had arisen during the summer vacation. Most of the students explained how the commune movement had increased production, how the famine had been eliminated, how a new future awaited the country. But my favorite student, a talented and thoughtful young man named Wang Ming, wrote instead about the failure of the Three Red Banners, concluding that conditions in the countryside remained difficult not because of unfavorable climatic conditions but because of mistakes in policy. Having presented his evidence, he argued that impatience to achieve the stage of communism had been very destructive, since without mechanization and a higher level of production, communism could not possibly be realized.

Because of my personal experience in the countryside during the years of famine, I agreed with Wang's conclusions and applauded his presentation, believing that his essay provided an opportunity to teach the students an important lesson about the mistakes of the past. In the revitalized Hundred Flowers period in 1957, similar criticisms had been aired, but no one had listened and three years of hardship and suffering had followed. Both because of Wang's argument and because his essay provided solid evidence, careful analysis, and thoughtful conclusions, I gave it a high grade and read it aloud to the class, praising its expository method and its organization.

I had known, of course, that it was dangerous to criticize the Three Red Banners, for Peng Dehuai* had argued at the Lushan Plenum in August 1959 that those policies had caused utter disaster in the countryside. He was harshly denounced by Chairman Mao, who had formerly referred to Peng as his close comrade-in-arms. My selection of Wang Ming's essay as a model was consequently fraught with risks, but I had felt that its conclusions warranted recognition. Besides, the essay was only indirectly critical, observing tactfully that something had gone wrong in our country and that change would be beneficial, since in some areas we had moved too fast. Moreover, I had tried to praise simply Wang Ming's technique as a writer and had carefully refrained from expressing my personal beliefs about the issues.

My praise of this essay was nevertheless singled out, when the Four Clean-ups Campaign intensified and all the teachers were subjected to renewed scrutiny, as behavior typical of a rightist who wanted to unite the young students and lead them in an anti-

---

*Peng Dehuai, a veteran revolutionary and China's Minister of Defense, vigorously attacked the Great Leap Forward, believing that it had brought socioeconomic disaster and undermined the nation's military security.

socialist direction. My case was treated as a serious example of class struggle, not only in 1965, but again in the following year, when the issue was revived to explain why the Cultural Revolution was necessary, and a third time, during the Clean the Class Ranks movement in 1969. Several teachers active in the Party branch I had once led delivered carefully prepared criticisms and accused me of taking advantage of my position as an instructor to attack the Three Red Banners. "A new tendency in the class struggle is apparent," it was variously claimed in the three meetings devoted to criticizing me, "when an enemy is allowed to go to the classroom and teach, there connecting with potentially dangerous elements among the students who want to overthrow the Communist Party. If the Four Clean-ups Campaign is not carried out thoroughly, there is no predicting what will happen to education in China."

"The stage of class struggle has obviously not ended," one teacher shouted, invoking Chairman Mao's famous injunction. "Yue Daiyun is a rightist who was dismissed from her job but was later generously allowed to return to the podium. Still she shows no gratitude and instead has tried once again to subvert the Communist Party." "If we are not constantly on guard," warned another, "our socialist country will surely be undermined by such class enemies who attempt to turn others away from the leadership of the Party."

The work team's threat that my rightist's cap could be returned any time, that I could once again be removed from the ranks of the people, was both frightening and profoundly depressing. I knew that what was really at stake in the Socialist Education Campaign, what accounted for the severity of my accusers, was the struggle for control of the young generation, who must be taught to repudiate the values of intellectuals trained under the old system. Clearly my student's essay was being used to illustrate the danger of Lu Ping's policies, which had allowed a person not yet completely reformed to assume teaching duties and thereby indoctrinate others to oppose the Party. Once again I was ordered not to return to the classroom.

That year everyone who taught composition got promoted one level and received an increase in salary of eighteen *yuan*, except me. My student was also disciplined, being denied access to Party meetings while he was investigated. His case was never resolved, however, because in the early weeks of the Cultural Revolution he was accused of a much more serious crime, of having as a friend a member of a Trotskyist group, a mysteriously undefined network of enemies whose identities were never revealed but with whom any alleged association was extremely dangerous.

Dismissed from my teaching work, I was assigned a few months later to gather materials for the new movement to criticize bourgeois literary viewpoints. One of the literary practices deemed totally unacceptable was the fictional representation of ordinary people, those who were neither heroes nor villains, the "middle characters." To portray a worker, peasant, or soldier character as anything other than exemplary was considered bourgeois, as such characters were supposed never to manifest deficiencies. Ambiguity was not tolerated in literature; the slightest indication of sympathy toward a villain was thought to confuse readers and lead them astray. My task was to search through newspapers and magazines to identify any articles that projected this and other "black viewpoints" so that their authors could be criticized. I performed my new task mechanically, knowing that such writers couldn't be shielded from the present campaign and that if I didn't assemble the incriminating materials, someone else would.

Again I was an alien figure, isolated from the students, whom I had allegedly poisoned, and from my colleagues. Believing that I could trust no one, I resigned myself to a solitary life and did whatever was asked of me. Just as the Spring Festival holidays approached in 1965, however, a letter from my cousin Gao Zhongyi, my father's sister's son to whom I had once been very close, made me realize that my own rebuke was slight compared with the punishments being imposed on others.

A student of English literature, Gao had been assigned to the China Information Headquarters as an interpreter after his graduation from Qinghua University in 1951. In this politically sensitive unit the reliability of every employee was thoroughly reevaluated during the Four Clean-ups Campaign, when all government organizations were trying to identify any unreliable elements in their midst, and one-third were ultimately classified as politically un-trustworthy and sent elsewhere. Despite the fact that he had al-ways been held in high esteem, Gao was one of those to be re-assigned, his new job that of a middle-school teacher on the remote Xinjiang border. It was not until 1968 that I understood why Gao's loyalty had been questioned and why he had been sent into virtual exile.

When I was fifteen, this cousin had returned to Guiyang from Southwest United University to spend the four summer months of 1946 at home while the three colleges were being reestablished on their former campuses. The vacation afforded us long hours to talk together, and I listened spellbound to his accounts of student resis-tance to the Guomindang in the Southwest and of the assassination of Wen Yiduo. Gao had seemed a person of revolutionary character and great integrity, and we had fallen in love. My family lived then in a large two-story house, with my bedroom downstairs, below my parents', beside a spacious tree-filled courtyard. Sometimes late at night Gao would throw stones over the wall, the signal for me to unlatch the gate, and we would talk in hushed tones for an hour or more before he slipped back into the street.

Our romance took on the qualities of one of the Western novels I was consuming so eagerly in my middle-school years, when I even read *Lady Chatterley's Lover*, and found myself infatuated with ro-mance itself, absorbed in experiencing the emotions of Jane Eyre or Tess of the D'Urbervilles or Scarlett O'Hara. Our moonlit meetings came to an abrupt end, however, when my mother discovered what had been happening and forbade me to meet Gao again. Frightened that I would repeat the unhappy pattern of her life, she wanted me to pursue a career, not fall in love at such an early age.

When Gao left for Qinghua, he reserved a post office box, and we engaged in a secret correspondence for the next two years. Through these letters we grew increasingly familiar, and our feel-ings for each other deepened. When I arrived in Beijing in 1948 to begin my own studies, he was waiting to meet me. I had looked forward impatiently to our reunion, but I soon discovered how far apart we had grown in our thinking. Influenced by my passion for foreign literature, he had changed his major from physics to Western languages, and one day took me to the home of his professor, Robert Winters, the American scholar who had taught English literature in China for many years. There we spent a pleasant afternoon drinking coffee and eating homemade biscuits in a foreign setting I found quite unfamiliar and appealing. I was intrigued by Gao's world and touched by the many ardent poems he wrote me, but I was also determined to become a revolutionary. Gao opposed my goal, urging me not to get involved in politics, saying that it was a nefarious business in which one could easily be taken advantage of. I still cared for him deeply, and my heart was pulled sharply in two directions.

After I had been in Beijing for nearly a year, just at the time of Liberation, Gao and I quarreled bitterly about the future. He wanted me to go abroad with him to study English literature, and planned for us to live with one of his sisters, either in France or in Thailand. I insisted that we could not abandon our country in such a time of need, but Gao believed we could do nothing to help the Chinese people and might as well save ourselves. From his father, a wealthy merchant and a Taoist and *qigong** expert as well, Gao had learned some mysterious methods of healing. In this conversation he also spoke of his interest in discovering whether *qigong* could be used as a method of contraception. I was insulted that he would mention such an intimate topic, and repelled that at this historic moment, when I believed everyone should be making a contribution to the construction of the new China, Gao seemed concerned only about his relationship with a woman. Moreover, I had already met Lao Gu, who was to become my revolutionary leader in the underground movement, and I couldn't help making comparisons between their attitudes and goals. After that quarrel Gao and I never met again.

Not long after arriving in Beijing in 1948, I had met Gao's close friend and classmate, Peng Yuanho, who worked as the assistant to an American journalist in the United States Information Service. At one time the journalist had returned to America on vacation, giving Peng, his friend and translator, use of his house. Several times Gao

Qigong is a system of deep-breathing exercises, its goal the cultivation of a person's vital energy.

and I had met Peng and his girlfriend there to listen to records, dance, and eat American chocolates from the refrigerator. Nearly two decades later during the Cultural Revolution, when investigations of alleged enemies were being carried out on a mass scale, Peng was attacked as an American spy. I was questioned several times in connection with Peng's case and instructed to confess what we had done in that house back in 1948, thus to make clear his crimes. I answered truthfully that we had listened to music, danced, and drunk fruit juice, but my bland replies made the Red Guards so angry they threatened to punish me for not revealing all I knew.

Finally, I understood that it was this friend's suspected crimes that had caused Gao's dismissal from his work in 1964 and consigned him to a small, backward school in Xinjiang where he spent his time teaching singing. What a waste of his talents and expertise, I thought sadly after receiving his letter, realizing with regret that if he had pursued his study of physics and not switched to foreign languages in response to my own love of Western literature, he would likely never have been vulnerable to such political suspicion. Had he gone abroad to study and not stayed in China because of me, he would have escaped years of hardship.

At the beginning of 1965 when Gao was to leave Beijing forever, he wrote asking me to meet him one last time at the Summer Palace. However, I was depressed after having been dismissed from teaching again and stung by the recent meetings to criticize me. So many political denunciations had made me reluctant to meet anyone who had known me earlier when I was a leading member of my department and a respected Party cadre. Having criticized Gao for his lack of revolutionary zeal, I didn't want to hear him reproach me or say we should have gone abroad together and avoided all of this suffering. Feeling sensitive about my own political disgrace, I preferred not to see him at all.

In Xinjiang Gao married a Uighur woman, and after twelve years received permission to return to Guiyang. When his wife refused to leave her native province, they were granted a divorce. In 1976 Gao married a widow whose husband, formerly a high-ranking Guomindang officer, had been sentenced to death by the Communist Party in the campaign against counter-revolutionaries in 1955. Settled in Guiyang with his new family, Gao was finally assigned to teach English in a middle school, his knowledge of foreign language at last put to some use.

As the Four Clean-ups Campaign progressed, I found myself increasingly bewildered, unable to determine which policies were correct, to distinguish right from wrong, or to see my own path clearly. The newspapers compounded my dilemma, for their articles regularly contradicted what I knew to be taking place. I would read about a farm that had recently produced a thousand *jin* of grain per *mou*, for example, an accomplishment hyperbolically compared to the launching of a satellite; or I would read about the success of the campaign to dig deep, a practice trumpeted as having greatly increased production. From my years in the countryside, I knew that the peasants just laughed at such inflated yield statistics, and I had seen with my own eyes the sand that lay beneath the topsoil. Unable to reconcile what I read with what I had learned at firsthand, I no longer had any sense of how to participate in my country's future.

Contributing to my dejection was my family situation, which had become more strained after Tang Yongtong's death. Lao Tang's mother's grief had not yet abated, and the family had to adjust to reduced financial circumstances now that she received a stipend of only 200 *yuan*, approximately one-third of my father-in-law's former income. Unable to maintain such a large household, we had no choice but to dismiss Daolan and another *ayi*, after which I assumed some of the burden of child care and housework. At my mother-in-law's request, I also took responsibility for the family's finances. Whatever decisions I made provoked complaints from my sister-in-law, who seized every opportunity to grumble about the quality of the food or about having to care for her two small children when their *ayi* was busy shopping or cooking. It seemed that in our family, as in the society as a whole, a previous period of optimism and harmony had disappeared.

For the moment unaffected by the political storms, my own parents had received permission in the summer of 1964 to move to Beijing for their retirement years. My sister had graduated that summer from Sichuan University and fortunately had been assigned a job in Beijing as a chemist in the Railways Institute, her relocation enabling them to join their three children in the capital. Overjoyed to have the family united again, my mother and father used all their retirement money to buy a small adobe house and plot of land from a peasant, midway between Beida and the neighboring Qinghua campus, where my brother taught physics. It was permitted to own your own home then as long as the property was not to be rented or resold, and my parents settled happily with my sister into their simple four rooms.

My mother remarked repeatedly that now all of her hopes had been fulfilled; her children had good jobs, her grandchildren lived nearby, and she could spend her remaining days caring for the vegetables, flowers, and grapes she had planted in her courtyard. I was delighted that she had finally found contentment. My father began to write his memoirs and to translate some of his favorite Somerset Maugham stories into Chinese. But this happy family routine lasted for only a year, after which I found myself back in the countryside, implementing the Four Clean-ups Campaign in a prosperous cabbage-growing commune east of Beijing.

During the same period that the political struggle was growing more heated on the campus, the campaign was reaching a climax in the countryside as well. Just as in the time of the land reform, intellectuals were being assigned to work teams to implement the government's policy in the rural areas. In September 1965, I left with the second group of sixty people sent out from Beida to participate in what was called the "second land reform." Our destination was Xiaohongmen, Little Red Gate, some three hours south of Beijing by truck. From there we split up into teams and traveled by horse cart to our assigned villages. On my team were five other people, a teacher from Qinghua, who was the leader, and four students, one from Quinghua, one from the Beijing Technical Institute, and two from my own department.

Because I was considered a rightist who had made a new mistake, I was not initially given any political duties but was supposed to spend my time observing the conditions in the village and becoming reeducated. What struck me most forcefully at first was the prosperity of this production brigade; life here was much more comfortable than in Zhaitang. On this fertile plain most of the cabbages consumed in the capital were grown. I looked admiringly across the carefully planted fields, observing the willow-lined irrigation canals that divided the land into patchwork patterns. The standard of living was much higher than in the more remote and mountainous region to the west of the city. Here in Xiaohongmen most of the families lived in three rooms instead of one, their central kitchen flanked by two bedrooms, their *kangs* connected by brick heating ducts to two large raised stoves in the kitchen. This village earned a substantial income from its cabbages, and the people wore clothing of good quality and lived in comfortable houses; but I soon learned that their lives were by no means happy.

The peasant family with whom I lived were members of the Hui, or Muslim, minority. The father, who had been blind for many years, prepared the food and took care of the household, while the mother and two daughters did the farm labor. These young women, who were seventeen and twenty, had been given no chance for education after primary school but were obliged to help support their family. Now they longed to become workers in the city. Every day when I went out with them to do labor in the fields, I listened to their dreams of moving away from the countryside, all the while trying to experience again the happiness I had discovered among the peasants in Zhaitang. It was far more difficult to lose myself in the routine of the countryside this time, perhaps because I was less isolated than before. Reading newspapers and listening to radio broadcasts each day, I could never entirely banish my apprehensions about the political situation developing in Beijing.

Before leaving campus, we had been provided with a list of the good peasants in the village—everyone except the rich peasants, the landlords, and those with a political problem—and each evening we went separately to their homes to eat. Always they provided us with the best food available, sometimes including even a portion of meat, wanting to earn our good will. But while the peasants were very welcoming and polite, they always viewed us as authorities, never as family members. The closeness I had known in Zhaitang was not to be repeated.

Each morning I would go out with the women to the fields, sharing their strenuous labor, sometimes breaking up the soil with a heavy hoe, other times planting seeds, loosening the soil around the new seedlings, or pulling weeds. After eating dinner in some village home, I would return to to my peasant family. As I followed this daily routine I learned a lot about Xiaohongmen, discovering that relationships among people were far from harmonious. If the peasants ever complained about injustices, however, the deputy brigade leader would punish them doubly yet invisibly. This was known as making a person "wear a tight shoe." The leader would simply claim that he needed someone to complete some difficult task far away.

After several weeks in the village, I understood how cruelly this deputy leader, now removed from his post, had treated the peasants. The young men whom he disliked, for example, he sent to work constructing highways, an unpopular assignment because of the distance from home, the low pay, and the many hardships. If anyone opposed this petty tyrant, he would become even more vindictive. The father of one middle peasant family had often quarreled with him, and the two men hated each other. That peasant always received the worst job assignments and the fewest work points—for example, being made to carry nightsoil on his back from the latrines to distant pits where it would ferment into fertilizer, a task especially odious on hot days and usually delegated to a former landlord. The man's request to move to his wife's family's village had been repeatedly denied, eliminating any possibility of escape.

The more I learned about Xiaohongmen, the more I believed in the importance of the Four Clean-ups Campaign. The two sisters in my family told about other instances of the deputy leader's oppression. A married woman in the village had refused his advances, insisting that she would remain faithful to her husband. To take revenge for this rebuff, the deputy leader had frequently assigned her work far from the village. Afraid that he would follow her and force her to submit to his desires, she had seen no alternative but to take repeated leaves and had earned far fewer work points than in any previous year. Moreover, when the peasants wanted to build houses for their children, thereby enabling them to marry, they would have to apply to the leading cadres for land. In order to obtain a good plot, the applicants would spend large sums on bribes and banquets, as the cadres were free to assign whatever quality of land they wished, entirely at their own discretion.

It was shocking to realize how strong the contradictions between leader and led had become. Such struggles as the women described to me, bent over in the fields, never to my knowledge occurred during the land reform period, when the peasants and cadres had worked side by side and owned the land together. After the collectivization movement, however, the peasants had become mere workers responding to their leaders' orders, taking far less responsibility for the productivity of the land than they had a decade before. When the peasants had felt they were the masters of their own soil, the cadres had been far less arbitrary and authoritarian, but circumstances had clearly changed.

Some of the village leaders had begun to behave like the factory leaders I had heard about before Liberation, oppressing and even beating their subordinates. No longer did the cadres participate in labor, but spent their time supervising others, issuing orders, and busying themselves with matters of organization, often taking advantage of their position to harass the village men and insult the women. They would sometimes even exaggerate the work points they were owed, falsifying the accounts and explaining dismissingly to the illiterate villagers that this year's wages would be lower than before. During the early 1950s, officials had been looked upon as caring parents, but now they were called "local emperors." Since there was no mechanism for controlling such abuses, I came to recognize that the Four Clean-ups movement was necessary to help the peasants improve their situation.

It was easy for us to see that conditions in the village cried out for reform. We had no way of being certain which local leaders were fair and which had abused their power, however, for the peasants were reluctant to confide in the work team members or divulge the cadres' offenses to outsiders. The villagers used China's two most popular bicycle brand names to explain figuratively their taciturnity. "The work team is just like the Flying Pigeon brand," they would say among themselves, "for soon it will be gone, while the local cadres are like the Everlasting brand and will be with us forever." The peasants were convinced, not without reason, that the cadres would in the future find some way to exact revenge against any who spoke out against them.

Assessing the situation in Xiaohongmen was therefore not easy, and some who had consistently been upright in their dealings with the peasants were hurt by our investigation. We had received instructions not to trust any of the rural cadres, but to assume that they were all followers of the capitalist road. Only after careful observation and inquiry would we be able to discover who was truly reliable, we were told. Thus on the very day of our arrival, our leader held a meeting to dismiss all the local officials from their posts, announcing that everyone in the village must from that day on draw a clear line to separate himself from those under investigation and must report to the work team anything that the cadres had done to harm the socialist cause. Next he ordered the village accountant locked up, concerned that if left on his own he might destroy his records before we could examine them for evidence of wrongdoing. The man's wife was allowed to bring food to the small room where he was confined, but she was always observed. I was amazed that a team from the universities could have such authority, but clearly its power was absolute. It was seen as the representative of the highest-level leaders, and thus no one dared resist its delegated authority.

Although the aim of the work team's investigation seemed to me crucial, its methods were undeniably harsh. In an effort to make the accountant admit that he had embezzled peasants' wages, for example, the three men from Beijing questioned him around the clock, refusing to let him sleep. Finally, he became so exhausted that he said whatever they asked and admitted all kinds of wrongdoing, although none of his crimes could ever be proved.

No one in our village was physically harmed, although elsewhere people were forced to "take a jet plane ride" by standing bent double at the waist, the head pulled back by the hair, the arms forced up high behind the back. Commonplace during the Cultural Revolution, this technique was first devised during the Four Clean-ups Campaign in a target village in Hebei province called Taoyuan, where Wang Guangmei, the wife of Liu Shaoqi, was the work team leader. Our team leader, more humane and reasonable than some others, never forced anyone into this excruciatingly painful position or hung anyone up by the wrists. Nevertheless, he did subject the local cadres to extensive psychological harassment, questioning them endlessly and making them lose face publicly by removing them from their jobs and casting doubt upon their veracity.

The brigade leader, it was later decided, had been very conscientious in his job, capable and honest, even though sometimes rough with the peasants. But when we arrived we dismissed him along with the others, wounding his self-respect and treating him like a criminal. We suspected him of secretly taking oil back to his home at night from the storage barn, to which he had a key, because some of the villagers testified that they had one day smelled the odor of deep-frying crullers coming from his stove. He maintained adamantly that he had been given an extra quantity of oil by his wife's family, that he would never think of stealing anything from the village. We ignored his protest, dismissed him anyway, and refused to converse with him.

During those early weeks we made many mistakes, sometimes trusting a cadre who in fact deserved punishment, dismissing the good cadres with the bad, and finding replacements who were ineffective, inexperienced, and lacking any understanding of how to run a brigade. The selection of new cadres was in fact our primary mission, as we had been told we would not be allowed to return to Beijing until a new set of responsible village leaders had been established. We tried hard to find people who measured up to the official criteria, authentic poor peasants who had suffered under the Guomindang and would therefore be loyal to the Communists, who had no prior connections with either the Guomindang or the recently deposed local cadres, and who were totally honest as well. But this was a difficult task.

A few weeks after we arrived, we appointed as the new brigade leader an old peasant who was honest and widely respected. Before long it became obvious, however, that he possessed none of the technical knowledge or administrative skill needed to oversee such a large production team. An expert in caring for the village sheep and cows, he had little experience with raising crops and was totally unsuited for his new responsibilities. We searched in vain for a replacement.

After six months had passed and the Four Clean-ups Campaign was drawing to a close, a group of county leaders came to Xiao-hongmen to investigate our progress. They inquired whether we had discovered any counter-revolutionary elements, whether the policy of opposing capitalism had been enforced, and whether any people with capitalist tendencies still remained in positions of authority. A peasant was considered to be a follower of the capitalist road if, for example, he was raising more than two pigs, although a small number of chickens and rabbits were still permitted in individual households at that time. The most important standard for evaluating the success of the work team, however, was the quality of the cadres we had chosen to run the village. This was a problem we had been unable to solve. In our village no one wanted to become a cadre, having seen the way we treated the former leaders. The peasant men feared that at some future time they too might be forced to say things against their will, be humiliated or punished, while the women asserted steadfastly that they would divorce their husbands if they became cadres.

During those months in the countryside, my principal assignment had been to work alongside the village women and learn their viewpoints. My first task had been the investigation of a woman in her fifties who was supposed to be a leader of a secret peasant religious organization named Yiguandao, the Way of Prevailing Harmony, that was considered still influential in the countryside of North China, even though most of its leaders had been labeled counter-revolutionaries and condemned to death in 1955. Because such secret religious groups had played an important role in previous peasant rebellions, they had been a serious target of attack. Nevertheless, in the area around Xiaohongmen, we were told before our arrival, not only had Yiguandao previously been very active, but the widow of one of the sect's leaders, who had died of illness just before Liberation, was continuing her husband's work.

My first task had thus been to find out what influence Yiguandao still exercised in Xiaohongmen, how many members it had, and what role this particular woman played in its organization. I made initial inquiries among the village women, but they were reluctant to respond until after I had worked beside them in the fields for several weeks. They would always laugh at me for not being able to squat as they did for long hours and would joke about my having to work on my knees, but they grew to like me and soon would chat easily about their children and about village affairs.

Before long I learned that Widow Huang was indeed an Yiguandao leader and that several years earlier a meeting had been held in her house, attended by Yiguandao members from the surrounding villages, at which her husband's former students had paid their respects to their deceased teacher. After lighting sticks of incense, the participants had designated three unmarried women between the ages of sixteen and eighteen as the three powers of heaven, earth, and man. These young virgins had then spoken mysterious sentences, pronounced secret oaths, and sat with closed eyes upon the *kang*, their incantations enabling them to serve as mediums. Through them the others had communicated with their dead leader, summoning his spirit to speak through them, to protect them, and to bring them peace.

It was also said that Widow Huang had an intimate boyfriend, a man who had formerly worked her husband's land, in whose house the couple had dug a secret underground tunnel should they need to flee the village. During the Anti-Japanese War elaborate networks of such tunnels had been constructed in that part of China with numerous entrances, sometimes concealed beneath the *wok* set into a family's earthen stove or beneath the water cistern. Widow Huang and her boyfriend had allegedly tried to connect their house with one of those old escape routes. Some of the women also told me that she kept a large knife in her home. After I reported these alarming rumors to the team leader, he pronounced the situation very serious and summoned the people's militia for a nighttime search.

In the storeroom of Widow Huang's house, we discovered a heavy coffin that she had prepared for herself, its cover the customary ten inches thick to safeguard the body from deterioration. The peasants had told us the coffin would contain guns secreted from the wartime years, and we watched breathlessly as the four militia members opened the lid. By that time we had all become very excited, but the casket was quite empty. A thorough search of Widow Huang's storage boxes did reveal the knife, which we seized triumphantly, despite her explanation that her husband, a watermelon merchant, had used this implement to slice open his watermelons for sale.

The next morning we descended on the house of Widow Huang's boyfriend, a strong, muscular peasant expert at martial arts, a tradition among secret society members. Although we dislodged his *wok* and moved his cistern, nowhere could we find any trace of a tunnel entrance. Next we divided our group, with three people dispatched to the fields to bring this Lao Zhao back for questioning, and four remaining behind to continue the search. Frightened that he might be arrested, Lao Zhao refused to come. Taking a stand with his back to the irrigation well, he held off the militia members with a shoulder pole. Several people were injured by the time he was subdued, after which he was taken immediately to the commune jail. Meanwhile, I was using a stick to scrape the earth floor of his house, finally discovering concealed beneath the dirt a hole covered by a board. The opening extended only a short distance, not beyond the walls of the house, but did contain, as had been rumored, a box of grain.

The next day Widow Huang was instructed to write down the names of the three young women who had served as mediums, as well as the names of any others who had participated in that ceremony. The list was given to the team leaders in the surrounding villages for investigation, and the three women were all subsequently questioned. Huang admitted that she was a member of Yiguandao but insisted that she had registered this fact at the time of Liberation, that she had concealed nothing, and that she had done nothing illegal. She also admitted having held a meeting and burned incense, but claimed the purpose was merely to pay respect to the gods. Yiguandao was really her dead husband's work, she protested, and the proceedings had been led by his former student, whose request for a meeting place she had felt unable to refuse. She swore she would never participate in such rites again.

We had hoped to find some evidence to connect the members of this sect to the Guomindang, who had controlled this village until shortly before Liberation. The Central Committee's warning that landlords, rich peasants, and counter-revolutionaries were using religious societies to carry out criminal activities had seemed especially applicable to Xiaohongmen, and we had known that we must be especially vigilant. Despite our suspicions, we never uncovered evidence of any political involvement. The women who had participated in the meeting were twice criticized and warned that their superstitions were dangerous, that they should be careful not to do anything illegal, but that was all. Finally, the team leader announced that the allegations had been thoroughly investigated, the affair settled, and he commended me on my efforts in resolving this difficult matter.

Meanwhile, the others on our team were busy poring over the brigade's financial accounts to discover whether any money had been stolen from the peasants. The accountant, who was kept locked up for some four months, was questioned repeatedly about how much he had embezzled and told that if he confessed his guilt, his problem would be quickly resolved. But the accounts were complicated, disorganized, and incomplete, and the accountant, a middle-school graduate and the only one in the village considered an intellectual, was a slippery fellow. He knew that once the work team left, nothing more would happen, so he confessed that he had stolen a large sum of money, perhaps far more than he had actually taken, and promised to repay it to the peasants over the next five years.

Unable to decipher the accounts sufficiently to establish whether there had actually been any misuse of funds, the work team members had to accept his confession. Finally, our leader had no choice but to release him, even though we had no way to enforce his promise and never learned whether the peasants in fact received any of the back pay that was allegedly due them. All we knew was that this kind of theft happened commonly, that the peasants, unable to read, were often cheated and exploited. A similar investigation to determine whether the brigade leader had stolen oil, grain, peanuts, and beans, diverting them from the collective storehouse to his own home, as one of his neighbors alleged, had also proved inconclusive.

My second assignment came in the late fall, harvest time for the large cabbages for which Xiaohongmen is famous. The entire crop must be gathered from the fields in just three days, after the cabbages are fully mature but before they have been damaged by the first frost. The pressure of time makes the harvest very intense, and every year a special system of wages is implemented to make work points dependent upon the number of cabbages cut, with one work point allotted for every one hundred heads picked. Given this clear incentive, some villagers, especially the women, go to the fields very early and return home late at night, thus earning three times the work points of an ordinary day.

In 1965, however, this piecework system was being criticized as a form of capitalist exploitation. The utilization of material incentives to stimulate production rather than reliance on the people's social conscience was condemned as a bourgeois and not a socialist practice. Accordingly, we decreed that work points would be distributed evenly, ten per day for men and eight per day for women, even though the women often worked harder than the men. While no one could openly object to our leader's insistence on following the socialist road, the peasants made clear their resistance by working very slowly. It quickly became obvious that the harvest could never be completed at this pace, and everyone worried that the cabbages would be ruined. Not wanting to take responsibility for the failure of the harvest, our leader relented and reinstituted the piecework system.

My job was to investigate what actually happened during the harvest period in order to determine whether the allocation of work points by the day or by the piece was preferable. It was obvious that the peasants uniformly preferred the second system, but since the work team still believed that this was capitalist and exploitative, my job was to find evidence to prove the official viewpoint correct. It was true, I discovered, that under the piecework system the peasants arose very early and rested very little, sometimes becoming completely exhausted, even volunteering to work in the fields at night by lamp. It was also true that the children were largely ignored and left without supervision, and were thus exposed to possible harm, that some women had collapsed in the fields from overexertion, and that once a house had burned down when there was no one to watch the cooking fire. But it was also true that the system of allotting work points by the piece was very effective. In the end, I submitted a balanced report, acknowledging that the allegedly exploitative system was sometimes injurious to the peasants' health and that it could be the cause of accidents, but explaining that it was nevertheless extremely popular and enabled the harvest to be accomplished quickly and efficiently.

My third assignment was the most difficult of all. Since the wives in the village were unified in opposition to their husbands becoming cadres, my task was to persuade them to compromise. Sometimes I would talk with a woman all evening, urging her to understand that if the most qualified peasants didn't assume positions of leadership, the jobs would be filled by less capable people and everyone would be harmed as a result. The women were adamant; someone besides their husbands, they insisted, could do the job. After the visit from the county leaders in May, this effort to establish responsible leadership for the village became the focus of our work. We visited many of the peasant families to inquire whom they wanted to see in positions of leadership, and we also went to the families of the deposed cadres to request that they return to their former jobs.

It soon became clear that many among the villagers believed the previous brigade leader was still the best choice for the task of running this production team. Despite his rude, arbitrary manner and his fiery temper, despite the fact that he had even struck a peasant once for some wrongdoing, he was known to be fair, knowledgeable, and experienced. This man could read; he knew when to plant the various crops and when to apply the proper amounts of chemical fertilizer. Thus the peasants wanted him to continue, believing him the most capable of raising the level of production, and thus the villagers' income.

This former leader's wife, famous for her strong will, insisted that her husband would not return to his post. I went to that family every day for more than a week, playing with his children, talking to his wife, building her trust and confidence, before finally she agreed to her husband's reinstatement. In the end, the brigade leader, the militia leader and the accountant were criticized and replaced by young men who had recently graduated from middle school. Although our task was finally accomplished, I never knew what happened after our departure. I suspected that inevitably the cadres who had been attacked during this half year would find some way to exact their revenge.

This time I was eager to return to Beijing. Not only had I felt excluded from the lives of the peasants in Xiaohongmen, but I was worried about what had happened in my absence. Month after month our work team had met twice a week to discuss the latest political developments. Back in November, shortly after our arrival, we had read in *People's Daily* of Yao Wenyuan's* attack on the historical play *The Dismissal of Hai Rui from Office*,† written by Wu Han, a vice-mayor of Beijing and a prominent historian. Then and throughout the winter months the play had been criticized in the most vehement terms, and with it were condemned several films, like "The Lin Family Shop," ‡ that I had seen and admired. Many points in those official diatribes I had been unable to accept—for example, that this particular film, which I considered among the greatest achievements of Chinese cinema, was attempting to lead people along the capitalist road. Even though everyone had felt too wary to venture an opinion, we had read the newspaper articles carefully, trying to comprehend what was prompting such attacks, certain only that it was something serious.

Throughout that spring the newspaper editorials had become

---

*Yao Wenyuan, a literary critic from Shanghai who earned the trust of Jiang Qing for his opposition to many writers and cultural leaders, later became known as one of the "Gang of Four."

†The play, published in 1961 and briefly performed, depicted a loyal Ming dynasty official who aroused the displeasure of other local officials by his efforts to alleviate the peasants' suffering and was subsequently dismissed by the emperor. The play was seen as an allegorical attack on the Great Leap Forward and the dismissal of Peng Dehuai.

‡"The Lin Family Shop," a film made in the late 1950s by Xia Yan, China's major screen writer, sympathetically portrayed the sufferings of a small shopowner brought to ruin by poverty, oppression, and the boycott of Japanese products in 1931.

harsher and more vitriolic. Then in May, Deng Tuo was attacked, a man I had long admired as a skillful writer, an exemplary leader. If Deng Tuo fell, I knew that those who had sided with him would also be in jeopardy, and Lao Tang would surely be among those assumed to be guilty by association. After rejecting the work team's conclusion that Beida was a "reactionary fortress," Peng Zhen and Deng Tuo had convened a conference on education at the International Hotel in Beijing in the summer of 1965. This was an attempt to reinforce the power of Liu Shaoqi by invalidating the opposition's claims. Some two hundred supporters of Lu Ping and eighty opponents were invited to those meetings to reevaluate the work team's verdict and pronounce final judgment on whether Beida was a bourgeois or a socialist institution. Eighteen people were invited from the philosophy department, among them Lao Tang and the Party secretary, a woman in her early fifties named Nie Yuanzi.

From the guarded comments in Lao Tang's letters to me in the countryside, I could guess his views of the political struggle. He admired Lu Ping for his role in the revolutionary movement since 1935 and for his efforts to promote the level of higher education, and could not believe that the university's former president truly possessed a bourgeois viewpoint or had been unfaithful to the Communist Party. Several times during this conference Deng Tuo had singled out Lao Tang for private talks, urging him to support Lu Ping and to help persuade others in the philosophy department that the work team's conclusion must be rejected. Such personal contact with the top leaders would surely implicate Lao Tang in whatever power struggle was unfolding, and I had sensed his growing anxiety. He wrote that on Saturdays he would always take Tang Shuang back to the hotel with him for rides in the elevator, a pastime that had brought our seven-year-old son such pleasure that Lao Tang had been able to escape briefly from the tension of those meetings. Trying to guess what lay between the lines of his letters, I had felt great concern about Lao Tang's health, knowing that he was exhausted from worry and lack of sleep.

After the conference ended, Lao Tang had returned to the campus and become ever more deeply involved in the political debates.

By then he had been appointed secretary of the teachers' Party branch in his department, a post that required him to lead discussions designed to bolster the support of Peng Zhen by stressing the progressive outlooks and approaches evident over the past decade in the teaching of philosophy. Meanwhile, Nie Yuanzi, the Party secretary of the whole department, was defending the opposite position, insisting that the work team's conclusions were correct and that the last ten years at Beida had been a reactionary period that must be thoroughly repudiated. But with the work team itself being denounced that spring by the Central Committee as ultra-leftist, Lao Tang for the moment actually had more power and influence than Nie Yuanzi.

My knowledge of those events was always sketchy, my ability to analyze their importance limited, since Lao Tang's letters could never be explicit. When on June 1, just ten days before our return from Xiaohongmen to Beijing, I received a letter describing in detail the recent events on campus, I became more alarmed than ever. Nie Yuanzi, Lao Tang's principal adversary within his department, had suddenly been thrust into the national limelight. On May 25 she had asked six others to join her in writing what became known as the "seven-person wall poster," a strident denunciation of Lu Ping, of the Beida Party Committee, and of the person on the Beijing Party Committee responsible for higher education, a man named Song Shuo.

"Many people look upon this poster as a rightist statement," Lao Tang had written, "and they have mounted their own posters to attack Nie Yuanzi. Perhaps some new campaign is developing," he reflected, "but there is no way to tell what will happen next." Nie Yuanzi's accusations reminded him of the claims made during the spring of 1957 by the students, eager to bring about reforms, that Beida's leadership, like that of the Youth League and the Party, had made mistakes. But Nie Yuanzi's attack was far more extreme, for she claimed that Lu Ping was an agent of capitalism, that Song Shuo, a strong supporter of Peng Zhen, had pursued a bourgeois educational line, and that all of Beida was in the hands of the bourgeoisie. Wall posters appearing in response to her provocative statements had denounced this pronouncement of May 25 as excessively negative, itself an attack on the leadership of the Communist Party. After reading Lao Tang's account, I found myself more than ever confused about what was developing and very frightened. Never in 1957 had anyone dared to attack such a powerful figure so openly, nor had anyone claimed that the Party's work at Beida had all been in error.

That same evening we were told to organize the peasants to listen to an important radio broadcast. My stomach tightened when the announcer declared that a revolutionary wall poster had appeared at Beida on May 25, and that this was in fact the first truly Marxist wall poster. Then the station broadcast the editorial that would appear in the next day's issue of *People's Daily*. Titled "Hail to a Poster at Beida," it elaborately praised Nie Yuanzi's poster and warned that "anyone who opposes Chairman Mao, no matter how old or how prominent, must be overturned."

Knowing only a little about Nie Yuanzi's background, I couldn't understand how she could have become so important. Previously a cadre on the Liaoning Provincial Party Committee, she had gone to the Liberated Areas and then had returned to the Northeast to assume a position of some influence in her native province. After her first husband was declared a rightist, she had divorced him and married a powerful member of the Central Discipline Committee, twenty years older than she, who had been very helpful to her career. After her marriage she had been assigned, presumably through her husband's connections, to her position at Beida. Also through her husband, I later guessed, she had become friends with Kang Sheng's wife, Cao Yi'ou, who had been sent to the campus for a few weeks in April and May to gather firsthand information about the situation at Beida. Apparently Cao Yi'ou had chosen Nie Yuanzi as the spokesperson for those attempting to destroy Lu Ping and his supporters, and this relationship explained why she was so trusted by the work team and its leader, Zhang Panshi.

I went to bed that night quite exhausted, trying to digest the news from Lao Tang as well as the radio broadcast and to absorb the official decision that Nie Yuanzi's poster had been deemed a Marxist and not a rightist statement. At the International Hotel conference Lao Tang had sharply opposed her, but now her position was receiving the highest validation. Always before, Lao Tang's letters had primarily concerned personal and family affairs, and his abrupt departure from this pattern signaled an inordinate concern about recent events. I could only be certain of one thing, that the situation was very serious, that without any doubt a crisis was near.

In the ensuing days I tried with increasing frustration and anxiety to comprehend the rapidly accelerating political struggle. The June 4 newspaper announced that the entire Beijing Party Committee would be reorganized, as would the Beida Party Committee, and that Peng Zhen had been dismissed from office. All of Beijing municipality, I read with alarm, was clearly "connected by a big black line to an anti-Party, anti-socialist clique." Again my mind reeled.

I had always felt great respect for Peng Zhen, ever since 1950 when I was in my second year at the university. Answering a knock at my door one midnight, I had found a messenger who said that Peng Zhen wanted to see me. Both frightened and excited, I had dressed hurriedly and walked to the waiting car. With three other students I was taken to his office, an impressive Western-style room with beautiful carpets and a big fireplace where a cheerful blaze warded off the winter chill. Again I had felt as if I were living out a scene from some Western novel.

Peng Zhen and his first secretary, Liu Ren, had greeted us, engaging us in conversation about the political courses in our curriculum. That year I was taking one class on Communist Party history, another on Marxism. I was asked whether we students liked our teacher and what kind of things he taught. "Tell me your feelings honestly," Peng Zhen had requested, patting my shoulder; "don't be afraid." I had replied that while the courses were obviously very important, they were not always very interesting, and that some among the two hundred students in the auditorium would often doze or read novels. After this talk we were served a delicious meal, even one dish made with peanuts, which were exceedingly difficult to buy then. I had formed a very positive impression of Peng Zhen, perceiving him as an official who genuinely wished to understand how others thought and who wanted to remain close to the people.

When the time for my graduation approached, the Beijing Party Committee had sent for my dossier, informing Beida that they were considering me for the post of Peng Zhen's private secretary. Thinking back to that time, I felt extremely lucky to have heard nothing further about this appointment, although my dossier was never returned. How could Peng Zhen be attacked as a person opposed to the Communist Party, I wondered, and what would this portend for Lao Tang, who was now publicly affiliated with both Peng Zhen and Deng Tuo?

After another *People's Daily* editorial declared that the decision to send teachers and students out to conduct investigations in the countryside was just a ruse to protect the leaders from criticism, I was not surprised when an order arrived instructing us to return to campus on June 10. After lunch that day I climbed into the back of a truck, terribly apprehensive about what awaited me. Expecting to find Lao Tang at the gate to help with my heavy bedroll, I searched the crowd for his face, but he was nowhere to be seen. As I entered the campus, I was assaulted by the shouting of slogans and by the shocking sight of the dormitory walls completely pasted over with posters. Long sections of bamboo matting had been erected to provide additional mounting space, and these too were plastered with pink and green paper. I wanted to read the posters instantly to learn what was happening, but I couldn't stop then with my cumbersome baggage. Finally, my daughter appeared with a bicycle, and I headed home as quickly as I could, dropping my things at the doorway to my bedroom, not even stopping long enough to wash after my journey or to ask about Tang Shuang. I simply greeted Lao Tang's mother and dashed back to the central campus to learn what the posters would reveal.

Unleashing the Violence

I HAD NEVER seen the campus so crowded or in such confusion. Classes had ended in May, and many of the students had not yet returned from the countryside or from factories where they were conducting the Four Clean-ups, but people from all over the city had flocked to this birthplace of the new revolutionary struggle. Contingents of workers, peasants, and soldiers, dispatched to support the May 25 poster, were clustered in small groups, shouting, "The workers, peasants, and soldiers applaud Nie Yuanzi's revolutionary action!" Using loudspeakers, delegations of students and teachers from other institutions cried out slogans, recited Chairman Mao's quotations, or proclaimed their solidarity with Nie Yuanzi: "We come from the Normal University; we support your revolutionary action; we shall learn from you!" The normally sedate campus was more raucous than any marketplace.

From the walls of the dining hall building, posters and slogans declared that "the bourgeois line of Lu Ping must be exposed" or, more fiercely, that Lu Ping's oppression of the workers and peasants was "a crime deserving a million deaths." The vehemence of the accusations struck fear in my heart, especially when my gaze fell upon the words, "Lock the murderer Hu Wenli in jail." The person so harshly condemned was a friend of mine, a pleasant, mild woman, a member of my graduating class, and a branch secretary in the nuclear physics department. She couldn't possibly have committed murder, I was certain, and I couldn't account for such threatening rhetoric. She was being held responsible, I later learned, for her department's failure to dispose properly of radioactive waste materials. Rather than being buried, the dangerous substances had been carelessly stored in the basement of a laboratory building, and several students had lost their hair as a result of exposure to this radiation. My mind spun as I read such denunciations, unable to comprehend what had taken place during my months in the countryside.

The posters in the area assigned to the philosophy department confirmed my worst fears. Ignoring the mobs of people, closing my ears to the din of voices, I moved in a daze from one accusation to the next. A special section of bamboo matting was devoted just to attacks on the International Hotel Conference, and Lao Tang's name was prominently featured. Some posters alleged that he was one of the leaders of that meeting, a member of the small group responsible for all that had occurred there, and insisted that he must confess publicly his role in that gathering. Others claimed that he had labeled Nie Yuanzi's May 25 poster a rightist statement, thus proving, now that Chairman Mao himself had written a poster to say that hers was the first Marxist-Leninist poster and thus genuinely leftist, that Lao Tang was himself a rightist. Still others accused him of having actually been a rightist back in 1957, when he had protected his wife, had refused to draw a line separating himself from her, and had written statements critical of the Party bureaucracy. The posters warned that he had slipped away that time and escaped punishment, implying that this time would be different, that now his true face would be revealed. Both of our names appeared with a bold red X through them, long an indication of the death sentence but now a signal that someone had been condemned as a political enemy.

Having read all the posters in the philosophy department section, I had no strength left to move on to the Chinese literature area, even though I desperately needed to know who were the main targets of attack among my own colleagues. After all that I had previously been accused of, I tried to reassure myself that it was unlikely any new charges had been leveled against me, but I couldn't be certain. It was growing dark, and my feet felt so heavy I could barely walk. As I headed home, I tried to face up to the perils of this new situation. At least when I was a rightist, I had known that I had a safe background, but Tang Yongtong's prominence could no longer afford protection. If Lao Tang himself fell down, there would be nowhere to turn for support.

When I returned from Zhaitang in 1960, I had not been completely without hope, clinging to the idea that the future might be brighter than the past, that I might still have a chance to do something to benefit my country. Returning from Xiaohongmen in 1966 was different, for I could see nothing to strive for, no hope, no future, only suffering. All that I had believed in was now being attacked, the whole seventeen years since Liberation said to be a "black line." In the anti-rightist period I had felt that the system was still right and I could try to change myself, but now I could find nothing to fall back on. It was a disorienting, depressing time, when everything I had worked for seemed to have been repudiated.

Feeling sick and unable to eat, I stayed in my room with Tang Shuang, aware that his sympathetic yet uncomprehending eyes never moved from my face. When dinner time passed and Lao Tang still had not returned, my anxiety became overwhelming. Finally the door opened, and as Lao Tang slowly crossed the room to sit beside me, he said only, "Now it's my turn."

In the midst of the utter confusion on the campus and the gnawing anxiety that permeated those days, a new kind of pattern, unfamiliar and frightening, began to emerge. Every morning Lao Tang had to report to his department to be interrogated about the International Hotel Conference by members of the work team and by Nie Yuanzi's supporters. Each night he would return, unhappy and silent. When the children had gone to sleep we would sit together, unable to read or make small talk, absorbed in our separate thoughts. Lao Tang never spoke of his ordeal or shared with me his pain, though he would occasionally comment upon the inability of human beings to control their own fate.

The day after my return I was told to attend a meeting in my own department. There the person in charge of our group of rightists spoke: "Now is a very special time to test your loyalty to the

Party," he announced, "a time when everyone must educate himself to understand what has happened. We are about to witness a great affair for the whole nation, an affair organized by Chairman Mao himself. You are not yourselves entitled to write posters," he warned, "but you are responsible for reading what everyone else has written. If you rightists have anything to reveal, you are to inform me and I will write your opinions down. Everyone must become involved, and this participation will reveal who is truly loyal to the Party. You cannot say or do whatever you like, but must follow these instructions, and I hope your willingness to reveal all that you know about followers of the capitalist road will once again earn you the people's trust." In this leader's speech, as always happens in China, a threat was issued alongside a promise.

I had already learned that a new work team, to replace the one sent in 1964 by Kang Sheng, had recently arrived at the request of Liu Shaoqi and the Central Committee to investigate and control the volatile situation at Beida. Wanting this second group to have no affiliations with the earlier work team, the authorities had drawn many of the new team members from outside of Beijing. The leader was the head of the Hebei provincial department of education and loyal to the policies of Peng Zhen and Deng Tuo, but in my department the work team head had formerly been the director of a film company in Changchun and was thus expected to be politically neutral and objective. The harsh denunciations I had seen covering the campus were written by the students but presumably initiated by the work team, whose goal was to contain the criticism by limiting its targets.

Nearly every day in the chaotic weeks that followed, I would see Nie Yuanzi appear in the central campus square near the dining hall to address the crowds, shouting, "We must all follow Chairman Mao and pursue to the end the Cultural Revolution, an event that will affect the whole world." People applauded her wildly, crying out slogans and chanting that they would follow Chairman Mao and oppose the capitalist road. As I watched the young people jubilantly carrying her on their shoulders, I thought about the absurdity of this situation. The new movement was allegedly to be carried out by the youth of China, yet here was this woman in her fifties wearing thick glasses, proclaiming herself their leader. "Chairman Mao has said that I am the first red banner," she would cry, "so anyone who opposes me opposes Chairman Mao himself." How arrogant she is, I thought; how curious that sometimes history pushes to the forefront someone so completely undistinguished.

Following the instructions issued at my department meeting, I would spend hours reading the two types of posters found on the campus. The outside ones were centrally located and open to the scrutiny of everyone. The inside ones, however, were mounted in the graduate students' dining hall in the more remote southern section of the campus and could be read only by those wearing Beida identification pins. Posters were thus sequestered from the public gaze either if they were written to express a tentative and unprovable accusation or if they were written to reveal errors committed by high-ranking Party officials, opinions that the authors believed should not be accessible to everyone.

Inside the dining hall my attention was immediately caught by an enormous enlargement, stretching from floor to ceiling, of a "black painting" that had appeared in *Chinese Youth* magazine. Observing only an autumn landscape depicting cheerful, industrious peasants harvesting rice and loading the grain onto carts, I could not understand why this painting was worthy of such attention. When I drew closer to read the accompanying explanation, I learned that the artist had included two but not three red flags in his landscape, a clear indication that he opposed the policy of the Three Red Banners. A stern admonition warned that the people must be vigilant, since in the area of culture many enemies were trying to undermine the Party.

On the opposite wall hung a large drawing that at a distance appeared to be merely a confused tangle of lines. Looking more closely, I saw that the grooves on an ordinary shoe sole had been painstakingly reproduced to show that they were actually rows of the character "mao," alleged to be an intentional insult to Mao Zedong and an indication that someone wanted the Chairman to be trodden underfoot. Out of curiosity I studied this drawing carefully, but I could find only a remote resemblance to the hallowed character that was supposedly being blasphemed.

In addition to such paintings and drawings, the dining room contained many posters, some attacking the International Hotel Conference, some mentioning Peng Zhen by name, which the outside posters would not dare to do because of his high position in the Party leadership. Here, away from public scrutiny, he was accused of wanting to protect the capitalist road and, a far graver offense, of being disloyal to Chairman Mao. Other posters accused not just Peng Zhen but Deng Tuo and other members of the Beijing Party Committee, ordering them to confess what they had done to oppose Chairman Mao. Since no one ordinarily would dare to criticize such powerful men, I realized that these attacks must have been authorized by someone important, an indication that the struggle was now being waged at a very high level.

On the morning of June 18, I was instructed to report to my department and remain there. Everyone had assembled, and we passed the time nervously reading newspapers, apprehensive about what would happen next. At nine o'clock a group of ten students burst in, their faces angry, their voices shrill. One of them shouted Chairman Mao's dictum that a revolution is not a time to embroider or serve tea, after which they seized Lao Chen, the department Party secretary who had offered me such encouragement in Zhaitang, calling him an enemy of the people, shoving a bamboo wastebasket on his head, and slathering paste on his back to glue on a poster that proclaimed, "Enemy of the People, Follower of the Capitalist Road." At first the paper wouldn't stick to his light-blue polyester shirt in the summer heat, so another student emptied the whole bucket of paste down his back, causing the sticky liquid to dribble down his legs. This time the poster stuck.

At the students' command we lined up along both sides of the corridor while they sought out the other enemies on their list. I happened to be standing beside the door to the women's lavatory and saw a young teacher dash inside. She was a favorite of Lu Ping's and had been disparagingly called one of his "five golden flowers," a term drawn from a popular movie title. Not only had Lu Ping selected her as an example for the other women teachers during the campaign to raise educational standards, but he had even chosen her to be a tutor for his children. Her husband was also a favorite of

Lu Ping's, and when Nie Yuanzi's poster had first appeared, this Lao Xiang had written down the names of those who had mounted supporting posters, denouncing Nie Yuanzi's allies as rightists. A class leader and therefore responsible for overseeing the students' political ideology, Lao Xiang had carried out Lu Ping's instructions, dismissing those students, usually from the countryside, who had inferior academic records and criticizing others for problems with their thoughts.

Several of the most militant students helping to organize the campus-wide parade of black gang members that day were members of Lao Xiang's class. Because of accumulated resentments, they wanted this couple, whom they dubbed "black teeth and claws," meaning that they were tools of the "black gang," to be paraded with the other more serious enemies. Guessing this, I stood casually in front of the lavatory door. The fiery students demanded whether I had seen this young woman, and I quietly said no. The prospect of being caught by these young rebels seemed so terrifying that I wanted to protect the young woman, whom I scarcely knew, but I dared not think what would be my own fate if I were caught in a lie. Miraculously, the students walked on; for the moment she was safe. Meanwhile, her husband, a tall man, had been forced to bend over so far that he looked like a curled-up shrimp, his face pale and sweating, a wastebasket on his head.

The idea of parading enemies had originated in the 1920s when the Communist Party, pursuing its work among the peasants, often forced the landlords to march in front of those they had formerly oppressed, every landlord wearing a tall, pointed hat bearing a description of his wrongdoing. Now in the frenzy of the moment, the students had no time to fashion enough hats, so they used wastebaskets instead, glued the posters onto the backs of their victims, and sometimes even threw ink in their faces to show the degree of contempt in which these former holders of academic power were now viewed. No evidence, proof, or discussion of guilt was necessary. People were being labeled as black gang members just for having some connection with Lu Ping, alleged to be part of the black line that extended to the Beijing Party Committee and finally to Liu Shaoqi himself.

Most of the targets in my department that morning were the responsible cadres, men like Lao Chen, Lao Xiang, and Lao Sun, the vice-chairman, as well as the members of the Party branch committee. By the time the students had finished, they had seized perhaps ten such enemies, all of whom were crowned with wastebaskets and branded with posters, some of which fell to the ground. Everyone was frightened, and I was certain that they would seize me along with the rest. Finally, they left, sharply ordering the rest of us outside to watch and "be educated."

Knowing that Lao Tang would inevitably be in this parade of Lu Ping's accomplices, I dreaded what would happen next. In my department the students had not struck anyone, but I had seen the young people from the history department use their leather belts and metal buckles to strap the legs of the person at the end of the line merely to make him speed up his pace. I had no idea what was happening in the philosophy department or what Lao Tang was being forced to endure. I only knew that whatever befell him, he wouldn't want me to know and that my watching his humiliation would greatly increase his distress. Finally, I seized a chance to slip back inside the building, hoping I wouldn't be caught. I waited there in the teachers' office for the next nightmarish hour, peering out the window as each new group of enemies was marched around our quadrangle, unable to block out the shouts of the students or the clamor of gongs.

At the head of the line of enemies from our building was Jian Bozan, a veteran Party member and prominent historian, famous for his early efforts to help Communist underground members establish connections with sympathizers in the Guomindang-controlled areas, for his protection of revolutionary students, and for his close relationship to Zhou Enlai. Now more than seventy, he had published many books and was held in high esteem, his very prominence, as well as his long association with the policies of Liu Shaoqi, having made him a primary target.

I could see columns of enemies emerging from the different campus buildings, flanked by jeering students wearing red armbands and shaking their fists. The striking of gongs punctuated their cries: "Come out and see the enemies," "Drag out the black gang and show them to the people," "Down with the warlords within the academic fields." Sometimes the victims' arms were twisted behind their backs or their heads roughly shoved down, and I saw stunned expressions on their faces.

When the parading had finished, the gongs finally stilled, I headed home. It was late, but I waited for Lao Tang, hoping he would return to eat lunch. When he finally appeared, he didn't speak, just hurriedly took off his jacket and dropped it in the basket for dirty clothes. I knew something must have happened, that perhaps his clothing too had been covered with paste, but I didn't want to ask. We ate in silence. Though he averted his eyes, I could see that his face was tired and expressionless, his thoughts far away.

That afternoon on my way to a university-wide meeting in the central dining hall, I passed many new posters denouncing the work team for following the wrong line and for showing compassion toward the black gang. "Down with the work team," "Expel the work team from Beida," "We will make revolution ourselves, without any nurse to help us," I read, shocked that the representatives of the Party's authority could be attacked so openly. A procession of students appeared on the platform when the meeting began, criticizing the work team vehemently, saying it was trying to bind them hand and foot and to prevent them from struggling against the enemy. The work team had been too mild, they accused; everyone knew that a mass movement must be violent. Challenging the work team to make clear its revolutionary viewpoint by supporting that morning's mass action, the students declared that either the work team must agree with their methods, whereupon they would conduct the Cultural Revolution together, or it must leave the campus immediately. The dilemma was clear: if the work team supported the students, more violence would follow; but if it opposed them, it would be regarded as opposing the masses.

Because of the work team's attempt to protect people from the students' violence, I hoped it would remain, but I could see that its authority had been seriously compromised. In the days that followed, its members tried to assert control, checking the identification pins of those who came through the gates and refusing

159

permission for students to gather and make speeches, but the revolutionary fervor had reached such a pitch that their efforts were in vain.

From the start, it appeared, there had been no way to contain this violence. When the students had first appeared in our department, the work team leader had tried to reason with them, offering to hold a meeting, a discussion, or a struggle session, but the impassioned young rebels had ignored him. Zhang Chengxian, I knew, had made many attempts to mollify and to divert the instigators of the June 18 parade, but events had achieved a momentum quite beyond control, resulting in some one hundred "enemies" being marched around the campus for more than an hour. Only later did I realize that the day's events had not resulted from a spontaneous outburst of revolutionary zeal on the part of the students, but had been engineered by Nie Yuanzi and Cao Yi'ou, who had the previous night organized representatives from each department to rally others to their cause in a concerted effort to destroy the power of the work team.

This June 18 affair, as it became known, marked the beginning of the violence that was quickly to engulf our campus and to spread from there across the city. Although this was the first time that people had been struck, shoved about, and paraded for all to see, the new method of revolution set an immediate precedent. At other institutions the students would sometimes act even more brutally to prove their revolutionary ardor.

A few days later I witnessed at close hand the cruelty that was rapidly becoming contagious. My department was to hold its first big struggle session, and everyone was required to attend. The auditorium was full, eight hundred people staring anxiously at Lao Chen, who stood on the platform surrounded by irate students shouting accusations and pushing his head down, then grabbing him by the hair to show the people his face, forcing his arms up high behind his back. He was responsible, they had decided, for all of the problems that had occurred in the Chinese literature department during the past year.

When a peasant student, the mother of a young baby, had failed to pass her exams, the department leaders had not taken care of her but had told her to return home, proving that they opposed the peasants. They had even admitted a Guomindang general's daughter as a student, obviously favoring a Nationalist's descendant over a peasant. Moreover, they had allowed a rightist to resume her teaching duties and thereby poison the students. Hearing this reference to the essay I had praised nearly a year before, I held my breath, waiting to become once again a target of attack, but the students were intent on Lao Chen's crimes and cared nothing about me at that moment.

Next they mentioned a student who was only twenty-three and had engaged in illicit sexual relations with a forty-year-old widow, a scandalous affair that had resulted, they charged, from the department's allowing students to read "yellow novels," which had corrupted their socialist morality. Furthermore, a man and a woman in the department had fallen in love and, each separately married, had committed suicide, jumping into the river bound together by a sheet. Another student had attempted to commit suicide, swallowing a bottle of sleeping pills and writing a poem by candlelight to say that when the candle had burned out, her life would have ended, and bidding the world farewell. Her roommate had returned in time to find the girl still alive and rush her to the hospital, but the example was said to reveal the debasement of the students' thoughts under Lao Chen's leadership.

They accused him of responsibility for all these random events, linking them together and claiming that his revisionist line had allowed poisonous literature to infect the department and make it a place simply to corrupt the younger generation. Others clamored that Lao Chen's past was also suspect, since in the Anti-Japanese War he had joined the Guomindang army and been sent to India for training. "A clear line must be drawn between the bourgeois thought of the Party secretary and true proletarian ideology," the students shouted. From my seat in one of the front rows at the far side of the auditorium, I could see Lao Chen clearly. Beads of moisture dripped from his face, betraying his humiliation and fear. Appalled at what was happening to this strong and committed revolutionary, I felt weak and helpless, sick with concern and apprehension.

By then Lao Tang had been proclaimed a "big black element."

This caused my sister-in-law to insist that our families take their meals separately, an effort to distance herself from a declared enemy. Without the help of the family's one remaining *ayi*, I had to prepare the meals for my children each day, and would routinely go out to purchase food at the nearby shop on my return home from my department. Late one afternoon I was surprised to see Lao Chen in the food shop, his face so dejected that I dared not speak to him, fearing that any contact might be dangerous for us both now that he was being seriously struggled against and I was a rightist. Despite all of his past reassurances to me in my own times of trouble, I could offer him no consolation, I thought bitterly.

I recalled how optimistic he had been when we young people had first traveled to Beijing, hoping in this revolutionary place to do something to help our country, and how he had sung songs the whole way, many of them tunes from the Liberated Areas. His diligence and sincerity as well as his warm personality had made him universally respected, even prompting Zhu Jiayu to fall in love with him during the land reform days. Now in his eyes I sensed something strange, a lost, blank, unseeing gaze that appeared not even to notice me. As I watched, he bought a bottle of strong, expensive liquor, nothing else. Knowing that Lao Chen never drank, I felt some alarm, and a flood of compassion for the extremity of his suffering.

The next day I heard the news of his suicide. After taking a bus to the Fragrant Hills, he had rented a room, rested awhile, and then walked in the mountains until late into the night, alternately drinking the liquor and a bottle of DDT. His body and the two empty bottles were discovered the next day by a park worker. The news of this tragedy spread quickly, filling all who had known and admired him with grief and anger. Those responsible for his struggle session announced stonily that Lao Chen had been unwilling to reform, choosing instead to remain an enemy of the Party forever. Moreover, they said, knowing that this was a nearly impossible task, his wife could retrieve his body from deep in the hills by herself. A strong woman, she went everywhere to ask for help as the weather was hot, the removal of the body urgent. At last she persuaded four grounds workers to help her carry the corpse to the nearest road and then convinced someone with a truck to transport her husband's body to the crematorium at Babaoshan. This was how the Cultural Revolution began in my department, with the loss of its leader. Such a warm, competent, devoted man would never again commit his talents to the revolution.

Refusing to countenance such acts of cruelty as the struggle session that had moved Lao Chen to end his life, the work team claimed that counter-revolutionary students were attempting to turn the Cultural Revolution in a wrong direction by using physical force rather than persuasion to steer people along the socialist road. Trying to maintain their previous authority, they singled out some students whose families had political problems or who had implied something unfavorable about the Communist Party and held these people up as examples of the counter-revolutionary trend. Such actions only turned the students who had participated most energetically in the June 18 violence more strongly against the work team.

On July 1, the birthday of the Communist Party, Tao Zhu, an advisor to the Central Cultural Revolution Group, came to Beida to conduct a mass meeting in the dining hall. Although he reiterated his firm support for the revolutionary activities of the June 18 affair, he was equally firm in his insistence that the work team would remain on campus to help the students conduct the new movement. In the weeks that followed, a majority of the students remained silent, uncertain what would happen next, but the most zealous, no doubt encouraged by Cao Yi'ou, continued to mount posters criticizing the work team's actions. Gradually, they attracted more supporters.

On the evening of July 22, a huge meeting was convened on the East Athletic Field, attended by some ten thousand people. Even though it was raining hard, everyone was told to be present. In addition to the Beida community, students from Qinghua and from Beida's attached middle school had joined the crowd. To my astonishment, Mao Zedong's wife, Jiang Qing, strode across the platform. It was her first public appearance. According to rumor, her agreement not to participate in political affairs was the bargain struck by Chairman Mao with high Party leaders to overcome their disapproval of his marriage in 1939 to a movie star notorious for her relationships with men, but now she was standing before us.

Although I was sitting far in the back and could see only a figure in a gray suit, I could hear clearly her voice, shrill and trembling with excitement as she shouted slogans. "All of Beida is under the dictatorship of the academic warlords," "Beida has been totally occupied by the bourgeois authorities," "It is time to overthrow the bourgeois academic clique," "Our hope lies in the younger generation," she proclaimed to thunderous applause. Soon a middle-school student, Wang Yawei, spoke, voicing the students' love for Jiang Qing, who was leading them in Chairman Mao's footsteps. As everyone clapped and yelled loud approval, Jiang Qing embraced this student and called her "a little red sun," echoing the term used to describe Chairman Mao himself. At this the crowd grew even more excited.

I found it impossible to share in this enthusiasm, for Jiang Qing's ensuing harangue about how she could not allow the class struggle to penetrate her own family left me depressed. "I won't let that woman be my daughter-in-law," she shouted; "I won't acknowledge her as a member of my family." She was furiously attacking Zhang Shaohua, the wife of Chairman Mao's second son Mao Anqing, and a student in my department. "That girl's mother is a traitor," Jiang Qing continued, alleging that this woman, who had joined the revolution very early, whose husband had died in the revolution's cause, was suspected of being a Guomindang collaborator, having surrendered to the enemy and then escaped to Yan'an with her young daughter. Somehow, according to Jiang Qing's logic, the suspicious circumstances surrounding the mother's escape implied that the daughter might also be a traitor who had married Chairman Mao's son for clandestine purposes. Hearing her talk on and on about such family matters, I wondered how I could ever admire Jiang Qing as a revolutionary leader when she seemed so concerned with personal vendettas.

Seated on the platform with Jiang Qing were Kang Sheng, the major emissary between Chairman Mao and his wife and another advisor to the Central Cultural Revolution Group, as well as Chen

Boda, Guan Feng, and Qi Benyu, all members of this important organization. When Guan Feng spoke, asserting that in this revolution the principles of the Paris Commune must be followed, that everyone must participate in elections and join in this great revolutionary movement, unprecedented in Chinese history and led by Chairman Mao himself, even I became excited, thinking that if the principles of the Paris Commune could be achieved, if everyone could receive the same salary and the high leaders be equal to the technical workers, then the cause of socialism in China would be greatly advanced. After all, the removal of privilege had been the rightists' main concern in 1957, and I still believed that a crucial goal. When Guan Feng emphasized that a revolution had begun, that it must necessarily be violent, that everyone must prepare for the outburst that would follow, I knew that my own family and friends would probably pay a high price. Still, I hoped that the new movement would prove an important step forward for the country as a whole.

At this point, with Lu Ping shut up in his room to write down his crimes against the people and the work team substantially discredited, no one could be said to hold power at Beida except Nie Yuanzi, whose support obviously came from the highest level. Tao Zhu's endorsement of the work team had been ignored, the slogan "Kick out the work team and leave revolution to the masses" emblazoned on more and more posters. Finally, on July 26 all one hundred work team members, these now ineffectual representatives of the Central Committee, were instructed to return to their units, there to pursue the Cultural Revolution and not to hinder its progress any further. Quickly, the Beida Cultural Revolution Preparatory Committee was organized, with Nie Yuanzi appointed its head. The other six signers of the original May 25 big character poster divided control of the university, selecting those whom they trusted to chair branch committees in each department. Jiang Qing's power was thus effectively consolidated at Beida.

In the oppressive heat of midsummer, more and more students began appearing dressed in olive green jackets, pants, and caps, with bright red armbands as their identifying badges of authority.

This garb was to become a standard uniform after Chairman Mao appeared in Tiananmen Square in August in an identical outfit to express his solidarity with the nation's youth. Calling themselves "Red Guards," a term coined by students from Qinghua's attached middle school, young people from across the city began to take the revolution into their own hands.

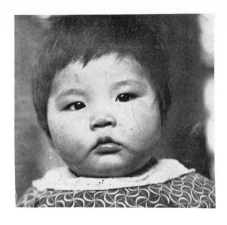

Yue Daiyun in 1932.

Yue Daiyun with her mother in 1933.

Yue Daiyun in Wudang, 1940.

Yue Daiyun (front row, second from right) with her middle-school graduating class, Guiyang, 1948.

Yue Daiyun as a first-year student at Beida, 1948.

Yue Daiyun after joining the Communist Party, 1949.

Yue Daiyun's poem posted on the wall at Beida, 1950.

Yue Daiyun (far left) at the Lenin Museum, Moscow, 1950.

Yue Daiyun (center) at the World Student Congress, Prague, 1950.

Yue Daiyun addressing 10,000 students at Beida after returning from Prague, 1950.

Beida's work team for land reform (Yue Daiyun, front row, third from right; Zhu Jiayu, front row, seventh from right; Lao Chen, fourth row, center, smiling; Fei Ming, third row, center, wearing cap and glasses), Jiangxi, October 1951.

Yue Daiyun (right) with new cadres selected by the land reform work team, including the woman in charge of women's affairs, Jiangxi, April 1952.

Yue Daiyun as a Beida graduate, 1952.

Yue Daiyun and Tang Yijie as newlyweds, the photograph that hung on their bedroom wall, 1952.

Yue Daiyun and Zhu Jiayu beside No-name Lake, summer 1956.

Tang Yijie's family, summer 1958 (back row, Tang Yijie's brother, Tang Yijie, Yue Daiyun; front row, his mother holding Tang Shuang, Tang Yongtong, Fourth Aunt; in front, Tang Dan).

Tang Dan and Tang Shuang; the photograph Yue Daiyun took with her to Zhaitang, summer 1958.

Yue Daiyun with Old Aunt and Old Uncle, Zhaitang, 1960.

Tang Yijie (center) with his father and another student, 1962.

Yue Daiyun's family, gathered for the wedding of her brother (standing, Yue Daiyun's sister, Yue Daiyun, Tang Yijie, her brother, her brother's wife, Tang Dan; seated, her mother and father with Tang Shuang), 1962.

Yue Daiyun's parents' house near the Beida campus, 1965.

Yue Daiyun and Tang Yijie, anniversary photograph in the midst of the Cultural Revolution, December 31, 1966.

Yue Daiyun, Tang Yijie, Tang Dan, Tang Shuang before Tang Dan's departure for Heilongjiang, summer 1969.

Tang Shuang, Yue Daiyun, Tang Yijie in front of Tiananmen, the day before their departure for Liyuzhou, November 1969.

Yue Daiyun in Nanchang to buy books for the worker, peasant, soldier students, 1971.

Tang Dan (standing) with a friend on the military farm in Heilongjiang, 1971.

Yue Daiyun (right) with three students in Anyuan, 1971.

*Tang Yijie, Tang
Shuang, Yue Daiyun,
returned to their home
from Liyuzhou, 1971.*

*Tang Shuang at home,
studying for exams,
1976.*

*Yue Daiyun and Tang
Yijie at home after his
release from detention,
1978.*

Long Live the Red Terror

During that August of 1966, with the work team gone and all constraints removed, the slogan "Long live the red terror" became the students' rallying cry. The Cultural Revolution Preparatory Committee's announcement that its primary goal was the smashing of the "four olds"—old ideas, old culture, old customs, and old habits—tacitly approved all forms of destruction and gave the young people license to conduct a self-appointed crusade to eradicate the past. With no limits imposed, no guidance offered, no one assuming responsibility for what occurred, and the Red Guards merely following their impulses, the assault upon their elders and the destruction of property grew completely out of control. Sometimes when the Red Guards searched for counter-revolutionary evidence, they would even demand money, knowing that their actions could not be challenged, that no one was in a position to oversee or reprimand them.

The primary targets of this revolutionary mission were the families that had already been identified as harboring black elements, and invariably our house was on their list. Late one night a group of seven or eight young people, none of whom I recognized, pounded on our door. Demanding that we open every glass bookcase, they strewed the contents about the room. The most vauable set of books in our library was the *Buddhist Canon*, only four copies of which remained in the country. Tang Yongtong had been collecting its many volumes throughout his life, but the students announced that all such books were superstitious, that religion was the opium of the masses, and confiscated one volume from each boxed set, declaring that these would be thoroughly investigated. The other books they shoved roughly back on the shelves, then sealed the glass bookcase doors with strips of paper to keep such poison from spreading further, and at the same time to keep us from destroying evidence.

Having finished with Tang Yongtong's books, they demanded that we produce all of our other counter-revolutionary possessions, such as stamps. I did have a stamp collection, but fortunately it contained nothing politically offensive. Because of my hatred for the Guomindang, I had never saved its postage, a prejudice that now served me well, for others I knew had been beaten for possessing Chiang Kai-shek stamps. When the search party demanded to see our records, I reluctantly brought out my precious stack of classical music, the small collection that Lao Tang had accumulated from second-hand stores in the 1950s. The Red Guards methodically shattered every disc with a large rock, then, satisfied with their revolutionary action, left the house. Numbly I picked up the useless pieces, piled them in a dustpan, and carried them out to the trash heap.

Throughout these proceedings my sister-in-law tried to disassociate herself from Lao Tang and myself, protesting that she and my mother-in-law were truly revolutionary and had nothing to do with Lao Tang, but the students ignored her disclaimers, announcing that our house was the home of a "reactionary scholar warlord" and that it would be used as an example for all the people to see. From then on our doors would remain open to the public until eight o'clock each night, and we would be prohibited from ever closing the rear courtyard gate, since Nie Yuanzi liked to use our yard as a shortcut between her room and the nearby student dormitory area.

Finally the students left, taking with them a beautifully boxed ceremonial knife and fork with lavishly decorated handles, made in India for the slaughtering and roasting of venison, a set that had been a gift to Tang Yongtong but that now was pronounced a dangerous weapon. Suddenly, I remembered the melon knife that we had seized on similar grounds in Xiaohongmen and thought how exaggerated and childish such gestures seemed. Several evenings during the next week we could see fires blazing in the student dormitory area and hear jubilant shouts as the rebels celebrated their victory by burning the books of their enemies. We never knew if Tang Yongtong's precious volumes were fed to the flames or just lost in the general confusion, but we never saw them again. I was glad my father-in-law had not lived to see this day.

Throughout the sweltering weeks of August, the Red Guards engaged in a frenzy of activity as they searched the homes of all suspicious families. A loudspeaker mounted on a high building kept the whole campus informed of what had been discovered in the raids. The Red Guards would report, for example, that they had found a Guomindang photograph, which would actually be a stamp from someone's collection picturing Chiang Kai-shek. Sometimes they would announce the discovery of a weapon, such as Tang Yongtong's venison knife, or a photograph of a Guomindang official, items they triumphantly declared indicated that the owner supported the restoration of Guomindang rule. Sometimes the Red Guards would find some "reactionary" novel or some incriminating historical data—for example, a diary that was said to contain comments unflattering to Chairman Mao. Perhaps the diary merely contained a remark about the famine in 1959 being worse than before, but the Red Guards construed such statements as evidence of dissatisfaction with the new society. Always the rebels claimed self-righteously that their findings proved that the class struggle must be sharp and enduring.

One of their most publicized raids was upon the house of a Mongol princess, the widow of a former Qinghua University professor. After her husband's death she and her two teenage daughters had been allowed to remain in their comfortable home, but now she was dubbed a representative of feudalism and was consigned to a small, shabby room close to my parents' house. I would often see her when I visited them, one-half of her head completely shaved in what was called a *yinyang* haircut, a humiliating punishment that the Red Guards had also inflicted on perhaps a half dozen people at Beida. It was terrible to see the pink skin of her partly exposed scalp, but despite this indignity she and her daughters retained their spirit, even decorating the windows of their crude quarters, previously a small shop and thus very close to the street, with brightly colored paper flowers. The Red Guards had confiscated from her former home two trunks of her clothing and shoes, saying derisively that the feeding of this parasite for so many years was truly a consequence of following the bourgeois educational line. Though she was spurned by many, my father detested such treatment and visited her often, taking sweets to the children to show his opposition to the harsh treatment she had received.

Terrified of these violent searches, people would naturally try to dispose of any items that they feared might arouse suspicion, but burning anything was prohibited. Even if people tried to burn their possessions in secret, they always had to fear that someone would smell the smoke or find the ashes and report this evidence to the Red Guards, who in turn would order the culprit to confess, believing nothing he said in his own defense. Despite this danger I had decided one day in July to burn all my poems, certain that a rightist's verses would inevitably be distorted or taken as evidence of some grave counter-revolutionary offense. Lao Tang had been very angry. "Someone will smell the smoke," he had reprimanded me, "and will come to check. The poems are not so important, but trying to explain what has been burned will be impossible." Still, I had taken the chance, and luckily no one ever noticed.

The uncertainty about where the Red Guards would appear next, who they would condemn, or what harmless possessions they would deem suspect, made everyone increasingly jittery and self-protective, placing a great strain on human relationships. Many people would volunteer incriminating information about others to the Red Guards, their assertions of loyalty a desperate effort to protect themselves from harm. Others would turn over large packages of potentially suspicious possessions, hoping to be spared the terror of a house search. My sister-in-law, eager to demonstrate her own political trustworthiness and to prevent any further attacks upon her family, went to the Cultural Revolution Preparatory Committee to declare she believed it unfair for her husband's mother to receive such a generous stipend after Tang Yongtong's death. Her suggestion that these monthly payments should be discontinued was praised as a revolutionary action. After this Lao Tang's mother had to live on her savings, supplemented by 20 *yuan* a month that we contributed.

In one of the classrooms, the parasitic nature of the capitalist class was receiving abundant testimony. There the Cultural Revolution Preparatory Committee had set up an exhibition of the materials confiscated by the Red Guards, and everyone, organized by department, paid an obligatory visit to this collection of photographs, paintings, books, artifacts, stamps, and identification papers of former Guomindang officials. On the walls were hung charts to reveal how many worker and peasant students had been dismissed from Beida and how many Guomindang descendants admitted, but most eye-catching of all was a string of high-heeled shoes captured from various homes around the campus. The expressed purpose of the exhibit was threefold: to reveal the seriousness of the class struggle at Beida; to make clear the sufferings of the workers, peasants, and soldiers; and to unmask the bourgeois lifestyle of the faculty and cadres. At the same time, Nie Yuanzi's group was bolstering its authority by assuming responsibility for the definition of the crimes committed by Lu Ping and the previous administration.

I knew that Tang Dan was one of the primary students selected to be an exhibition guide, perhaps because of her school achievements or her ability as a public speaker, perhaps to make her a model for other young children with enemy parents, to show that such young people could still carry out the revolution, despite their family background. When I arrived and saw her gesticulating with a pointer, explaining the significance of one of the exhibits, I felt a burst of pride. Seeing her capability, her independence, I hoped that such qualities would enable her to survive in this chaotic world. Tang Dan was describing how intellectuals, ignoring the fact that their livelihood depended on the labor of the peasants, continued to discriminate against the working class.

As I walked past the displays, I was amazed to see on one table Tang Yongtong's knife set, beside which had been spilled drops of red ink to indicate blood, the caption explaining that members of the capitalist class, hoping to "recover their heaven," the comfortable life they had known before Liberation, even kept weapons in their homes with which to fight against the proletariat. After seeing the necklaces and earrings, the embroidered silk dresses, even a candy tin made in America, I left the exhibit with contradictory emotions. I knew that many of the explanations were grossly exaggerated, having seen nothing that offered proof of counter-revolutionary activities, but I also realized that the gap between those in positions of prominence and the common people was undeniably large.

Another effort of the Cultural Revolution Preparatory Committee that summer also touched my own life. Told that they had been exploited by their employers, the household workers on the campus were being organized and encouraged to itemize the various ways in which they had been abused. They had not been given time off on Sundays, for example, had not been given vacations, had not eaten the same food as their employers, and had received no compensation for medical care. If an *ayi* had worked for a family for many years, she was now owed a large sum of money. The leader of this Family Assistants' Committee, as it was called, was the *ayi* who had worked for more than ten years in the household of my uncle, the chairman of the geology department. Although my aunt was in poor health, from that time on the *ayi* refused to help at home and spent her time organizing the others to demand compensation from their employers. She asked for 1,000 *yuan*, an enormous sum, to recompense her for the years she had been exploited, but my aunt stubbornly refused to pay. As a result she was accused of being a bourgeois lady and warned that a struggle session would be conducted to teach her that she could no longer pose as superior to her *ayi*. Frightened by those threats, my aunt at last paid the amount demanded, after which her capitulation was publicized as a great victory for the working class. From then on my aunt prepared the meals for the *ayi*, who returned home from her meetings and revolutionary activities only to eat, a situation that made my aunt bitterly unhappy. Just over a year later she died of a cerebral hemorrhage.

The vice-leader of the Family Assistants' Committee was the *ayi* of Meng Kun, the professor under whom I had worked as a teaching assistant and who had been for several years my supervisor. Because Meng Kun was not a department head but just a professor, his case was initially considered less important, but his *ayi* too demanded a large sum. He had not been branded an "academic warlord" and, assuming his position to be less dangerous, had refused to pay. In response the *ayi* leaders decided to find some way to put down such an arrogant member of the upper class and force him to change his attitude toward the workers. One day Meng Kun's *ayi* took a crumpled piece of newspaper containing a large picture of Chairman Mao to the Red Guards in our department, declaring that clearly Meng Kun hated Chairman Mao, since he had thrown this newspaper into his bathroom wastebasket after defacing Chairman Mao's photograph with black ink. The Red Guards went immediately to Meng's house and took him into custody, declaring that a very serious political affair had occurred and summoning the whole department to a meeting. Each day we teachers were required to stay in our office, reading newspapers or having discussions, and I was told especially to attend this particular meeting because it concerned my professor.

In the courtyard the Red Guards made Meng Kun kneel down before them. One accused him of being a traitor to the Communist Party, claiming that as a Qinghua student during the Anti-Japanese War he had joined the Party and less than a year later been arrested by the Guomindang and jailed. Before long he had been released, which proved that he had betrayed the Party to secure his freedom. Meng Kun explained that his release had been brought about by the cooperation between the Communists and the Nationalists, but the Red Guards sharply dismissed his comments, asserting that after his release from jail he had devoted himself to academic work, never participating in Party activities again and even letting his membership lapse, a clear sign that he had been a traitor to the Party.

Far more impassioned, however, was their accusation that he had insulted Chairman Mao, a matter so serious that it could not even be uttered again. To clinch the case against him, Meng's *ayi* reported how she had found this crumpled newspaper in his trash basket, after which the Red Guards intensified their shouting of

173

slogans, proclaiming that no one could be allowed to insult Chairman Mao in such a way. Then they began to beat Meng Kun brutally with their leather belts, and all the while I was in the front row, forced to watch. My teacher was in his late fifties and known to have diabetes, yet for some ten minutes those students struck him in turn, sometimes with their belt buckles leaving huge red welts across his face. I could do nothing to help him. After declaring that this is what happens to one who insults our leader, they sent Meng Kun home.

Meng Kun's ordeal continued after his return home, for his children posted a sign on his house saying that his family members were all drawing a line to disassociate themselves from him. His relationship with his wife had long been strained, and because he was a strict father, his son and daughter also had felt distant from him. Now the children wrote a poster saying that their father had been a fascist in the family and that they would have no further connection with him, a denunciation they delivered to the Red Guards in our department. For an entire year, until he was put in solitary confinement in the campus building called the "cow shed," Meng Kun was never allowed to share his family's meals but was given simple fare such as steamed buns in his own room.

The unexpected became almost routine during those weeks, and crises became regular events in our lives. One evening after dinner a boy of thirteen, the grandson of Zhou Peiyuan, who was then vice-president of Beida, appeared at our door shouting angrily for Lao Tang to come outside. Zhou Peiyuan's situation was at that time the best in our neighborhood because he had vigorously opposed Lu Ping and was now considered a loyal revolutionary. His grandson and my daughter were close friends, having grown up together as neighbors and classmates in school. The boy had always been a frequent visitor in our house and a favorite of Yang Yongtong's.

When Lao Tang went outside to see what was the matter, this boy stuck a poster on our wall declaring Tang Yijie to be a black gang member who had always opposed Chairman Mao and demanding that everyone draw a line to separate themselves from him. A totally conventional poster, the work of a child, it ended with the slogan, "Down with the black gang." When he spoke, however, this child assumed all the vehemence and bravado of a Red Guard, insisting loudly that Lao Tang confess what crime he had committed and ordering him to speak up quickly. Lao Tang just said, "Yes, yes, I committed a crime," and the boy left, looking fiercely proud and satisfied because he had acted like a real Red Guard, putting up a poster, struggling against a black gang member, and even pushing his head down once or twice. Shocked and shaken, I looked on in disbelief at the sight of this child treating an elder and a family friend in such a manner. Still, I knew there was no recourse but silence, as protest would surely have unleashed more and greater violence, with this child reporting to the Red Guards that Lao Tang had resisted being struggled against. No one even dared to remove his poster, although after several days the rain and wind wore it away.

More distressed than either Lao Tang or I at this episode, however, was Tang Dan, who had just witnessed her childhood friend attacking her father. In her eyes I could read her emotions, although she never spoke of her feelings. She seemed changed after that moment, unable to shake off the memory of such humiliation. Every day during that summer she had come home to sleep and eat, and even though I knew she had been told to draw a line between herself and her family, she had never been rude to us or unpleasant. I never asked where she went during the days, knowing that she would want to follow the mainstream and not be isolated from her friends, and that to keep her place at the top of her class she would have to demonstrate her loyalty to the Cultural Revolution. But after this attack upon her father, she always seemed less confident, less optimistic, less able to remain detached from the problems at home.

The "theory of revolutionary inheritance" had become very prominent by then, and a popular slogan warned, "If a person is a dragon, his son will be a dragon, but if a person is a rat, his son can only dig a hole and climb into it." Another similar couplet declared, "If the father is a hero, the son will also be a hero, but if the father is a reactionary, the son will be a rotten egg." Because of these widely repeated slogans and the incident with Zhou Peiyuan's grandson, I began to feel increasing concern for my children, knowing how much bitterness and pressure they must feel because of the supposed crimes of their father. To protect them from such unpredictable attacks upon their family, I decided to take them to live temporarily with my parents, away from the violence at Beida. My mother agreed immediately to my request, and my brother also offered to help with my children's care, but my father complained, saying they would be noisy and prevent him from studying. He needed some peace and quiet in this time of chaos, he protested, but in the end, after my mother argued bitterly with him, he consented. I was hurt by his reluctance, but decided this was still the best way to shield my children from the violence.

Another day I returned home to find a poster with the commanding words "legal order" on the wall outside my house. In smaller characters the announcement declared that the people within had no right to live in such surroundings and must give up their fine living quarters to the working class. We were to move all our belongings into three rooms, leaving the rest of our house vacant. To comply with this sudden order, we worked feverishly through the night, apportioning the reduced space as best we could. Lao Tang and I kept one-third of the large living room and what had been Daolan's room, his brother took two of the bedrooms, his mother one bedroom, and his aunt the other servant's room.

After two days a second "legal order" was posted beside the first, this one declaring that we would no longer be allowed to shelter a landlord in our house and that this enemy must be sent away to be supervised by the peasants. This time my heart froze. To give up my living space mattered little to me, but to send Lao Tang's aunt away, to break my last promise to Tang Yongtong, was too bitter to contemplate. I knew that she had nowhere else to turn, for Fourth Aunt's daughter, long widowed and responsible for her own children, was already overburdened, and the concubine's son had been declared a rightist and thus could have no influence on her case. The policy stated that landlords must be returned to the place where they had formerly exploited the peasants, necessitating that Fourth Aunt go back to the Wuhan area where she had lived with her husband.

We all realized the perils of such a journey, since everywhere landlords were being beaten and forced to do hard labor. I could only hope that the Red Guards would forget about her, as that would sometimes happen in their ardor to rush on to yet another revolutionary deed. My sister-in-law warned, however, that we could not try to conceal a landlord under our roof, as the Red Guards would surely return to do all of us greater harm, only to make Fourth Aunt leave in the end anyway, so she might as well leave before such things happened. Reluctantly Lao Tang agreed with his sister-in-law, since everywhere we knew the five black types were being dragged out and sent off to the countryside. Finally, unable to conceive of any way to protect this old woman for whom I felt great affection, I told Fourth Aunt with great sadness that she must go, as we could find no alternative. Her tears made my heart nearly break.

Knowing her fate was sealed, she set off one day, telling no one, for my mother's house where she had never been before, the half hour's walk a difficult journey on her bound feet and a dangerous one because of the unpredictable outbursts of violence on the campus. Tang Shuang, trying to keep busy while shut up in the house, since children risked injury if they were allowed outside to play, had been sitting on the bed amusing himself with flies, trying to obey the order not to disturb my father and unable to pass his time reading as Tang Dan did. After catching some flies in a glass bottle, he had covered it with paper and was listening to the insects buzz as they tried to escape, having already pulled off some of their wings and glued on bits of paper to see whether the insects could still fly. Bored with this solitary play, he had been delighted to find his beloved aunt, who had taught him to recite many Tang dynasty poems, at the door. But her face was grave and as she folded him in her arms she wept, saying she would never see him again. "Why?" Tang Shuang had asked innocently; "I'll be coming home soon so just wait there for me."

Feeling powerless to avert Fourth Aunt's fate, I took one day's leave to accompany her to the train station. There we found a scene of total chaos, the huge building mobbed with people, everything dirty and disorderly. Chairman Mao's instruction that the nation's students should "exchange experiences" and learn from each other's revolutionary actions was being carried out with such enthusiasm that the transportation system had been totally disrupted.

As young people poured into the capital by the hundreds of thousands to take advantage of the free food and lodging and eager for the coveted opportunity to see Chairman Mao in person in Tiananmen Square, students from Beijing took advantage of the opportunity to see parts of the country they would never otherwise get to visit. No fares were charged for trains or buses, and despite desperately crowded conditions, the young people piled themselves into train cars, some even riding on top, and many incurring injuries along the way. With schedules abandoned, we had heard of trains crashing, of hundreds being killed. Seeing for myself the chaotic conditions at the railroad station, I was grateful I had forbidden Tang Dan to travel to South China to exchange experiences, even though I had incurred her anger and resentment, since her cousin the same age had been allowed to go.

The outsides of the train cars were covered with slogans, often attacking some individual as a counter-revolutionary, and inside the coaches I could see bodies crammed together. The young people on the platform all wore their olive green outfits, their jacket sleeves rolled up nearly to the shoulders in the summer heat, heavy belts at their waists, canvas bags carrying food and their copies of Chairman Mao's quotations slung over their shoulders. Some had bound their pant legs with light green cotton strips, and all displayed proudly three or four different buttons with pictures of Chairman Mao. As they greeted each other, their Red Books held high, they seemed oblivious to their surroundings, so fervently did they feel about being vested by Chairman Mao with unlimited authority for waging revolution.

After standing in a long, unruly ticket line, I pushed a path for us through the crowds to the platform. Red Guards were streaming in and out of the train windows, and I had to shove Fourth Aunt into the car, squeezing her into a corner, since all the seats had been long since occupied. The car was filthy, the lavatories crammed with youthful travelers. I had to fight against tears thinking what this seventy-six-year-old woman, her feet bound, her hair pulled back neatly into a bun, would face in the days ahead. I had given her some money, and I knew that she would try to locate a relative in Wuhan, another landlord's wife, to live with. Every month I sent ten *yuan* to that woman's address, but I never received a response. Even without any information, I was certain that her life must be very hard. Then about a year later I received word that she was dead.

In 1970 on a visit from Beida's cadre school in Jiangxi to the provincial capital of Nanchang, I quite unexpectedly met Fourth Aunt's husband's concubine's son, who had remained in the countryside after his condemnation as a rightist. During her year in Wuhan, he told me, she had been too ill to write. Although her daughter had been able to visit her occasionally with some food, no one could shop for her or provide regular care after she fell ill. He had only been allowed to travel to Wuhan to arrange for her cremation. We both knew that with proper care her death could have been prevented.

Lao Tang's own situation had made him unable to offer any assistance to his aunt. Every morning he was picked up to be criticized in his department and then was sent out to do labor on the campus with the other black gang members, some of whom were elderly professors. Their task was to clean the streets or pull up grass and weeds under the hot summer sun. With Red Guards from all over the country descending on the university to exchange experiences, the campus was always crowded and littered with melon skins, peanut shells, and sunflower seed husks. While Lao Tang and the other black gang members cleaned up this refuse, the zealous Red Guards could ask them questions whenever they wished.

Curious to know what these famous "academic warlords" were like, the young people from the provinces would command them to stand up and answer questions: "What crime did you commit?" "Why are you opposed to the Communist Party?" "What poison have you fed to the students in your classroom?" Lao Tang was subjected to this harassment every day; I and the others who had been accused as rightists were now considered to be "dead tigers" and spared this intense abuse.

Those assigned to do physical labor that summer were divided into two categories. In the first group of "active counter-revolutionaries" were people like Lao Tang, those who had held responsible positions, like departmental Party secretaries, or those with close ties to Lu Ping. In the second group were people like me, former rightists or those who had been labeled "sprouts of revisionism" or "helpers of Lu Ping" or "tools of the black gang." In my department there were three in the first labor group and eighteen in the second. We members of the second group did not have to work on campus, but were sent to help with the construction of a new building for an affiliated primary school. There we assisted the regular workers by carrying bricks and removing dirt in huge baskets suspended by ropes from our shoulders. Before we were sent to this project, however, we did some labor in the outlying areas of the campus, so I had heard the questions with which the revolutionary young people were haranguing the more serious enemies.

The black gang members could of course give no satisfactory answer to their interrogators. They would just bow their heads and say, "Yes, I have committed a crime, and I beg your pardon." One professor from the Western languages department, reputed to be the best English speaker at Beida and formerly Zhou Enlai's interpreter when the Communist Party and the Guomindang had negotiated in front of the Americans after the Anti-Japanese War, was one of those accused of being a "reactionary authority." He was sent every day to collect papers and garbage from the streets. This distinguished academic, then in his early fifties, had suffered from high blood pressure, and the stress of the Red Guards' questioning plus the physical strain of constantly bending down to pick up refuse caused him one day to succumb to acute heat prostration. After breaking into a profuse sweat and collapsing from dizziness, he was taken to the campus hospital, where he died two hours later.

Violence, brutality, tragedy became commonplace at Beida that August. Every day and night small groups of four or five would be picked up to be criticized in their departments and then paraded through the campus to "accept struggle from the masses." The targets of these "mass ground struggle sessions" would always be forced to balance on one of the high, narrow dining hall benches and told to answer questions. If the answers were considered unsatisfactory, the person's head would be pushed down or he would be instructed to bend low or he would be held in the agonizing jet plane position, continually begging the people's pardon for his past offenses. Because I lived in the area of the student dormitories, I would see several groups of some twenty or thirty people conducting these struggle sessions every night when I went out after supper to read the latest wall posters by lamplight. Usually the abuse would last for about an hour, then the victim would be allowed to return home.

One evening I had gone out to read the new posters when I came upon a group of students surrounding a teacher from the math department, a woman who had graduated in the same class as I, standing on one of those benches, her hair disheveled and a big placard across her chest announcing that she was an active counterrevolutionary. She had once remarked that the Cultural Revolution was wrong, I learned, and when her comment was reported, she was taken into custody and held somewhere on campus, perhaps in a classroom building. Suddenly out of the crowd I heard her husband's voice declaring with icy piety that he could never live with her again, that their relationship was finished, that she was no longer the mother of their three children. Following his denunciation, the Red Guards commanded her again to admit her guilt. Provoked by her silence, they shoved her head down very low, knocking out all of her hairpins and causing her hair to fall forward and cover her face. I had seen such scenes of humiliation and abuse many times by then, but never had I heard such a heartless repudiation by a husband.

Witnessing such daily cruelty had a numbing effect. One evening when I returned home after doing my labor, I saw my neighbor's cook and lifetime friend sitting on the threshold weeping. The neighbor, the chairman of the physics department and an especially kind old man who had never married, had returned home that day after a particularly harsh struggle session. The cook had discovered him with a scarf tied around his neck, hanging from the ceiling. Hearing the news of this latest tragedy, I recalled how after I had been condemned as a rightist, when I was shunned by everyone, this professor would always smile warmly at me and say hello when he worked in his courtyard, and how he had tried to save his favorite student from being exiled to the countryside. I thought bitterly that it was better for him to be dead, as he was now over seventy and couldn't bear such harsh treatment. His body was quickly taken away to be cremated, and no one mentioned him again.

Another neighbor, even more prominent, was less successful in attempting to end his life. Feng Ding had been a high-level theorist in the Party, which he joined in the 1930s, before becoming chairman of the philosophy department at Beida. Famous for his book *The Communist View of Life*, which had formerly been required reading for the younger generation, he was now being harshly attacked as a revisionist and betrayer of Marxism. An unusually thin, slight man, he, like Lao Tang, was assigned to the first labor group and forced to work cleaning the campus grounds. Because of his fame, the visiting Red Guards were always curious to see what he looked like and endlessly ordered him to stand up and answer their questions. They even interrogated him at night, I knew, as his house was just opposite ours. He had finally become so depressed that he swallowed a large overdose of sleeping pills, but his son found him and rushed him to the hospital. He tried to kill himself three times in as many months, but his son, who was very devoted and caring, saved him each time. Somehow he survived that ordeal and lived until 1983.

Shortly after Feng Ding's first suicide attempt, harsh knocks pounded on the door to our bedroom one morning at six o'clock. A group of angry Red Guards rushed in and seized Lao Tang without saying a word. I was desperately frightened that they would beat him as punishment for some unknown crime and feared that since his health was poor, a serious beating would be fatal. I followed the students outside, but they pushed me away, preventing me from following, and I could do nothing. No matter how terrified I was for my husband's safety, I had to report for labor with the others in my group and spend the day carrying heavy loads of dirt at the primary-school site with no way to find out what had happened to Lao Tang. Finally, at about eleven o'clock that night, he opened the door. I could see no traces of physical abuse, and he said that he had not been beaten but that something very serious had happened.

A picture of Chairman Mao, torn in half, had been found on our courtyard door, and the Red Guards were treating this as a grave counter-revolutionary offense. Lao Tang had explained to them that it would have been impossible for him from the inside to glue such a picture on the outside of his courtyard door, but they had closed him in a room to wait, giving him no food all day. Finally, late at night they had told him he was free to go home, never informing him about what had been decided. Much later I learned that this picture had been pasted on the closed door by Feng Ding's son to keep people from walking through the courtyard and disturbing his father. No one would dare to open a door that had been sealed with a picture of Chairman Mao, the son had reasoned, but he had not thought about the possibility of someone's opening the door from the inside and unknowingly ripping the picture in half, which is what must have happened.

In addition to the events that touched me personally during those summer months, I was also shaken by reports of the tragic violence occurring elsewhere. Lao Tang's cousin, a teacher in the nearby Normal University's affiliated middle school for girls, came to us one time to report what had happened when those students tried to follow the example of Beida's revolutionary actions. Filled with passion for the new movement and eager to conduct the struggle against their own enemies, they had forced the president of their school, famous as one of the first Chinese women to be educated, to climb through a narrow underground cement drainage pipe. When she finally emerged, they had brutally beaten her to death. Most of the girls at this middle school were from high-ranking intellectuals' families and thus, I guessed sadly, felt compelled to demonstrate their commitment to revolutionary goals. These teenage girls, ordinarily shy, mild, and gentle, had somehow become capable of unimaginable cruelty.

The leader of that group of militant school girls was the daughter of a Central Committee member and had been invited to stand beside Chairman Mao in Tiananmen Square during his first appearance before the Red Guards on August 18. During that event Jiang Qing had asked her name and she had replied, "Hu Bing-bing," a given name that means "very mild." Jiang Qing had told her this was a name appropriate to a high-class lady, not to a young revolutionary, and had said she would give the girl another name, Hu Yaowu, which means "desiring a soldier's strength." Having been singled out so specially by Jiang Qing, the girl tried to live up to her new identity and became very fierce.

People died so easily during those weeks. Almost every day we heard news of suicides. A poster would appear announcing that someone had refused to be reformed and had decided to remain an enemy permanently. We knew then that the person had allegedly killed himself, but we never knew if the death was really self-inflicted or whether such a person had in fact been killed or forced to commit suicide by the Red Guards. After the body of the famous novelist and playwright Lao She was pulled from a Beijing lake, for example, the Red Guards insisted that he had taken his own life, but people always believed he had been beaten to death. By the end of August the situation had become so terrible that we could see no end, no future, no hope. People just tried to survive day by day.

My own daily routine had by then become very regular. Every morning I would leave before eight o'clock to report to my labor, taking along a piece of steamed bread for lunch. At the primary-school construction site I would see the neighborhood children, completely unsupervised and without anything to occupy their time since all schools were closed, playing and fighting among themselves. Sometimes they would grow bored and would come to ask us what crime we had committed, happy for a chance to make us bend our heads and confess we had done something wrong. At the end of the work day when we walked in a line back to campus, they would often spit at us or stop us to make us sing the "howling wolf song," a chant devised especially for black gang members and class enemies. Those at the head of the line would be told by these children to stand still and sing:

> I have committed a crime against the people;
> I am an enemy of the people;
> I understand my crime;
> I will be reformed by the Party.

One day an elderly professor was ordered to sing these words, but he could not carry a tune and merely recited the lines instead, after which the children made him sing it again and again as punishment for his initial disobedience.

The first few times we were made to sing these words we felt so humiliated, so demeaned, so angry, that the indignity was hard to bear. Later we simply treated the children's demands as a joke, and often a member of our team of eighteen would voluntarily start to sing very loudly whenever the youngsters approached. We three women in the group were never able to treat the matter so light-heartedly, but many of the men would take the initiative themselves, shouting, "So, you want us to sing for you again today," and then launch robustly into the melody, singing lustily and laughing at the children all the while. Soon the children would laugh along with us, and though they still followed us with insults or threw stones, I could not remain angry with them. One day a young boy had come up to the person beside me in line to ask, "Uncle, could you give me a cartridge shell?" Hearing his guileless question and realizing how starved these children were for playthings and for companionship, I realized they were still innocent underneath the veneer of insolence engendered by the political situation.

At the end of my labor, I would walk straight to my mother's house to see my children, often carrying home extra food she had prepared to save me the trouble of shopping and making dinner just for Lao Tang and myself. But one day when I arrived at their small house, I found my mother in tears. The street committee had visited her that afternoon and announced that these children were the "bastard offspring of the black gang," and that if they continued to remain in her house they would be forced to wear cardboard placards declaring them to be the "spawn of dogs." Then everyone would know their true identity, and they would be prevented from spreading their contamination any further. My daughter was crying as well, although Tang Shuang, only nine years old, was happily turning somersaults on the bed, oblivious to this new crisis.

My own heart turned over; I didn't know what more I could do to shield my children from abuse. I thought of Hawthorne's image of the scarlet letter, the brand that Hester Prynne could never remove. To attack innocent children, to punish them so cruelly, seemed too much to bear. My father, desirous as always of peace, said I had better take the children home again. After talking with my mother until late at night, I finally concluded I had no other choice, and set out, carrying their quilts in a drenching rain.

When we arrived home, wet and tired, I discovered that I had forgotten to take my key, and saw from the darkened windows that Lao Tang was not yet back from his struggle meeting. We always used the back door to our house, but this time I knocked at the front door to ask Lao Tang's brother to let us in. No one responded to our knocks or calls, and as I stood outside in the downpour, I felt utterly lost and alone, anxious in addition about Lao Tang, as he was always home by this time. My daughter grew more enraged as the moments passed, and began pounding on the window and shouting for her grandma. At last Lao Tang's mother, who was in poor health and spent her days lying on the bed, heard us and told her daughter-in-law to open the door. As my anger burst forth, I spoke sharply to my sister-in-law, asking how she could have been so heartless as not to let us in. She countered that I was still as arrogant as before, and that such an attitude was most inappropriate to one in my situation. I called her a cruel woman and said that I hoped someday she would realize how mistaken she was about my family.

When Lao Tang finally returned home, she told him that I was arrogant and offensive to have spoken so rudely to her, which drew him into a terrible argument with his brother, who then worked at the Ministry of Coal. The quarrel lasted for an hour, and when it was finally over Lao Tang wept bitterly, in a way I had never seen before. Frightened by the intensity of his emotions, I said nothing more. Their angry contention that they had undergone much suffering because of us while remaining always on the side of the people, and that we should humbly apologize to them for what they had endured on our account, could have no possible answer. We finally swallowed our anger and resentment and tried to sleep. By then it was three o'clock in the morning, just three hours before we would have to get up to prepare for our labor at eight. Tensions had reached such a peak, passions become so inflamed, that our family relationships had completely broken down. Resentments festered and on the slightest provocation could erupt with great intensity.

On September 12, the day before our wedding anniversary, my mother announced she would prepare some special food for us that evening. When I arrived at the end of my work day, a generous container of red stewed pork was waiting for me, its aroma filling the room. Such a dish was a great luxury when meat was in short supply, and I gratefully took it back home to share with Lao Tang and the children. Even though they no longer lived with her, she often prepared the evening meal for us, as it was difficult for me to shop and cook each night after finishing my labor. We had a special feast that evening, but the feeling of well-being was short-lived. At six the following morning we awakened to a knock at our door, always a frightening occurrence in those times of Red Guard intrusions, but this time I found my sister, looking pale and distressed, saying that my mother was very sick and had been taken to the hospital in the middle of the night.

By the time I arrived at her bedside, my mother was unable to recognize me. I gazed disbelievingly at her ashen face and stared at the hideous tube in her mouth that was helping her to breathe but making her face look misshapen and distorted. She was just fifty-six, and had always been healthy and vigorous. My brother, in a fury, told me that at eleven o'clock she had complained of a piercing headache, and that he had set her on the back of his bicycle and pedaled her to the hospital. The examining doctor had said there was nothing seriously wrong and had given her some pills and sent her home. But after a few hours she had felt much worse and begun to vomit. By then she was too weak to ride behind him, and he had cycled about desperately to find a taxi that would drive her to the hospital. At that time she was in great pain but still alert.

I could see how much the Cultural Revolution had disrupted this hospital. The walls were covered with posters, and many of the most competent medical personnel had apparently been taken away to await judgment by the Red Guards, who were investigating whether or not they had engaged in any activities that could be judged counter-revolutionary. Only a few doctors remained to staff the hospital, their patient load totally unmanageable in this time of widespread illness and injury. The one who treated my mother was young and inexperienced, and he initially diagnosed her illness as encephalitis. To confirm his judgment, he ordered a spinal tap, a test that proved fatal. What she had suffered was a cerebral hemorrhage, a condition that might under better circumstances have responded to treatment. However, the spinal tap had increased the damage to the brain, we were told, causing a blood vessel in her head to burst. By the time I arrived at her side, her eyes were open but she was unaware of anything that was taking place.

After telephoning my department to ask for leave from labor for that day, I remained beside her with my father and brother, hoping she would at least be able to recognize us once again. For a day and a night we took turns at her bedside. Although her eyes remained open, she never responded to our presence. Alone at midnight in the hallway with my brother, while my sister sat with our mother and my father was at home resting, I felt sadness beyond expression. Human life seemed too painful to bear. When my brother burst into tears, I knew his grief was not only for my mother but for society, for all those who had suffered so much. The sobs came from deep within his breast, a grief for which there was no consolation. With my mother gone, the only one who had really loved him, who understood the unhappiness of his own marriage, he would lose someone terribly precious, and at the same time have to assume the burden of the family on his shoulders. I reached out to hold his hand, knowing that no words could assuage his sorrow, and tried to concentrate on a poetic line that my father had written to me after I had been declared a rightist. "Everything is temporary, nothing is everlasting," I repeated over and over to myself in that moment of anguish. My mother died early the next morning.

We covered her body with a white sheet, placed her on a cart, and wheeled her to the hospital morgue. The room was filled with bodies. Soon a nurse wheeled in another cart on which lay the body of a young girl of middle-school age who had been terribly beaten. Since she had been dead upon arrival, no one had bothered to cover her with a sheet. Across her chest were two paper banners, one announcing her identity as a "counter-revolutionary bastard dog" and the other proclaiming, "Anyone who opposes the Cultural Revolution will come to no good end." Her face and hair were matted with blood.

We had put my mother's body in a refrigerated drawer, but every other such compartment was filled, and there was no space for that young girl. No one had come to care for her body, and the nurse was asking how to dispose of this corpse, since the weather was very hot. Another nurse replied, "Never mind, just leave it; perhaps later it will be taken to the crematorium. It is only a counter-revolutionary little dog anyway." I felt sure that she was the daughter of black gang parents and had been beaten to death, perhaps because she had defended her parents or disagreed with the Red Guards in an effort to protect them. They were presumably being held somewhere under supervision, no doubt unaware of their daughter's fate. In a panic I thought of what could befall my own children as well, and of my utter powerlessness to protect them from harm. The young people had become the innocent victims of this mad violence, I reflected helplessly as I looked at the body of that young girl.

Then began my own long and heartrending struggle to see to the disposition of my mother's body. First I went with my brother to the hospital administrators to make the preliminary arrangements, but so many people had died that we had to wait in a long line. Finally, the secretary of the hospital informed us that we must remove the body in two days because the morgue space was needed for others. So we set out by bus for Babaoshan, located far to the southwest of the city. Always a terrifying place, now it seemed more horrible than ever, with so many frantic people needing to arrange for the cremation of their loved ones. At the office we were finally told that my mother's ashes could not be buried there in the revolutionary section of the cemetery, since in order to qualify a person must be a cadre above the thirteenth degree, whereas her retirement certificate stated that she had attained only the rank of fifteen, the average rank for teachers. We could not argue, so just asked what to do. Unless we wished to take her ashes home with us, the indifferent official replied impatiently, we would have to go to the other part of Babaoshan, the section for common people.

We followed a dirt road off the highway for some distance before arriving at a hill with many steps leading to a Japanese-style building on the top. Built by the Japanese as a memorial mausoleum for their soldiers, this structure was now in disrepair, the red painted doors and window frames faded, the surrounding grass brown and sparse. Inside the small office we were told that my mother's body would be cremated along with the others. If we wanted her to be cremated alone, we would have to produce a certificate verifying that she had died a natural death, since anyone who was a black gang member, who had been beaten to death, or who had committed suicide, was not entitled to the privilege of individual cremation. My father had begged us to find some way for her to be buried and not burned at all, saying that this was his last wish, but we knew there was no way for this to be done. The most we could hope for was to keep her ashes separate, even though obtaining the necessary documentation would not be easy.

The death certificate issued by the hospital stated only the date of death and did not specify the cause. Finding a doctor willing to assume responsibility for certifying the cause of death seemed an impossible task, and in any event the crematorium insisted upon a document from someone's work unit. Since my brother had not been labeled either a black gang member or a class enemy, I urged him to request the necessary certificate from his department, although I agreed to try at the same time myself.

Returning to campus, I found the secretary who was responsible in my department for all personal matters, such as obtaining cloth coupons when a baby was born, producing a letter authorizing leave, or certifying that a body could be burned after death. I had always had a good relationship with this man, and to my relief he fulfilled my request without question, even offering to arrange with the department's Red Guard leader for me to take several more days of leave. I could not express the depth of my gratitude at a time when such considerate treatment, such human understanding, had all but disappeared, and when we had thus far encountered nothing but coldness and indifference in dealing with my mother's death. My brother, on the other hand, could find no one in his department willing to issue such a certificate, for any action in those days could later be construed as constituting some crime and everyone was reluctant to assume responsibility for matters that would normally be considered routine.

With the necessary document in hand, we returned to the crematorium office, presented our certificate, and bought a small black box to hold the ashes, but still we had found no way to transport the body the long distance from the hospital. Having exhausted every other alternative, we decided we would have to wait in line at the one nearby truck station, where finally we were told that no vehicle would be available until the next day. We couldn't wait, however, as the hospital would keep my mother's body no longer. Hoping to persuade that secretary to allow her body to remain for an additional day, we returned to the hospital, greatly upset at having to request a favor from such a heartless functionary. After listening impassively to our story, he gave us a qualified agreement, saying that if the space was not needed, they would keep her for an additional day. If another body arrived, however, they would have to take her out. Knowing this to be a very unreliable guarantee, we returned to the truck station to beg the driver for an earlier vehicle, and at last he agreed to transport the body during his two-hour lunch break. Exhausted, we accompanied him to the hospital one final time and successfully delivered the body to be burned.

The truck stirred up clouds of yellow dust as it bumped along the dirt road and drove up behind the mausoleum to the small cement building where a huge chimney produced a continuous stream of smoke. Many bodies lay on the ground, awaiting their turn. We were not permitted to observe the actual cremation, just to watch the workers place the body in an iron box and push it by machine into an adjoining room. When I saw my mother for the last time, her eyes were still open, as if she had been observing this macabre chain of events. Five minutes later we were handed a cloth bag filled with charred chips. I never knew whether these were indeed the remains of my mother's body, but we put the ashes into our box, realizing that doubts were pointless, and walked back to the mausoleum.

It was a gloomy, musty place, its many large rooms lined with narrow shelves, some twenty to each wall, divided into small compartments. The spot assigned to us, the last vacant one, was on the very top row, so I climbed onto a ladder and placed the small black box in the empty niche. All this time we were surrounded by grief-stricken people, many of them bewailing the lack of space which meant that their boxes of ashes could not be stored and must be taken back home.

We paid thirty *yuan* for our spot for a three-year period, after which time, we were told, our box would be placed in the earth and buried in a collective grave. Somehow this eventuality unleashed all of my father's pent-up emotions, and he began to sob, saying that we knew our mother couldn't bear any kind of communal housing. At the agricultural university in Guizhou where she had taught, he reminded us, she had even refused the offer of a three-room apartment on campus, preferring to live in their small house and walk twenty minutes each morning to reach her classroom. It was unbearable to think of her having to be forever crowded together with strangers, he told us bitterly, and begged us to find some alternative.

It was not until I returned from the countryside four years later, having extended the time for her ashes to remain in the mausoleum, that we were able to fulfill my father's plea. A cousin had introduced us to the man responsible for the forests in the entire Fragrant Hills area, and told me that this man was very fond of wine. I managed to purchase three bottles of expensive liquor, using the coupons I had saved from the previous Spring Festival, and offered him this gift together with a substantial sum of money, whereupon he agreed to find us a piece of land where we could bury my mother's ashes.

The plot he provided was a beautiful spot on a mountainside from which we could see all of Beijing. Behind her grave was the mound of a famous Chinese violinist, and behind that the grave of Mei Lanfang, China's most celebrated opera singer. At last my father was comforted, saying that perhaps in the moonlight my mother could enjoy their music and sing songs with her neighbors. The plot was about one yard square, and we carried up cement and water to fashion a simple headstone. Two years earlier my father had married a classmate of my mother's whose husband had died in jail, a rightist who had refused to admit any crime. It was my mother's old friend who inscribed the characters of my parents' names in this spot where they would someday lie together, a place where they could both find peace.

Throughout the emotional strain of those agonizing days surrounding my mother's death, I never shed a tear, so great was my numbness after all that had happened. I merely tried to cope with what had to be done, attending to my mother's body and assuaging my father's grief. It had been just over three months since I returned from Xiaohongmen, but in the brief span of those chaotic weeks unimaginable pain and suffering had been inflicted on my own family and those around us. My husband had become a major target of attack, my teacher beaten, my children threatened, my family divided, Fourth Aunt sent to face unknown hardships, my leader, my neighbor, my mother all dead, while around us had been unleashed a kind of madness, a level of violence and cruelty so extreme that it was impossible to absorb, intolerable even to contemplate. I had no thought about the past or the future, just a kind of dogged determination to help the rest of my family survive.

Heaven and Earth

EVERY AUTUMN Beida takes on a special beauty, the burnished red of its maples, the bright yellow of its willows and ginkos brilliantly reflected in No-Name Lake. The air is sharp and clear, free for a few weeks of the dust that often dims the blue sky. Always in October we would take time out from our work to visit the Fragrant Hills with our children. After walking in the valley to admire the foliage, we would sometimes spread out a picnic, other times splurge on a meal at a nearby Western restaurant that served such unusual dishes as chicken Kiev and cream of vegetable soup. This year was different. When people looked at the small island in the middle of the campus lake, they saw not colorful foliage but a huge signboard, its black characters painted against white squares commanding, "Sweep away all the ox ghosts and snake spirits." All around the lake, all over the sides of buildings, hung posters, often dominated by a large red X through an enemy's name. In this atmosphere autumn passed unnoticed. Lao Tang and I reported each morning for labor, our children were absorbed in revolutionary activities, and in addition I still felt deeply shaken by my mother's death. No one thought about the scenery or about setting off for an excursion to the hills.

By September hardly a family at Beida remained untouched by tragedy. With Chairman Mao continuing to appear before millions of impassioned Red Guards in Tiananmen Square, his encouragement further inflaming their revolutionary ardor, it was clear that the acts of appalling violence we had witnessed were receiving the highest sanction. But over the summer months, a new situation had begun to develop, one that would in two years time compel Mao Zedong to take drastic action to curb the anarchy he had encouraged. A controversy over the leadership of the burgeoning revolutionary movement had already begun to polarize the Beida community, with opinions sharply divided over the issue of Nie Yuanzi's authority. By late fall two major factions had emerged, their intensifying rivalry the impetus to a further escalation of the violence.

At the same time that Nie Yuanzi was handpicking her supporters to staff Beida's Cultural Revolution Preparatory Committee, the ideals of the Paris Commune were still being widely publicized throughout the country. Such a blatant discrepancy between ideal and actuality was disturbing to many, who could see that while Nie Yuanzi was voicing her support for the selection of leaders by vote to ensure that they were truly the servants of the people, she was nevertheless appointing only those whom she trusted to positions of power. This was just a preparatory committee, she contended defensively when challenged about her methods, not a formal leading body, so it was not necessary for a vote to be taken. Despite her disclaimers, it was apparent that her committee had arrogated absolute power unto itself.

To express opposition to her authoritarian approach, a few radical students began to write posters and slogans criticizing Nie Yuanzi's committee and protesting that her group was illegal, since it had not been chosen by the masses. Those who dared to challenge her power were members of three of the many spontaneously formed Red Guard fighting and struggle groups that had taken shape that summer, detachments calling themselves the Beijing Commune, the East is Red, and Red Flag Waving. Although these students and young teachers originally had agreed with Nie Yuanzi's opposition to the work team, now they began to repeat their earlier slogans with a different target, claiming that they didn't want her to be their nursemaid and that they would conduct this revolution themselves. Emboldened by the heady victory won when the work team was disbanded, they wanted no replacement for that representative of higher authority and turned their tactics against their former ally. One of the slogans that expressed this opposition sentiment urged, "Act on your own initiative; don't be controlled by a dictator." Out of this early opposition to Nie Yuanzi from the most radical students grew the division of the campus into two warring factions.

Contributing to the emerging resistance to Nie Yuanzi's authority was a growing emphasis on the importance of independent thinking. Even Yao Wenyuan and Zhang Chunqiao* had criticized the old educational system for producing overly obedient students who cared only about high grades, the "5+ obedient sheep."† Chairman Mao's assertion that people must "use their own heads" was being frequently cited in an effort to make the nation's young people more independent of their elders, more thoughtful and critical. Continuing this theme was the excoriation of Liu Shaoqi's previously venerated tract *How to Be a Good Communist*, first published in 1939 and reprinted in 1962, but now denounced for such things as encouraging slavishness and making people simply into submissive instruments of the Party.

Hostility toward Nie Yuanzi derived most directly, however, from her policy of identifying large numbers of teachers, cadres, and students as enemies, a practice that many began to feel would bring permanent ruin to the university. Every day, it seemed, the loudspeakers would announce the name of someone new who had been targeted as a member of the enemy camp, labeled either a "reactionary academic authority" or a "capitalist roader." In response to such continuing attacks, the Red Guard group called Beijing Commune, first organized in the chemistry department, mounted a provocative poster criticizing Nie Yuanzi's policy openly and claiming that in making so many people enemies she was not following Chairman Mao's instructions, but was seeking to advance her own authority without regard for the welfare of the university.

---

*Zhang Chunqiao, originally a journalist, became head of the Propaganda Department of the Shanghai Party Committee, then a member of the Central Cultural Revolution Group, and finally the member of the "Gang of Four" whom many expected would become China's next premier.

†In China's marking system, 5+ is the highest grade, equivalent to A+.

More radical even than this group, and made up largely of students from the law department, Red Flag Waving soon publicly asserted the necessity of following the principles of the Paris Commune and requiring the whole university to vote for the members of the Cultural Revolution Preparatory Committee.

By then Nie Yuanzi had her own Red Guard organization, called the New Beida Commune, a group that had rallied around her leadership the previous June in an effort to overturn the influence of Lu Ping and his supporters. Dominated by Party cadres and by students and teachers from peasant or worker backgrounds, New Beida attempted to discredit any who had supported the old educational methods, denouncing those people as members of a black gang, and subjecting them to humiliation and abuse.

In response, the three radical Red Guard groups boldly staged a demonstration outside the central dining hall, sitting down on the ground and refusing to leave until their demands were acknowledged. The sit-in attracted surprising support, with many previously silent students joining the ranks of the more daring Red Guard initiators. For several hours the demonstrators, perhaps two hundred strong, sang revolutionary songs and read aloud Chairman Mao's words, attempting to force Nie Yuanzi and the Cultural Revolution Preparatory Committee to treat them equally with New Beida, to provide them also with supplies of paper and paste, and to call for a campus-wide vote. Claiming that Chairman Mao himself had written the characters for New Beida's name, calligraphy that had been proudly reproduced on posters and lapel buttons and used for the masthead of her own campus newspaper, called *New Beida*, Nie Yuanzi had tried to deny any legitimacy to the radical coalition that opposed her. But now this major demonstration made clear the growing strength of her opponents, proving that they were a force to be reckoned with.

By winter the radical groups, joined by other organizations, even some early Nie Yuanzi supporters who had grown disillusioned, united to form the Jinggang Mountain Corps, named for the famous mountain stronghold of Chairman Mao's Red Army in Jiangxi province, and committed to the overthrow of Nie Yuanzi's leadership. Subsequently this alliance established a Jinggang Mountain Headquarters with its own loudspeaker and its own news-paper, called *New Beida Daily*, for which the opposition students also appropriated Chairman Mao's calligraphy, announcing de-fiantly that his script was intended for all of Beida and not just for one group. Even though it had no influence at first, the Jinggang Mountain coalition kept growing. Its leaders made great efforts to attract supporters by asserting that they would resist the policies of Nie Yuanzi, that her denunciation of so many faculty members was wrongheaded and excessive.

During those summer months my own children had become closely acquainted with the Red Guards who opposed Nie Yuanzi. Although just thirteen, Tang Dan was passionately concerned with political affairs, almost fanatical, and she had become especially friendly with the members of the radical Red Flag Waving Corps. Her intense opposition to Nie Yuanzi arose partly because this woman was her father's enemy and partly because of her own rebel-lious personality and instinctive affinity for the oppressed side, qualities we shared. Though not old enough to participate directly in the rebels' activities, she had become an eager assistant, even taking Tang Shuang along to help her carry tea and boiled water from our house to the sit-in participants when they demonstrated outside the dining hall.

Many other children who were just primary school graduates also allied with the opposition side, often in response to Nie Yuan-zi's persecution of their families. Jinggang Mountain declared that a person could be a revolutionary whatever his family background; even though he could not choose his parents, he could certainly choose to promote the revolution. However, New Beida spurned the offspring of "bad families," denouncing them as the "spawn of dogs," and admitted to their ranks only the children of the "five red families"—workers, peasants, soldiers, revolutionary cadres, and revolutionary martyrs.

Among those children affiliated with the Jinggang Mountain side, three became especially prominent that fall for their continu-ous and very visible support. This group of "little revolutionary generals" consisted of Tang Dan, the daughter of a prominent pro-fessor of history, and the daughter of the Party secretary in the history department. All of them were children whose fathers had been vehemently denounced as enemies. Proud to be treated by their elders as revolutionaries, these three girls had been given red armbands and were allowed to assist the Jinggang Mountain members in a variety of ways, pasting posters on the walls, selling the *New Beida Daily*, passing out handbills and urging passersby to study them carefully. When they saw new posters penned by the other side, they would argue vigorously against their opponents' assertions to anyone who would listen.

Tang Shuang, then nine, would assist his sister with some of these tasks, sometimes climbing onto a high roof to drop a large sheaf of handbills to the crowd below. After he had demonstrated his climbing skills, he was recruited to steal loudspeakers, all of which initially had belonged to the other side, since Nie Yuanzi had refused to allow her opponents such an important propaganda weapon. Along with several other young people, Tang Shuang would go out at night when the loudspeakers were unprotected, cut their wires, and carry the prized equipment back to Jinggang Mountain headquarters. When I learned of my children's activities, I felt proud of their independence and determination but very worried about their safety. Tang Shuang might fall from a tree or from the window of a high building; worse yet, he would certainly be beaten severely if he were caught. Sometimes when he went to other campuses to sell the Jinggang Mountain newspaper, I would follow him secretly. If he were beaten, I might be able to offer some protection, or at least go for help. When I tried to dissuade him from his revolutionary exploits, he always brushed aside my maternal caution, afire with the importance of the tasks entrusted to him.

By the end of 1966, factional loyalties had grown intense, even though real distinctions between the groups were often unclear. With both sides claiming to represent the masses and both therefore justified in seizing power from any they considered reactionaries or capitalist roaders, the rivalry grew ever more antagonistic. Each group was determined to prove its loyalty to Chairman Mao, its commitment to carry the Cultural Revolution through to the end; each was determined to demonstrate its unyielding opposition to the enemies of the Party and the people. In this climate of hostility, an unspoken competition developed over who could display more revolutionary fervor, more devotion to Chairman Mao, more hatred for political adversaries. It was a chaotic and fluid situation, with new struggle groups forming, and people shifting their allegiances from one detachment to another they believed to be more truly dedicated to the goals of the Cultural Revolution, however vaguely those might be defined.

At Beida the two major factions were composed of many such subsidiary teams, which coalesced whenever a group of people decided they shared similar views. The new detachments would announce their existence by means of a poster, and only later decide to ally with one of the coalition groups. In my department the strongest Jinggang Mountain team of teachers called itself the Mountains Are Thoroughly Red, while the strongest New Beida teachers' team had taken the name Massive Cudgel, recalling Chairman Mao's reference to the fabled monkey king's stick in his poem "Changsha." Neither organization had more than ten members. The people who united into these small groups would take upon themselves spontaneously decided tasks, like the searching of a prominent professor's home or the interrogation of a vulnerable cadre, although not all of the teams' revolutionary acts were violent.

The Lu Xun Team in my department, made up of seven teachers, undertook the project of organizing all of Lu Xun's quotations into categories, separating his remarks about revolution from his comments about other topics, such as intellectuals or workers. Students in another department formed the Reveal Things Thoroughly to the Bottom Detachment, assuming the task of investigating every aspect of the lives of high government officials. The membership of these fighting and struggle groups was always shifting, the teams themselves forming and reforming, their spontaneous nature and self-imposed responsibilities an illustration of how the Cultural Revolution emerged from the consciousness of the people. Despite the catalytic effect of Chairman Mao, Jiang Qing, and others at the highest levels, actions were often initiated at the bottom rather than assigned from above, a major departure from the normal pattern of political movements in China.

As these groups at Beida established connections with comparable organizations at other universities, where the students, faculty, and cadres were becoming similarly polarized, two principal coalitions emerged in Beijing. Xin Beida assumed a prominent role in the Heaven faction, so named because its leader Han Aijing was a student at the Aeronautical Institute and also because Nie Yuanzi was said to be able to "touch heaven"—to have special access to the top leadership. In response, Jinggang Mountain affiliated with the subsequently organized Earth faction, named because its leader, Wang Dabin, was a student at the Geology Institute. During the months from September 1966 to January 1967, when the whole country was becoming riven, these young people spread out across the city to exchange experiences, descending first upon schools, later upon government institutes and factories, to organize the students and workers, fan the winds of revolution, and at the same time extend their own group's influence.

Even with the students absorbed in making revolution outside of the campus, Lao Tang had to attend many evening meetings in his department, each one conducted like a trial. The interrogators wanted to learn what had happened at the International Hotel, and I was constantly worried, aware that after these sessions some people were locked up and kept in confinement to write their confessions, while others were beaten. Always I would sit on the top step of the stairway outside the room at the end of the second floor corridor, hoping to overhear what was happening inside. I wanted to know where Lao Tang would be taken if he were to be locked up so that I could provide him with clothing and food, but fortunately, night after night, he was allowed to return home. Sometimes the meetings would last until nine-thirty, sometimes until midnight, and I would just sit there waiting, wondering what our fate would be.

Even at this time when suffering and misery were so widespread, however, life went on. In December I discovered that I was pregnant, but instead of being joyful at the prospect of a new baby, I became deeply depressed. Feeling that I could not add to Lao Tang's burdens by telling him this news, I could see no recourse but abortion. Finally, I went to the hospital to state my request, only to have the hospital authorities demand that either my husband or my department sign the necessary forms. To tell my department was equivalent to making my condition public, so my effort to shield Lao Tang from additional distress was in vain. When I told him of my decision, he urged me to keep the baby, cautioning that we might later regret having prevented the birth of this child. I wanted to yield to his urging, but I could not imagine being pregnant at this moment when the future seemed utterly unpredictable. After all, I reminded myself, even though the second labor group had been dismissed, I could be reassigned to such work at any time, and if I were pregnant, not only would my health and that of the baby suffer, but I would be vulnerable to special taunts and insults by the Red Guards. The normally joyful prospect of pregnancy seemed an impossibility under such circumstances, so I persuaded Lao Tang to sign the form.

We went together to the hospital one afternoon during the rest period just after lunch so that he would not have to request leave for such a purpose. After signing the papers, Lao Tang hurried back to his labor and I entered the hospital. Performed by the suction method, the abortion took only an hour and was much less painful than I had feared. It was over before I could really grasp what had happened. But back at home I felt weak and faint from the loss of blood. All I could do was to lie on the bed, utterly drained and unable to move. When Lao Tang returned, his mother came to ask why I had not prepared the evening meal, and her solicitous tone made me weep inconsolably, my feelings of pain and loss finally released. When I told her what I had done, she was aghast, reproaching me that an abortion was immoral, that I should have discussed the situation with her, that I should never have done such a thing. She was deeply distressed, and we wept together. The next day I felt strong enough to get out of bed and resume my normal activities despite the stabbing pain in my heart. I could not shake off the thought that I had killed my own child.

As the months passed, I would often regret my decision. The factional struggle so engrossed the Red Guards in late 1966 that I was left on my own; time hung heavily on my hands. Because many others also had nothing to do, no compulsory labor, no classes to teach, no academic work of any sort, other women intentionally became pregnant. No one had an interest in reading books, both because the atmosphere was too tense to permit concentration and because such academic pursuits seemed useless and irrelevant in those days. Some people used this period to learn English, but I thought it likely that I would return to the countryside to live with the peasants. I wanted to escape from this environment where intellectuals were constantly abused, where relationships among people were so cruelly antagonistic. As I spent my days attending meetings, reading Chairman Mao's quotations, preparing food, washing clothing, sewing Tang Dan's worn out pants into overalls for Tang Shuang, many times I thought sadly how precious it would have been to have a new baby after all.

But as the tumultuous months of 1966 drew to a close, life had seemed so unpredictable, danger to my family so imminent, that I had been unable to consider giving birth to a new child. The stress and anguish of those weeks showed clearly in the photograph that Lao Tang and I had taken on the last day of 1966. It was our annual custom to sit for an anniversary photograph, but that year our wedding date had coincided with the death of my mother, and we had completely forgotten our usual practice. Not wanting to abandon our tradition, we walked to a small photo shop in nearby Haidian on New Year's Eve. When we picked up the photograph, I realized with a shock the toll that the past six months had taken. My face looked haggard and gaunt after the abortion, my mouth drawn into a stiff, artificial smile, while Lao Tang appeared frightened, his eyes staring widely, as if seeing a world he had never known. Even in the anti-rightist period his life had not really been disturbed, but this time he had not escaped. Nevertheless, as we walked home with that picture and remarked upon all that had befallen us in those months, we still felt fortunate. Both of us were alive, after all; we had not been beaten or locked up like so many of our friends, and Lao Tang had even been allowed to return home every night, a necessary restorative after the stress of labor and countless struggle sessions. Whatever the misfortunes of our family, we knew that many others had suffered far more.

In January 1967, following the "January seizure of power" when Zhang Chunqiao, Yao Wenyuan, and Wang Hongwen* seized control of Shanghai municipality, Chairman Mao took another step to solidify his power over the country. Grateful to his supporters in Shanghai, he praised their revolutionary action, after which a front-page story appeared in *People's Daily* urging the whole country to follow this example and overthrow the capitalist roaders in the government. Such an enthusiastic response to the Shanghai radicals encouraged widespread imitation, and most of the Red Guards who had not already set out to fan the winds of revolution left the universities, eager to travel and exercise their mandate to seize power.

Young people wearing red armbands, badges of authority donned at will, flocked to government offices, determined to overthrow anyone in power, following the lead of their Shanghai mentors. After the top leaders had been taken away for interrogation and imprisonment, the older cadres would be locked in a separate room and ordered to read Chairman Mao's Red Book, instructed that thenceforth the Red Guards would assume all authority. In such revolutionary actions, the two factions would compete for influence and control.

When the Heaven faction rebels arrived at the Ministry of Education, for example, they joined forces with sympathetic fighting groups inside that organization, herding into one room all of the older officials said to have political problems, such as prior connections with the Guomindang, denouncing them as enemies and assigning them such demeaning tasks as the sweeping of hallways and cleaning of toilets. Hours later the Earth faction forces arrived to connect with their supporters and accomplish a similar take-over of power, only to find themselves preempted by their rivals. Their only recourse was to recruit into their own ranks any staff members ignored by the Heaven faction.

Perhaps only 2,500 people remained on our campus by that point, about a quarter of the previous population. With the exodus

*Wang Hongwen, a worker and middle-level cadre at a Shanghai textile mill, became a member of the Central Cultural Revolution Group and one of the "Gang of Four."

of the militant students, there were few Red Guards left to supervise even the first labor team. Tired of this job and eager to participate in the excitement of making revolution, the remaining Beida
militants decided to send the black gang members to the countryside where they could be supervised by local Red Guards. Only a
dangerous accident prevented Lao Tang from being sent out with
the others.

One particularly cold day, anticipating that Lao Tang would
want a bath when he came home, I had warmed the bathroom for
an hour before his arrival, after which he gratefully disappeared
into the tub. The only ventilating outlet was in the living room, and
we were always watchful when we moved the coal stove because the
fumes could be fatal. When Lao Tang stayed in the bathroom for an
unusual length of time, I went in to see if something was wrong
and found him unconscious in the tub. In a panic I shouted for
Tang Dan and Tang Shuang and together we managed to lift him
out and wrap his dripping body in a thick padded coat. It was urgent that he get fresh air immediately, so with the children each
holding one leg and me supporting him under the arms, we half
carried, half dragged him out to the courtyard. After covering him
with quilts, we could do nothing but wait. Finally, after half an
hour, he revived, and after two more hours, when he could sit up,
we were able to help him to bed. From the moment he regained
consciousness, however, he complained of extreme pain in his
back. In our haste to get him outside, we had unknowingly dislocated a vertebra in his lower back.

For three months he remained at home, unable to move, suffering from constant pain. All the while I reproached myself for having acted so hastily, for not thinking of some better way to carry
him. Still, the accident was in one way fortunate, as the doctor said
he could not be moved to the countryside. We had heard that the
labor there was very strenuous, harder than what I had been subjected to as a rightist, but only later did we learn how much the
others suffered. The young peasants had been organized as Red
Guards and told that these black gang members were the ultimate
enemy, thereby justifying the cruelest kinds of treatment. So while
Lao Tang escaped that ordeal, his back injury was very painful, and

I could not even stay at home to care for him, since just at that time I was assigned some new work.

The campus was much quieter now that so many students and young teachers had left. Not everyone was waging revolution, however. Perhaps half the members of my department had simply returned home, not wanting to participate in the struggles. Called "free and unfettered people," those who stood outside the frenzy of activity even devised homonyms for Chairman Mao's three instructions that were so inflaming their fellows with revolutionary zeal. Chairman Mao had said that in the Cultural Revolution everyone must do three things: struggle (*dou*), to put the enemy down; criticize (*pi*), to learn what is right and wrong; and transform (*gai*), to change the wrong ways into right. Those students who remained uninvolved, their numbers swelling as the fighting intensified, declared that they would *dou*, which also meant play with children; *pi*, which also meant chop wood and do housework; *gai*, which also meant bring about changes in their personal lives, like learning carpentry to build a new sofa or table. In my department this group of students, along with some of the young teachers who had remained on campus and enemies like me who were not presently doing labor, were, one day not long after Lao Tang's accident, put to work printing materials.

Some were assigned the task of printing all of Chairman Mao's unpublished statements, while others were told to print documents seized when the Red Guards searched the houses of high officials. We printed records of meetings, for example, and Red Guard indictments of high officials' crimes, such as the one hundred pages of accusations against Li Xuefeng, head of the Beijing Party Committee after Peng Zhen. Similar publishing efforts were taking place in many of the universities and factories, and the resulting leaflets were sometimes exchanged, sometimes sold on the street. Because my calligraphy was not as legible as that of some others, I was set to work spreading the black ink while the other rightists from my department actually cut the stencils. Then I would help with the printing and binding, tasks that kept me busy every day for eight hours. We all worked very hard, and I learned a great deal from reading Chairman Mao's statements, the allegations of high officials' corruption, the reports of other kinds of wrongdoings discovered by the Red Guards, and the criticisms of "poisonous" literature.

Meanwhile, the factional fighting was becoming more and more heated. Both sides now had loudspeakers and every night would engage in a battle of words using Chairman Mao's quotations as weapons. If the New Beida loudspeaker proclaimed that we must have a people's dictatorship over the enemy and that revolution was not a tea party, then we knew that a new victim would be seized or at least a new enemy's name announced. Quickly, Jinggang Mountain would retaliate with another quotation, asserting that Chairman Mao had said we must unite the people and not pronounce so many as enemies, and attacking New Beida for acting independently and ignoring Chairman Mao's instruction that only 1 to 3 percent of the people were bad. Every evening after dinner the loudspeakers would blare, and always we would be bombarded by two different quotations. The pattern of verbal abuse was always the same: New Beida would announce the name of some additional enemy, accusing Jinggang Mountain of protecting such people, after which Jinggang Mountain would claim that New Beida considered everyone an enemy and prevented people from uniting to make revolution.

The name-calling intensified as well. Jinggang Mountain would call Nie Yuanzi "Old Buddha," a term used for the empress dowager and considered very insulting in this revolutionary time. Playing on the name of Jinggang Mountain's leader, Niu Huiling, New Beida would call its opposition "ox head mountain," a derogatory allusion to the general with the head of an ox traditionally depicted alongside the emperor of the underworld. Then Jinggang Mountain would call Nie Yuanzi a "broken down shoe," meaning someone who bestows sexual favors freely, applicable because Nie had recently married her third husband, a high official who was soon to be attacked as a confederate of Liu Shaoqi and put in jail. When that happened and Nie knew her house would be investigated by the Red Guards, she personally escorted a group to conduct the search, proving how early she had drawn a line between herself and her husband. Before long she got divorced again. Meanwhile, her brother, Nie Zhen, who had been a vice-president of People's

University and had married the divorced wife of Liu Shaoqi, was put in jail, after which Nie Yuanzi announced that she would draw a line between herself and her brother. As the months passed, Jinggang Mountain made insulting jokes about such developments, proclaiming that now she was ready for her fourth and fifth husbands. All of this abuse was very noisy, the loudspeakers' volume set at a high pitch, the accusations continuing usually until eleven o'clock at night. If either side ran out of denunciations, its broadcasters would stop talking for awhile and play revolutionary songs. No one who lived in the central campus area could get to sleep until the din had finally subsided.

In the mornings the blare of loudspeakers would resume. Very early we would hear about the actions taken by the Red Guard teams during the night as well as the names of any new enemies. Then our regular daily routine began. At nine o'clock all of us remaining on campus would report to our departments to "receive instructions from Chairman Mao." Our meetings would always open with the leader's selection of some quotation from Chairman Mao, a passage that we would first recite together and then sing to music. We had all been taught to believe in the importance of "reading Chairman Mao's book, listening to Chairman Mao's words, and being Chairman Mao's diligent students." Most people genuinely believed that since we were engaged in a revolution, such collective obedience was necessary. Any who did not share this belief went along, following the mainstream, knowing that to survive, belief in Chairman Mao was essential, divergent thinking a grave risk.

After the recitation and singing of Chairman Mao's thoughts, we would analyze the particular selection in detail. The proceedings had the air of a Bible class as we recited together, for example, "It is right to oppose reactionaries," and then discussed why this was true. Or perhaps we would discuss why a revolution was not a time to serve tea and confess what we might have thought before, such as that one should be humane toward his fellows, asserting that we now understood the necessity of struggling fiercely against class enemies. Thus our discussion meetings always involved some self-criticism, some investigation of how we had held incorrect thoughts before, and some explanation of why we had come to accept the new viewpoint acquired from Chairman Mao.

At eleven o'clock would come our break, and everyone, even the older professors, would participate in a dance of loyalty, accompanied by music from the omnipresent loudspeakers. You could not just stand aside and watch, as it was dangerous to differentiate yourself from the group. Even if you could not dance, you would move your arms and feet in time to the music. The purpose of the dance was to make everyone remember what Chairman Mao had said and to demonstrate collective loyalty to our leader. The steps had their origin in a Xinjiang folk dance, but the words were new:

> Beloved Chairman Mao,
> We have so much in our hearts to tell you,
> We have so many songs to sing you;
> A thousand, thousand red hearts leap for you,
> A thousand, thousand red hearts face the red sun;
> We wish you long life forever.

Many professors disliked this procedure, feeling foolish enacting the dance routines, but I always enjoyed the chance to be outside in the fresh air, to sing and dance and escape from the tedium of the meetings. Others who felt as I did would try to prolong the time for this break, stretching it from ten minutes sometimes to as long as an hour. Besides, I still felt devoted to Chairman Mao, so for me the words to this song were uttered sincerely and with heartfelt emotion. After the break we would return to our meeting until noon, spending the latter part of the morning reading the day's newspaper or some propaganda leaflet, or studying the new posters mounted outside.

In the afternoons we were free to walk about and study the wall posters. Sometimes we would be organized into groups to visit other institutes, like the Association of Literature, which was located in a large building downtown, its walls plastered with slogans and denunciations. Sometimes we went to the First and Second Foreign Language Institutes or to People's University to read their posters. The leaders wanted us to be familiar with the propaganda displayed in places besides our own campus so that we would understand how many enemies were in our midst, how much in our society needed to be changed, and thus how essential was the Cultural Revolution.

Everyone during those months in late 1966 was expected to memorize three essays written by Chairman Mao, the "three old essays": "The Foolish Old Man Who Moved the Mountain," "In Memory of Norman Bethune," and "On Serving the People." Sometimes in the street a Red Guard would randomly stop you and make you recite a line. When you wished to make a telephone call, the operator would not say "hello" but "serve the people," and you would have to respond "thoroughly and perfectly." Only after this exchange would she ask what number you wanted to call. If you were unable to reply with the appropriate words, you would be told to go back and study Chairman Mao's works. When you went shopping, you would inevitably meet some shop attendants who were Red Guards and would ask you something about the three essays or about the Red Book. Before you could make a purchase, you would have to respond with the appropriate quotation. This was called "popularizing Chairman Mao's teachings and making them known to everyone."

Such excessive adulation of Chairman Mao, such enforced conformity, didn't offend me at the time. I wanted only to follow the group, knowing that as an uncapped rightist I could easily be singled out for special criticism once again, that Lao Tang could be arrested at any time, that my children could be cruelly beaten. I thought only about how to get through this period safely and was far less contemplative, far less evaluative, than in Zhaitang when I had pondered all that was happening around me. Like everyone else, I was terribly frightened. Everything was new, unpredictable, threatening, and I had neither the motivation nor the energy to think about current policies or to question why people were acting in these ways. Besides, I didn't trust myself and believed my own opinions might be unreliable, since everyone around me was acting in unison. And of course I knew that to think independently was dangerous, for we had repeatedly been told that if we harbored any deviant thoughts, our guilt would be plainly evident. This warning was an effective deterrent. Most of the time I didn't think at all, just moved through the days with everyone else, doing what was expected.

At the same time that uniformity of thought and action were being instilled in us all, the violence on the campus was escalating, a result of the bitter factional rivalry. Whenever Jinggang Mountain announced that it supported someone to join the ranks of the revolution, New Beida would counter that the person had committed many errors and was clearly a counter-revolutionary. This struggle for ascendency had terrible consequences.

Knowing that to run a university, professors and administrators could not be eliminated, and hoping to take charge of the educational process once again when the Cultural Revolution had finally ended, Jinggang Mountain often accepted into its ranks some of the most famous professors, the same academic authorities who were being struggled against by Nie Yuanzi. In retaliation, New Beida would try to discover some political errors committed by any who received support from the rival group. If incriminating evidence could be found, then New Beida could allege that Jinggang Mountain was a counter-revolutionary organization.

Before joining the Jinggang Mountain side, Pang Wenjun, the history professor whose daughter was one of the three "little revolutionary generals" with Tang Dan, had been in the second labor group like me. He probably would have remained relatively inconspicuous had he not become centrally involved in the factional rivalry. Because of his bourgeois background and the fact that many of his family members had been officials before Liberation, he was singled out by Nie Yuanzi's supporters as a primary target. Jinggang Mountain claimed, however, that this professor had always supported the revolution, that he was a loyal comrade, and that a person must be judged not on the basis of his family background but on the record of his deeds.

Hearing Jinggang Mountain's endorsement, New Beida decided to prove Pang was an enemy of the people in order to deny the legitimacy of his supporters. Its members worked long hours in the library, reading every article Pang had ever written to unearth some proof that he had been opposed to the Communist Party before

Liberation. Finding nothing that would indict him as a "reactionary academic authority," they went to his home, searched all his belongings, and finally just took him out to be struggled against in a big parade.

One very cold day, perhaps in February 1967, I saw this man who had received a Ph.D. degree from Harvard, being marched around the campus with two or three others. A heavy wooden signboard hung on his chest, suspended by thin wires that had cut bleeding welts into his neck. The sign proclaimed him a "reactionary power"; the characters of his name were obliterated with a red X. A more ingenious indignity had been devised for another of the academic luminaries in that parade. Chairman Mao had once said that "at Beida the temple is not so large but the Buddha is very tall; the lake is very deep and the turtles buried in the mud are many," a warning about the university's influential role in the society and about the many enemies who lurked there. Responding to those metaphors, the Red Guards had forced the second enemy, a prominent professor of Indian philosophy and languages who had received his Ph.D. in Germany, a former vice-president of Beida, to carry on his back a huge iron *wok* used for boiling porridge in the student dining hall. The pot was tied with ropes around his neck and hips. His stooped form supporting the heavy *wok* was supposed to represent one of the turtles that had been successfully dislodged from its hiding place at Beida.

The students accompanying the five or six enemies being thus displayed to the people struck a gong loudly and shouted, "Down with these reactionary powers," "They must pay for what they have done," "Jinggang Mountain supports these reactionaries and is responsible for their crimes." Those of us who were accidental onlookers simply stood by woodenly, unable to say or do anything to stop such abuse. Anyone was free in those months of revolutionary activism to punish and criticize an enemy, and none of the bystanders wanted to provide any excuse for which they could themselves be attacked.

Jinggang Mountain had no way to protect its members from such treatment, but it could take revenge. In retaliation for this particular incident, it singled out a former vice-secretary of the Beida

Party Committee who from the beginning of the turmoil had been supported by New Beida because of his opposition to Lu Ping. Now this person's history was thoroughly checked by Jinggang Mountain members, who learned that he had joined the Party early and had subsequently been arrested by the Guomindang, only to be released a year later. This fact proved, they claimed, that he was a traitor and an enemy of the Party, and since New Beida wanted to protect this reactionary, then clearly it was trying to shelter the enemies of the people. Because of his powerful position in the New Beida faction, this man was locked up and interrogated, some said very cruelly, to make him divulge the plans of the New Beida organization. Then in 1968, when even the propaganda teams sent to calm the violence pronounced him a traitor and he believed there was no hope of reversing his judgment, he became so depressed that he jumped into the campus swimming pool and drowned. In such cases Jinggang Mountain's tactics were just as harsh, its claims just as exaggerated, as New Beida's.

Because of Nie Yuanzi's power as head of the university's Cultural Revolution Preparatory Committee, the New Beida faction controlled almost the entire campus, and with it, supplies, food, and transportation. The Jinggang Mountain members had managed to occupy three student dormitories where they slept and held almost continuous strategy meetings, trying to devise ways to counter their opponents and expand their own power. The two rival headquarters were only a three-minute walk apart, and each group had mounted on its rooftops powerful slingshots made of bicycle inner tubes with which to fire large stones, bricks, and other projectiles. It was very dangerous to walk in this area, which was just adjacent to our house, and I worried constantly about my children, never knowing where they went during the days.

That spring of 1967, perhaps in May, the violence reached a new height when finally the New Beida members beat a young man to death. They claimed that a member of Jinggang Mountain had come to their office to steal documents and that they had been trying to make him confess who had sent him and why he had come. During their questioning they struck him repeatedly with a bicycle chain, angered by his unsatisfactory answers. A day later he died from his injuries. Later it became known that the victim was a middle-school student in search of reading matter who had sneaked into a library adjacent to the New Beida propaganda office. Not being familiar with the conditions at the university, the youth had not known that he was in danger and had merely broken in to look for a book, some said a "yellow" book, but that was mere conjecture. After this, Jinggang Mountain attacked New Beida even more vehemently, posting huge announcements that these people were responsible for a blood debt. Everyone was very upset, but New Beida insisted that the young man had been a spy and an active counter-revolutionary.

Once Jinggang Mountain had acquired a degree of influence and had accumulated evidence about the wrongs committed by New Beida members, Nie Yuanzi's group made even greater efforts to crush the opposition. The excuse was a poster written by the East Is Red team, a subsidiary of Jinggang Mountain, criticizing Lin Biao (then Mao's "closest comrade in arms" and designated successor) and saying that if capitalist roaders existed in the government, they must also exist in the army, and concluding that everyone must remain vigilant. Perhaps this Red Guard group contained high military officials' children who wanted to influence the power struggle within the PLA, but New Beida could assert that counter-revolutionaries within the Jinggang Mountain faction were trying to promote divisions in the army. Thus they demanded that Jinggang Mountain turn over all members of the East Is Red group to the Cultural Revolutionary Preparatory Committee, which would investigate the situation and force those responsible for this poster to write confessions.

Next, New Beida issued an ultimatum. If the East Is Red members were not surrendered, New Beida, which now numbered perhaps 1,500 supporters, would have grounds for claiming that the whole Jinggang Mountain group, some 500-strong, was counter-revolutionary. The Jinggang Mountain people knew this threat could not be carried out, that it was impossible to prove that so many were truly counter-revolutionary. Nevertheless, one young East Is Red member, a student in her second year in my department, was terribly frightened about what would befall her if she were turned over to her enemies, especially now that they had beaten one victim to death. The day after the ultimatum was issued, she jumped from the stone boat that decorates the campus lake and drowned. People said that she could no longer bear the constant turmoil, the pressure, the feeling that all her revolutionary efforts were apparently futile.

Determined to eliminate its opposition and assume complete control of the campus community, New Beida continued to press Jinggang Mountain. When its members caught a Jinggang Mountain supporter, they would lock him up, beat him, and demand information. The struggle was growing daily more intense. Members of both factions looked like remnants from the European Middle Ages, decked out in firemen's helmets, thick vests, and shin guards because of the danger of unexpected skirmishes. Whenever New Beida needed supplies, it would raid the athletic department or other storage facilities on campus, sometimes making requests from the Heaven faction members at the Physical Education Institute nearby. Jinggang Mountain similarly acquired protective equipment from Earth faction members in other parts of the city, but clearly it was on the defensive.

Always New Beida tried to discredit any Jinggang Mountain members who were in some way distinctive. One evening the loudspeakers announced the name of someone new whom they had targeted as a "black offspring," as "dog's spawn," and as an active counter-revolutionary, a fourth-year student of physics noted for his academic excellence named Deng Pufang, the son of Deng Xiaoping (who, along with Liu Shaoqi, was a prime target of the Red Guards). This Jinggang Mountain supporter, the loudspeakers threatened, would be captured and forced to reveal all that he knew. One evening a large group of perhaps thirty or forty militant young people wearing armor and helmets, carrying spears, arrived to lay siege to the Jinggang Mountain building in which Deng Pufang lived on the third floor. The New Beida warriors began to search door to door, determined to find such a distinguished quarry. Badly frightened, Deng decided to escape by jumping from the window that faced Haidian Avenue, hoping to blend in with the crowd outside of the university wall and get away. He did succeed in thus evading his captors and was reportedly hidden in someone's home, but his back was so severely injured from his fall that he remained permanently paralyzed below the waist.

New Beida's attacks were unrelenting. A young man in my department, a capable student and the best violinist at the university, had at the start of the Cultural Revolution written a poster claiming that Lin Biao had in fact committed some errors, that he had spent much of the Anti-Japanese War in the Soviet Union, that he was not really as important a military leader as people had been led to believe. One day New Beida announced that this young man, whose father was vice-president of the Minorities Institute, had opposed the army and must be captured so that Lin Biao could be protected. The young man, who was living at home, knew that if he was caught, the consequences would be dire, so he decided to attempt an escape.

On the evening that New Beida announced its plan to arrest him, the most attractive young woman in our department, a New Beida member, quite unexpectedly declared her love for him. She told him she wanted to flee with him to his relatives in the Northeast. From a sympathetic teacher, a neighbor who had learned of their plans and told everyone, we learned the next day of her bold declaration and found that this girl, nicknamed Laughing Eyes, had in fact disappeared with her friend. Some two years later in the Clean the Ranks movement, the young man was discovered, brought back to the campus, and struggled against as a counter-revolutionary. Laughing Eyes stood by him loyally throughout his difficulties, waiting for him when he was sent to the cadre school in 1969 and placed under the supervision of my work team. Finally he was rehabilitated after the fall of the Gang of Four, the two were married at last, and the husband was given a job teaching Chinese literature at a university in the Northeast.

As New Beida attempted to suppress the activities and destroy the legitimacy of Jinggang Mountain, such attacks became more frequent. Unimaginable events, like the condemnation of a vice-chairman of our department, a man whom everyone had assumed to be above reproach, became commonplace occurrences in those unpredictable days. Previously the head of academic affairs at Beida, but eager to teach Chinese poetry again and not remain an administrator, this man had been sent to our department to replace the chairman, ill for many years. Like many of Nie Yuanzi's supporters, he had come to Beida from the Liberated Areas, but nonetheless his sympathies were with Jinggang Mountain. The day after he had routinely led a departmental meeting, New Beida suddenly announced that he was a traitor. When in the Northeast with the Red Army, his accusers alleged, he had been captured by the Guomindang and had done secret work as a collaborator, writing slogans on walls and even signing a confession testifying he would never return to the Communist Party. For those previous crimes, he was sent to the dreaded "cow shed," the crowded prison set up in 1967 in a one-story temporary classroom building for the most serious enemies of Nie Yuanzi.

In this unheated cement structure perhaps a hundred people, eight from my department, were kept under guard through the bitter Beijing winter. Forced to rise very early every morning to study Chairman Mao's quotations, to do labor in the day, and then to attend interrogation sessions until late at night, these professors and cadres, some of whom were imprisoned for nearly a year, would be beaten severely at the slightest excuse, such as their Red Guard supervisors not liking their responses to questions. How fortunate Lao Tang was to escape this fate, I realized later. Perhaps it was because of his back injury or because he was always obedient and submissive, writing endless confessions at the request of his philosophy department interrogators.

In that brutal summer of 1967, even people without any political problem or any question of past disloyalty became victims of the factional strife. One of those attacked by New Beida simply because of his prominence, even though he had no "bread to be cut," as was said in the idiom of the day, was Zhou Peiyuan, considered by many the most important leader of Jinggang Mountain, and perhaps the only person over sixty to be a member of a Red Guard organization. Zhou had never been associated with the Guomindang, had never written anything that could be construed as opposed to the Communist Party, and had vigorously opposed Lu Ping. In the period before Nie Yuanzi's May 25 poster, he had been allied with the anti-Peng Zhen group, but later he had joined forces with the opposition. Perhaps he had felt sympathy for the Jinggang Mountain students whom Nie Yuanzi oppressed, perhaps he thought Nie Yuanzi was dictatorial and arbitrary, perhaps he guessed that the Jinggang Mountain faction would win in the end; no one could know, but his allegiance changed and he became a symbol of Nie Yuanzi's opponents.

Not wanting to allow Zhou an opportunity to escape, New Beida did not announce its intentions in advance this time. One night at about ten o'clock two of its struggle teams just appeared at Zhou's house, as I saw from my doorway, to conduct an investigation, obviously hoping to discover some kind of incriminating evidence. The Red Guards looked very menacing. I knew how those young students had to work themselves up before conducting such searches, encouraging each other and shouting revolutionary slogans, insisting that they must fight resolutely against their enemy, to banish their misgivings and kindle their anger. This pattern, which I had first observed months earlier in that meeting to criticize Meng Kun, seemed especially true of the young women, for whom such violent actions would ordinarily have been intolerable.

On this night I saw the students hit Zhou's wife on the face, once on each side. Once known for her beauty, her wealth, and her arrogance, she may have said something to provoke this abuse, but I could not hear. I just saw the Red Guards push her into a corner and stride off to find her husband. Their mission was a failure, however, for Zhou had been advised of their plans and had gone into hiding. Each side, we knew, had spies in the other's camp. Later we learned that Zhou had sequestered himself in a small pavilion in a remote corner of the Summer Palace, where the Earth faction was the dominant group and where sympathizers had agreed to conceal him. After ransacking his house, the New Beida group left, empty-handed.

One evening the loudspeakers blared with an unusual intensity as the two factions threatened each other, warning that a big struggle would take place that very night and that everyone must be careful. There was much activity in the area near our house, and we could see that the Red Guards had all donned armor and helmets. They were carrying handmade spears and daggers, even martial arts swords, all of which were easy for New Beida to obtain since they had occupied the athletic department and the metal shop. All through the night we waited tensely for some decisive confrontation. By morning the danger had passed, but our proximity to this violence made me resolve to find some way to relocate my family. The other half of our house, which we had vacated so rapidly in compliance with that official order, still remained empty, and I made up my mind that the time had come for us to move out of our once comfortable home into some surroundings farther away from the Jinggang Mountain headquarters, which were the focus of the factional struggles.

My decision was confirmed when one Sunday morning I was routinely washing the family laundry in a large metal basin. Emptying the pockets of my daughter's jacket, I found inside a letter from a young man named Xia Zhang, a Jinggang Mountain leader whose name always appeared prominently in the wall posters. A talented geology student, he was skilled at electronics and had almost single-handedly assembled all the Jinggang Mountain loudspeakers. Tang Shuang idolized Xia and for him scaled tall trees and climbed out of top-story windows to steal the enemy's broadcasting equipment. I knew that Xia was a good person, but I was quite unprepared to read that he had fallen deeply in love with Tang Dan. Strongly opposed to her having a love affair at fourteen, I worried as well that Xia's prominent position might bring my daughter some harm. Aware that she would be angry to learn I had discovered her secret, I thought for a long while about how to react. Finally, I wrote her a note saying that she had just graduated from primary school, that in this period of turmoil anything could happen, that I hoped she would be careful, and that I trusted she would conduct herself in such a way as not to bring any further difficulty to our family or to herself.

At the same time I recalled my own first experience with romantic affection when I was her age and my family had moved to Huaxi outside of Guiyang to escape from the Japanese air raids. Every Sunday afternoon three priests, one Italian and two Chinese, would stand in the small village square to show the people Bible pictures, explain scripture verses, and sing hymns. Each Sunday I would climb a hillside to wait for the priests to appear, following them into town. Their gentle words and beautiful voices always moved me, and the young Italian priest became the object of all my youthful fantasies. In my heart a passionate love blossomed, even though the priest never even knew my name. After my family returned to the city I never saw him again, but his face, his carriage, his voice remained precious. Not wanting to hurt my daughter's feelings or deprive her of the bittersweet experience of young love, I decided just to express my concerns about the family's vulnerability during this intensely unhappy period. Having put my note on her desk, I watched for some clue to her response when she sat down for dinner, but I could see nothing. I never learned whether she had even read my note.

However, there was no longer any doubt in my mind that we should move when, just a few nights later, the loudspeakers announced again that a decisive battle would be fought to resolve definitively which faction was in the right. The announcers each claimed their side's affiliation with Chairman Mao, their approval by Jiang Qing, and both predicted total victory. Again and again they warned that everyone must prepare for this final contest. When my children didn't return for dinner that evening, I grew increasingly alarmed. All the while I could see people piling up stones on the rooftops and carrying clubs toward their respective headquarters. By eleven o'clock when the children still had not come home, the atmosphere on the campus had grown unbearably tense. "Overturn New Beida," "Overturn Jinggang Mountain," "This will be the last battle," the loudspeakers dinned shrilly as I grew more and more anxious. Unable to bear the tension, I decided to go myself to Jinggang Mountain headquarters to find my children. Since I was a rightist and Lao Tang a black gang member, I knew my presence would not be welcome, especially at this explosive moment, but I decided to take the risk. Lao Tang, trying to focus his attention on the Red Guard newspapers I had collected, was too distracted by the children's unusual absence to be able to concentrate.

At the back gate of our courtyard, I hesitated, worried that maybe the group's members, already on the defensive, would think I was a spy. I knew that even if I attempted to gain entrance to the Jinggang Mountain building, I would be unlikely to find my children. Finally, I just plunged ahead, too worried to debate the outcome any longer. To my relief, the guard at the door had earlier been my student and responded politely that my children were indeed inside preparing a back-up broadcasting system and that I could go in to see them. I found them on the third floor assisting Xia. Tang Dan asked in a frightened voice what I was doing there, but Tang Shuang shouted angrily, "I'm not a child and I don't want my mother checking up on me." His dignity insulted, he vowed that he would never return home, that he was a Jinggang Mountain loyalist, that he would fight to the death with his comrades. Still I insisted that the children come with me, announcing firmly that I would stay there, even help them, until they agreed to return. To break the tension, Xia said that the task was nearly finished and he was ready to go to bed. "If we need you," he said to my son, "I will come to your house to call you, for I know how loyally you support Jinggang Mountain." At last the children consented.

Even though the threatened battle again failed to materialize, I knew the beatings and kidnappings would continue as before, so I went the next morning to my department to request less prestigious housing. The New Beida people, eager for good living quarters, agreed immediately. All I had to tell them was that my family had no right to live in such a luxurious house, and that besides the rent was too high for us to afford any longer. A week after my application had been approved, we scheduled our move. It was only then that I allowed myself to feel any emotions about this decision or to absorb the fact that a crucial stage in my life was being left behind.

I had paid some peasants at a nearby commune eighty *yuan*, more than a month's salary for me, for three carts to transport all of our possessions, most of which were books. Many people had sold their books that year at the going rate of seven *fen* per *jin* if they were in excellent condition, four *fen* if they were old or damaged, even if they were valuable. Such decisions were made for various reasons, because extra people had been thrust into a family's living

221

space, because people thought books no longer had any use, or because they no longer wanted to be intellectuals, but we had kept ours, and now they, along with the heavy glass bookcases, must be moved. Lao Tang had taken three days' leave, and the drivers helped us with the heavy loads.

A light rain was falling as I sat on a mule cart behind a load of plastic-draped books, thinking about the years I had spent in that house, aware that a part of myself was also being left behind. Since my marriage in 1952 all my joys and sorrows had been experienced within those walls, and now I was voluntarily bidding my past good-bye and starting anew. Nothing I had planned for in my life had been accomplished, I realized sadly, nor did my hopes seem to stand much chance of fulfillment. It was with a heavy heart that I had closed the door behind me on those familiar rooms.

The Naked Flagpole

OUR NEW HOUSE was on the outskirts of the campus, a fifteen-minute walk away from the student dormitory area. Even though a loudspeaker was positioned very near to our door, this narrow lane was physically removed from the factional rivalry. Our quarters were small, half the house of another professor who had been condemned as a reactionary and ordered to consolidate his family in half of its former space, but for the first time in my life, I shared my home with just Lao Tang and my children. My spirits began to lift as I stitched some new curtains, tidied up the courtyard, and thought about the flowers and vegetables I would plant as the weather grew warmer, grateful for this sense of asylum from the chaos of the central campus.

Thinking back, I realized we had witnessed acts of violence nearly every day for a year and a half, what with wall posters provoking angry debates, people being seized and struggled against on the campus, and Red Guards trying to intimidate each other with words and blows. Now not only had we moved away, but in 1968 the violence at Beida abated in response to urgent instructions from the highest leadership. We knew that the people locked in the cow shed were still being cruelly beaten, but attacks were not occurring openly with such frequency.

The Cultural Revolution had reached such extremes of violence in the summer of 1967 that a major propaganda campaign was under way to promote the formation of "big alliances." Red Guard leaders at Beida could not but heed these exhortations for fear of being accused of opposing Chairman Mao's directives, so for a brief interim we noticed a lull in the fighting. It was a welcome respite, even though we guessed it could not last, knowing that the hatred fueling the flames had by no means abated.

The revolutionary movement that had begun as an attack upon bureaucratic privilege had by then evolved into a power struggle in the broadest sense, with everyone competing for advantage and trying to carve out a sphere of influence, creating in the process a level of anarchy that in many places approximated civil war. Originally, most of the competing groups had genuinely professed noble aims, believing that they were more loyal to Chairman Mao than a rival faction, that they could better help China combat its revisionist tendencies and progress toward true socialism. The various Red Guard groups, heeding Lin Biao's slogan, "You can forget everything else but the word 'power,'" had attempted to seize power for the proletariat, which they believed would otherwise be destroyed by the bourgeoisie. But the factionalism had spread, the designation of enemies grown out of control. Not only did friends, classmates, and co-workers support different sides, but members of the same family would sometimes turn against each other, a husband taking documents belonging to his wife to his own faction, for example, as evidence to be used against her. Disputes had become so bitter that production was interrupted at many factories while the workers conducted their struggle sessions, even, as in the Guizhou airplane-manufacturing plant, using their machinery to produce automatic weapons.

We all had heard reports of intense fighting in many areas of the country, like Guizhou, Sichuan, and Yunnan, the "three provinces on the plateau." There artillery bound for the war in Vietnam had been seized from the PLA and was being used in bloody internecine battles. I learned at firsthand of the bloodshed in the provinces from a cousin, a middle-school teacher in Sichuan, who had traveled to Beijing to exchange revolutionary experiences and connect with other Earth faction groups. As head of her Red Guard detachment, she had tried to persuade my father to rent his house to her group as a headquarters, but he wanted no part in the struggle, and she was instead staying with me.

Worried about the fighting in the provinces, weary from the violence on campus, many people had become depressed as the New Year of 1968 approached. The initial revolutionary goals had long vanished, forgotten like the ideals of the Paris Commune. There seemed no end to the nightmare we were engaged in, no hope of resuming a normal life. The middle schools officially began instruction, but the teachers were continually struggled against by the students, and the principals were either in jail, under house arrest being supervised by the masses, or waiting to see what would happen and unwilling to risk action of any kind. Even if a school was actually holding classes, the children could choose whether or not to attend. Often when a teacher tried to conduct regular lessons, the students would interrupt with embarrassing questions or find some other way to disrupt the class. Some young people were serious about learning and hated the turmoil, but they were usually in the minority.

Ever since the fall, when Chairman Mao had returned from a tour of the provinces and seen the results of the deadly factionalism, he had been attempting to restore order. Day after day the loudspeakers had repeated his new instructions: "Unite together," "Among workers there can be no fundamental contradictions," "Carry on the revolution but return to classes." But high school and university students alike were dispersed across the country, doing whatever they pleased in the name of promoting revolution, and for months no one had been able to control their movements or their actions. Even stern directives from the highest leaders that the Red Guards should stop exchanging experiences and return immediately to their units had been ignored. To no avail had Chairman Mao tried to open the universities, and we had all grown more anxious in realizing that even he was not in charge.

While not accomplishing its desired result, Chairman Mao's call for resuming the educational process did prompt each faction at Beida to recruit more cadres and teachers in an effort to ensure the ascendency of its side when classes finally did begin. Many important people previously oppressed by New Beida were deciding to ally with Jinggang Mountain, and a famous wall poster had appeared, known as the "32 cadres-and-teachers' poster." Its thirty-two signers, all formerly influential on campus, had joined together to assert that Jinggang Mountain was following the correct line in trying to unite the people and in opposing those who did not adhere to Chairman Mao's instruction. The poster had been organized by the vice-chairman of the Chinese literature department, a black gang member assigned to the first labor team with Lao Tang, who had decided to speak out in response to Jinggang Mountain's repeated offers of cooperation with teachers and cadres. Lao Tang was another of the signatories. Because the support of these thirty-two people was considered essential to the reopening of the university, Jinggang Mountain's legitimacy was greatly bolstered by this public endorsement.

At the time of our move away from the central campus, the command that disputing factions must unite into revolutionary alliances was being constantly reiterated. In response, each faction at Beida steadfastly declared its intention to cooperate with the opposition, but at the same time retained its weapons and continued to occupy its fortified buildings. In February 1968, as a result of mounting pressure within the campus and from the highest leaders, Nie Yuanzi even declared her willingness to cooperate with Jinggang Mountain in accordance with Chairman Mao's directive, but still she maintained that some of the groups within that rival coalition were counter-revolutionary organizations. While many of the participating students were true revolutionaries and would be welcomed into New Beida, she pledged, the leaders must first offer their self-criticisms, and members of groups like Red Flag Waving must be punished. Despite such ostensibly conciliatory words, Nie Yuanzi's actual intent, I guessed, was to force her opponents to admit they had been wrong and agree to accept her authority in the future.

The Jinggang Mountain leaders replied warily that theirs was truly a revolutionary group desiring to unite with New Beida, but that first Nie Yuanzi must relinquish control of the university and allow a new Cultural Revolutionary Committee to be elected by the people. Only under this new leadership, Jinggang Mountain asserted, could the university again begin to operate. New Beida countered that Jinggang Mountain must admit the incorrectness of its stance, for only then could the two groups cooperate and run the university together. Nie Yuanzi must offer a self-criticism, explaining how she had oppressed the masses, Jinggang Mountain insisted; Niu Huiling must be interrogated, New Beida declared. With each side unwilling to yield to the other's demands, all hope of unification dissolved. The situation continued to deteriorate, and fighting flared up again.

In a place called Hanzhong in the mountains of Shaanxi, where Beida maintained a branch campus for the study of applied physics, the factional struggle had grown particularly violent. Nie Yuanzi had sent Gao Yuanping, one of the signers of the original May 25 poster, to enforce her authority on this campus. Using a loudspeaker, he had commanded the Earth faction stalwarts to lay down their weapons, but they had occupied a multi-story building and fortified it, even shooting from its windows with guns. Deciding to take the building by force, Gao ordered the use of fire bombs. In the ensuing blaze some people were burned to death, I was told, while others died jumping from the fifth-floor windows. Altogether twenty-one people perished in that battle. Gao Yuanping's attackers were victorious, but after the fall of the Gang of Four he was tried and condemned to death for his crimes, although his sentence was suspended. No doubt he believed that he was protecting Chairman Mao and struggling for the truth, while those who opposed him felt so convinced of their cause that they were willing to fight to the death.

In this period of escalating struggle, Nie Yuanzi decided the moment had come to seize power over all of Beida and then to begin the educational process once again. Accordingly, in May 1968 she delivered an ultimatum. If within two weeks the Jinggang Mountain faction did not surrender all of its weapons and cooperate with New Beida, she would cut off the electricity and water from its five buildings and surround those enclaves with New Beida students armed with slingshots. The Jinggang Mountain response to her threat was predictable: its leaders announced that their supporters were heroic, that they would never surrender or submit to the dictatorship of Nie Yuanzi, that they would endure her oppression to the end, even if they must shed their blood, until the last person in the buildings had been sacrificed. Immediately, Jinggang Mountain began to augment its defenses. Working day and night, the young people constructed walled bridges, designed by the architecture and engineering students, using timbers from the dormitory roofs to connect the central building with the buildings on each side. At the same time they dug tunnels to connect the two outermost buildings with this central network.

Every time a car would arrive carrying sacks of rice and other provisions, a battle would break out. Some of the Jinggang Mountain students would initiate a diversionary skirmish on one side of their enclave, while the students on the other side would prepare to receive supplies from a hole they had chipped through a wall. People like Tang Dan, a familiar figure, since she would walk by these buildings every day to visit the shops on Haidian Avenue, could often slip through a door to bring in small supplies of food for the Jinggang Mountain defenders, but anyone New Beida considered suspicious would be captured and interrogated if caught attempting to enter the Jinggang Mountain stronghold.

One day a geography student named Liu Wei returned from Anhui where he had been contacting other Earth faction supporters. Trying to enter the Jinggang Mountain headquarters, he was captured and accused of being a spy by the New Beida students who stood guard. Under intense interrogation he was beaten repeatedly to make him divulge information, such as the location of the tunnels and other details about the fortifications. The beatings were so cruel that he died of his injuries. Liu Wei was thus the third student killed by New Beida supporters, for shortly before, a young man named Ying Wenjie had been similarly caught, interrogated, and beaten to death. These events shocked the whole campus community, inured though we were to violence by the early summer of 1968, and persuaded still more people to support the Jinggang Mountain side.

One night very late I saw a light in Tang Dan's room and found her making a flower wreath out of crumpled paper and silk, all in white. On the testimonial ribbons that hung from each side, she had written, "For the martyr Liu Wei, from your comrade-in-arms Tang Dan." She had known the young man only slightly, but she sat gazing at her memorial, lost in thought. I realized at that moment that my daughter, though only fifteen, was now fully grown, that she had her own views, her own imperatives, her own life. My emotions were a complex mixture of sympathy for her grief, pride in her fervent commitment to a cause, and anxiety about her future. She told me that evening that she had decided to join the young people within the Jinggang Mountain stronghold, that she would participate in their final battle. I urged her instead to continue providing food from the outside, insisting that this was a crucial task, but tears welled in her eyes as she told me passionately that she would fight to the end beside her valiant comrades. All I could do was urge her to consider again how she could best contribute to their struggle, and tell her to be careful.

Not long after Liu Wei's memorial service in early June, Nie Yuanzi carried out the first part of her threat and turned off the electricity in the Jinggang Mountain buildings. Undaunted, the students under siege, only two hundred and fifty strong now that all but the most courageous had left, refused to surrender, and at two o'clock the next morning took action themselves. First a team slipped through the doors and overpowered the unsuspecting New Beida guards, locking them in a room. Then a second team sprinkled the adjacent Haidian Street with baskets of tiny dried pea-shaped beans, a defensive tactic characteristic of battle scenes in traditional Chinese novels. Finally, two young men set out to restore the electric power. Carrying a large covered basket specially woven by their comrades and a rope fitted with a pulley device made by the Earth faction students who controlled the workshops at the Geology Institute, one person used a ladder to climb up the nearest utility pole and affix the pulley while the other sat in the basket, allowing himself to be hoisted to the top. Midway up, however, the pulley broke, plunging him to the pavement. Taking great risk, another Jinggang Mountain loyalist grabbed a ladder and climbed to the top of the pole where, despite the hail

of missiles from New Beida slingshots, he managed expertly to disconnect the high voltage wires and attach a second lead that would
provide electricity to the besieged building.

By then the New Beida leadership had been alerted and many
students had rushed to the scene. The beans were so slippery, however, that no one could get close to the pole. It had taken nearly
twenty minutes to connect the buildings to the high voltage wire
and convert it to regular current, a feat accomplished by the technical workers, engineers, and science students inside the Jinggang
Mountain headquarters. Suddenly all three buildings' lights blazed
simultaneously, and everyone cheered so wildly that I could hear
the shouts from my house. The New Beida loudspeakers crackled
with the frantic announcement that its members had been attacked,
a tactic to muster supporters. Hearing the shouts, Tang Dan and I
went outside. When she dashed off to learn what had happened, I
worried that some harm might befall her, but in a short while she
returned with exuberant reports of victory. I shared her excitement, marveling at what these young people could accomplish. My
generation had always been obedient, had endured whatever befell
them, but these young people were different. They would resist,
they would struggle for what they believed in, they would even
fight, and I admired their resourcefulness, their determination,
their courage.

This event received great publicity, and many people said it
caused Nie Yuanzi to be criticized by Chairman Mao, whose instructions stressed unity, whereas she, by cutting off the electricity, had fostered greater antagonism. Seemingly she dared not attempt such a confrontational tactic again or increase the pressure
on her adversaries, for her threats were heard no more. Moreover,
her aggressive methods had aroused sympathy for the Jinggang
Mountain side from people previously unallied with either faction.
Still the hostilities continued, however, and no one could see an
end or a resolution.

For several months we had been hearing reports of the success
of the army and workers' propaganda teams sent to several important Beijing factories riven by factional fighting. Instructed to pro-
pagandize Mao Zedong thought, those teams were supposed to

unify the warring factions and thus restore order and revive production. In our study meetings every morning we discussed the propaganda teams' accomplishments, always glowingly reported in the press, to determine whether a similar cessation of hostilities could be accomplished on our own campus. Just as a bowl of water must be kept level to prevent it from spilling, so the two sides must now be treated equally, charged the editorials.

As we studied the newspaper accounts and evaluated the achievements of the propaganda teams, I felt renewed admiration for Chairman Mao. Having used the power of the students to ignite the flames of revolution, he now had turned to the workers and soldiers. Like many intellectuals, I had a high opinion of the PLA, for I remembered gratefully the liberation of Beijing and the triumphant entry of the soldiers through the Qianmen Gate. I also respected the workers, believing them to be the true proletariat and wanting to expand my relationships with them. Like many others, I felt optimistic that this combined force would restore order and bring an end to the factional battles.

But not everyone shared my enthusiasm. Especially on the neighboring Qinghua campus, Red Guard opposition to these intruders, this new group of nursemaids, was violent, as my father described to me in a shocked voice one night in late July. He had been taking his customary daily walk near the university that morning when he saw a huge red banner carried by a group of workers. Divided into two teams, they were shouting their determination to persuade each faction to lay down its arms, to use reason not violence. But Qinghua's Heaven faction, also named Jinggang Mountain and led by the fiery Kuai Dafu, decided to deny these mediators access to the campus, and assaulted the workers with rocks, spears, and hand grenades. Five of the unarmed workers were killed in the fray, hundreds of others were injured.

How could those defenseless workers, Chairman Mao's own representatives, be attacked so brutally, my father asked, and we all began to wonder whether even this tactic could bring an end to the bitter fighting. The next night, long after we had gone to bed, we heard a car's loudspeaker demanding, "Kuai Dafu, where are you? Chairman Mao wants to meet with you. He has something to tell you. Please return to your university." Later we learned that Chairman Mao had summoned the city's five major Red Guard leaders to a meeting, and that he criticized them very harshly for having divided the people and caused so much bloodshed and destruction. Then suddenly everything quieted down. Just as in a cockfight, people said, once a cock fails, his comb falls over and he puts up no more resistance.

That same week everyone from Beida came out with gongs and drums to welcome the soldiers and workers, who had arrived at our gate quite suddenly, a tactic designed to prevent opposition by the Red Guards. The teams were soon divided into small groups, one for each department, usually with a PLA member as the leader. We all hoped we would now see an end to the fighting, and a resumption of classes. I was again convinced that a new future was not far off. The siege of the Jinggang Mountain headquarters had already been lifted, the young people were able to come and go freely without fear of being kidnapped, and now both sides were required to turn in their spears, pikes, knives, and slingshots. At last someone was responsible for what was happening, someone was in charge, whereas previously there had been no place to turn for help, no authority detached from the rivalry. Thus people felt safer than they had for a long time. My optimism extended to thoughts about my own family's fate, for I trusted that the propaganda teams, as outsiders, would view the entire situation anew and undoubtedly more fairly than had the Preparatory Committee. Perhaps Lao Tang's label as an enemy would even be removed.

The leader of the army propaganda team, Wang Lianlong, was a vice-political commissar of the elite 8341 PLA unit responsible for guarding Chairman Mao and his compound at Zhongnanhai, his high position signaling the importance that the Central Committee once again attached to Beida. Five factories had provided the workers to lead this new movement on our campus, the largest number coming from the famous February Seventh Locomotive Plant, while the soldiers had been sent both from the 8341 unit and from the 68th division in Hebei province, thus representing the central and the local government. Even in my department, at the basic level, an army cadre, the political instructor of an 8341 company, had been put in charge, so we all knew that the team's mission was considered of the greatest significance, and found its authority very imposing. When the Beida team leader announced the dissolution of the cow shed and the dismissal of all those still imprisoned, as well as an immediate ban on any use of weapons, any beating or physical punishment, the army's presence seemed to confirm people's hopes. Still, we knew that reunification would be difficult to accomplish, that neither side had relinquished its desire for power, and that negotiations about how to create some new organization to run the university had reached no conclusion.

After the team began its work in my department, we all assembled in a classroom every morning to discuss Chairman Mao's instructions and consider how best to implement them. The most emphatic directives declared that we must all unite together and conduct revolution while returning to our studies, and that the working class would thenceforth be the leaders, with the intellectuals receiving reeducation from the workers, peasants, and soldiers. Whenever a new teaching from Chairman Mao was announced, there would be a parade on campus with people beating gongs and cheering. We would all go outside and shout our support, perhaps two or three times a week, often late at night after some friend at a newspaper office had conveyed the latest development by telephone. We would then dutifully get out of bed to join the demonstrations, for people still competed to profess their loyalty and devotion to Chairman Mao.

Once the propaganda teams were established, a movement to Clean the Class Ranks began. It was deemed essential before the university could reopen to discover who was trustworthy and could be allowed to teach and who was truly an enemy. Since so many people during the Cultural Revolution had been designated as "black gang members" and "academic warlords," it was difficult for the propaganda teams to determine who to place in positions of responsibility once again. As they supervised the three-stage process of struggle, criticism, and reform that was to terminate the Cultural Revolution, these carefully selected groups of soldiers and workers were officially accomplishing the transition back to ordinary life. The Clean the Class Ranks movement, we were told, would be conducted very strictly; the lessons learned at Beida and at Qinghua—as always, designated "breakthrough points"—would subsequently be applied to other universities around the country.

A few days later we learned just how strictly this new campaign would be implemented when we were suddenly instructed to move out of our homes and into the dormitories, where teachers, cadres, and students would live together, organized by department, taking their meals from the central dining hall. The announced reason for sequestering us on campus was that we must all concentrate single-mindedly on the new movement, undisturbed by the distractions of daily life. The unspoken reason was that we could be more easily controlled and the exchange of information and opinions prevented. Since four people were assigned to the same room, not only would it be impossible for anyone to speak privately, but roommates were expected to supervise each other and report any suspicious behavior or attempts at private conversation. The propaganda teams' announcement was met with reluctance, since arranging for the care of our homes and families was difficult, and most people did not relish the idea of such collective living. Grateful that the propaganda teams had put an end to the Red Guards' license to abuse teachers and cadres in whatever way they wished, however, we continued to hope that the presence of the soldiers and workers would improve the situation of the intellectuals, despite this ominous initial development.

My immediate concern was with practical matters, like the feeding of my children, since Lao Tang would be similarly housed with the philosophy department members. My only choice was to ask my sister-in-law, who would be staying in the dormitory assigned to library workers, but who still employed an *ayi* with Lao Tang's mother's money to help with their family's meals, if my children could stay in our old home. I was relieved when my request was accepted, as then I could just lock our house and move in with the others from my department.

While we were all trying to make such necessary preparations, something happened to alter the atmosphere of trust and optimism. It was perhaps three days before we were to move into the dormitories that a new directive from Chairman Mao was announced one evening. Unlike other such instructions, this one was never printed in the newspapers but was passed by word of mouth from the upper levels of the leadership down to the people. The bourgeois revisionist viewpoint of intellectuals must be seriously criticized, we were told, "to make such people understand their parasitic position in society." Intellectuals, especially the older, influential ones like Jian Bozan, would "first be criticized and second provided with a means of subsistence." Initially I thought this was good news, indicating a more relaxed attitude toward intellectuals, who would at least be allowed the necessities of life. It was said that they could keep 60 *yuan* per month as a salary, enough to live simply, and I felt relief that they would not be beaten in struggle sessions or subjected to abuse any more. Then I heard the shocking news of Jian Bozan's suicide.

A close friend of Lao Tang's father and a vice-president of the university, Jian, the man who had led the column of enemies from my building in the June 18 parade, had long been respected as an eminent Marxist historian and a committed member of the Communist Party. During the War of Resistance he had taken substantial risks under Guomindang rule, thereafter devoting his life to the service of the revolution. Then in 1965 he was criticized. His theory that historical development results not from moments of violent popular struggle but from the landlords' periodic peaceful concessions to the peasants' demands was said to indicate his opposition to the Party, indeed to Chairman Mao's own view of history. Because of this past criticism, Jian was an obvious target for the students at the start of the Cultural Revolution, when he was further accused of being an important link in the "black line" because of his work with Liu Shaoqi in the Guomindang-controlled areas in the war against Japan.

Jian and his wife had subsequently been removed from their comfortable house on campus and assigned a small, shabby, one-room structure on the same lane as the Mongolian princess. I often passed by their house and could see the difficulty of their living conditions. They had no kitchen, for example, and had to keep their coal stove outside, underneath the porch roof just beside the street, because of the danger from fumes if they were to cook inside. Just to harass this elderly couple, neighborhood children would shout, "Since you are counter-revolutionaries, it is better that you don't eat," and throw handfuls of water or dirt onto their stove to put out the cooking fire. Following these insults, Jian's wife would have to go through the tedious and costly task of using more fuel to relight the stove.

When the propaganda teams had first arrived on campus, we learned from a friend in the history department, they had visited Jian to ask what they could do to improve his situation. He had replied that he needed just two things, first to have the children stop putting out his cooking fire, and second to have his research materials returned. In a few days Jian and his wife were moved to a better house with two rooms and a shared kitchen, and their salary was increased to 200 *yuan* per month. Everyone thought that their life would begin to improve, but then the new policy toward intellectuals was announced with Jian Bozan mentioned by name as an example.

Although he had endured the attacks of the Red Guards, the harshness of his living conditions, the insults of passersby, and repudiation by his own children, the announcement by Chairman Mao had apparently been more than he was willing to bear. In China a strongly established tradition dictates that if you do not want to cooperate with the government, you do not accept its favors or the food it offers you. A famous story, for example, relates the defiance of an ancient Shang dynasty prince who, when the empire was destroyed, went into the mountains to eat wild ferns, weeds, and seeds, living as a recluse rather than accept the favors of the conquering rulers. This principle, known as "the refusal of food from an immoral government," has been a precedent respected by intellectuals for centuries. Thus Chairman Mao's new instruction, I guessed, was an intentional insult, an effort to humiliate intellectuals in order to prevent them from resuming their traditional role as a potent force to criticize government policy. Jian must have felt so deeply offended by the implication that from then on he would simply be kept alive, being fed by the state, that he had made the strongest protest conceivable.

The very next day he and his wife were found lying side by side on their bed, dead from an overdose of sleeping pills. His favorite student, a friend of Lao Tang's, told me sadly that he had seen the bodies, their clothes neatly arranged, their faces peaceful and in an attitude of repose. Everyone talked about this tragic event, which began to alter people's attitudes about the presence of the soldiers and workers on campus. Initially, the propaganda teams' arrival had been viewed as presaging a time of greater relaxation, a termination to the intellectuals' plight, but now we feared that a new period of oppression might follow.

Sharing my grief with Lao Tang, I wondered aloud what it would be like to make Jian Bozan's choice, what he would have thought about, what sentiments he would have expressed to his wife in the hours before they ended their lives. Joint suicides had happened before, of course; Fu Lei, for example, the famous translator of Romain Rolland and father of pianist Fu Tsong, had committed suicide with his wife amid the terrible violence of 1966. Neither of us could imagine making such a decision to die together, but we saw the recurrence of such tragedies as a kind of omen, auguring that the army's presence would not be so beneficial as we had hoped nor the resolution of our country's problems so easily achieved.

It was with this tragic event fresh in our minds that we began life in the dormitories. The first stage of the cleansing of class ranks, the stage of struggle, would decide who was in fact an enemy and where the necessary lines should be drawn. Our initial goal, instructed the propaganda teams, was to ferret out the enemies in our midst and make them stink so badly that they could never exert their influence over the people again. When this task was accomplished, we were told, we would attend to the problems within the ranks of the people, engaging in self-criticism and arriving at an understanding of the correct path to follow. Then we could move from the stage of criticism to the stage of reform and devise a new system that would enable us to resume our regular lives, marking the end of the Cultural Revolution. With this goal in mind, we began the process of identifying our enemies.

When the movement began, however, it was so fiery, so violent, so opposite to my expectations, that at first I couldn't believe what was happening. Although the Red Guards could now only execute decisions made by the propaganda teams, they were still allowed to conduct the struggle sessions, to put enemies on a platform, make them admit their crimes, force them into the jet plane position, and isolate them from the masses. Not only did we all fear how we might be treated if singled out as such targets of struggle, but even more we feared the ultimate consequences. Previously, if the Red Guards branded you a counter-revolutionary, you knew that the verdict was unofficial, but now if the 8341 PLA leader assigned you this label, your fate was officially, permanently sealed, and you would spend your life outside the ranks of the people. Contributing to this constant pressure was the vagueness of the criteria for designating counter-revolutionaries. We knew that in his famous essay "On the Correct Handling of Contradictions" Chairman Mao had defined six ways to identify an enemy, but these criteria could still be very flexibly applied. An enemy was said to be "one who opposed the Communist Party," for example, but no one knew what kind of activity or attitude would be construed as opposing the Party. The uncertainty was constantly intimidating.

One morning when our department meeting opened at eight o'clock, a very capable teacher, a specialist in the history of the Chinese novel, was told to read a quotation from Chairman Mao. This was normal procedure, for always people would read quotations in turn and discussion would follow. That morning the atmosphere was particularly charged, as no one could anticipate what would follow or who would be accused as an enemy. Afraid that he might be the next victim, this Guo Yanli mispronounced one syllable, and instead of reading, "Chairman Mao is our great leader, our proletarian revolutionary teacher," he inadvertently switched one syllable and pronounced the word "bourgeois" teacher. Immediately the team leader jumped up, declaring that this was exactly the kind of counter-revolutionary person that must be dragged out, that this teacher was an enemy pretending to be a loyal Party member, that we now could see his true face.

Guo had good reason to be so nervous. Perhaps a year and a half before, seeing so many people on campus being labeled as enemies, so many old cadres jailed and maltreated, he had grown skeptical about the Cultural Revolution and had voiced his concern one night to his wife. The present conditions, he had remarked, reminded him of a historical novel describing the Han or Song dynasty. In those ancient times when a person was named emperor, he wanted to rule absolutely and to get rid of any who had known him previously, just as those who now wielded political power wanted to destroy any who had known them before they achieved prominence. Also in her thirties, his wife worked in a publishing house and was a committed Red Guard in her own work unit. Frightened to discover that her husband harbored such disloyal thoughts and believing that such suspicions were exceedingly harmful for a Party member, she sought advice from the vice-secretary of our department, a woman she had known when she was herself a student. Her husband was known to all as a loyal and reliable person, honest and sincere in both his academic and political work and always faithful to the Party. Thus the vice-secretary had taken no action, advising the anxious wife just to urge her husband to overcome such incorrect and dangerous thoughts.

Aware that his wife had talked to this vice-secretary and revealed his early misgivings about the Cultural Revolution, and that the team leader surely would have been briefed by the department leaders about any who concealed dangerous thoughts, Guo had been unusually nervous that morning when called upon to read. After the team leader shouted that such a mistake was not an accident but a revelation of true feelings, another person in the department, someone trusted by this leader, stood up to say that Guo clearly had opposed the Cultural Revolution. A third accuser, not even a Party member but someone who had earlier been criticized for following the "white and expert way" and who undoubtedly wanted to protect himself in this new campaign, stood up to declare that Guo was indeed a devious person. Once when they had been watching television together and some people on the screen had begun the loyalty dance to Chairman Mao, Guo had walked away, indicating his disapproval. And furthermore, this accuser continued, one morning when everyone else had stood in formation to sing Chairman Mao's quotations and shout, "Long live Chairman

Mao, Good health to Lin Biao," waving their Red Books together in rhythm, Guo Yanli had not joined in the slogans.

Following this indictment one of the perhaps ten young activist teachers in the department who were completely trusted by the propaganda team declared that Guo Yanli was truly a counter-revolutionary and must be placed under supervision. Others shouted, "Make him stand up," and grabbed his arms to force him into the jet plane position. I saw his face beaded with sweat, tears welling up in his eyes. He knew his fate. He was roughly led away and locked in a small room in the dormitory. Having wanted only to help him understand the Cultural Revolution and return to the revolutionary way, and hoping the Party would help him not to make a mistake in the new movement, his wife regretted this outcome bitterly, having never expected that her confidential words would be used as a condemnation. Later she was allowed to take him some clothing and a bedroll, and people said the two clasped each other tightly in a tearful embrace.

Most people in 1966 had not dared to criticize the Cultural Revolution, even to their spouses or dearest friends, for fear of some unforeseen consequences. But after the PLA arrived, when we thought the violence was over, that intellectuals had less to fear, Guo's example was chilling. Widely regarded for his scholarship and always eschewing political entanglements, Guo had nevertheless been designated an enemy, his years of obedience ignored. Even though he had never expressed any misgivings openly, he was accused of having reactionary thoughts. The Cultural Revolution must influence not just people's bodies but their hearts as well, we were told. It was becoming clear that the propaganda teams' unspoken goal was the permanent destruction of the whole group of teachers and cadres formerly esteemed by Lu Ping. Guo was said to be one of those turtles that Chairman Mao had charged lay deeply buried in the mud at Beida.

The next morning when another person, someone even less politically involved than Guo, was branded an enemy, we all grew increasingly nervous about our own fate. This man, Mei Kewen, a successful scholar of experimental phonetics, was highly respected, and when he was declared a counter-revolutionary, we were all stunned. Seeing our surprise, the team leader announced triumphantly that this should be a lesson for us, that even a person who had never spoken about political matters could be an enemy in his heart, in his blood. Such inner convictions could not long be concealed, he warned, and we should all realize that remaining silent would not protect us, that our true feelings would inevitably make themselves known.

Mei was being accused because of a single comment he had made to his roommate in November 1968, after Liu Shaoqi had been branded a "big traitor," a "big thief in the working class," and a "big spy," triple allegations that were widely publicized in the media. Mei had remarked aphoristically that when one is in the ocean of public office, he sometimes floats very high and sometimes sinks very low, just as Liu Shaoqi had once been the leader of the nation and was now despised as a traitor. Presumably to establish himself as a loyal member of the department, this roommate had repeated Mei's single sentence to the propaganda team leader, claiming that Mei apparently did not agree with the Party. As a result, the leader proclaimed Mei an active counter-revolutionary and had him taken away to the same small room as Guo, using him as an example that no one can escape from politics.

Each day when we went to the central dining hall for lunch and dinner, we would see the enemies that had been thus far ferreted out from each department being marched past in a line to get their food, supervised by Red Guards carrying spears. Such treatment is considered very serious in China, since it isolates this group from the rest of the people, humiliating them by displaying them as outcasts and separating them from the masses. At every meal we would see them, these people who had always before been respected members of our departments. The propaganda teams were proud of their successes, proclaiming that they had picked out many turtles from the mud and taking special pride in displaying enemies who had never been previously suspected of any political error. It was not the people already identified as capitalist roaders who concerned them, for they were not interested in "beating dead tigers," but to find fault with someone new was deemed an important way of warning the rest of us to be obedient and banish any dissident thoughts from our minds.

In my department they accused eight people who had never been attacked before, concentrating on four who were academically distinguished and labeling them all "active counter-revolutionaries." Although the evidence was transparently flimsy, the most brilliant, loyal, and obedient intellectuals were now being condemned as counter-revolutionaries. Receiving instructions from Jiang Qing and her associates, the propaganda teams, we guessed, were intent upon destroying permanently the power of any potential opposition. The unspoken goal of the struggle stage of the Clean the Class Ranks movement at Beida apparently was to gain control over the black clique formerly associated with Lu Ping, the group that Jiang Qing feared and hated the most.

It was a confusing time, violent and terrifying. Each one of the enemies must be struggled against, so the propaganda team divided the departments into groups, combining students and teachers together to indicate that none of the older intellectuals could be trusted, and standing those who had been accused in front of these groups for criticism. The hostility in the air was unmistakable, but in my department the meetings were conducted without much physical abuse. The accused teachers were made to stand and admit their guilt, while others criticized them and cried out slogans. The intellectuals could of course never provide satisfactory responses to the exaggerated charges.

Each day we attended three of these sessions. From eight o'clock to eleven-thirty each morning we read Chairman Mao's quotations and discussed their meaning, after which an enemy would be identified, made to stand up, and questioned to extract some admission of guilt. Then from two o'clock until five and again from seven o'clock until ten we repeated the procedure, sometimes with the same enemy. Because the accused persons had so little to reveal, they would just stand silently while the students shouted at them and tried to force them to confess, threatening that if they would only admit their wrongs, the policy toward them would be lenient, whereas if they refused, it would be very strict. When no one could make the enemy speak further, we would read more quotations from Chairman Mao.

I was assigned, along with three other teachers, to a group of twenty-five second-year students. At every meeting we teachers would remain silent, waiting nervously for our turn to be attacked, while the students conducted the criticism. During this first stage of the movement, however, I was never singled out, since officially I had taken off my rightist cap and was classed on the side of the people. Like Meng Kun, I was considered a dead tiger.

Each night when I returned to the dormitory I would try to comfort my roommate, a young worker from Shanghai who had completed just three years of middle school. She was the department's Party vice-secretary, the person who had reported Guo Yanli's misgivings, and was just my age. After coming to Beida, perhaps because she was somewhat awed by her surroundings, she had been very obedient to anyone in power, a loyal follower of Nie Yuanzi, a member of New Beida, and the Preparatory Committee's representative in our department. Now she too had become a target, accused of many kinds of wrongdoing and of desiring to seize power away from Chairman Mao's propaganda team. She had always been so obedient that during the Cultural Revolution she would put her small son to bed, then lock him in the house in order not to miss the evening meetings. Now she repeated to me the same words over and over every night: "How could I be opposed to Chairman Mao or to the working class when I am a member of that class, I am a worker?" I could not reply consolingly that I knew she was loyal, because then I would be going against the opinion of the propaganda team, and I knew she would tell them anything I said; I could not profess that she was indeed opposed to the working class, because I knew that was not true. So night after night I would simply counsel her to be patient, to wait until later when everything would become clear. Still she reiterated her questions, utterly preoccupied, and both of us grew very depressed.

The propaganda team accused her of trusting in Nie Yuanzi and warned her to change this dangerous viewpoint, claiming that she was responsible for everything that had happened under the Cultural Revolution leadership. For several days the team members harangued her, the students shouted at her, and she made a self-criticism. I guessed that their purpose was the repudiation of everyone who had been loyal to Nie Yuanzi, fearful of future opposition to their authority, a situation that made me recall the land reform period when anyone previously influential in a village had to be overturned.

The main enemies were treated much more seriously than such people as this department vice-secretary. Those people identified as having "big problems" had been assigned individual groups to handle each of their cases. Shortly after the new movement began, the propaganda team leader had announced that those who signed the 32-person poster were all counter-revolutionaries, their purpose the seizure of power over the entire university, their goal to lead Beida away from Party policy and make it return to the capitalist road. This was a crime, the 8341 cadres declared, indicating that some people still wanted Lu Ping's dynasty restored. Lao Tang was, of course, among them.

My dormitory was close to my mother-in-law's house, so often I would dash over to see my children if time permitted after a meeting had ended. One day I heard shouts from the central dining hall and looked through a window to see what was happening. To my horror, Lao Tang was standing on the platform, his arms twisted behind him, his head thrust down, his body bent nearly double. I was stunned to see him there, alongside Lu Ping, Feng Youlan, and others of the most prominent academics on campus, being singled out as a "big enemy," far more important than when he was just one among many black gang members. In this mass struggle session being conducted jointly by the history and philosophy departments, the victims were being treated with unusual cruelty. Red Guards were forcing all of their arms up high behind their backs, shoving their heads down very low. Never before had Lao Tang been physically abused to this degree, and the expression on his face was an indescribable mixture of pain, fear, and sadness.

My heart felt icy cold, frozen in my body. The students were sitting on the floor, lustily raising their fists and shouting slogans. It was a nightmarish scene. I didn't want Lao Tang to see me, knowing that would only increase his humiliation, so I turned away. Unable to face my children, I walked in a daze back to my dormitory room. How distant my recent optimism seemed. With Lao Tang singled out as a major enemy, there could be no hope for my family. This decision had been reached by Chairman Mao's personal guards and meant that our fate was permanently sealed.

The Clean the Class Ranks movement had defied my every expectation. I had hoped for a turning point, an end to the cruelty, an improvement in the situation of intellectuals, but instead more people were being attacked than in the earlier stages of the Cultural Revolution. In the countryside as well the violence was continuing. A friend of Lao Tang's, whose parents were peasants in Daxing county not far from Beijing, had told us of terrible brutality in one production team. The local militia had in one night killed all of the "five bad types," along with their family members, even their children, supposedly to cleanse the village of its enemies. This action was immediately condemned by the government, we read in one of the small Red Guard newspapers, but nonetheless it struck fear in our hearts. Even at the height of the red terror we had never known of such a massacre.

The day after seeing Lao Tang's abuse I went with a heavy heart to visit my children, concealing from them any news about their father and trying to reassure them about their own daily concerns. I knew they were becoming steadily more discontented with their own situation, for one day Tang Dan had burst into my dormitory saying that she could not bear to live under her aunt's roof any longer. She couldn't stand having to listen to any more complaints about how our family's problems had made her aunt's work in the library difficult, or to observe her aunt's rudeness to her grandmother, or to cope with her two young cousins. Tang Shuang was also angry. He had taken his pet rabbit with him to his aunt's house, but she abhorred this animal and one day had found him giving his pet not the tough outer cabbage leaves to eat but some tender center ones. In a rage she had screamed at him for offering such precious food to an animal, leaving him greatly offended. Because of all these problems, Tang Dan insisted that she and her brother must move back home, declaring that she would take her grandmother with them. Finally, I agreed reluctantly that she and Tang Shuang

245

could live alone, but I could not allow my mother-in-law to depend on them, as I knew she needed the *ayi*'s special care.

Not long afterwards, when the daily struggle meetings had been taking place for perhaps a month, it became obvious to everyone that this tactic would never produce satisfactory results. Not only were we exhausted from the constant tension and uncertainty, but we were all growing increasingly concerned about our homes and our children. Since it was no secret that all the adult members of the campus were sequestered in the dormitories, many homes had already been robbed. Finally, after the propaganda teams had been besieged with multiple requests, they decided that everyone except the enemies could return home to sleep and just attend the three meetings each day. This decision created a slight relaxation in the tension, and we were told to move on to the second stage of the campaign.

Lao Tang was still confined in the separate room in his dormitory set aside for enemies, but it was only about two weeks later that he was also, without explanation, allowed to return home. Perhaps the leaders had decided they had collected too many enemies, although Lao Tang and the others were told sternly that their cases were not finished, that there was as yet no final conclusion, that they would be subjected to an ongoing investigation to observe how they responded to criticism, that their behavior would influence their final verdict. But at least we were all living at home together once again.

The decision to move people back to their residences didn't stop the wave of petty thefts on campus. One day when I returned from a meeting, I found our door ajar, the lock broken, and all of our storage boxes overturned. It was just after the sixteenth of the month, the day that salaries and ration tickets for grain and oil were distributed. The house was empty, I couldn't find the children, and I felt totally at a loss about what to do. In a few minutes Tang Dan appeared with two men from the campus security office who had come to examine the evidence. They took photographs and fingerprints, and I showed them where my salary and all of our ration tickets had been taken from a drawer. When Lao Tang returned, he discovered that his father's gold pocket watch, a prize

Tang Yongtong had received at Qinghua in his student days, was also missing. Tang Shuang found his cherished radio gone, a set that he had painstakingly assembled from parts purchased with great difficulty at local markets. The security officers said that they would investigate the crime, but meanwhile, since our bank accounts were still frozen, we had to borrow some cash to cover our month's expenses.

Many other people had been robbed as well. To our surprise and relief, however, our own case was solved after two months. The thief, the son of a Qinghua professor, was ordered to return our possessions. Some of the money and all of the ration tickets had been spent, but we got back the watch, the radio, and some sweaters, so we felt very grateful. The boy, like many other unsupervised teenagers who had turned to petty theft, was sent to jail for his crime.

This was a period of great stress for everyone. Sometimes the night meetings would last until eleven o'clock, and I often walked home with a neighbor, Lao Wu. To prevent people from asking the next day what we had been discussing, we never spoke together, but one very cold night, perhaps in February 1969, when most of the others were riding bicycles, something I dared not attempt in the dark, Lao Wu suddenly spoke, as if talking to himself. "Why am I regarded as a counter-revolutionary? I cannot understand this accusation when I have never wanted to harm either the Party or our country. Do you really view me as an enemy?" A coal miner before coming to the university, he had begun his studies much later than I, although we were the same age. Although he had had some doubts about Lin Biao's ability to lead the nation, he explained in low tones, and had once remarked that Lin Biao's health might perhaps prevent him from carrying on as Chairman Mao's successor, he had always considered himself a loyal member of the working class. He had certainly never tried to bring harm to Lin Biao or the Party.

To my surprise, Lao Wu continued to speak. "I always knew in my heart that you were not a rightist," he said, "and I sometimes wondered what you thought about during those years, how you managed to accept the accusations, how you dealt with the situation of being classed as an enemy." Lao Wu had always seemed very self-contained to me, and I would never have thought he would speak so genuinely, so openly. Above his face mask I could see only his eyes, so hollow, so filled with sadness and disappointment. I was touched by his sincerity and wanted to provide some support, some alleviation of his distress.

"Sometimes you cannot help what happens to you," I replied, "but it was very painful for me to be peeled off from the main trunk of the Party like a piece of bark." I tried to encourage him, saying, "This is a revolutionary time, and in such moments of upheaval people cannot be as careful as they should," explaining to him my metaphor of the surgical procedure and commenting gently, "it is inevitable for some healthy tissue to be excised along with a cancerous growth. Like me," I continued, "you are a piece of that healthy tissue which has been cut away and sacrificed for the revolution." To my amazement, Lao Wu wept as we walked. It was so unusual to see a man cry that I was frightened and urged him not to worry so much. It was dismaying to see such a strong man reduced to the tears of a small child, and I turned sadly toward my house, understanding what he felt and carrying on my own shoulders the weight of his burden. From that evening on we felt a kind of bond with each other. Although we would sometimes chat on our walks home, we never again mentioned anything about politics, as such topics were simply too dangerous.

As the second stage of the campaign gathered momentum, the students turned their attention to us teachers. Meng Kun was the first in my group to be accused, his indictment as a traitor to the Communist Party based on the same evidence that had earlier caused him to be beaten by the Red Guards and confined in the cow shed. As the students rehearsed his arrest by the Guomindang, his release, and his subsequent aloofness from Party activities, they demanded that he admit his mistakes and confess his guilt. He never responded. For three days they accused him and criticized his famous study of modern Chinese literature, and all the while he kept silent. When they had finished, they turned to me.

In threatening tones they declared that I had been a rightist before and that they had done me a great favor in taking off my cap, but it was clear that I still opposed the Party, so they must put my cap back on again. I had opposed the Three Red Banners from the podium, they charged, and had encouraged students to denounce the commune movement and thus to disagree with Chairman Mao's thought. By praising a reactionary student essay, I had demonstrated my wish to poison the minds of the younger generation. By this time the students' ire was aroused, their allegations greatly exaggerated, their language vehement. I had heard all of their accusations before, the evidence seemed irrefutable, I could think of no defense. Believing that they had the power to reimpose my cap and class me as an enemy any time, I grew ever more depressed. When they ordered me to stand up and listen to their criticism, all of my resilience, all of my inner reserves, seemed to ebb away. Not only Lao Tang was an enemy, but I was too.

That afternoon as I headed home under a darkening winter sky, my gaze fell upon the flagpole that had been the gift from my graduating class in 1952. The once gleaming marble base was now scratched and dusty and no one any longer thought of flying a flag. Suddenly all the strength left my body, I could not continue. Tired of the whole ordeal of living, I thought for the first time about death, wondering if that might save my children from ruin. Perhaps if their parents were dead, the shadow we had cast on them would be removed and their future would not be like ours, empty of all hope. As I sank onto those marble steps, I tried to remind myself that life had not so long ago seemed full of promise. But the happiness and confidence of those earlier years was now scarcely within the reach of memory.

Overcome by desolation, I cried bitterly, weeping not only for myself and my children, but for my country, for all the waste, the loss, the suffering of those fourteen years. Even when my mother died I had stifled my emotions, but at this moment I was so exhausted from the pressure of the recent weeks that I broke down completely. Finally, I roused myself and headed home, knowing that another criticism meeting awaited me that evening and that in the meantime I must cook for my children.

An hour later I was back in the classroom listening to more accusing shouts, more threats about reimposing my cap. Through it all I sat motionless, having nothing to say. Yet a third meeting was devoted to my case the next day, and again the students reviewed my whole history, stressing the reasons I had been named a rightist and the way I had ignored the Party's generosity in removing my cap. The next morning they moved on to the next victim.

We four teachers had no recourse but to sit passively, submissively, knowing that since the propaganda teams were the personal representatives of Chairman Mao, their verdict would be final. Over and over I wondered what punishment would be given to me this time and whether I would spend the rest of my years in isolation as an enemy of the people. Then, like the earlier stage of the campaign, this one was suddenly declared finished, and we were instructed to begin considering how to reform our university. For the moment I seemed to be safe from immediate danger, but I could summon no enthusiasm. The memory of all that our flagpole had once symbolized remained painfully lodged in my heart.

Learning from Hardship

THE CLEAN THE Class Ranks movement, unable to accomplish the transition from revolutionary upheaval back to normal life, had lost its momentum by the early summer of 1969, and we began to hear rumors, nervously exchanged, about further changes. People continually discussed the likelihood that the entire Beida community would be moved to a May 7 cadre school, in accordance with the directive issued by Chairman Mao on that date in 1966 instructing that intellectuals should be reeducated by the workers, peasants, and soldiers. Called "the highest instruction to the people from Chairman Mao," this decree stated that intellectuals, presently unable to raise their own food or even distinguish grain from weeds, must undergo reform in the rural areas, the factories, and the army. Popular wisdom interpreted this to mean that we all would soon be sent down to the countryside.

In order that Chairman Mao's directive could be implemented, every university and government agency sent representatives to search for someplace to establish its cadre school. The task was difficult. Not only was all arable land in the countryside long since under cultivation, but the intrusion of such large numbers of urban intellectuals into established peasant communities seemed a virtual impossibility. Besides, the peasants opposed an influx of city dwellers, protesting that the newcomers would use up scarce food and land and provide only an unskilled and unnecessary labor force in return. Because the new policy would enable the propaganda teams to separate out any whom the leaders distrusted, to observe these people in a carefully controlled situation, and at the same time to clear the campuses and ministries of any who might obstruct thorough reform, the peasants' opposition was disregarded. Later the teams would be able to recall to the city those who had demonstrated their loyalty to Mao Zedong-thought and leave permanently exiled in the countryside any who might oppose the renovation of the old system. The policy was referred to as "preserving the cadres for later use."

A group of the army's propaganda team leaders at Beida and Qinghua returned to their native Jiangxi province in search of an appropriate cadre school site. Having fled with Mao Zedong from the Jiangxi soviet republic to Yan'an in the 1930s, these veteran soldiers hoped to find in the revolutionary base area some territory where the two university communities could be relocated. Finally, they selected an expanse of muddy ground adjacent to the vast Lake Poyang, a site that year after year had been inundated by late summer floods. The peasants had abandoned their efforts to reclaim this land because of the difficulty and expense of maintaining the thirty-foot-high dike they had built some years before along a mile or so of the shoreline. Recently the army had begun preliminary repairs of this huge mud retaining wall, and it was decided that our two universities would undertake a permanent reclamation project. At the end of 1968, the first group of workers and administrative staff, maybe fifty or more, had set out for Liyuzhou, named Carp County after the plentiful local fish, to assist with the repair of the dike and prepare for the arrival of the cadres and teachers.

In addition to the sick, the disabled, and the elderly whom Chairman Mao had exempted from such arduous reeducation projects, some specially chosen teachers and cadres, perhaps twenty percent of the faculty and staff, would remain on campus to deliberate ways of revolutionizing the system of education. These were usually people from the study groups already established for that purpose in each department, groups that were composed of supporters of Nie Yuanzi, opponents of Lu Ping, and activists in the

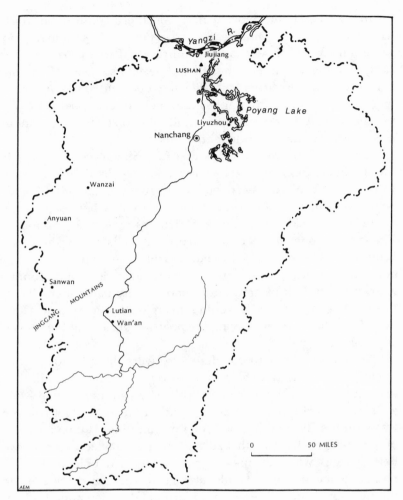

Jiangxi Province

Clean the Class Ranks movement. It was these groups who would work with the propaganda teams and supervise those students not yet assigned jobs or sent to the countryside. Perhaps because Lao Tang's mother was in poor health and needed someone to care for her, or perhaps because I had been very obedient in the preceding months, fearful that my rightist cap might be reimposed, my department leaders asked me if I would like to stay on the campus and assist with the educational reforms.

Lao Tang urged me to stay so that Tang Shuang could remain in the city in my care, but I hesitated and one day discussed my reservations with Lao Wu, my friend and neighbor. If I stayed, I knew I would remain in a very subordinate position, whereas if I went to the countryside, after my experience among the peasants in Zhaitang, I would surely be able to excel at the labor. Furthermore, I could be more relaxed in the countryside, away from the pressure of politics. Hearing of my doubts, the propaganda team responded angrily to my lack of gratitude, removing my name immediately from the list of those who would remain in the department. However, I was happy to be leaving the political tensions of the university behind.

The months prior to our departure were difficult, for no one knew how to anticipate the circumstances we would encounter, no one could predict the outcome of this new venture, no one could guess when or even whether we would return. My first concern was with the effect of this move on my children, but then I learned of the policy instructing that all sixteen- and nineteen-year-olds in Beijing, those who were the ages to have finished junior and senior middle school in 1969, would also go to the countryside. Even though Tang Dan had received no further education after graduating from primary school in 1966, she would be sent to the far northern province of Heilongjiang unless she wished to join relatives elsewhere in the countryside. A few young people, high officials' children, for example, were able to utilize the "back door" and get accepted into the army, but Tang Dan had no such connections. Her only alternative was to go with us to the cadre school in Jiangxi.

After long discussions about which option would be preferable, her desire for independence was decisive. Declaring that she didn't want to be a swallow always hovering around its nest, that she wanted to be an eagle soaring freely in the sky, she stated her intention to go with her fellow students to a military farm in remote Dedu county, some 130 miles from the Soviet border. The leaders of this farm were all men who, either because of behavior, attitude, or age, were considered unfit to remain in the army. The more I learned about her destination, the more anxious I became, but Tang Dan's mind was made up. When she was issued an army greatcoat as protection against the winter cold that commonly reached −40°C, she felt great pride, her revolutionary mission confirmed. Tang Dan was just sixteen and very small for her age. Knowing that unimagined hardships inevitably awaited her, I watched with sadness as she set off with her fellow students in the open trucks that would carry them to the railroad station, their young faces animated with the excitement and importance of their revolutionary venture.

Once Tang Dan had left, we turned our attention to practical arrangements. Some people, unwilling to pay their monthly rent for an indeterminate period of time, were giving up their homes and selling their furnishings and books, but we decided to live as inexpensively as possible in order to afford the rent for our house, not wanting to dispose of our library. The rent was a small sum, only 5 *yuan* per month, but we had no idea whether we would ever be able to return, so the decision to retain our home was a calculated risk. The other difficult choice was whether to take Tang Shuang with us to Jiangxi.

Since the land we would be working had all been reclaimed from the lake bottom, parasites posed a major health problem. Those blood flukes lived in snails and entered the human body through the pores, traveling via the blood to the bladder and intestines where they laid their eggs, causing the often fatal illness known as snail fever, or schistosomiasis. I had been to an educational exhibit concerning this danger, and I knew the symptoms, with the liver becoming hard, the abdomen distended, and the skin yellow. Because we would be working in the rice paddies with our feet bare, the risk of infection would be high, and we debated leaving Tang Shuang in Beijing with his grandmother. He pleaded to go with us, however, and in the end we decided not to separate what was left of our family.

In October 1969, while we were making our preparations, Lin Biao announced that the Soviet Union might at any time launch an attack on China and issued his "number one order" to prepare for war. Anyone not needed in the northern cities must be evacuated to the South, we were told, as North China would be the primary battlefield. We must be more disciplined than ever before, because only if the people resolutely obeyed all orders from the leadership would China be strong enough to resist its aggressor. No doubt this instruction was partly a device to make the people nervous and blindly acquiescent, but we sincerely believed that strict obedience was necessary to safeguard the security of our country. Thus when the specific order to leave our homes was finally given in November, we assumed that war was imminent and hastily packed up our belongings, locked the door of our house behind us, and climbed aboard the appointed train bound for Jiangxi province with the rest of our group.

My first impression of Liyuzhou was of a monochromatic yellow landscape relieved only by the blue of the sky and the white of the fishing boats' sails on Lake Poyang. The dried grass, taller than my head, and the brown sugarcane stalks appeared coated with yellow dust. Curiously, as we walked along the small road that led to our new home, we were standing at the bottom of the retaining wall, looking up at the sailing junks that seemed to float in the sky. The sight made me think of a traditional folk song about the Milky Way in which the moon was likened to a sailboat traveling along a silver river of stars. Climbing up the sloping ramp to the top of the dike, we walked along a tree-lined road just broad enough for two trucks to pass, but aside from these occasional touches of green, all else was yellow in this flat countryside as far as the eye could see. Having so often heard Chairman Mao's exhortation that we intellectuals must learn from the workers, peasants, and soldiers, I had expected to find some kind of village nearby, but aside from the four huge sheds constructed by the Beida workers in preparation for our arrival, all else was wasteland. It was in one of these sheds that I spent my first night in our new school.

Constructed almost entirely of bamboo, which I knew from my land reform experience grew plentifully in Jiangxi, these crude barracks had frames of vertical bamboo posts lashed together with iron wire and a roof of bamboo poles thatched with the tall, tough local grass. The walls were formed of woven bamboo strips plastered with mud from this land that had once been lake bottom, a readily available mortar that stuck like glue. Inside, bamboo pillars and boards made a suspended sleeping loft, lined, like the damp ground, with low wooden platforms on which we spread our mats and stored our few personal belongings. The packed earth floor was so wet that often in the morning we would find toadstools growing and frogs hopping underfoot. Two of these temporary dwellings housed all two hundred women and most of the children, who climbed the ladders excitedly to the loft, making forts out of our bedding and waging exuberant pillow fights, completely ignoring our reprimands.

The construction of more permanent housing occupied all of our time during those initial weeks. Our first task was to cut the grass that grew abundantly in that area, carrying load after load back in heavy shoulder baskets to provide fuel as well as thatch. Next we had to transport the bamboo poles that had been rafted along the lake for our use. Sometimes twelve feet long, these poles were heavy and cumbersome, but we learned how to balance a single trunk on our shoulders, as well as how to carry two smaller poles by lashing them together in front and supporting them on a carrying pole. Next some of the poles would be sectioned with a special knife and split into narrow half-inch strips to be woven into a wall. None of us had ever done such work before, but we managed to complete our new dwellings in just over a month, and we moved in before the mud had even dried on the walls.

At that point the cadre school instituted a military organization, with families separated according to their university departments and everyone divided into squadrons of ten people, with ten squadrons constituting a company. In the seventh company, to which I belonged, the 106 people, drawn from the Chinese literature department, the library, and the clinic, were separated into two buildings, one for men, the other for women and children. My sister-in-law would have been in this group except that a recent illness had kept her on the campus. Tang Shuang stayed with Lao Tang in the eighth company, made up of some 100 people from the history and philosophy departments. Although I could walk to Lao Tang's company in half an hour, we were allowed to visit each other only on holidays, which at the start of our stay in the countryside came very infrequently.

We outfitted our new barracks as comfortably as we could, making stands to hold our wash basins and hanging up ropes at regular intervals for drying our clothes. At first we curtained off our sleeping spaces with plastic sheeting, but the leaders refused to allow such privacy. Despite our efforts, the new sheds remained inadequate. Inexperienced at thatching, we never managed to prevent our roofs from leaking, and during a rainstorm could only position our wash basins beneath the worst drips. On those nights we slept beneath plastic sheets tied to the bamboo supporting poles, waking to empty these canopies when they filled and all the time listening to a symphony of dripping water.

With seventy of us women living crowded together in this crude dormitory, the most pressing task was still the construction of better housing. This was essential, for the winter winds were notoriously strong on this treeless plain, and the leaders doubted whether our present bamboo lodgings could withstand the buffeting of the winter storms. My first assignment was thus to make bricks, a use for which the dense soil in this area was perfectly suited. Our brick-making team numbered twenty people, mostly men, but because of my experience in Zhaitang, I was considered robust enough to participate in such heavy labor. It was exhausting work. The first step was to dig up the dense, hard clay with a spade and then to carry water from the canal that had been dug beside the dike and mix the water with these rocklike clods of earth. After a thorough soaking, the clay turned into clumps of slippery mud that could be broken down only by hours of stamping with our bare feet. Later we purchased a buffalo from the local peasants, since even our feet were no match for the stubborn clay. When at last the mud was soft, we slapped it by handfuls into rectangular wooden molds. After the bricks had dried, we could carry them to the kiln and fire them for two days, moving them at last to a building site.

Every day I participated in this same work, which, despite its monotony, was strangely satisfying. Always before I had devoted my time and energy to abstract tasks, never creating anything with my own hands. Even in Zhaitang I had never seen the fruits of my labor, but had carried rocks for a reservoir that was never finished, cared for pigs that only grew thinner, worked in the fields along with many others. Here in Liyuzhou I could for the first time see the results of my efforts. I could produce by myself a hundred bricks a day, hold them in my hands, so smooth and even and red, and know that my labor was of immediate benefit to the community.

As I worked, I reflected upon the lot of the peasants. If they led such a life, I decided, why indeed shouldn't we intellectuals live in a similar fashion. It was refreshing not to have to think about anything, not to have any worries, not to be assaulted by political concerns, but just to fulfill simple menial tasks. I didn't want to remember the past or recall the suffering we had put behind us; I wanted merely to rest and savor the peace of this simple life. I was thankful that in the cadre school our past histories were ignored, and even Lao Tang, so recently denounced as a major enemy, was treated equally with the others. We all were expected to participate in the labor together, with only a few singled out for punitive treatment.

On that day in July 1968 when the propaganda teams had come to restore order on the campus, Nie Yuanzi had been taken into custody, along with her principal assistant in the philosophy department, and placed under supervision by the Beida authorities. Although she was not imprisoned, she could not leave her room without permission. Twice in subsequent months I had met her in the clinic, her face sallow and expressionless. At the cadre school she was one of the few to be given particularly onerous labor. Her task was to empty the heavy buckets of urine collected nightly in each dormitory, a splashing load that she would carry on a shoulder pole to the fields, where it would be fermented and used for fertilizer. One other woman, Peng Peiyun, was also assigned this

strenuous and unpleasant work. Formerly the assistant Party secretary for Beida under Lu Ping and later considered a big black
gang member, she and Nie Yuanzi had previously been bitter adversaries. Now, ironically, they were both considered serious enemies by the propaganda team, which wanted to destroy the power
of Lu Ping's supporters and of the Cultural Revolution leaders as
well. As I watched the two women carrying such heavy burdens of
nightsoil, I always felt compassion for their suffering.

The rest of us were treated equally, eating the same food and
receiving 16 *yuan* apiece from our monthly salaries, which we gave
to the cooking group to pay for our meals. This small sum was adequate, since our food was supposed to be comparable to that eaten
by the peasants, their way of life supposedly our model. The rest of
Lao Tang's salary and of mine was deposited directly into the branch
of the Beida bank recently established in Liyuzhou. We could accu-
mulate our regular pay even if we could not spend the money, and
many of us acquired a sizable savings during our months at the
cadre school.

Even though I felt relief, even happiness, during this initial period away from the turmoil of the campus, life was not easy. In the
late summer and fall of 1969, after the growing season for vegetables had passed, we had as much rice to eat each day as we
wished, but nothing else except a thin soup made out of water and
soybean oil—no meat or vegetables. The group responsible for running the kitchen would try to vary our meals, providing us with lo-
cally caught fish from the peasants perhaps once or twice a month,
but there were few other foodstuffs available, since there were no
markets, no shops, no peasant villages nearby. To purchase provisions meant crossing the lake, and although the advance group
sent out from the university had bought several of the small, flat-
bottomed boats used by the local people, none of us were yet able
to manage those unwieldy craft.

One day before our arrival seven people from that original
group had decided to make a crossing to purchase some staple
goods and had been caught in a squall in the middle of the lake.
Unable to handle the boats after the wind had whipped up the
waves, the men had all been drowned. This frightening story re-

mained fresh in our minds, and no one wanted to risk another lake crossing after such a tragic mishap. Consequently, the only way to get provisions was to walk the three hours to the nearest town of Tianzimiao, named Temple to the Son of Heaven because of the temple built there by Zhu Yuanzhang in the Ming dynasty in gratitude for his life having been spared after his boat had overturned in a storm. The difficulty of transporting even such necessities as rice, salt, soy sauce, and oil this distance on a carrying pole made us willing to subsist on a basic diet of rice and soybean oil soup for several months, after which the university invested a substantial sum of money in the cadre school. After the purchase of a steam launch and two trucks, we could transport such provisions as wood, flour, and rice by boat and drive to the nearest market town for vegetables.

During those first two months our labor continued seven days a week, nine or ten hours a day. So many urgent tasks awaited completion that we would even be obliged to participate two or three times a week in what was called "night fighting," which meant continuing to work for three hours after dinner on jobs requiring less light, like moving bricks out of the kiln or carrying supplies from the lakeside to the kitchen. The climate added to our difficulties. As the nights grew cold, the water in our mud pits often froze into a thin layer of ice by morning. The buffalo could still work, but some of the women were troubled by stiff and painful joints from using their bare feet to mix the clay in such temperatures. Miraculously, I never suffered from these problems.

When the first holiday was announced one Sunday, everyone was overjoyed. This was the first time that I could spend together with Lao Tang and Tang Shuang, and we decided to walk to Tianzimiao, a simple outing that was to be our chief excursion in the coming months. As we walked, we talked at length about our present life, looking ahead with little regret to the prospect of remaining peasants forever, remote from the complexities and tribulations that we had known as intellectuals in the city.

In this local town we bought popsicles and stale cookies, both of which tasted delicious after two months with scarcely any sugar. Because of its many flies and dirty appearance, we avoided the wine shop that served meat and ate a simple lunch in the town's single small restaurant. To provide goods for the soldiers at a nearby military garrison, Tianzimiao even offered a small grocery shop and a rudimentary department store. Despite the popsicle wrappers and cow dung that littered the street, this was the closest to civilization we had come in many weeks. As we walked back along the dusty road, passing fields of sugarcane and tall, yellow grass on both sides, we could occasionally glimpse above the dike the white sails against the blue sky, the only spot of color in this otherwise monotonous landscape.

Worried about our diet in the countryside, Lao Tang's mother often in those first two months sent us small parcels of dried beef and sugar. In the city she had catered to her grandson's love of meat and his dislike of vegetables and had even allowed him to stir a spoonful of sugar into his glass when he drank water. Many other people also received supplies regularly from concerned family members and friends in Beijing; and as the meals at the cadre school got worse and worse the volume of parcels steadily increased. Finally, the local post office protested that there were not enough postal workers to handle all these goods and announced that from then on they would deliver only a notice that a package had arrived. The recipient would have to go to Nanchang, two hours drive away, to collect his parcel. Far from being a hardship, the arrival of a postal notice became like an invitation to a festival, giving the recipient an excuse to request a half-day's leave and passage in the supply boat or one of the trucks, after which he could enjoy the pleasures of urban life and restaurants for a few hours.

Such opportunities did not last, however. Before long we were told to inform our relatives immediately to stop sending packages. After two weeks we would be prohibited from collecting any further parcels, and subsequent postal notices would be delivered directly to the leader of the propaganda team, who would then display the contents of all packages in a public exhibition. Our beef and milk, our sugar, candy, and cookies, our walnuts and peanuts, our canned foods would all be lined up beside the name of the intended recipient to show how greedy that person was, how much food he craved, and how unwilling he was to share the lifestyle of the peasants. The warning was effective, as no one wanted to be so humiliated. After our packages stopped arriving, the occasional trips to Tianzimiao became even more enjoyable.

Although the purchase of the steam launch significantly improved our diet, it imposed the arduous task of unloading supplies via a long and precarious dock that had been constructed across the expanse of shallow water near the shore. It took perhaps five minutes to walk along those narrow, undulating planks from the boat to the safety of dry ground, and we women had to carry on our shoulders sacks of flour weighing some forty pounds while the men carried hundred-pound rice sacks. We also had to unload bags of cement used to repair the dike, each company taking responsibility for this labor in turn. Dreading those trembling planks and certain with each step that I would lose my balance and plunge into the parasite-infested water, I found this work the most burdensome of all the tasks I was assigned.

My company was housed farther from the boat landing than any other, a distance that became a great disadvantage in the autumn when heavy rains turned the hard-packed clay into treacherous expanses of slippery mud. Having been sent to the cadre school to be reeducated, however, we were expected to learn things from hardship, so we would always be sent out to unload supplies from the boat in the rain. The ideal held out for our instruction was "the greater the difficulty, the greater the necessity of accomplishing a task." Garbed in our rain gear of knee-length plastic coats, ankle-high boots, plastic leggings tied with rope, and large plastic hats, all in bright shades of red, orange, and green, we trudged along in a line through the cold rain, appearing like vestiges of some medieval European past. But while our outlandish costumes may have appeared somewhat humorous in their incongruity, our task was serious and difficult. Many people slipped and fell, ending up coated with mud as they struggled on under their heavy loads.

One of my friends, a neighbor at Beida and a woman who had long suffered from high blood pressure, tried hard to keep up with the others. Believing that she should set an example as a Party member, Tao Qun had volunteered to go to Liyuzhou despite her physical weakness, but once there she was accorded no allowances for her disability. Obliged to carry her allotted bag of flour whatever the weather, she would fall repeatedly on rainy days. I could do nothing to help except walk behind her and lend a hand when she slipped in the mud. On such days the hazardous journey from the boat to our company's barracks took nearly two hours instead of the customary thirty minutes. We all could readily testify to the aptness of the local peasants' adage, "When the sun shines, the ground is as hard as iron; when the rains come, the ground oozes like pus."

The leaders continually found ways to test us, always assigning us outdoor tasks when it was raining, choosing that time to have us move bricks from the kiln to a building site if there were no supplies to unload from the boat. Carrying fourteen to sixteen bricks at a time on a shoulder pole, the seventy to eighty pounds expected of a woman, was an exhausting task even without the rain, but the leaders liked to demonstrate their power over us and to teach the intellectuals that life was not as easy as they had always assumed in the city. We were always reminded of the slogan that was supposed to govern our thoughts: "We do not fear discomfort; we fear not even death."

Our labor certainly made us understand quickly the hardships of peasant life in that part of Jiangxi province. If we ever complained, however, our army leader would berate us for our weakness, declaring that our previous lives had always depended on others who had carried our provisions for us, and that now it was time for us to learn what their work was like. At our hour-long morning meetings, when we would assemble to study Chairman Mao's thoughts or to discuss an article in the newspaper, our brick-making team leader would elaborate this theme, commanding us to recognize our weaknesses and to learn from the example of the masses. At other times, however, the leaders were polite to us, even occasionally initiating a conversation to assuage their own loneliness. But we could tell that despite their surface demeanor the cadres had scant respect for intellectuals. In their eyes we had only one useful function, to serve as a model for the workers, peasants, and soldiers regarding birth control, for we typically had only one or two children in our families.

The leader of the five-person committee that ran the cadre school clearly believed it his duty to make our lives difficult and thereby accomplish our reeducation. Once, for example, after an exhausting day of labor, after we had washed our hands and feet and climbed into bed, the trumpet shrilly called us back from sleep. It was eleven o'clock, and the wired radio was broadcasting a message from headquarters that a military drill was about to begin. We were shrilly instructed to appear at the door to our company's office, our quilts packed into bedrolls on our backs, within five minutes. This accomplished, we were to run with our heavy loads to headquarters, a fifteen-minute trek. When finally we had all assembled and were seated on our bedrolls, exhausted and disoriented after being roused from sleep, we were told we would be entertained with a movie from Albania, titled "Wound."

Although a foreign film would ordinarily have been a rare treat, at this point we were in no mood to enjoy it, and Tao Qun just fell asleep beside me, snoring. Deciding to seize this chance to join Lao Tang and Tang Shuang, I searched unsuccessfully through the crowd, and ended up watching the movie by myself. It told the story of a young Albanian couple training to be doctors. The husband wanted to go to the countryside to practice medicine, but the wife, preferring to pursue her medical research in the city, agreed to accompany him only after much discussion. Her wounded spirit had been healed at last.

The film accomplished the opposite of its intention, leaving me upset instead of inspired. The glimpse of another world where people lived in comfortable houses and ate at restaurants made me feel utterly remote in this place where we were struggling to carve out a meager subsistence for ourselves amid such adverse and primitive conditions. Even though many of us agreed with the Albanian doctor and believed that we should dedicate our lives to serving the people, this was hardly what we were doing. Since coming to Liyuzhou we had not even seen any workers, peasants, or soldiers. How could we be reeducated by these exemplary types when we were totally isolated from any factories, farms, or military bases? The only workers and soldiers we met were our leaders; otherwise we were in the exclusive company of intellectuals. The whole idea behind the cadre school suddenly seemed to me totally unreasonable, to serve no purpose, to be of no help to society. I wondered what the others were thinking as we stumbled back to our dormitories, allowed finally to sleep.

The harshness of the leaders did not usually stem from cruelty or vindictiveness. Many of the propaganda team members were simple, honest people who believed in Chairman Mao's teaching and sincerely wanted to help the intellectuals learn from the laboring people. Although some of the leaders undoubtedly harbored anti-intellectual prejudices, many felt that they were acting in our best interests, helping us to get rid of our pride and overcome our separation from the masses. Their policy, I believed, was not altogether wrong; some intellectuals did feel superior to everyone else in society, and some, especially the academic men, were indeed quite helpless, unable even to boil water to make tea, so accustomed were they to being cared for by someone else.

Because I agreed with many of the goals of the cadre school, I rarely felt resentment at the way we were treated. Even though we were not doing anything to benefit the people, I thought we were learning something of value. I actually enjoyed rising to the challenge of our labor, successfully passing the leaders' tests, and training myself to live by my own efforts. I found it gratifying to supply our own food and become self-sufficient, for I believed that Chinese intellectuals had become weak after centuries of assuming someone else should provide for all of their material needs. Agreeing that intellectuals should become more productive members of society, I seldom joined in the bitter complaints of many of my colleagues.

When the rainy season passed, replaced by the freezing temperatures of winter, our brick making stopped completely and the team members were assigned to new duties. Along with three others, I was put to work as a cook in the company kitchen. I knew I was envied, my new work considered far more desirable than, say, carrying bricks, but I also knew I had been chosen because of my stamina. In the kitchen I would often work thirteen hours a day, beginning at four-thirty every morning when we started preparing porridge. First we would collect grass and twigs for fuel, then light the cooking fires, then bring huge pots of water to boil. Meanwhile we would cut mounds of turnips into thin strips to be salted, a tiring task requiring skill with a cleaver. Finally, we would carry the steaming porridge outside in two large buckets on a carrying pole. Equally demanding, however, was the need to be able to stand up to complaints, as people grumbled constantly, some claiming the food was too salty, others insisting it was too bland.

In all twelve of the school's companies, the kitchen groups were raising two pigs to provide meat for Spring Festival eve. As the holidays approached, our pigs had grown very fat, and we devoted much thought to how the precious pork should be served. After all the care that had gone into their raising, with even the rice-washing water being collected and mixed with yeast to add to the cooking scraps, we wanted the feast to be a memorable one. The problem was that no one knew how to slaughter the pigs.

Our leader decided to use this opportunity to teach the intellectuals another important lesson, to confront them with the realities of life. Accordingly, he chose the two most highly trained intellectuals in our group to be part of a team of four who would learn from the nearest peasants how to kill a pig and then instruct the others about this necessary skill. Each of these two men had received a Ph.D. degree; one was a mathematician trained at Cambridge, the other a physicist trained at Moscow University. After observing the peasants' technique, these professors came first to our company to demonstrate their new skills.

The mathematician, a person always obedient to the propaganda team, announced that he had learned a lot from the peasants and that killing a pig was not really difficult if you followed three steps. First, you must stick a knife into the windpipe; second, you must hang the pig up to bleed; and third, you must fill the pig with air, plunge it into boiling water, and remove the bristles. As he talked, I could tell that he was trying to bolster his confidence. It was evening and the day's labor was completed; everyone had gathered in the small assembly space in front of the dormitories to watch. I was busy boiling large cauldrons of water, but I saw on the

faces of these professors expressions alternating between seriousness, nervousness, and disgust at the task they were about to
perform.

With slightly trembling hands, the mathematician determinedly
plunged a long, sharp knife at the throat of the first pig, but the stab
was not precisely aimed and the knife stuck fast. The enraged animal struggled violently, suddenly breaking loose from the con-
straining ropes, and began darting about wildly, spurting blood
everywhere. As the crowd scattered, the leaders shouted vainly for
someone to grab the pig. The two professors seemed immobilized,
uncertain how to intervene in this travesty for which they were responsible. Finally, several people managed to tie the frantic animal,
now tired from its exertion, and the mathematician dealt it a final
blow with his knife. The second pig was despatched on the first attempt, the carcasses at last ready for the kitchen staff.

I worked until late that night to clean the pigs and scrape away
their bristles, but when the time came for the banquet the next day,
I had no appetite. As my mind replayed that bloody scene, I could
not eat. Perhaps I was just overtired, but even the smell of the cooking meat made me feel ill, and I saved my share of the pork for Tang
Shuang. After the pig-killing fiasco, one of the teachers from our
department wrote a crosstalk* called "Two Doctors Kill a Pig,"
which quickly became famous. It poked fun at the two professors
who had studied so diligently at prestigious universities and had
acquired so much knowledge, but who still could not kill a pig. The
leaders liked the parody so much that they broadcast it repeatedly
over the radio at mealtimes.

When the planting season arrived, preparing the paddies required all our attention. First, we had to plow and flood the fields,
then break up the lumps and smooth the mud. This was accomplished by one person pulling a board on which another person
stood to weigh it down. Next, we spread the fields with nightsoil,
already collected and fermented in a pit with straw and grass. Finally, we all had to wade into the plots barefoot to transplant the
seedlings by hand. To reduce the risk of infection, we covered our

* A popular form of comic dialogue that uses understatement and ambiguity to
satirize contemporary life.

legs with a medicinal oil intended to close the pores, but even with this precaution many people contracted snail fever.

In our two years, more than four hundred people from the neighboring Qinghua cadre school fell ill; the number from Beida was much smaller, only because there happened to be fewer snails on our land. The cure for snail fever was itself dangerous, as the medicine that would kill the parasites was such a strong poison that it placed a strain on the heart. Treatment required hospitalization at Nanchang, and total rest and quiet. One library worker from Qinghua who was receiving this medication, allowed a visit by his wife from Beijing, became overly excited during her visit and died within a few days. Knowing this risk, some people preferred to forgo treatment and just wait, aware that the original parasites could only live within the host organism for seven years, and that their eggs could never hatch.

One of Tang Shuang's classmates fell seriously ill with this disease, suffering from a high fever and a pain in her liver. Her worried parents decided to have her undergo the treatment, despite its risks, and the loudspeakers broadcast the young girl's courageous words to the whole cadre school. "When I take the medicine, I feel most uncomfortable," she explained, "so I think about how much more uncomfortable the parasites inside me feel. Knowing that I am killing them, I take heart. I am Chairman Mao's little red soldier, confident that I shall win a victory."

During this transplanting season we all worked feverishly, trying to keep our thoughts on our task and not to worry about the possibility of infection. Since all the transplanting must be accomplished within four or five days, we held a competition to see who could plant the most seedlings in the even, grid-like pattern that would insure their healthy growth. After a whole day of bending over in the fields, we could barely straighten up. Still, I won third place in our company; in fact, I was the only woman to place among the top ten, and I was given two towels and an enamel mug at the end of the competition.

The planting season was especially hard on the weaker ones, however. Tao Qun, who suffered from an inflammation in her knees, had been exempted from work in the rice fields and assigned instead to work in the vegetable plots, a task relegated to the older people and to those too sick for heavy labor. The leader of that group, an assistant professor specializing in early Chinese texts, himself walked with a limp and had given Tao this assignment as a special favor. But still she could not squat to do the hoeing, so she took with her to the fields a small stool on which she could perch while loosening the soil around the plants. Her action provoked a storm of criticism.

In some other companies, I had been told, the leaders were more sympathetic and concerned, but in ours they believed that intellectuals should suffer some discomfort to compensate for the easy lives they had led before. "You intellectuals have been sent to the countryside for reeducation," she was reminded sharply, "and if you are afraid of pain you will never be reformed." Unwilling to resort to praise and flattery in order to win favorable treatment as others did, she just kept silent, and consequently her weakness of will became the topic of several of our evening meetings. The pressure on Tao Qun was intense, with some people arguing that her use of the stool enabled her to accomplish her job and others maintaining that the labor was a test of a person's resolve and could not be made too comfortable. When we walked back to the room in the brick house that she and I by then shared with six other women, she wept as she told me she had only been trying to do her best.

As the spring of 1970 turned into summer, the heat became our major concern. Because the land for our cadre school was below the level of the lake, a blanket of hot, humid air hung over us without relief. In that damp, boggy area, mosquitoes thrived, and we suffered not only from the heat but from the swarms of insects. Three times a week after dinner we had to attend a meeting to discuss the day's newpaper articles or to consider someone's conduct, and we would have to douse ourselves in oily, smelly mosquito repellent to sit through those outdoor discussions. Then later, when we climbed beneath the mosquito nets that covered our beds, we were greeted by a wall of hot air that had been trapped inside the protective cloth. I was often so hot, my body so sticky, that I could not sleep.

Once when I felt I could no longer bear the heat, I took my bed board outside, planted four spades at each corner on which to hang my mosquito net, and slept on the ground. After the stifling closeness of our small room, I felt much more comfortable outside and managed to sleep quite soundly under the stars for two nights, despite the other women's warnings that I would be eaten by wolves if I ventured out of doors alone in the dark. It was true that often we could hear wolves howling in the distance, but now we had electric lights burning all night and I decided to take the risk in order to get some sleep.

My experiment seemed a total success, until the work team leader learned of my aberrant behavior. Saying that I lacked all sense of discipline, he reprimanded me sharply, observing that if everyone acted according to his own whims there would be no way to run the company. I had no choice but to obey and sleep inside with the others. Always in those weeks of summer, I would get up in the morning after a restless night to find my woven grass mat completely drenched with sweat. How I wished for a bamboo bed like the ones the peasants used, and for their freedom to sleep wherever they wished.

Adding to our misery was the difficulty of bathing. Because of the danger of parasites, we could not use water from the lake or the canal and had to draw all of our water from a deep well. We would fill a basin and let the cold water warm all day in the sun, but having washed once after our labor, no one had the energy to wash again before climbing into bed. Tang Shuang would plead with me to let him swim in the canal, but I forbade this temptation strictly, fearful that he would become infected, yet hating to deny him such a pleasant relief from the oppressive heat. I tried to remember how much more difficult bathing had been in the winter months. Because both the well water and the fuel to warm it were precious, we were each allowed only half a basin, two large dippers full, every two weeks during the cold weather. With this small amount we would first wash our hair, then our bodies, finally our clothes. Each season seemed to bring its accompanying problems.

Despite the difficulty of the climate, of our labor, of our living conditions, I could generally keep my spirits fairly high. Compared with the tension and suffering of the Cultural Revolution, life in the cadre school seemed peaceful and pleasant, and I had quite genuinely found a kind of contentment. Tang Shuang was even receiving an education now that a primary school had been set up in Liyuzhou, drawing upon the university faculty for its teachers. Dedicated to her task, the principal found many people willing to contribute part of their day to the education of the children, and Tang Shuang's instruction, especially in math, was better than he ever could have gotten in Beijing. This opportunity to study seemed so precious after the disruption of the schools for more than three years that it helped make up for the fact that he had been ill with malaria three times. On balance, I was glad that we had decided to take him with us to Jiangxi.

For a whole year we had been exhorted to think only about living the life of the peasants and remaining in the countryside forever, but at the end of that steaming summer we were told to redirect our thoughts to matters of education. An order had been received that Beida and Qinghua would both resume instruction in the fall of 1970 and that each university would establish a branch school for worker, peasant, soldier students at Liyuzhou. To prepare for this important change, we would reflect upon the year spent in the cadre school, draw some conclusions based on our experience, and report them at a summing-up meeting for our company.

When it was my turn to speak, I could attest with complete sincerity that I had basically enjoyed these months in the countryside, that I had found pleasure in being a laborer and making a tangible contribution to society. When I had engaged in academic work before, I had never known how my lectures or articles would be received, whether they would be viewed as a contribution to society or as a crime. By concentrating only on "developing my limbs and making my brain simple," I could feel strong, healthy, useful, and at one with nature, I concluded, and thus I welcomed the leaders' encouragement that we settle here in the countryside and become a new generation of peasants. At the end of my remarks, I read a simple poem:

Growing melons and beans in front,
Raising chickens and pigs in back,
Setting out red pepper chains and pumpkins on the step,
This is indeed a good life.

The leader liked my ideas about the advantages of settling down in the countryside and asked me to be one of seven people to address an assembly of the whole cadre school, all twelve companies and seven hundred people, at what was called a "big conclusion meeting." However, he reproached me for being too passive about politics, advising me that intellectuals must continue to play an active role in the country's future, that it was insufficient just to enjoy a simple life, that I must seriously think about how to contribute once again to education.

At that meeting one speaker discussed the importance of intellectuals renewing their concern with education; another described how he had overcome bitterness and reached a new kind of happiness in the countryside; a third asserted that even in this remote place people must remain informed about national affairs. When my turn came, I suggested that life could be lived in a variety of ways, and that if so many peasants devoted their days to laboring in the fields, we surely could find a sense of purpose in such a simple existence. Then I read my poem and concluded, since the leader had told me I must add something more, that we intellectuals must go on to make some new contribution to education. After the speeches each company presented some form of entertainment. I sang a song, Tang Shuang sang with his primary school, and Lao Tang joined in the collective recitation of a poem. When the meeting concluded, the effort to transform intellectuals into peasants had come to an end.

Too High a Price

Our leaders treated the arrival of the first group of students in the fall of 1970 very seriously, announcing that these young people must gain an entirely different impression of university life than had previous classes entering Beida. With exams abolished, every pupil had been admitted on the basis of recommendations from his factory unit, commune, or army battalion, a policy intended to make the advantages of higher education available to those who would never before have had a chance at admission. Inevitably, the children of high officials were accepted in the process, but most of those privileged young people, knowing that we had no books and no educational facilities, refused to go to the countryside and instead enrolled at the Beijing campus. Thus in our branch school most of the students would be genuine workers, peasants, and soldiers, although even they had some connections to the lower-level cadres at their factories and communes. At neither campus, because of the previous domination of the universities by the intellectuals, could their children be accepted.

To instruct this new generation of students, ten teachers from each of five departments—philosophy, history, literature, economics, and international politics—would be released from much of their labor. Called the "five-same-thing-teachers," the chosen faculty members would do the same things as the students in five ways: eat together, live together, labor together, study together, and

274

reform their thoughts together. In order to qualify, a teacher must be in good physical health, have sufficient academic knowledge, and have a correct political attitude. Both Lao Tang and I were selected.

In anticipation of the students' arrival, preparations began to transform our facility into a permanent campus for the education of cadres, teachers, and students. The faculty would be given rotating assignments, a stint at teaching to be followed by a period of going out to work at a factory or commune, then a period of doing labor on the cadre school site. Committed to this new plan, the leaders began the construction of additional housing, expanded the electric power station, purchased a second steamboat and even a machine to make popsicles, much to the delight of Tang Shuang and the other children. Trees were planted, and a campaign to wipe out snails was begun. Encouraged by the slogan "Depend on the masses," we all were given one day off from labor to go to the muddy edges of the rice paddies and the foot of the dike to collect snails. In this competition some people managed to fill half a rice bowl with the small conical shells, an activity that greatly excited the children. Liyuzhou would be transformed into a new village, far more attractive, far more comfortable than in the past, a setting worthy to receive the new and much vaunted students.

During this period policies at the cadre school became somewhat less strict, with attention at last paid to people's family lives. Several rooms were created for a new use, some formed by partitioning off a small space in a collective dormitory with a bamboo wall, and one created at the side of a barn. In such makeshift quarters all the couples in the school were to be allowed to live together for two weeks at a time in rotation. Some couples chose to leave their children in the dormitory, but when our turn came, we three were happy for the chance to live together as a family once again.

We were assigned the room in the barn, a large mud-walled shed with a thatched roof. Separated by a shoulder-high mud partition from the two oxen who were the barn's permanent occupants, this space had served as sleeping quarters for the peasants who had earlier attempted to raise animals on this land. The room had been recently outfitted with a small table and with boards and benches to form a sleeping platform. Despite the smell of the oxen and the crudeness of the surroundings, we eagerly took our quilts and moved in, grateful for this relative privacy. After completing our daily work and finishing our evening meetings, we would walk back from our separate companies to meet at this barn. For half an hour I would wade through the tall field-grass with only an occasional building shedding some light in the darkness, eager to join Lao Tang and Tang Shuang.

On one side of the barn, the flat fields stretched endlessly toward the horizon, on the other we could see the high wall that held back the waters of the lake, the lights of the fishing boats above our heads often indistinguishable from the stars. As we lay side by side, talking about our new life and ruminating about someday having our own house here at Liyuzhou, we could hear the howling of wolves in the distance. With pleasure I talked at leisure with my son, now twelve years old and ready to form his own viewpoints about life, and looked forward to teaching once again.

A big celebration was planned to commemorate the arrival of more than one hundred students in Liyuzhou. As a first lesson in self-reliance and withstanding hardship, the students would walk the thirty-five miles from Nanchang to the cadre school, while the strongest among those chosen as teachers would meet them at the midpoint of their trek. The late summer weather was still very hot, more than 100° F each day, so the students' departure was scheduled for eleven o'clock at night. Eleven teachers, including myself and one other woman, a doctor who would be available in case of medical emergency or exhaustion, set out at four o'clock in the afternoon to walk some eighteen miles to meet the students.

At midnight we finally reached the designated midpoint, a carefully selected spot beside a river where a monument recorded the heroic deeds of a PLA soldier who had died rescuing some drowning children. The local government had also been instructed to treat the arrival of these new students seriously and had organized the peasants all along the route to prepare tea, set off firecrackers, and beat gongs as a sign of welcome. Even though I knew the demonstrations had all been prearranged by the authorities, I still appreciated the warm atmosphere. Every half hour we would reach a new village, and the night air would be filled with festive sounds. While we walked, we sang songs, mostly Chairman Mao's quotations set to music, as well as the lyrics that had become our cadre-school theme song:

> We never fear discomfort,
> We fear not even death,
> We will conquer every hardship,
> We will march to victory.

The cadence of this tune was perfect for walking, and we sang it many times. At six o'clock in the morning, exhausted but nonetheless exhilarated, we arrived at the cadre school.

The whole community had lined up on both sides of the street to welcome us with applause and slogans: "Long live Chairman Mao," "Greetings to the new generation of students," "Move forward with educational reform." I was filled with enthusiasm, thinking about how different this group of students would be from any I had known before, older and far more experienced. The teachers were different now too, no longer stiff, formal, or arrogant, but prepared to learn from the students how to improve their thoughts and at the same time help the students increase their knowledge. The prospect of participating in this shared educational endeavor was thrilling, and I felt proud to be a teacher again.

Thirty students had been admitted to the Chinese literature department, their ages and educational backgrounds varying widely. The youngest was eighteen, the oldest thirty-eight, and some had attended only six years of primary school. Such discrepancies only contributed to the excitement of our experiment, and to the hope that we could accomplish something significantly new here in this remote and backward area. I quickly learned that many of the students, disappointed and skeptical, did not share our enthusiasm. Eager for an education, they found themselves in a place without classrooms, books, libraries, even paper. Some of the young women discussed their misgivings frankly with me as I accompanied them to the school's best brick building where we would live together. I tried to reassure them that certainly we would have books later, reminding them that representatives had already been sent to Jiangxi

University, still closed after the Cultural Revolution, to borrow books on Chinese literature. Even though I knew this request had been met with an evasive answer, I didn't tell that to the students. Perhaps they didn't know that the library had been used as a military barracks during the previous two years or that most of the books had been removed, many of them lost and others burned because of their alleged counter-revolutionary or pornographic contents. If for some reason this provincial library could not provide us with books, I told the students, we would surely receive some from Beida.

The first week was considered an indoctrination period during which half of our time was devoted to labor, hoeing the corn and bending over barefooted in the flooded rice paddies to pull out weeds. Both were exhausting tasks. Strict regulations were enforced regarding the application of snail medicine before working in the paddies, but a few students became infected despite these precautions. The other half of our time was spent in discussions to familiarize the students with the purpose of our new experiment in education. Meanwhile, the faculty met together to try and decide what to teach the new students. Despite our eagerness, no one had any idea how to conduct this much-heralded new educational venture.

We had held long discussions even before the students arrived, trying to interpret the terse orders received from the Beida authorities that the starting point must be to criticize the old educational system and the old literary policy, making the students understand that their goal was to pursue a new direction. Such a brief statement gave no indication of how to proceed, however, or how to put the new policy into practice. During the rest of that first month, we in the literature department decided to divide our time between study and labor, and to use as our first text the "Yan'an Talks on Art and Literature," since everyone owned a copy of Chairman Mao's collected works, known then as "the steering tiller, the principal weapon, and the staple food."

When I learned what was to constitute the rest of the lesson in that first month, however, my initial enthusiasm was quickly dispelled. The leader of my teaching group instructed that as part of the students' orientation, I would give a talk explaining why I had become a rightist, why I had opposed Chairman Mao's literary thought, and why my former attitudes had been dangerous and harmful. As I listened aghast to this suggestion, he continued to say that my life had followed a zigzag course and that I had made a big mistake, one that could now be used as a valuable lesson for the new students, an example of how the old educational system had led people to become enemies of socialism.

"When you were a student leader," he elaborated, "you made many contributions as a true revolutionary, but then, because of your education under the old system, you failed to place sufficient trust in Chairman Mao's literary line and became an enemy of the Party." Knowing that I had always talked about foreign literature in my classes, and that I had read many foreign novels during my middle-school years, he also told me to explain how the corrupting influence of Western bourgeois literature had undermined my morality and made me change from a revolutionary to an enemy. Then after I had developed all those points, he concluded, the students would discuss them.

Having thought that this would be an opportunity for me to start a new life, to develop a relationship once again with the students, I felt stunned. I couldn't bear to tell the newcomers I had been labeled an enemy, to expose before them my past humiliation, to reveal that I still bore the stigma of an uncapped rightist. My elation drained away. Apparently I had been selected as a teacher not because of my abilities but because I was someone from outside the ranks of the people who could be held up to the students as a warning.

After my cap had been taken off, I had tried to think as little as possible about my condemnation as a rightist with its accompanying shame. When I did think back on those two years, it was with the sense of having been unjustly accused. I could accept the newspaper reports that some people had in 1957 genuinely opposed the Communist Party, but I knew in my heart that I was not one of them. Such blasphemous thoughts could never be revealed to the students, of course, because the price of taking off my cap had been to admit my mistakes and confess my guilt. To claim publicly that I had been innocent would be to repudiate the decision made by the Party. But if I could not speak honestly, I had no idea what else to say. I was given three days to prepare my talk.

When I stood before the students, I modified my story as much as I dared. First I discussed how the old educational system had been harmful because it automatically excluded worker, peasant, and soldier students, and considered a candidate's academic record to be the only criterion for university admission. "We were not taught Chairman Mao's literary thought with sufficient thoroughness," I continued, "and I failed to study it earnestly enough or to apply it in every aspect of my life." Acknowledging that I had been declared a rightist and an enemy, I explained that even though subjectively I had thought I was doing something good and acting as a revolutionary, objectively I had worked against the people's benefit, failing to make literature serve the needs of the workers, peasants, and soldiers. "Now is a new era and we have a new educational system," I concluded; "we must study Mao Zedong's thought with great thoroughness to prevent any return to such a dangerous path." Afterward the leader expressed his dissatisfaction with my remarks, reprimanding me for avoiding the issue of my own guilt and neglecting to explain how Western literature had corrupted me. Fortunately, there was no opportunity for me to address the students again on this subject, and the criticism passed by.

Even though the leaders were dissatisfied, the students were very interested in my comments. The peasant girl who slept beside me in the dormitory, herself only a primary-school graduate, asked me in hushed tones one night whether I thought the study of literature dangerous, since it seemed so easy to make a serious mistake. I had no idea how to respond. She filled the silence by suggesting that perhaps it was better not to study literature at all but instead to do something more concrete, something less subject to conflicting interpretations. While others expressed fewer trepidations about engaging in literary study, many asked my opinion about what difficulties might befall them in the future. To my relief, only a few seemed fearful of being contaminated by a former enemy or eager to maintain a distance from me after that talk.

After the first month had passed, we teachers agreed to concentrate on criticizing the old ways of thought, especially the "eight black viewpoints" defined by Jiang Qing in February 1966, at the start of her efforts to revolutionize Chinese culture. With the students we would criticize these viewpoints in turn, explaining why it was an error to write about "middle characters," ordinary people who were neither heroes nor villains, or to interpret realism as a license to expose society's deficiencies, or to explore new ways of thinking that might provoke a rejection of Marxism and Mao Zedong-thought. After one teacher had discussed an issue, the others would all participate in self-criticism, explaining how they had themselves previously been influenced by such dangerous viewpoints as a result of insufficiently studying Chairman Mao's literary theory.

For two months we analyzed how the wrong line in literature had been harmful, but no one knew what to do next. As we still had received no books and it was nearly October, time for the first rice harvest, the propaganda team leaders decided to suspend all study, freeing everyone to participate in this important labor. The machine that had been purchased to help with the harvesting ran day and night, and we all became coated with yellow dust, for the rice must be reaped in just a few days, after it had fully matured but before the grains became too ripe and fell from the stalks. The harvest was a great success, and we averaged 650 pounds of rice per *mou* of land. A big feast was planned in celebration.

The leader of the cadre school wanted the harvest to provide a lesson as well, so he instructed that on the night before we tasted the fruits of our labor, we would have a "meal to remember former bitterness." Before Liberation a meal of rice alone would have been unthinkable in the countryside, and the precious grain would have been mixed with husks and wild plants to fill people's stomachs. Thus for dinner that night the kitchen staff prepared steamed buns made of corn flour, rice husks, and wild greens, producing a dark green, coarse, bitter bread. Everyone was told to eat at least two of these unpleasant buns without wasting a crumb. For me such unpalatable fare was familiar enough after the famine years in

Zhaitang, but I felt sorry for Tang Shuang who had been fed meat and butter all through those months of hardship. Lao Tang and I had tried to take him often to Tianzimiao during the past year to provide him at least occasionally with meat and sugar, but this time he could not escape and would have to eat the bitter fare along with the rest of us.

The next day we feasted on fish and rice grown with our own hands. Even in the city I had never tasted rice fresh from the fields, as it is customarily stored for a number of years before being sold. The steaming bowls had such a delicate fragrance, such a sweet flavor, that the meal truly was memorable. I invited Tang Shuang to come to my company for dinner that night, sharing half of my fish with him and requesting Lao Tang to save the portion of meat that our son would otherwise have been served in the eighth company.

As winter approached, the labor was reduced for everyone, providing abundant time for study, so we asked the students to read newspaper articles out loud, a task they could have performed just as well in silence by themselves. Then we conducted discussions about current affairs, and at last decided to have the students write. Three groups were formed for this purpose: one to write essays about the "eight black viewpoints," another to write essays about their personal lives before coming to the cadre school, and the third, for which I was advisor, to create a dramatic performance. Our goal was to instruct them in three kinds of composition: argumentation, narration, and literary creation. Since we had so few books, they would have to produce their own texts, then exchange them to benefit from the efforts of the others.

The initial problem facing my group was the construction of a plot suitable to our assigned topic, the reasons why the old educational system needed reform. After much discussion we decided to write a drama about a male student from a remote rural area who had been admitted to Beida because of his outstanding academic ability. At the university he studied very hard, and at the same time fell in love with a girl from an urban intellectual family. Enamored of her family as well, he grew ashamed of his humble origins. One day his father came to visit him, shabbily dressed, smoking a crude pipe, looking very rustic. The boy felt abashed when his girl friend entered unexpectedly. Instead of introducing the old peasant as his father, the boy said that this was a visitor from his native village.

Behind our plot lay a popular saying: "The first year a shabby peasant, the second year a city slicker, the third year a stranger to his parents." Our goal was to illustrate the way people became corrupted by bourgeois influence, in this case not through the fault of the young man but because of the educational system to which he had been exposed. Finally, after returning to his village for a visit, the young man understood the error of his ways. Our play concluded with the new worker, peasant, soldier students arriving at a recently established university in the countryside and the admiring young man expressing his certainty that they would never follow the wrong road as he had done. We performed our play, titled "The Five Withouts Thatch-roofed University," in the style of a dance drama, combining traditional Jiangxi folk tunes with our own lyrics. Our accomplishment was greeted with such enthusiasm that the script was later staged by the propaganda troupe on the main Beida campus.

That second autumn in Liyuzhou we had other problems to cope with besides devising a new curriculum, for the rains were unusually heavy, the threat of flooding severe. The water level in the lake had risen so high and the pressure upon the dike grown so intense that even a small hole would have caused the entire structure to give way. The leaders, realizing that many lives lay in their hands, grew increasingly nervous. Every day we worked to shore up the dike with the help of the PLA, piling up sandbags and checking for cracks in the cement. The local government, eager to please the leaders in Beijing who viewed our cadre school as a model, at one point sent a hundred thousand peasants to assist with this crucial task. For three nights at the peak of the crisis we got little sleep. Patrols were strictly organized, with white lines drawn every thirty meters and two people given responsibility for each small section. We took our patrol duties very seriously, knowing that any carelessness could cause the whole cadre school to be covered by water.

On the night that it was my turn to stand watch, the moon was full and the sky clear. With Lao Wu, the neighbor who had so openly inquired about my feelings that night after his own criticism meeting, I stood gazing out over the lake, now threatening in its beauty. Waves occasionally broke over the wall, so high was the water level, and our clothes soon became drenched with spray. As we walked back and forth in the moonlight, Lao Wu began to confide in me again, this time about his personal problems. His wife, a much younger woman who had stayed behind in Beijing to continue her work as a middle-school teacher, was asking for a divorce. Knowing that she tried to avoid appearing in public with her husband, a man of slight build and severe features, I suspected that she had married him only because of his academic reputation and because of the royalties he received for his many published books. Now she had fallen in love with another middle-school teacher, a handsome but slippery and unfaithful fellow, and Lao Wu was very upset. Hearing him speak wearily about the bitterness of life, I could think of no adequate consolation and urged him not to torture himself about things that could not be solved. Once again our hearts were close, our understanding deep.

Such an open, personal conversation would have been inconceivable in the tense atmosphere of Beijing, where political movements had followed one after the other since the Anti-rightist Campaign, destroying the trust, the sincerity, and the openness that had once characterized our friendships. Here in the cadre school, I realized, the bonds between people were closer than they had been at any point in the previous decade. With everyone facing the same conditions, doing the same labor, sharing the same housing, eating the same food, receiving the same monthly stipend, the competition for economic and political gain that had so undermined relationships at the university was greatly reduced. Our ingrained responses of suspicion and mutual distrust had begun to disappear. In addition, everyone knew the importance of cooperative effort, realizing that if the wall gave way, we would all share the same fate, becoming food for the fish at the bottom of the lake together.

After the flood danger abated, our teachers' group again had to face the problem of finding some ongoing method of instruction. Our leader argued that the students could not spend all their time in the midst of sent-down intellectuals when the principal distinction between the old and new systems of education was the goal of serving the people. We all agreed that the Jinggang Mountain region, the old guerrilla base area, would make an ideal spot for a new kind of learning to take place. Even though a whole day's travel was required, the higher leaders approved our request for two trucks for transportation to this revolutionary shrine.

By that time a brick building roofed with tile had been constructed for the use of married couples in the cadre school, and just as the trip to Jinggang Mountain was being planned, my turn to spend a month together with Lao Tang and Tang Shuang was announced. While I was loath to leave halfway through this precious family time, I had no choice, and I was also eager to see Jinggang Mountain, a place of legendary significance in my mind. I arose early to be ready for the eight o'clock departure and said good-bye to Tang Shuang, telling him I would be away for perhaps a month or two. He replied confidently that I would not really go away but would surely return that very night. I took this as a sign of his reluctance to have me leave, and patted him reassuringly as I pulled on my boots. An unusually heavy rain had been falling for almost a week, leaving the ground so slippery that I had difficulty walking to the departure point. Despite the weather, my spirits were high.

Poor health prevented the leader of our teaching group from joining our expedition, and a young teacher who had graduated in 1966, previously a staunch follower of Nie Yuanzi, had been put in charge. Formerly the editor of the Red Guard newspaper for all of Beijing, this avid young activist vowed that we would continue with our mission despite the downpour, that nothing could deter us from reaching Jinggang Mountain. If, as our song proclaimed, not even death could frighten us, how could we be stopped by a simple rainstorm, he demanded. This kind of argument was unassailable, even though many of us had misgivings about starting out in such weather. After our plastic-wrapped bedrolls had been loaded onto the truck, we arranged ourselves as comfortably as possible, agreeing to sit down on our quilts in rotation because of the limited space. Those in the second vehicle seemed far more fortunate, protected from the rain as they were by a canvas cover stretched over a metal frame, while our truck was completely open to the elements.

Our difficulties began immediately when the trucks could not negotiate the muddy ramp leading up to the road atop the dike, the only access to the world beyond our stretch of reclaimed lake bottom. Nothing could shake our leader's resolve, however, and he summoned a tractor to tow the trucks up the slick incline to the road bed. Despite the plastic rain gear that covered our cotton padded overcoats, we were all quite wet by the time we finally got under way. In addition to this discomfort, we were apprehensive, aware that the steady rainfall had begun to erode the edges of the embankment. Now that the flood waters had receded, no one was concerned with the condition of the dike, and the road had become barely wide enough to allow two trucks to pass.

Perhaps half an hour after our departure, as we approached the Qinghua cadre school, we met a truck carrying a large load of wood. Although the road could ordinarily accommodate two vehicles, we watched with mounting anxiety as our driver inched to the very edge of the embankment to let the oncoming truck pass. With a sigh of relief, we settled down again, watching with some continued concern our friends in the truck behind. Their driver also moved cautiously toward the edge of the road, but somehow he misjudged the distance. Before our eyes the truck full of students plunged over the side, turning over twice before it stuck against a pile of bamboo logs. Screaming in terror, we ran from our truck and slipped our way down the slope to the wreck. Most of our friends, though bruised and covered with mud, were trapped but not seriously hurt; but the two who had been standing just behind the cab were pinned beneath the heavy metal frame that supported the canvas top. Seeing their faces the color of pig's liver, I knew at once that they were dead. We struggled desperately to release them from the crushing weight, but the truck was too heavy. In a frenzy, we began to dig away the mud beneath the chassis in order to free the others, finding some four or five people seriously hurt. Messengers by then had returned from the nearby Qinghua headquarters with a tractor and another truck to transport the wounded and the sheeted bodies of the dead to the nearest hospital.

Everyone was crying. One of the dead was a student in my group and a favorite of mine, the eldest son in a worker's family, himself a worker from a machine factory in Shanghai. The other victim was a teacher who I had watched bid a fond good-bye to his wife and two children at the cadre school a half hour before. I felt dazed with grief and shock.

When there was nothing more to be done at the scene of the accident, we walked the short distance to the Qinghua dormitories where we were given cups of steaming ginger water with brown sugar. Somewhat revived, we headed slowly home, supporting those who had been bruised in the accident, deeply shaken by what had just occurred. Tang Shuang's parting words rang in my head like an omen. Remembering my friends now dead, I realized how easily it might have been my truck that had slipped over the edge. Human life seemed to depend on the merest chance.

The head of our group walked along in stunned silence, aware that he was responsible for this tragedy. Many of the students, their grief turned to anger, complained bitterly that they had been brought to Liyuzhou for an education, but so far had learned nothing, and now this terrible accident had occurred. I returned numbly to the room I could share for two more weeks with Lao Tang and Tang Shuang, grateful to have their company, trying to come to terms with my grief and my doubts. Chairman Mao had said that when you strive for revolutionary goals you must expect to have some victims, but I felt that the price we had paid, both today and over the past years, was too high. Always we had victims, but rarely any accomplishments. Had some of us spoken out that morning and voiced our misgivings about setting out for Jinggang Mountain in such weather, we could perhaps have prevented this loss of life; but to speak out against the school's slogan would have been tantamount to opposing Chairman Mao's instruction. Everyone had kept silent.

The news of the accident was received grimly at the cadre school headquarters, where the leaders were anxious not only because of their own accountability for the tragedy, but also because they must find some explanation to give the stricken families. The leaders telephoned Beijing immediately to report the situation and receive instructions, knowing that the incident would be viewed very seriously. Since our school was supposed to be a model, an accident like this might influence the fate of the whole new educational program.

The following morning we were assembled and told not to be disheartened, since Chairman Mao had warned us that struggle would inevitably bring losses, but to recover quickly and continue to move forward. These two people had sacrificed themselves for our new system of education, the leaders continued; their deaths were not in vain, because the accident had occurred in the pursuit of important innovations. Thus we must always remember our loyal friends and honor them at a big memorial meeting to instill the lesson that change cannot be accomplished without sacrifice.

Back in my dormitory I was told to organize my group of students to write poems and prepare memorial songs and essays. Suppressing my emotions and doubts, I called the group together to recall Wang Yonggan's warm personality and the things he had said and done. I wrote my own poem for him, which was later read in the memorial meeting. The words genuinely expressed my grief and sense of loss but concealed the questions in my heart. I could not believe that his sacrifice was in fact worthy, and I held that Red Guard leader responsible for what seemed to me senseless deaths. My poem just said that to offer up one's life in the pursuit of important goals was indeed a noble act.

At the end of this week, we assembled all of the commemorative essays, working long hours to prepare a memorial book for our two comrades. Everyone who helped with the stencils wrote with great care, each stroke filled with emotion and grief. When the family of my student was brought from Shanghai for the memorial meeting, I was asked to be responsible for his mother, but I declined, knowing that I could not possibly offer words of revolutionary encouragement in the face of her grief. As we brought her tea in our room, she related her high hopes for her first son, the only member of her family ever to attend a university. She told of how he had gone to work after junior middle school to help support his family because his father had been ill for several years, about how happy and proud she had been when she had bid him farewell at the Shanghai railroad station. Now only his ashes remained, she sobbed. My heart ached, but I could think of no words of comfort. Some human misery cannot be assuaged, and at such times silence seems preferable to hollow condolences.

The memorial meeting was conducted by Wang Lianlong, the vice-commissar of the PLA's 8341 unit and the army propaganda team leader at Beida, who had arrived the afternoon after the accident to take charge of the necessary arrangements. The proceedings were brief. The victims were bestowed the honored title of revolutionary martyrs, and a eulogy was delivered to remind everyone that these deaths had not been meaningless. Later the families were given financial compensation for their loss, a subtle message that they should inquire no further into the reasons for their loved ones' deaths. All of us understood that we were not to mention this unfortunate incident again. Nonetheless, we later learned, the families continued to demand that someone be held accountable for the tragedy. Ultimately, the former Red Guard leader from our department was issued a warning from the Party for his over-zealous conduct and disastrous judgment.

In December our objective of reaching Jinggang Mountain was revived. Chairman Mao had issued a new instruction, specifically directed to the PLA but interpreted more broadly, urging more rigorous training to prevent the military from becoming just a group of "young master soldiers," unable to withstand hardships and accustomed to comfort and idleness. Training must be conducted with firm discipline, even in peacetime, we were told; marches and bivouacs would improve our fitness. As always, people were eager to put Chairman Mao's instruction into practice, and our leaders, determined that our model cadre school should serve as an example, announced that the students would undertake a long march. Called "camp and field training," the expedition would start at Nanchang and finish at Anyuan, the coal mine where Chairman Mao had organized the workers in 1922. The leaders of the Chinese literature department decided to continue on to the Jinggang Mountain area, anticipating that if we walked eight *li* per hour, eight hours per day, we would complete our march in seven days.

The morning of our departure was cold and gloomy; a light freezing rain chilled us through as we completed last-minute preparations. Despite the low temperature, we all chose quilts of just medium thickness to carry on our backs, preferring to be cold at night than to carry a heavier burden during the day. Except for the elderly and the sick, everyone above the age of ten was expected to participate. In our company only some ten people stayed behind, among them Tao Qun. I had worried about Tang Shuang, but found him elated at the prospect of this revolutionary outing, proud that he was being treated like a man and allowed to join in the execution of Chairman Mao's latest orders. I saw his excited face as we gathered in formation, the primary school students in the lead, my company in the middle, and Lao Tang's somewhere near the end.

We marched two by two, the whole cadre school together demonstrating a collective loyalty to Chairman Mao. I was chosen to be one of the six members of a cheering squad that would sing songs, read passages from Chairman Mao's thoughts, and shout slogans to inspire and encourage the marchers. Because my job was to walk back and forth alongside the group, I was able to go forward to the front ranks to check on Tang Shuang, my trips increasing in frequency when the rain began to fall heavily. Proud of his adult role, he resented my appearances and told me sharply that he didn't want his mother always watching him. Still, I could not overcome my concern, especially when the leaders called for a "rapid pace march," making us walk three and a half, sometimes four miles per hour to increase our fitness. Such a stride, exhausting even for the adults, left me extremely hungry by afternoon every day.

We were not permitted to buy anything to eat along the route, even when we passed a shop, the purpose of our march being to train us to endure hardships. Seeking out bitterness, we had been told, would test our mettle. But once I had a chance to fall behind the rest of the marchers and purchase a small packet of hard candies in a village store. As soon as I could, I passed them secretly to Tang Shuang, cautioning him to keep them in his pocket and suck on one when he felt particularly exhausted. He rejected my offer instantly, saying that he was a class monitor, he wasn't weak, and he certainly wasn't going to do anything prohibited for the others. Disappointed to have my maternal concern so sharply dismissed, I nonetheless realized that it would have been difficult for him ever to slip a sugar piece into his mouth unobserved.

The regular kitchen staff was responsible for providing our meals along the way. Lao Ding, the only person in our literary history group who had not been condemned as a rightist, was now the leader of the kitchen group, and he carried a shoulder pole with a large iron *wok* suspended from each end. Tall and strong, our cook kept up a rapid pace, the perspiration caused by his exertion making steam rise up from his bald head to create a comic effect. Beside him another person with a shoulder pole carried both of their bedrolls. An American jeep left behind after World War II and given to the cadre school accompanied us in case someone should fall ill or collapse from exhaustion. Its driver would proceed ahead of the column to purchase rice for our meals from villages along the route, thereby reducing the quantity of supplies that had to be carried. Although the food never seemed sufficient, so hungry were we from walking, we were given white-flour buns and turnips for lunch, sometimes even meat and vegetables for dinner, far more luxurious food than our daily fare in Liyuzhou.

Many in our group had never seen the South China countryside, and even for me this scenery was new. So unlike the dusty yellow plain of North China, here the soil was red and compact, the hillsides dotted with pine trees. The two-story brick houses, with the family's living space above its storeroom, bore no resemblance to the low adobe houses typical of villages near Beijing. We saw many rivers, buffaloes plowing flooded rice paddies, fields showing the first broad-bean shoots, none of which could be found in the North, where the parched ground would still be frozen solid.

At night we would sleep in a village primary school, our itinerary having been planned to make such lodgings available at the end of each day. The first night it was raining and very cold when we stopped for dinner, and everyone had developed painful blisters from the unaccustomed marching. The cooking group provided us each with one gourd full of warm water, enough when two people joined together to fill up a wash basin, into which we gratefully plunged two pairs of tired, aching feet. I wrote several couplets to express our appreciation for all that the cooks were doing to make us more comfortable.

The first-aid team came around later and with a disinfected needle drew a single strand of our own hair through the most painful blisters, causing them to drain during the night. Then we spread some straw on the ground, covered it with our bedding, and climbed under our quilts and overcoats, falling into an exhausted sleep despite the cold. Marching was far more difficult the next day because everyone suffered from painful blisters, and we could hardly wait to stop, this time at a former temple, now a school, which again provided a welcome if hardly luxurious shelter. We emptied the classrooms of their tables and benches, carried in armloads of straw, and after a hasty dinner fell asleep.

On the third night we were unable to reach our planned destination because of heavier rainfall, slippery roads, and accumulated fatigue, all of which had slowed our pace. Instead, we stopped unexpectedly at a village so small that it had no primary school, no obvious place to accommodate so many weary travelers. Our leaders decided that just as the PLA had stayed at the homes of the peasants during the battle for Liberation, so would we divide up and disperse ourselves throughout this village.

Three students and I were assigned to the ancestral hall, a large, high-ceilinged room that offered utterly uninviting surroundings. It was almost seven o'clock by the time we reached our quarters, and by the light of a small kerosene lantern we could just make out the figures of two old men sitting in bamboo reclining chairs. With their white hair and wrinkled faces, they looked almost like corpses as they sat motionless, expressionless, in this dark and unventilated room. An oppressive smell greeted us from behind the door where wooden buckets of urine were waiting to be dumped into the cesspools the next day. The several people sitting about looked at us with unfriendly, fixed stares, obviously displeased at our intrusion. Knowing that there would be no warm water for our feet that night, we just climbed under our quilts, unable to make any requests of these unwilling hosts.

Before falling asleep, I thought about how little the peasants' lives had changed since the days of the land reform, and about how much different our reception had been in 1952, when we students had been welcomed as saviors. Never in that period had I sensed such hostility from the peasants. They had been grateful for our help, happy to receive such prized possessions as the quilts and mattresses we distributed from the former landlords' houses. In those months the peasants had looked forward to a bright future, but now their confidence and trust seemed to have disappeared. I saw nothing but resentment in the eyes of the people clustered around that kerosene lantern. The next morning our leader explained that all of those people were former landlords and rich peasants who had been turned out of their houses and forced to live in this ancestral hall, so of course we couldn't expect them to be hospitable. However, I could not so readily dismiss my impressions of the peasants' altered expectations.

The fourth day of our journey was intended as a test of our endurance. It was New Year's Eve, and starting at two o'clock in the morning everyone, even the children, marched at an exhausting pace that at times reached four and a half miles per hour. Although we stopped for rests, many could not keep up, and by four o'clock that afternoon when we arrived at the town of Wanzai, only Tang Shuang and one other middle-school student were still marching. The others had been picked up by the truck that was carrying all of our *woks* and cooking equipment for that single day. The village militia had been alerted to extend to us a warm welcome, after which we settled down to wrap the traditional New Year's dumplings, our mouths watering at the generous quantity of meat provided for the filling, a reward for our exertion. As we prepared this holiday feast, we talked of how we would surely never again spend a New Year's Eve in such unusual circumstances. After consuming the dumplings, we listened to inspirational speeches about the goals we should set for the year ahead and sang some songs, but everyone was too tired to participate with much enthusiasm. Nevertheless, Tang Shuang announced to me proudly that he felt like a hero for having proved he could keep up such a pace for so many hours.

On New Year's Day we reached Anyuan, where a welcoming committee promptly came out to greet us, joining us in revolutionary songs to celebrate our arrival at this historic place. We even used the school's equipment to prepare a stenciled pamphlet praising those who had shown unusual strength and endurance during the march, and I was proud that all three members of my family were cited on this list. For nearly a week we stayed in this small mining village, turning over our meal tickets and eating in the canteen with the workers. Twice we visited the mines, once to see the most primitve working conditions, where the laborers still chipped away at the coal with pickaxes and carried the heavy lumps out in shoulder baskets, and once to see the most advanced conditions, where the workers used carts on small-gauge tracks. The leaders told us that once we had seen the hardship of these workers' lives, we would always remember that the coal we used so heedlessly in the city had been produced with great difficulty, and we would therefore be conscientious about conserving fuel.

The miners' situation was indeed very moving, and I thought often about their lot, working underground in such adverse circumstances, covered with coal dust, for eight hours each day. It had been nearly fifty years since Chairman Mao had visited this spot to uplift the workers with his revolutionary vision, but many of them still worked under the same conditions. I could see how much our people were still suffering and wondered what I could possibly do to help. When we visited the miners' families, they all talked about how Chairman Mao's visit had been like a lamp lighting their way, but I knew our hosts were not old enough to have remembered his stay.

Realizing that everyone was too exhausted to attempt the march back to the cadre school, the leaders ordered trucks for the return trip. Our literature department decided, however, that since we were already halfway to Jinggang Mountain, we should push on to visit this even more hallowed revolutionary site. Also, we knew that if we were to return to Liyuzhou with the others, we would immediately face the problem of having nothing for the students to do. Again I said good-bye to my family, aware that Lao Tang would soon set off on a similar excursion with the philosophy students, leaving Tang Shuang behind in Liyuzhou. Concerned about my son but knowing I had no alternative, I left a second time for Jinggang Mountain.

After several days we reached Sanwan, where Mao Zedong in 1927 reorganized the scattered troops that would soon be known as the Red Army. Many memorials had been built to commemorate his and Lin Biao's achievements. The places where Chairman Mao had announced the "eight forbidden things," establishing the standards of discipline for this army, as well as where Lin Biao had slept and where the soldiers had lived, had all been carefully restored. Sanwan was just a village, without even a street and with just two small shops run by the local commune, but it was a beautiful spot. Spring had already come to this subtropical area; the apple trees had begun to bud, and the fields of yellow rape, dotted with purple wildflowers and ringed by high mountains, created a beautiful backdrop for these revolutionary monuments.

The peasants here seemed warm and honest when they expressed their strong devotion to the Red Army, in which many of their children had assumed positions of some rank. Thus we decided to spend a few days in Sanwan, seizing this opportunity for the students to truly learn from the people. Divided into groups of three and accompanied by a teacher, they would visit the peasants and ask them to recall songs, poems, and folk stories as well as their own family histories, later developing these rich materials into essays. At the cadre school they had been able to write only about their own lives, but with the experiences of these peasants as a resource, the students could begin to develop their understanding of Chinese society. Seeing a great improvement in their writing, I thought that perhaps we had finally found a successful new way to teach.

After three more days of continuous walking, we reached the Jinggang Mountain region. All along the road from Sanwan we had passed memorial buildings commemorating events in revolutionary history, most of them restored ancestral halls that preserved, for example, the bed where Mao Zedong had slept, the mosquito netting he had used, or the table where Lin Biao had eaten. Every day during our stay, we visited some site of special importance, such as the large, white, moss-covered stone where Chairman Mao had often sat to make important decisions and to contemplate the future of China. Always a guide would explain the significance of the spot, educating the visitors about the history of class struggle. Now that so many people were carrying out Chairman Mao's call for "camp and field training" by engaging in similar expeditions, the guides had grown quite experienced.

In one huge memorial hall we viewed an enormous oil painting of Chairman Mao meeting Lin Biao, but everyone knew this representation to be historically inaccurate, for it was actually Marshall Zhu De who had met Mao at this spot. In Beijing many of us had seen the original painting, but in this copy Zhu De's face had been changed to that of Lin Biao, while every other detail had been faithfully reproduced from the original.

We also made several visits to a home for the elderly, all people who had made some contribution to the revolution in their early years. When asked to recall the past, these old men grew animated and provided the students with abundant material for their compositions and poems. But after almost a month had passed, we felt that the experiment could not be extended indefinitely. Many of the young people had grown restless, complaining that they had nothing to read and that they could not write endlessly without having some kind of textbooks against which to test what the veteran revolutionaries were telling them. Again feeling that we were not teaching the students adequately, we decided to return to Liyuzhou and try to provide them with a more thorough understanding of revolutionary history.

Returning to the cadre school by truck via Nanchang, where I had gone to order books for the worker, peasant, soldier students, I set out as soon as I could for Tang Shuang's dormitory, alarmed to find him very thin and recovering from a recent bout of tonsilitis. From Lao Tang, who had returned before me, I learned that the situation had been far more serious than my son revealed. Each day Tang Shuang had remained behind in the dormitory when the others went out to do their labor, and Lao Tang had found him lying there, just one small body amid all those empty beds, his face flushed with fever. Beside him was a small stool on which stood a cup of water and half of a tomato, the best sustenance his friends could offer when they left for the day. Lao Tang's voice grew strained as he remarked that anything could have happened with Tang

Shuang unattended in that dormitory; had he felt faint, he could never even have called for help. At least when he was a small child and had fallen ill there had been someone to care for him, if not his mother, but this time he had been completely alone. Sharing Lao Tang's distress, I felt I could never leave my son again.

Some five days later, however, a telegram arrived advising us that Lao Tang's mother was seriously ill and that we should return to her bedside. Knowing that the travel expenses were too great for us all to go, I insisted that Tang Shuang accompany his father, even though his fever had not completely disappeared, so that he could receive medical care in Beijing. As I stood sadly watching the steamboat pull away from the dock, I could see Tang Shuang waving to me from the crowded deck. Worry flooded over me, for his health, for his future, and for the untold difficulties my rightist label would cause him in the years to come.

In just two weeks a decision was announced that all the worker, peasant, soldier students would proceed with their teachers to the Beijing campus, since the educational facilities at the cadre school had proven inadequate. Many of the students had written letters back to the university protesting that they had neither books nor equipment, that they even had no access to peasants, and that with so much of their time spent doing labor, they had little opportunity to study. Finally, the authorities had agreed that these objections were justified. By then it was March 1971. During the next two months I packed up all of my family's belongings and assembled the various teaching materials we had accumulated.

Our departure was scheduled at night, the daytime temperatures already prohibitively hot in late May. The whole cadre school gathered cheerfully to see us off, knowing that they would soon follow. As we bounced along in the back of a truck, proceeding on that narrow road atop the dike for the last time, lights sparkled gaily from the fishing boats, matching the students' mood but not my own. The young people talked excitedly, many having never been to Beijing except perhaps for a brief stay as Red Guards exchanging experiences. But despite the tranquility of the lake at night and the welcome prospect of returning home, my thoughts were somber. I kept recalling our earlier trip along this road and the two who had died in that overturned truck, their ashes remaining buried forever beside this lake. I thought also of the others who had died, seven in the capsized boat, two from snail fever, two from amoebic dysentery, two from suicide, not to mention the money and effort that had been wasted to build a power station, an irrigation system, and buildings to house and supply us all.

In midsummer those remaining at the cadre school received orders to prepare for their return to Beijing. Apparently, the announcement prompted an immediate cessation of labor and the beginning of a kind of holiday spirit. With discipline relaxed and everyone concerned only with thoughts of going home, the pigs were all slaughtered, and "hundred-chicken banquets" held to consume the fowl. The community so laboriously constructed out of that forbidding lake bottom was dismantled, and arrangements were made to sell the steamboats and the farm machines cheaply to a nearby commune, to disassemble the electric power station, to take the trucks and as much other equipment as possible back to the campus. Many items had no further use, however, and the school became a vast carpentry shop as bed boards were fashioned into couches and desks, tables and bookcases, to utilize the wood that was still so precious and difficult to obtain in Beijing. However, the dormitories, the brick factory, the paddy lands could only be abandoned. Our battles against the snails and mosquitoes, against the oppressive heat and the treacherous rains, were totally wasted. Both the human and the economic costs of constructing Beida's cadre school were just to be forgotten.

The New Generation

THIS WAS MY fourth return from the countryside, yet when the truck deposited me with all my belongings once again in front of the main dining hall, I looked around with shock and dismay at the signs of disrepair and general neglect. Never before had the campus appeared so shabby and untended. The crimson flag that had once flown so proudly, symbolizing my classmates' hope in the future of our country, was nowhere to be seen, and paint peeled forlornly from the flagpole.

The Jinggang Mountain buildings that had been connected by tunnels at the height of New Beida's siege were now surrounded by mounds of dirt and rubble, dumped hastily on the walkways when the first-floor rooms were suddenly ordered cleared of the residue of battle and readied for occupancy once again. For two years those buildings had lain vacant, their damage so extensive that the propaganda teams had simply ignored them. But the decision to bring more than a hundred students back to campus from the cadre school had made additional dormitory space necessary, and the worker, peasant, soldier students were being assigned to these battered quarters.

From one corner of the former Jinggang Mountain headquarters a rope festooned with old, broken-down shoes still dangled, a crude reminder of the insulting allegations of Nie Yuanzi's promiscuity which no one had bothered to remove. On many rooftops the

stout rods that had served as slingshot mounts peered down ominously, and at the top of the campus heating plant's huge chimney,
a faded threat still proclaimed, "If the enemies don't surrender,
they will all perish." As my gaze was caught by this reminder of
previous propaganda battles, I wondered idly how anyone could
have managed to paint those characters so far above the ground.
Some of the walls boasted fresh slogans, declaring, "Beida warmly
welcomes the propaganda teams," or "Return to the classroom and
continue the revolution." On other walls, faded but still prominent, appeared lingering testimony to the ferocity of bygone campaigns. "We must smash Lu Ping's dog's head," I read, recalling the
terror occasioned by the appearance of an alleged criminal's name
so harshly obliterated by a large red X.

The side porch of the philosophy building stood empty, the sign
now unheeded that proclaimed it a "platform for criticizing ghosts."
But my memory peopled this makeshift stage once again with the
frightened faces of teachers and cadres, many of them my friends
and colleagues, painfully posed in the jet plane stance. Everywhere
the grass, now brown in early summer, grew uncut. Hardly a win-
dowpane remained intact, the jagged shards of protruding glass
now shrouded with cobwebs and dust. Surrounded by these grim
reminders of times past, I wondered if all that had happened since
1966 could perhaps have been a bad dream, some nightmare from
which I had finally awakened.

The others who had returned with me from Liyuzhou, occupied with the immediate task of transporting their scattered belongings, were attempting to borrow bicycle carts on which to load
the possessions that had served them during the past two years.
Seeing no available carts, I set out to look for Lao Tang and my son.
My mother-in-law, recovering from a broken hip, looked pitifully
old and weak and greeted me tearfully, expressing words of relief at
my return and pouring out her desire to move in with my family at
once. I reassured her as best I could and turned to greet my daughter, on vacation from Heilongjiang to be reunited with her parents,
her face somber as she spoke of the difficulties of life on the military farm.

I had last seen her leaving for the Northeast nearly two years before, optimistic and eager, determined to soar like an eagle and help develop the frontier. Now she spoke only about returning to Beijing and about the oppression of those once enthusiastic young people, who had in the intervening months encountered the realities of bribery, blackmail, and rape. I was shocked at her size. Noting with alarm that she had not grown any taller, I was fearful that she had been ruined physically as well as spiritually by her experiences.

My brother-in-law and his wife were far more polite than when I had seen them last, for Lao Tang and I were teachers, selected from among the whole faculty, and we thus occupied positions of honor once again. Still, I felt fortunate that we had paid rent for all those months, as now we had a home of our own to return to. Many others, believing they would surely spend the rest of their lives in the countryside, had given up their housing and were being allocated space in student dormitories, sometimes crowded in with five or six people to a room.

Trying to absorb a flurry of initial impressions, I hurried back to the dining hall to claim my belongings. A young teacher from my department, seeing my need for a cart, came up and offered to help. This unexpected gesture of assistance from a Party member filled me with the hope that perhaps others would now treat me as one of the people. A renewed sense of equality and acceptance, plus the prospect of being a teacher once more, helped dispel the gloom created by the physical appearance of the campus and by my mother-in-law's and daughter's somber spirits.

I had returned many times to this same spot in the center of the university, but somehow, strangely, I felt more optimistic than on any of those earlier occasions. After the ordeal we had undergone, this seemed a new beginning, for our country which had weathered such crippling storms, for the university with its new educational goals, and for my family now that Lao Tang and I had been reinstated as teachers. Even though the people around me seemed depressed, the campus badly damaged, some irrepressible new hope surged within me.

Nevertheless, I could see that the process of reconstruction would be long and difficult. Rebuilding just the physical facilities would take much time. After unpacking, I visited the students who had been my roommates in Liyuzhou to invite them for a meal. Their room was badly scarred, the cement floor chipped, the broken windowpanes covered by newspapers that rustled in the wind, the once white walls blackened from cooking and heating fires that had consumed most of the dormitory furniture. On top of the boards covering one of the tunnel entrances a table had been placed, but the bed boards and benches still stood in piles about the floor. It would be two months before the dirt piled outside the windows was loaded onto trucks and carted away.

Clearly, the past five years had brought devastating changes to more than just the university's physical plant. Only the worker, peasant, soldier students remained on campus, since nearly the entire Red Guard generation had been sent out in 1968 and 1969, many to military farms in the far reaches of Gansu and Guizhou. The fate of those former students, so recently touted by Chairman Mao as the hope of China's future, epitomized for me the enormous waste of the Cultural Revolution. Those thousands of young people still seemed worthy of our respect; their courage, resourcefulness, and resilience had all been amply demonstrated. Their idealism, their fervor, their desire to contribute to their country, as well as their loyalty to Chairman Mao, were surely incontestable. Yet now their reputation had plummeted, and I wondered what their future would hold. Lacking skills as well as education, habituated to an absence of discipline and a disrespect for authority, they were considered undesirable by leading officials in the army and the factories alike, and were consequently just sent away to do labor in remote areas of the countryside.

Moreover, although the goal of the Cultural Revolution had been to renovate Chinese culture, there now seemed to be little of our cultural heritage remaining at all. Certainly the educational level of the student generation had plunged far lower than before. The worker, peasant, soldier students, while capable and eager to learn, were difficult to teach because of their limited educational backgrounds. Many had attended only primary school; a few were unable even to write Chinese characters with ease. It worried me to realize that both groups—the worker, peasant, soldiers being given a chance for higher education, and the "educated youths" remaining in the countryside to create a new generation of peasants— were largely ignorant of Chinese culture. They knew so little about "today and yesterday, [things] Chinese and foreign," they had so little appreciation of their cultural heritage, that I feared for the future of my country. Thus there was much to counter my optimism.

Many others shared my misgivings about current policy, my doubts about the consequences of the past five years, but no one could speak about such things. The newspaper editorials and radio broadcasts daily proclaimed the importance of the Cultural Revolution, which had been led by Chairman Mao himself. "Long live the Cultural Revolution," "Down with anyone who opposes the Cultural Revolution," were repeated refrains. Despite this propaganda effort, however, it was during this period that the young generation, recently so fervently committed to revolutionary goals, their passion now spent, began to reflect on their altered circumstances and to develop a new consciousness about what had gone wrong.

Another change had occurred at Beida in 1970 when Chi Qun, the former political commissar of an 8341 division, was appointed to head Qinghua's revolutionary committee and given responsibility for the educational reforms at these two universities, having previously assumed similar responsibilities in the Ministry of Education. Although only in his mid-thirties, this assertive and strong-willed young man commanded wide respect. I had met him one drenching day at Liyuzhou when he appeared in our dormitory dressed in a shabby military uniform and a straw hat, looking not at all like an important official. His manner was easy and solicitous; he asked us what problems we were encountering and seemed genuinely eager to help. Xie Jingyi, also from the 8341 PLA unit and formerly the personal secretary of Jiang Qing, now deputy head of Qinghua's revolutionary committee, was with him. Impressed by their air of self-confidence, we formed an initial impression that these new leaders were capable, accessible, and concerned with the welfare of the Beida community. Later, when Chi Qun announced in the summer of 1971 that the Jiangxi cadre school would be dissolved, he gained further support among the faculty.

The propaganda teams still retained positions of leadership at all levels, although their original members had been replaced now that peace was restored. Most of the workers were either very young and inexperienced or very old, near retirement, and although often kind and pleasant, they knew nothing about education. Their function was to carry out the instructions of the PLA cadres in authority.

The main goal of Chi Qun's administration was the implementation of a new educational policy based on Chairman Mao's instruction in 1958 that students in the humanities and social sciences must use society as the laboratory in which to test their theories. During the past seventeen years, we were told, the main problem with education had been the "three separations," the separation of the university from the worlds of practice, of politics, and of manual labor. Scientists were said to perform sophisticated experiments with wheat in a test tube, but to be unable to recognize wheat growing in a field; intellectuals in general pursued their research goals without consideration for the needs of the people. To eliminate such problems, students were to be prohibited from following the old pathways; they were no longer to walk the old trail from the library to the dining hall to the dormitory, called the "three points in a straight line," or to isolate themselves in the university like snails hiding in their shells. Nor were they to be stuffed with useless information, like so many Beijing ducks for roasting; instead, they were to be encouraged to think for themselves. Their term of study was simultaneously to be shortened, the five-year program in Chinese literature reduced to three years, the physics and math curricula taught in four years rather than six.

While these new policies were in many ways sound, they posed difficult problems. The teachers, having just recovered from an intense period of criticism, struggle, and humiliation, were hesitant to offer lecture courses. They preferred instead to lead discussions, not wanting to risk being labeled "bourgeois academic authorities" in the future, but their reticence hampered their ability to impart knowledge. Furthermore, no one knew how to utilize society as a laboratory, even though we all could agree on the goals. Meanwhile, viewing their years at the university as a precious opportunity to learn, the students wanted to spend their time studying, not just taking repeated trips to communes and factories.

We set about reforming education as best we could. My own assignment for that fall semester of 1971 was to teach a course about the struggle between bourgeois and proletarian literary theory from the May Fourth Movement in 1919 to Liberation in 1949. One tradition, exemplified by such poets as Xu Zhimou, who was influenced by Mallarmé and Baudelaire, was seen as leading people to decadence; the other, exemplified by such celebrated writers as Lu Xun and Guo Moruo, was thought to encourage people in their revolutionary struggle. In addition, I led the students to analyze the errors in the literary line of the past seventeen years, explaining that Zhou Yang's policies were bad because they had caused literature to become separated from the workers, peasants, and soldiers, and that Jiang Qing's policies promoting the model operas were good. The workers, peasants, and soldiers must be portrayed as heroes in every literary work; they must be presented as "tall, valued, and perfect."

This assignment was difficult for me. For the sake of my children, I wanted to be a good teacher, to satisfy the leaders and earn their praise, but being a "five same-thing teacher" was not easy. In the cadre school I had been obliged to fabricate an explanation about how I had opposed Chairman Mao's view of literature, and now I must teach the virtues of the model operas when I knew that workers, peasants, and soldiers were not perfect, and that the more we insisted on their flawlessness, the more people would distrust the new literature. Since Jiang Qing had said that this elimination of "middle characters" was the main difference between the old bourgeois line of Zhou Yang and the new proletarian line, however, I had no choice. Gathering materials from newspapers and magazines, I based my comments always on these reflections of official policy rather than on my private thoughts, so that no one could criticize my viewpoint.

Such ongoing concerns were suddenly interrupted by an event of the greatest importance. A young woman student who had grown quite close to me and whose father was a high naval official came to me one night in mid-September, just after the anniversary of both my marriage and my mother's death, with a shocking story. Lin Biao, she told me breathlessly, had plotted unsuccessfully to assassinate Chairman Mao, and his airplane had crashed while he was trying to escape to the Soviet Union. Her story seemed totally preposterous. Lin Biao was, after all, Chairman Mao's closest comrade-in-arms, and daily I had waved my Red Book in the air and repeated rhythmically, "Chairman Mao, may he live ten thousand years; Lin Biao, may he have good health forever."

Although in retrospect such ritualized devotion seems difficult to imagine, at the time we chanted this paean seriously and enthusiastically. My student's excited words thus left me aghast and terrified, and I warned her that surely such a sensational story was only a rumor. Fearing that she might place herself in grave danger merely by repeating this unconfirmed account, I urged her not to spread her news any further. What I had heard seemed too terrible to be true, yet too fantastic to discount. I could only guess that some new struggle might be unfolding, some serious rift within the highest leadership. That evening Lao Tang agreed that the news could not possibly be true, since Lin Biao was Chairman Mao's closest ally; like me, Lao Tang believed that a conspiracy of such dimensions could never happen within the Communist Party.

The rumors spread rapidly, and soon everyone was talking secretly about the news. Within a few days we had heard many details about these shocking, indeed unimaginable, events. Supposedly, Lin Biao had wanted to kill Chairman Mao in his train, but at the last minute Lu Min, the person responsible for executing the plot, had become frightened and had felt overwhelmed by guilt at the prospect of killing such a great man, perhaps remaining a criminal forever in the eyes of history. However, Lu knew that he would himself be killed if he failed to perform his appointed duty, so he went to his sister, an eye doctor, and told her that he must immediately be admitted to a hospital. She gave him some drops that blurred his vision, making his eyes red and swollen, and he entered the hospital. Thus the deadly explosion was averted.

At this point, according to the story we were told, Lin Biao became very frightened that people would learn of the aborted plot, especially since Lu Min's brother was the chief editor of *People's Daily*. Panicked, Lin decided to move rapidly, but he was uncertain how to carry out his plan. His treachery was stopped only by the revelations of his daughter, Lin Lihen, a student in my department while I was in Zhaitang, who had access to the red telephone used by high officials and called Chairman Mao's office to reveal her father's intention to flee with his accomplices to Canton. From there, bolstered by many supporters, he would resist Chairman Mao's forces in the north, and with the help of the Soviet Union split China in two. Unable to find his daughter, and guessing that she had informed on him, Lin Biao decided to escape immediately to the Soviet Union. Some people even said that his wife, Ye Qun, lost one of her high-heeled shoes on the tarmac while running to board the airplane.

To foil this conspiracy, Zhou Enlai was sent to the Great Hall of the People where, on a huge radar screen, he watched Lin Biao's airplane take off, but he could not order it shot down over Chinese territory, as people might accuse him of conspiring to overthrow Lin Biao. Only when the plane flew out of Chinese air space and crossed the boundary into Mongolia, did Zhou make a decisive downward gesture with his fist, the signal for a missile to destroy its target. This was a great victory for Zhou Enlai, who was likened to a god for handling the affair so efficiently.

In the plane, supposedly, were Lin Biao, his wife, his only son Lin Liguo, and a secretary, while some distance behind them flew a helicopter carrying the three people responsible for executing the coup. Also aboard the helicopter were many top-secret Air Force documents, as well as large sums of American money. Zhou Enlai decided not to shoot down the helicopter, because the affair might still look like a conspiracy if there were no one left to tell the story, so he sent up three planes to force the helicopter to land. His plan was successful, and all the documents were saved. The three criminals aboard, deciding to commit suicide simultaneously, each held a pistol to his own head. At the signal two pulled their triggers but the third hesitated; he was caught alive and later reported everything that had happened. There was no way to determine how much of this elaborate story was fact, how much had been embellished in the telling.

News of Lin Liguo's unsavory activities also spread quickly, and everyone gossiped excitedly about how he had wanted to find a beautiful wife and about how his mother had helped him in this search. People from all twenty-eight provinces, seeking advancement, had sent him photographs of attractive young women, and even at Beida the Party secretary in the politics department had selected a particularly attractive student in the attached middle school, sending the girl's photograph to Ye Qun, an action for which the secretary was harshly attacked after the fall of the Gang of Four. However, Lin Liguo had allegedly chosen a comely nurse from Wuhan and sent her to Beijing to train to be the wife of a high official.

Some particularly lurid accounts told how he tried to force her to accompany him on the airplane to the Soviet Union and beat her severely when she refused, then locked her in a dark room. In the preceding months, people testified, he had traveled repeatedly to Canton where he could watch television shows broadcast from Hong Kong, Taiwan, and the United States. Every night he would select a different mistress, always a stewardess from either the military or civilian airlines. I even heard through the rumor mill that Ye Qun had carried on a private relationship with Huang Yongsheng, the PLA chief of staff. There seemed no end to the gossip.

How could Lin Liguo, a young man of just twenty-four, be trusted with such a high position as head of the Operations Department of the Air Force; how could he be given the authority even to initiate acts of war on another country; how could the fate of the entire society be controlled by such an inexperienced, degenerate person, I queried. In my mind the relationship between leaders like Mao Zedong and Lin Biao had seemed so pure, so unshakable, a friendship forged in hardship and warfare, almost a holy alliance. How could these two now be trying to kill each other? I knew that the accounts I had heard were unreliable, but still the rumors made me question how such intrigues could occur within the highest levels of the Communist Party. Even though I had been dismissed from its ranks, I still idolized the Party, believing it to be almost sacred. During the Cultural Revolution I had seen ample evidence of corruption in the private lives of high officials, but I had dismissed this as an individual problem, trusting that after awhile such weaknesses could be eliminated. Now it seemed indisputable that the corruption permeated the whole system.

The revelations were shattering for me. I could not sleep at night, thinking that if all this had never been revealed, Lin Biao would have remained a lofty, hallowed figure. No one would have known what was happening "behind the screen," or that the corruption reached to the very core of the Party. So many of us had dedicated our lives to the future of our country, but what use were our efforts when the society was being directed by people like Lin Liguo? Both Lao Tang and I were disillusioned, aware that something was fundamentally wrong with the system in which we had believed so devotedly. I guessed that we were not the only ones whose faith in the Party wavered, but no one could communicate his misgivings.

The prevailing assessment of Lin Biao changed very rapidly after news of his plot against Chairman Mao was revealed. Earlier we had been told of his heroic accomplishments in the Anti-Japanese War, of the great contributions to his country he had made while the youngest commander in the Red Army. Although rumors had circulated in those years that he was addicted to opium, we had dismissed this gossip, concerning ourselves only with his military feats. Then when he was presented as the intended assassin of Chairman Mao, people's adulation changed overnight to hatred. Believing Lin Biao to be utterly ungrateful for all of Chairman Mao's trust, I shared in the shift of popular opinion. No one doubted Lin Biao's guilt; the photographs of the airplane wreckage provided indisputable evidence of his crimes.

As I pondered the disillusioning revelations about the man who had been named in the 1969 constitution as Chairman Mao's successor, I thought sadly about a woman named Ma Mingzhen, a chemical worker in Guiyang who had been arrested after speaking critically about Lin Biao. Ma had even written a wall poster querying that his designation as successor was a feudal practice, unsuited to the spirit of the Cultural Revolution. My stepmother had known this young woman, read her poster, and seen her paraded in an open truck through the city streets. Uncowed after her arrest, Ma had declared in her jail cell, "I speak the truth, although it may be too early; later everyone will acknowledge the validity of my words." To prevent her from uttering further heresy, her captors had dislocated her jawbone, then displayed her to the people en route to her execution. She was shot in 1969 on her thirtieth birthday. With Lin Biao's exposure, Ma Mingzhen's allegations were corroborated, two years too late to save the life of this promising young scientist.

Aware of the depth of popular misgivings after the Lin Biao affair, the leadership mounted a massive educational campaign to prevent the Party's image from being tarnished. At Beida, Chi Qun instructed the small writing-and-criticism groups within the humanities departments to turn their attention away from such previous targets as the old educational policies or the literary line of Zhou Yang and begin a thorough criticism of Lin Biao in order to exonerate the Party. Perhaps two months later, he established the Beida Big Criticism Group, drawing together some eight people from the existing departmental groups to organize materials criticizing Lin Biao, to discuss his plot, and to propagate a correct viewpoint on this recent crisis.

In response to signals from the highest levels of the Party, this university group pronounced the abortive coup an unfortunate affair, but not such a terrible occurrence that it could not be surmounted if confronted in the proper manner. Lin Biao, the group explained, was not a leftist, even though he appeared so outwardly, but rather a rightist in essence. The attempt by Chi Qun and Xie Jingyi to create an impression of unity and confidence was remarkably successful. Having observed how they organized the central criticism group so efficiently, initiated discussions at all levels so swiftly, and formulated their opinions on this potential disaster so convincingly, nearly everyone became persuaded, if not of the accuracy of their conclusions, at least of their effectiveness as leaders. Perhaps the Central Committee was indeed still solidly united, Lin Biao's treachery an isolated event, an aberration.

While we were pursuing our discussions of Lin Biao's crimes in department meetings, debating the various newspaper editorials that pronounced him alternately an ultra-leftist, then a rightist, or a leftist at the outset and a rightist at the end, or a leftist on the outside and a rightist in essence, we were also trying to set the university in operation again. I was given various assignments during those first two years after returning from the cadre school.

For awhile during the winter and spring of 1972, I worked on the air raid shelters being constructed on campus in response to Chairman Mao's call to "dig tunnels deep, store grain everywhere, and never seek hegemony." To provide for our needs in the event of nuclear war, we were tunneling out classrooms, a dining hall, even an underground library, all of which would connect with the vast labyrinth of tunnels being constructed beneath the city. First, we removed vast quantities of earth using shoulder poles and wheelbarrows; then, we hauled in tall steel-reinforced concrete arches on small handcarts; finally, we replaced the dirt to conceal our shelters from view. Everyone contributed a full month of labor to this collective project.

Later I spent my time attending political meetings, preparing a new course on Lu Xun, writing brief articles to explain his essays to the worker, peasant, soldier students, and supervising their research papers. This was, in fact, my most challenging assignment because the students' level of knowledge was low, their experience in writing a literary essay minimal. That fall the students became deeply engaged in the study of Marxism-Leninism and attended many lectures on four of Marx's works. I was responsible for supplementary lectures on two of these books, the *Critique of the Gotha Program* and the *Communist Manifesto*, after which I would meet with a group of students in their dormitory to help them resolve any questions they had on the lectures.

By the early summer of 1973, we were ready to set aside theory and begin using society as our laboratory. Because of my previous experience teaching writing, I was assigned to the journalism group within my department, and set out with ten students and two other teachers to Shijiazhuang, a six-hour trip by rail, to live at the offices of the *Hebei Daily*. There the students would train to become reporters.

I was reluctant to leave home this time and, like many of the other teachers, felt some envy for the more settled, stable life of the university office staff. Lao Tang's mother had decided not to live permanently with us, despite her strained relations with her other daughter-in-law, as the space in our house was cramped and we had no *ayi* to help with her daily needs. Still, she enjoyed coming for short stays, and I regretted that my departure would deny her these happy intervals with her grandchildren. Tang Shuang, now fourteen, would miss me even more, for his father was preoccupied with meetings and came home only to sleep. I arranged for my son to have a meal contract at a canteen that catered to students at the nearby Academy of Sciences, having no choice but to leave him again essentially on his own. Sadly I recalled how little I had been able to care for my son, not even able to nourish him with my milk when he was an infant.

During the half year away from campus, I lived together with the women students in the newspaper offices, sleeping on the floor in a bedroll and eating in the staff canteen. I settled into a comfortable routine, collecting information with the students and helping them compose their articles during the day, and at night, when they were busy with their work, immersing myself in Western novels, mostly Balzac and Dostoevsky, borrowed from the well-stocked newspaper office library. Absorbed in my reading, I would continue by flashlight under my quilt after the lights went out at eleven o'clock.

My group was responsible for reporting on education and agriculture, and we had just begun to familiarize ourselves with the situation in Shijiazhuang when the Zhang Tiesheng affair occurred. Earlier in 1973 reform of the university admissions system had been urged by many who believed that acceptance should be based not only on recommendations but on test scores as well. In response to this pressure, examinations were reinstituted that summer, but the new policy was unpopular among the high cadres, whose children would no longer be admitted automatically, and among young people prominent in the Cultural Revolution, who were politically advanced but had a limited educational background. One prospective student, a former Red Guard from Liaoning province named

Zhang Tiesheng, took the required examination on agriculture and, unable to answer the questions, instead wrote that such requirements constituted a return to the old way of education. The tests, he continued, were designed to exclude the worker, peasant, soldier students, to prevent them from "occupying the heights [above the battlefield]," and instead allowed this strategic spot to be captured by bourgeois intellectuals. The examinations were simply a means of oppressing the young generation and shackling their thoughts, Zhang Tiesheng continued, proof that the people responsible for instituting such a procedure should be overthrown.

When many high-level leaders, including Chi Qun, applauded Zhang's assertions, the newspapers published both his comments and numerous articles praising him as a hero who opposed the old educational system. My group from the *Hebei Daily* was sent to interview middle-school teachers, students, and workers to learn their views of this controversy. Some of those interviewed said that Zhang's response was correct, that those entitled to an education should not be determined by test scores, but others queried how someone unable to answer any test questions at all could be held up as a hero.

I personally disagreed with Zhang's argument, but the leader of the newspaper had requested that we treat this affair as an important example and had announced that Zhang Tiesheng was protecting the right of all the workers, peasants, and soldiers to an education. The educational level in the Shijiazhuang area was quite low at that time, and the leader wanted us to present Zhang Tiesheng as a hero who was preventing both a return to the old way and the creation of a "spiritual aristocracy." Not all the students agreed with the leader's position, and we discussed the problem at length.

One of my students, a worker from the model oilfields at Daqing, insisted on presenting both sides of the issue and refused to report only the approving comments, but her article was never published. The newspaper officials, asserting that such a balanced judgment was not appropriate at this time, advised the students to make their articles support the "newborn things" from the Cultural Revolution and strive to improve whatever they found deficient. Having been criticized once before for defending a student's right to analyze the failings of official policy, this time I deferred to the leader's judgment.

When I returned home for Spring Festival, many faculty members, I learned, had criticized the effort to turn Zhang Tiesheng into a "blank paper hero." Determined to correct their attitude, Chi Qun had secretly organized an examination that would humiliate these arrogant professors, purposely including many questions that required the recall of specific, even trivial, information. One afternoon the teachers were all told to attend an important meeting from which no one could request leave. When they arrived at their department meeting rooms, each was given a test paper with questions covering the teacher's academic field as well as political theory. So angry were many of the professors at such demeaning treatment that one simply wrote, "I would like to take a score of zero and learn from Zhang Tiesheng." Chi Qun's purpose was to make the teachers feel humble, to demonstrate that one examination was not an accurate test of a person's ability, and to enforce the lesson that the destiny of the young generation should not be decided on the basis of a single test. Instead of reducing the faculty's sense of superiority toward the students, however, the episode succeeded instead in reducing the faculty's esteem for Chi Qun.

I was in Shijiazhuang at the time and therefore did not take part in the exam, but in 1975 I watched a movie recreating this event, with the teachers in my department serving as actors. Titled "Counterattack," the film's purpose was to embarrass the intellectuals, many of whom were thought to have remained arrogant when classes had resumed after the Cultural Revolution, to have seized this chance to retaliate for past injustices and make the worker, peasant, soldier students feel inadequate and inferior. As the simulated exam progressed, my eye was repeatedly caught by Lao Ding's bald head as he sat before the camera staring at his test paper, unable to answer any questions, and I thought how convincing he was in his designated role. The film would have been circulated throughout the country except that the Gang of Four was arrested before the movie had been distributed.

While in Shijiazhuang I accompanied the students on several trips to the countryside. After observing the peasants, we would return to discuss our findings and decide how to analyze our data. In August we traveled five hours by bus to a commune west of the city to report on the peasants' advanced approaches to planting cotton. Eager to reveal how productive and prosperous they were, the commune leaders assigned us a room in a new house built by a couple about to be married. The villagers were so welcoming that they even let us use the betrothed couple's new quilt and bedding, hoping that such special treatment would encourage us to publicize their accomplishments. We took a lot of photographs, and they felt grateful for the chance to display their achievements.

One evening during our stay in this remote village, I heard a news broadcast reporting the events of the Tenth Party Congress. Immediately my attention returned to the national political scene. Wang Hongwen, the staunch ally of Jiang Qing and formerly the chief of security at a small Shanghai factory, a man with only a middle-school education, had been named deputy chairman of the Politburo, a position immediately below that of Zhou Enlai, and thus officially acknowledged as Chairman Mao's successor. I knew that this announcement signaled that the Gang of Four would take charge after Chairman Mao's death. Believing that the Cultural Revolution had amply demonstrated the failings of this ambitious group, I glanced at the veteran reporter who had accompanied our group to this commune. From his eyes I could feel that he shared my apprehension, but we both remained silent.

When I returned home from Shijiazhuang in early 1974, not only did I hear about the recent exam that had so offended the faculty and about the increasing disaffection for Chi Qun and his attempts to revolutionize the university, but I also found myself in the midst of a political campaign. Waged by Jiang Qing against old intellectuals and cadres, the movement against "right deviationists" was primarily an attack upon Deng Xiaoping, who had recently been returned to power after spending seven years working at a cadre school and in a factory. At Beida this campaign to expose "those who put on new shoes but follow the old trail" involved an investigation of people's thoughts and actions since 1971. The goal of the investigation was to determine which teachers and cadres had revealed any inclination to revert to feudalism, capitalism, or revisionism, and which ones were genuinely faithful to the needs of the workers, peasants, and soldiers.

When the students checked the notes they had taken at lectures given during that three-year period, they found many professors to criticize. Wu Zhuxiang, a novelist known especially for his descriptions of the countryside in the 1930s, for example, had once stated that some human emotions are universal and unaffected by political circumstances. He was harshly denounced for his explanation that a person would feel sympathy for any grief-stricken widow, whether her husband had died from disease, had been killed in battle, or had been executed as a landlord. Another professor was bitterly attacked for not alleging that class struggle was, as Chairman Mao had stated, the major theme of the classic eighteenth-century novel *Dream of the Red Chamber*.

Meetings were organized by the propaganda team leaders in each department with the students encouraged to identify any teachers who had harbored incorrect thoughts, or had led the young people in an academic direction and made them indifferent to politics, or had opposed the Party's educational policies by favoring the students' remaining on campus rather than going out to learn from society. Sometimes the class monitor would assemble small groups of students to write accusing posters, and advise them which problems in the department were the most urgently in need of reform.

During those weeks in February when the campaign was at its peak, three posters eventually singled me out for criticism. In Shijiazhuang, they claimed, I had spent my time reading bourgeois Western novels rather than establishing connections with the worker, peasant, soldiers. Furthermore, I had discussed those poisonous books with my students, thereby leading them astray. In the two meetings to criticize me, three students, all Party members, stood up to testify that my thoughts had deep rightist roots. One warned me never to relax and be tempted by such ideas; another shouted that I should never be allowed to teach again, as I would surely continue to corrupt the minds of the students. Just as in the Anti-rightist Campaign, it was the students closest to me, those who had wanted me to teach them about literature outside the

regular course work, who were the ones to attack me. I knew that
these young people would soon graduate and thus needed to establish their loyalty to the current movement to obtain good job assignments, but nevertheless their denunciations saddened me, as I
had tried to maintain a close relationship with these young worker,
peasant, soldiers. Their criticisms were not terribly serious compared with all that I had been accused of in the past; still I felt depressed at this new testimony to the unreliability of human relationships in the aftermath of the Cultural Revolution.

Then suddenly, after perhaps a month had passed, the criticisms stopped and the movement was dropped; no one knew why.
Later we would guess that the Gang of Four had been unsuccessful
in its attempt to remove Deng Xiaoping from power, but at the time
we just said that, like other initially threatening but abortive campaigns, this one had the "head of a tiger but the tail of a snake." My
errors were never again mentioned, and I was sent out with a
group of students to train for a month with a PLA regiment.

Another effort to pursue the revolution in education, this assignment was intended to make the students learn from the soldiers their discipline, their correct political thought, their simple
and frugal lifestyle. I was intrigued by the prospect of seeing what
life was like in the army. After traveling for several hours by jeep,
followed by the students in an open truck, I reached the regimental
headquarters in Changping county, and was immediately impressed
by the orderly arrangement of the buildings. While the natural setting was uninspiring, a basin surrounded by dry, rocky mountains
that reminded me of bald heads, the symmetry and tidiness of the
installation was appealing.

At first the students and I were assigned to a group of ten ordinary soldiers with whom we ate each meal, ladling our individual
portions of beans, vegetables, and salted turnips out of a common
basin. After the first week, however, the teachers were given the
privilege of eating with the officers, and I found myself in a totally
different environment at mealtimes. Seated at a round table, I would
be served plentiful helpings of four dishes, one of them always containing meat, another often sprinkled with peanuts. This was my
first contact with military officials. While some of them were affable,

asking about the worker, peasant, soldier students on our campus or about our families at home, others were arrogant and aloof, refusing to speak with us and silently conveying their antipathy toward intellectuals.

The first week of our training was physically very taxing, as we novices had to learn to march carrying heavy packs and weapons, an exercise we practiced for five hours a day. Three times during that week a trumpet blared at midnight, the signal for us to pack our quilts and equipment in five minutes and prepare for battle. To my embarrassment, I never could complete this assignment successfully, but would always lose my things in the dark and be late for roll call. When the drill was finished, we could go back to sleep.

The second week the students began rifle and pistol practice, an assignment I thought exciting, but I was asked instead to teach writing to a group of army correspondents. Thus when the students went out for target practice, I spent the whole day in the classroom. I grew very fond of my new pupils, however, and often would go out with them after dinner to practice shooting, feeling great delight when one or two of my bullets would hit the target. These shy, sincere young infantrymen, all peasants from the countryside, came several times to visit me after I returned to Beijing, eager for me to check the articles they had written for the PLA newspaper. Some, like Xiao Pan, a modest, earnest young man of nineteen from a peasant family, were avid to learn and hopeful of someday attending a university.

It was perhaps May 1974, after I had rested for several weeks at home, that I was sent out from campus yet again, this third time to accompany a new group of journalism students for their apprenticeship. This time our base was the nearby *Beijing Daily*, an assignment that allowed us to return home on weekends. Despite this advantage, I felt less relaxed here than at the *Hebei Daily*, both because our leader was from the 8341 unit on campus—a high official's son who had completed only junior middle school and disliked intellectuals—and because my group was responsible for investigating the new achievements in industry. Among the peasants I had always felt relaxed and confident, but on our first visit to a metal-refining plant, I immediately grew tense at my inadequacy in the presence of huge and unfathomable machines. The journalist accompanying our group often looked critically at me, realizing my ignorance about factories. Although I was eager to learn, even the briefing sessions, with their statistics about rates of production, were not easy for me to follow. Determined to become familiar with industrial production and the concerns of the workers, I tried to overcome my ignorance and worked hard with the students to turn their comments into publishable articles.

Responding to the students' discontent and to their arguments that they could not write endlessly about the society without deepening their knowledge, we teachers finally scheduled one day each week for lectures and discussions about Lu Xun. My topic was his literary thought, while others would discuss his poems and novels. The enthusiastic response made us feel that finally we had discovered an effective educational method, instructing the students while they were at the same time immersed in the society. Our experiment was considered so successful by the university leadership that it was later recommended as a model for other departments.

As in Shijiazhuang, I developed a close relationship with those young people, who knew that I was not a Party member, that I was understanding and not very strict. Sometimes they would confide to me their private thoughts. The official regulation that students were not allowed even to discuss the subject of love, a rule that conflicted unrealistically with the natural impulses of these young people in their late twenties, caused several of them to seek out my advice. After several months I became aware that a young man I had known from the Liyuzhou campus was trying to win the affections of a girl who lived in the room next to mine. Sometimes in the evening when the students would gather around the single television set, I would see him pass notes to this girl, whom I knew to be interested in another young man. Even though he was not especially talented academically, the boy came from a peasant family and had been a coal miner before joining the PLA. He was proud of his impeccable worker, peasant, soldier credentials and rather arrogant.

319

One Saturday afternoon when I was correcting papers, after most of the students and newspaper staff had left for the weekend, I heard sharp screams and cries for help coming from the side stairwell. At the third floor landing I found this girl, terror-stricken, running toward me with blood streaming down her face. The young man was pursuing her with a knife. While the others surrounded her assailant, fearing that in his crazed state he might do further harm to himself or others, I rushed the girl to the nearest hospital. I later learned that her angry suitor had crisscrossed her cheeks with eight gashes, determined that if he could not have her himself, he would spoil her beauty so that no other man would ever want to marry her. In ten days her wounds had nearly healed, but she felt so demeaned and humiliated that she could no longer face her fellow students and returned to Tianjin where she had formerly been a worker. I never heard from her again.

The boy was declared a traitor to his worker-peasant-soldier class, and the entire Beida community was summoned to a meeting to denounce him. As he stood on a platform, three people analyzed how he had come to act in such a way, observing that his arrogance had made him willful and selfish. The leadership wanted to make him an example, to illustrate that even a respected member of the working class can become a "bourgeois successor," commit immoral acts, and bring about his own destruction. After the meeting had gone on for two hours, a jeep arrived carrying several uniformed policemen, who handcuffed the young man and dramatically led him away. He spent a year in jail and was then returned to his coal mine as a laborer.

Despite the effort to attribute the boy's crime to his own character, the incident was troubling for many of us. It seemed natural to me for these young people to fall in love and obvious that the official policy of prohibiting romantic emotions had contributed to this tragedy. When I tried to convey my concern to another teacher, querying whether love could in fact be denied by official regulation, he urged me not to discuss such matters, saying I would only get into trouble. But I knew the explanation for this terrible incident was more complex than the leaders had admitted. Clearly, the habituation to violence that was the legacy of the Cultural Revolution, plus utter ignorance and inexperience about how to handle the turbulent emotions of love and jealousy, had precipitated this disappointed suitor's cruelty. The young generation had perpetrated the turmoil, I reflected sadly, but they seemed destined to pay a higher price even than we, the revolution's intended victims.

Revolution's Wake

LIN BIAO's attempted coup d'etat in the fall of 1971 was never satisfactorily explained. Confusing articles continued to appear in the newspapers, alleging that Lin Biao was only a leftist in form but a rightist in essence, yet neither these statements nor repeated political study sessions had restored people's faith in the Party leadership. The Central Committee urgently needed some way to isolate and renounce Chairman Mao's chosen successor, to condemn Lin Biao without condemning as well the Cultural Revolution that he had so publicly championed. Among the people most eager to define the parameters of his conspiracy and thus eschew any connection to Lin Biao's treachery was Jiang Qing, whose close relationship to the late vice-chairman was fixed in the popular mind. Everyone knew that she owed her emergence as a public figure to the February 1966 conference on PLA art and literature at which she had, under Lin Biao's auspices, delivered the key address. Nor had people forgotten the photograph of Lin Biao in his study that was reproduced in all major newspapers, that conspicuously credited to photographer Li Jin—Jiang Qing's pen name.

Even the three sets of documents, complete with photographs of the airplane wreckage, compiled by the Central Case Committee had not laid people's doubts to rest. These materials had vividly chronicled Lin Biao's previous wrongdoings and exposed the elaborate details of his recent plot, but a definitive analysis of why he had so betrayed the Party's trust was still needed. When in August 1973 Chairman Mao remarked, in response to materials submitted by a study group at Qinghua, that it was correct to link the criticism of Lin Biao with that of Confucius, Jiang Qing no doubt recognized an opportunity to assign her former mentor's perfidy an academic coloration, distancing it from the contemporary scene by associating it with issues safely lodged in the remote past. Dissatisfied with the fourth set of Lin Biao documents then in progress, she decided to enlist the aid of scholars, aware that extensive new research and rethinking would be required to establish convincingly the correspondence between Lin Biao's errors and those of Confucius.

That fall, while I was still in Shijiazhuang, Chi Qun and the Party committees from the nation's two most prestigious universities had selected twelve scholars who would be relieved of all other duties to concentrate on an assignment of the utmost importance. Lao Tang, already a member of the writing group within his department working on the Lin Biao affair, was one of the six from Beida to be chosen for this task force that became known as "Liang Xiao"—a shortened form of the official title, Beida-Qinghua Two Schools Big Criticism Group, and a term that simultaneously meant "two schools" and its homonym "good effects." By December the group had moved into the beautiful Pavilion upon the Lake, formerly the residence of Yanjing University president John Leighton Stuart, their luxurious quarters an indication of the high esteem in which these scholars were held. Here in this tranquil setting they would be able to concentrate without distraction on their project to revise the fourth set of Lin Biao materials.

Learning by mail of Lao Tang's new assignment, I was pleased that he was considered one of the most academically learned and politically sophisticated members of the faculty. I naturally hoped that his appointment to such a distinguished group might help erase the stigma of his former "black gang" label and the shadow that both of our past histories had cast on our children's future. Impressed by the group's prestige and by the prospect that it would dictate policy for the whole country in the movement to criticize Lin Biao and Confucius, I had not the slightest premonition that membership in this elite body would ultimately bring disaster instead of benefit to my family. The effort to repudiate Lin Biao, who had brought such harm to the country, and to criticize Confucius, whose insistence on ritual and the subjugation of women I had always detested, seemed a necessary step to restore unity and promote progress.

During the spring and summer of 1974, after the group had been expanded to thirty-two members and moved to larger quarters in another lakeside guest house, the scholars enjoyed unusual privileges. Each was assigned a private room, a great advantage for people like Lao Tang who at home had no separate space to work away from the noise of the family. Moreover, they were all given, in addition to their regular meals, a daily stipend to purchase special foods like fish and eggs, items still in limited supply for the general public. Whenever they needed materials from the library, they had only to write down the titles and books would be delivered to their rooms. Thus ensured of physical comfort and freed from interruptions, they could devote their energies with total concentration to the task at hand.

More important than such tangible benefits was the special access they were given to places, people, and information. One weekend, for example, they visited Lin Biao's residence at Maojiawan near Beihai Park to conduct an investigation. Lin's reading notes, the marginal comments in his classical texts, his calligraphy, were all examined for evidence of Confucian influence. One notebook, for example, contained the comment that China must benefit from its Confucian heritage, and a scroll hanging on the study wall announced in Lin's calligraphy the Confucian maxim, "Restrain oneself and recover the rites." Both were seized as indications of Lin's desire to restore capitalism, and later incorporated in the fourth set of critical documents. To each paragraph the Liang Xiao scholars added supplementary comments to clarify why Lin Biao had made such reactionary remarks and why there was no doubt about his rightist nature.

What astonished Lao Tang even more than this documentary evidence of Lin Biao's reactionary viewpoints was the magnificence of his compound, which boasted a swimming pool kept at a constant temperature throughout the year and a toilet seat that always remained at body temperature. Ye Qun's closets were stuffed with expensive clothes and high-heeled shoes, her room adorned with satin quilts and thick carpets. The house contained two projection rooms where the family could watch whatever films they fancied, as well as television programs beamed from Hong Kong by satellite. The scholars left armed with scrolls, books, and note cards, as well as with shocking impressions, given the Cultural Revolution's recent attempt to eliminate bureaucratic privilege, of the material prosperity of China's highest leaders.

The Liang Xiao members also accompanied Jiang Qing on trips to factories, communes, and military bases where she professed her concern for the welfare of the workers, peasants, and soldiers. In June 1974, for example, Lao Tang and nine others from the group traveled in her specially appointed, armored train, stopping in Tianjin for two days, then at the model commune in Dazhai, and finally at an army base in Shanxi. In the carpeted coaches each person was assigned a separate sleeping compartment, whereas ordinary travelers, if they could afford a berth at all, would sleep in tiers of three pallets, some sixty passengers to a car. In Tianjin the group was settled overnight at a hotel maintained for high-ranking officials, where the food was of superior quality and the pool heated year round, even though few Party officials could swim. At Dazhai where Lao Tang and the others worked in the fields to show their closeness to the peasants, Jiang Qing even shoveled manure to demonstrate her willingness to share in the most burdensome physical labor. At Shanxi they toured the base of the PLA's 63rd division and then participated in an evening's entertainment. Jiang Qing sang a piece from a model opera, while Lao Tang sang one of the popular military marching songs, "I Am a Soldier and I Come from the Common People." On a subsequent inspection trip in July, he visited a naval base where he was taken to see a submarine, something that impressed these scholars enormously, for no civilian had ever seen such a secret vessel before. As an ordinary citizen Lao Tang would have had neither the time, the money, nor the reason to travel, let alone to enjoy the accommodations of the highest leaders.

His brief encounters with Jiang Qing left him with initially favorable impressions. On that first tour, intent upon winning the respect of her chosen scholar companions, she had appeared receptive, humble, eager to learn, announcing with seeming sincerity that she wanted these professors to be her teachers. She had asked one scholar to analyze for her the classical poem, "Encountering Sorrows," another to explain the meaning of Marx's *Gotha Program*, and Lao Tang to teach her about Laozi's *Daodejing*, which Chairman Mao had said was an important military text. Lao Tang had been impressed by her ability to recite many Tang poems perfectly, even some that he didn't know, and by her calligraphy, which was carefully modeled after the Chairman's, but he had also noted the narrowness of her learning and the arbitrary nature of her judgments.

Such access to Jiang Qing and through her to Chairman Mao himself made the authority of the Liang Xiao group unquestionable, its members said to be able to "touch heaven." Yao Wenyuan kept Chi Qun and his assistant Li Jiakuan informed about policy decisions at the highest levels, apprising them immediately of Chairman Mao's latest instructions, which they could then interpret and embellish in their articles. Enjoying the apparent support of the entire Central Committee, they received other kinds of privy information as well, such as the composition books written by Lin Biao in his school years. These documents were forwarded to Liang Xiao by Zhou Enlai, an act that seemed to convey the Premier's endorsement of their work. This kind of access to inside information in a society dominated by secrecy contributed crucially to Liang Xiao's prestige and ensured that the pieces they wrote, collective efforts often published in *People's Daily* or *Red Flag* and signed with one of the group's pen names, were automatically accepted as definitive.

I knew that Lao Tang's work had begun to bring him national recognition after the Beida Party Committee asked him and Pang Wenjun, also a Liang Xiao member, to deliver a talk explaining the significance of the fourth set of Lin Biao documents. Their presentation was deemed such a helpful analysis of Lin Biao's thought and of the similarities linking him to Confucius that Lao Tang and Pang Wenjun were requested to deliver it again at a meeting of top cadres held in Capital Arena at New Year's, 1974, shortly before I returned to Beijing. By order of Jiang Qing and Zhang Chunqiao, a tape recording of this address was subsequently distributed for discussion at political study meetings across the country, and when I returned to campus, people often spoke to me admiringly about Lao Tang, praising his skillful clarification of such complicated issues. A few people made ironic, even cynical remarks, indicating that they found the presentation of Lin Biao as an "out-and-out disciple of Confucius" less than convincing, but I just overlooked the skeptics, believing that Lao Tang's speech was above reproach. Indeed, the fourth set of Lin Biao documents had by then become the first directive of the Central Committee, further testimony that the authority of Liang Xiao was being given the highest confirmation.

Having been catapulted into a position of such power and prestige was at times unsettling for Lao Tang. His close affiliation with Jiang Qing and her supporters could someday prove disadvantageous, he knew, for the question of Chairman Mao's successor was by no means resolved. After the movement against "right deviationists" early in 1974 when I had been attacked, in fact, he had begun to wonder whether the Liang Xiao publications were by innuendo being directed against Deng Xiaoping, and one weekend returned home from the guest house to say that he wished to leave the criticism group and resume his former teaching position in the philosophy department. I had tried to reassure him and had urged him not to worry.

That fall when the campaign to "evaluate Legalism and criticize Confucianism" was well under way, I became engaged in the intellectual issues that had been Lao Tang's concern for more than a year. Chairman Mao, not wanting to repudiate all of traditional Chinese civilization, had recently praised the Legalist thinkers as a replacement for Confucian philosophy, and all the students that semester were studying those two schools of thought. The movement's major theme was that Legalism, because it advocated struggle rather than moderation and because it insisted on the formulation of laws to govern conduct rather than relying on the inherent morality of the people, would help society progress. Most of the older professors in my department, stung by the attacks against veteran cadres and intellectuals the previous February, were finding excuses not to teach, and I was among the five young faculty members assigned to give this course.

The topic was largely unfamiliar, despite my earlier forays into traditional literature, so Lao Tang helped me select materials and formulate my ideas. Having always disliked Confucianism, I was intrigued by my new assignment, and the students were excited as well. Delighted at last to learn about Chinese history and philosophy and to study the classical language, they worked very hard, taking advantage of their first opportunity to analyze the texts of the ancient philosophers, but one semester of such academic work was all they were allowed. In the spring semester we were told to resume our discussion of the educational reforms.

In January 1975, Lao Tang reached the pinnacle of his recognition when he was selected as a delegate, along with one other Liang Xiao member, a prolific young scholar from the history department, to the Fourth National People's Congress. A photograph on the front page of *People's Daily* showed him to be not just an ordinary member of the presidium but seated with other dignitaries on the platform. This special honor was an acknowledgment of Lao Tang's distinctive position in the criticism group, as well as a kind of restitution for his sufferings during the Cultural Revolution. He was considered one of the two Liang Xiao members most abused during those years, and Pang Wenjun had already been made a delegate to the Tenth Party Congress in August 1973. Lao Tang was proud to be able to follow in the footsteps of his father, who had been a delegate to the First, Second, and Third People's Congresses as a representative of the intellectuals, and I was pleased at his prominence, hoping it would help improve the future prospects of my children.

During the next few months, grateful for the honor accorded him, Lao Tang voiced apprehensions about his membership in Liang Xiao less frequently, but his worries could not long be disregarded. During that spring of 1975 the entire society waited nervously for Chairman Mao to name his successor, but his allegiances seemed to fluctuate, keeping everyone on edge. In April, for example, he warned Jiang Qing not to form a "Gang of Four," and not long afterwards, having received information allegedly from Zhou

Enlai about Roxanne Witke's interviews with his wife,* criticized her sharply for revealing so much of his private life to a foreigner. As a result she even moved out of the Chairman's compound at Zhongnanhai and into the state guest house. Also that spring Chairman Mao had criticized Yao Wenyuan's report asserting that empiricism, the approach for which the pragmatic Deng Xiaoping was most noted, was the main threat to the Communist Party. As a result of these indications of disapproval of Jiang Qing's faction, rumors spread widely in the early summer that the Gang of Four was losing power. Again Lao Tang began to consider ways to disassociate himself from the criticism group.

Even though my own concern about Lao Tang's affiliation with Liang Xiao was mounting, what absorbed my attention far more in those early months of 1975 was the danger facing Tang Dan on the distant Heilongjiang frontier. After his return to power, Deng Xiaoping had taken steps to enable some among the educated youths to return to their homes, find jobs, and resume their previous lives. While we all applauded this new policy, we had also heard how local cadres were able to implement it to their own advantage. The situation had apparently led to widespread abuses of power and created opportunities for bribery and sexual harassment.

Tang Dan's accounts of cadre misconduct on her military farm made me feel desperate to bring her home as quickly as possible. The farm leader had pressured some fifty girls into sleeping with him, I learned to my horror, warning them that this was the only way they could secure his permission to leave. Arrogant and unafraid, this regimental leader had even persuaded the daughter of a high official to submit to his advances. However, her father, who along with many other cadres was soon reinstated in his former position, learned from his daughter all that had happened. Outraged, he personally conducted an investigation into the matter, resulting in both the regimental leader and the vice-leader being found guilty of gross misconduct. The leader was summarily executed, his subordinate given an extended jail sentence.

Tang Dan had also explained the other ways in which students

---

*The biography, *Comrade Chiang Ch'ing*, was published by Little, Brown in 1977.

managed to obtain transfers or university recommendations. If a military farm needed a truck or a machine or some electrical equipment, for example, any parent who was able to provide such items could be assured of having his child sent back to the city. As news of these practices spread, many parents, like me, became obsessed with securing the safe return of their children, giving gifts if necessary and paying frantic calls on anyone who had some connection to the leaders on the communes and military farms where the educated youths had been living since 1969.

Tang Dan seemed to me especially vulnerable. Having always been conscientious about her labor, first making bricks, then feeding pigs, then caring for the farm's horses, she had been placed in charge of provisions for her regiment. This privileged assignment enabled her periodically to leave the farm and travel by tractor to the nearest market town to purchase supplies of oil, salt, and soy sauce. Rumors about what could befall young women in the remote countryside, where vast stretches of prairie separated one village from another, filled me with alarm. Her other job, providing food for the night workers in the early spring when tractors were plowing day and night, also seemed to entail some risk. Every evening she would carry steaming buns or noodles on shoulder poles to the workers in the fields, an assignment that hardly allayed my maternal fears.

For the past six years she had been struggling to acquire an education. Late into the nights she would read by kerosene lantern, ruining her eyesight but managing nevertheless to complete all the texts required of a middle-school graduate. This accomplishment had not been easy. Several times she was criticized for following the "white and expert road"; her leaders complained that her attachment to books betrayed her desire to leave the countryside behind rather than to settle there permanently. Unafraid of criticism, she persevered, and in recent years even extended her annual month-long vacations in Beijing without permission so that she could read more books. By then discipline had become more relaxed, as the cadres were preoccupied with their own material gain.

When Tang Dan had volunteered to go to the border area with her classmates rather than moving with us to Jiangxi province, she had been committed to the progress of the country and filled with revolutionary zeal. Over the years, like most of her friends, she had grown disillusioned. No one in a responsible position, she felt, cared genuinely about developing these remote areas of the countryside. Under Japanese occupation in the 1930s, Dedu county where she worked had been a productive area. Its rich soil, its farm machinery, some left by the Japanese, some purchased from the Soviet Union, were now supplemented by an abundant labor supply, as the young people from the cities were eager to work. Despite these resources, the farm operated every year at a deficit. Because of inept leadership, the seeds and fertilizer would often arrive late for planting, and when the crops did finally mature, the harvest would be delayed, resulting in much of the yield being wasted. The leaders sent the young people out to work each day, but apparently cared little about whether their efforts bore fruit. Repeated examples of negligence and mismanagement had made the majority of young people grow disheartened. They believed their efforts to be pointless, their hope of contributing to the border areas futile.

After I learned about such conditions, especially about the unscrupulous demands leaders were making of the young women in their charge, I became terribly worried about what might befall Tang Dan. But with a rightist for a mother I knew she had no chance to be recommended for university education. The only way for her to return to Beijing was either for Tang Shuang to join the army, thus leaving me with no children at home and legitimizing my request for my daughter's help, or for Tang Dan to be declared physically unfit to remain on the military farm. Further thought made me decide to pursue the latter option. The army might well not admit Tang Shuang because of my classification as politically unreliable, nor could I ask him to give up his middle-school education for his sister.

Ever since Tang Dan had been exposed to the intense cold of the Northeast, her menstrual periods had stopped, and we agreed to use this potentially serious health problem as grounds to request a medical release. As early as 1972, on her annual month's vacation, I had gone with her to a doctor but had learned that although her uterus was underdeveloped, this condition was not classifiable as a disease, since it could not be cured by medicine. Discouraged, we had abandoned this approach, but now it seemed the only hope. To obtain a certificate testifying that Tang Dan was ill, we went first to the Beijing Women's Hospital, where a doctor gave the same diagnosis and the same opinion. Later we paid several visits to a doctor at the Hospital for Traditional Chinese Medicine, a woman to whom I had received an introduction through friends. After several explanatory visits and expensive gifts of wine and foreign cigarettes, I asked for her help. Having a daughter in Mongolia herself, she was sympathetic and advised that a change in climate would perhaps help Tang Dan's condition to improve. She knew that constant exposure to those harsh winters, especially in the latrines where urine would freeze almost as soon as it left the body, had caused many young women to suffer menstrual disorders. When we left, she provided Tang Dan with a certificate recommending her transfer and with herbal medicines to help alleviate her problem.

Optimistic at last about my daughter's chances, I waited impatiently for news. However, the cadre on the military farm curtly dismissed Tang Dan's certificate, claiming that her condition was not actually an illness and that if he were to send Tang Dan home for this reason, he would have to send back most of the other girls as well. I refused to give up hope. I would have to find some other way to secure her release.

Tang Shuang's future was also very much in doubt. The math aptitude he had demonstrated in Liyuzhou continued when he started junior middle school, and always he received the highest grades in his class. Consequently, he had been made the leader of a group of seven students selected by a professor of mathematics from the Academy of Sciences who, worried about the future of the sciences in China, had in 1974 received permission to set up a special class to study calculus. This teacher had told me several times that because my son was exceptionally gifted, I should help him develop his talents, but such encouragement only increased my frustration. I knew that the double stigma of being from an intellectual family and having former enemies as parents meant that he could never attend a university.

Worry about Tang Shuang's blighted prospects, about Tang Dan's continuing exile in the Northeast, and about Lao Tang's dangerous involvement in the political struggles of the Gang of Four weighed heavily on my mind as I left for Daxing county in the late spring of 1975 to help with the wheat harvest. Here some three hours drive from Beijing, Chi Qun had arranged for Beida to take possession of part of a prison farm for young offenders. At this site the faculty members not trusted to resume academic duties were continuing their reeducation, and the students were given experience doing physical labor to prevent them from once again following the "three points in a straight line." Under the policy of half work, half labor, the members of the literature, history, and philosophy departments were sent to this new cadre school in six-month shifts, and my turn had come.

The setting of the Heavenly River Prison Farm bore no resemblance to its name. From the bus window I saw groups of teenagers at work near the road. They wore coarse gray clothing, their heads were shaved, their eyes seemed empty of all expression. Most of them had been convicted of theft or vandalism, but some had committed political crimes.

The environs appeared as blank and expressionless as the inmates' eyes. A few stubby trees broke up the flat, monotonous landscape, but aside from such touches of green, all that met my gaze was brown and dry. Low buildings with high, barred windows stood in rows along streets of yellow dirt. When I had gone to the countryside before, I had lived at least in some proximity to the peasants, but here, I thought dejectedly, my only neighbors would be criminals. I tried to generate some enthusiasm, noting that the living conditions were far better than we had encountered in Jiangxi. At least brick houses and a large kitchen had already been constructed for the prison's use, and the fields were already under cultivation.

In addition to our work harvesting wheat, we faculty members had to teach two days a week. At first we had no books, and a single lecture would be followed by long discussion sessions. The policy was for the students to assist with the instruction, so an important part of our task was assisting them in the preparation and delivery of lectures on the struggle between the two literary lines.

The students continued to resent their situation, however. No matter how much we discussed the "two erroneous viewpoints"—one that knowledge was a private possession, another that education could disregard politics and the shaping of thought—they remained dissatisfied with the new policy of alternating education on campus with physical labor. They simply wanted to return to the university to study. Since these worker, peasant, soldier students could not be reprimanded for their incorrect attitudes, two teachers were singled out instead for criticism. These faculty members, who had indeed expressed some sympathy for the students' concerns, were suddenly accused of having instigated the young people's erroneous views. One of the teachers was my personal friend, and I became very depressed at such an obviously unwarranted attack.

The criticism of these two teachers contributed to the already ample tension of life in Daxing county. Three or four days a week we would do labor in the fields and then at night check the students' papers and assist with the preparation of their lectures, tasks that often kept us up until midnight. Since the site was planned as a permanent extension to Beida, much money and effort were being spent on development, and several times a week trucks carrying lumber and bricks would arrive after the regular labor was finished. Sometimes as late as eleven o'clock at night we would have to go out to unload supplies for the construction of new classrooms and dormitories. The lack of sleep coupled with worry about my family, whom I could not return home to see, began to affect my health.

I had no idea what was happening to Tang Dan in Heilongjiang, nor what would happen to Lao Tang, who had become ever more prominent since the Fourth People's Congress. Once before while I was in the countryside he had been singled out, by Peng Zhen and Deng Tuo in 1965, and he had paid bitterly for that recognition. Now he was even more famous, more closely allied with some among the highest leaders. Anxiously I recalled the proverbial statement that the protruding rafter is always the first to rot away.

This unrelieved stress brought about a recurrence of the thyroid disease I had suffered from shortly after Tang Dan's birth in 1953, when I had been so busy writing articles and studying modern literature while carrying on my political work. Then my illness had necessitated an eight-hour operation; now more than twenty years later the symptoms recurred. I had been in Daxing county for only two months, but my inability to eat, my elevated pulse rate, and my tendency to break into a sweat at the slightest exertion made the doctor order me back home for a rest.

At the end of the summer, the students also returned to campus, permitted during their last semester finally to concentrate on academic research and write a short literary paper before their graduation. Even though this group had been so highly valued, I doubted whether they had benefited very much from their years at the university. Many of them were far more skeptical than I. One student remarked bitterly that, first, his generation had been the victims of the Cultural Revolution, which deprived them of a good education; next, they had been part of an educational experiment that failed; and third, they would after graduation just be merchandise offered for sale at a cheap price. The worker, peasant, soldier students from my department, however, were assigned very desirable jobs, often as university teachers or research workers in institutes, for they were looked to as the new force to oppose the capitalist road. It was not until after the autumn of 1976, when Jiang Qing and her supporters had been removed from power, that this young man's cynical prophecy was confirmed and nearly all of those young people were removed from their prestigious jobs and reassigned. In my department, for example, eight worker, peasant, soldier students had been originally retained as teachers, but all were subsequently given less demanding and less privileged work.

The tension that had brought on a recurrence of my thyroid illness in Daxing provided obvious testimony to the difficulties that once again confronted my family. This time I was merely a bystander, helpless to influence Lao Tang's situation or Tang Shuang's future and unsuccessful in my efforts to bring my daughter home. As new perils seemed to confront us on all sides, I found it far more difficult to stand by uselessly as an onlooker than to endure my own hardships in the past.

During those months of 1975, Deng Xiaoping continued to consolidate his own political base and returned to office large numbers

335

of cadres deposed after the attack against Party bureaucrats began in 1966. Aware of this threat to their political future, Jiang Qing and her allies intensified their efforts to overthrow their rival. In August they seized upon Chairman Mao's brief criticisms of the popular historical novel *Water Margin*, whose accounts of peasant rebellions had always before been highly praised, to attack revisionism and capitulationism. In this thinly veiled assault upon Deng Xiaoping, the bandit hero of the novel was accused of surrendering his revolutionary principles and betraying the welfare of the people. Naturally, Liang Xiao, the Gang of Four's principal propaganda organ, wrote many articles to further this campaign against the "surrender faction," a reference to those who had once been revolutionaries but had later surrendered to the capitalist road.

By then many people had come to realize that all of Liang Xiao's pronouncements about history, literature, and philosophy contained a contemporary political message, and that the very creation of the group had been part of Jiang Qing's attempt to defeat her adversaries. The *Water Margin* campaign was unmistakably being waged not just against Deng Xiaoping but against Premier Zhou himself. All along many people had felt frustrated at having to accept whatever explanations Liang Xiao formulated, but in recent months cynical remarks had become far more frequent.

Having been criticized for ongoing rightist tendencies in 1974, however, and wanting to do nothing that would bring further harm to my children, I had willingly accepted at face value Lao Tang's work to criticize Lin Biao and Confucius, and I had even tried to quell his misgivings. Now the enormity of Lao Tang's predicament could no longer be ignored. He couldn't in good conscience continue to participate in a group that had become simply a tool of the Gang of Four, nor could he withdraw, since any manifestation of disloyalty to Jiang Qing or Chairman Mao would risk the direst consequences. From that time on, we both began to feel acutely how isolated were the members of Liang Xiao.

Ironically enough, my own life that fall was progressing with uncharacteristic smoothness. My new assignment to teach a course on modern Chinese literature for foreign students was viewed by my colleagues as completely undesirable. Not only would I be

teaching a simplified view of Chinese literature to uninformed foreigners, not only would I be in a situation fraught with political
risks, but I would be denied any contact with the worker, peasant,
soldier students, whose recommendations were influential at times
of academic promotion. None of those concerns mattered to me,
however; I was grateful for this chance to distance myself from politics. With this truly international group of twenty-two young people
from Europe and Canada, Korea and Japan, Africa and the Middle
East, I could discuss writers and their works with far greater freedom than ever before. To be spared the political constraints that influenced the presentation of literature in a Chinese classroom, to be
able to discuss ideas and interpretations with students of such different outlooks, was like awakening from a long slumber.

Over the course of the semester, I developed such a warm relationship with my students that they selected a representative during the last meeting to convey their gratitude and present me with a
souvenir of our work together. With some difficulty they had purchased a record of Beethoven's violin concerto in Hong Kong, a gift
that made me aware not only of their appreciation but of how much
had changed in the past decade. For a moment my mind wandered
back to the night the Red Guards had descended upon our home in
the summer of 1966, smashing every vestige of the old culture.
Now I could listen to Beethoven once again.

Entertaining foreign guests was not permitted at that time, but I
still hoped to give a farewell party for those students in my home.
Going first to the people in the university foreign affairs office, then
to my department vice-chairman, I finally received permission to
submit a preliminary report. Later I was notified that someone
would come to inspect my house to decide whether it was adequate
to receive foreigners, and I spent a hectic day washing walls and
organizing books neatly on their shelves in preparation. A few days
later I returned to the foreign affairs office to inquire whether permission had been granted, only to be told that my house was ac-
ceptable for foreigners but the environs were too unsightly because
of the trash area beside the main path. Undeterred, I asked Tang
Shuang to help, and together we carried the garbage to a new site,
close by but concealed from view. At last the authorities consented,

337

even offering to reimburse me for the cost of entertaining. Wanting this to be my own party, I replied that I would prepare something very simple and would not need repayment.

When the day arrived, I served a large bowl of eight-precious-ingredients rice, a symbol of the union of many different elements in a united taste, along with fruit and tea. As we discussd the students' ideas about modern Chinese literature and their fascination with the richness of the May Fourth period with its multiple foreign influences on Chinese writers, I became more than ever excited by the idea of expanding my own horizons and studying Chinese literature in a world context.

In addition to discovering this important new focus for my academic work, I also gained from these foreign students a sense of friendship unknown for many years. With my worker, peasant, soldier students, relationships had necessarily remained somewhat distant, with caution exercised on both sides because of continuous political pressures. Because my new students had no part in Chinese politics, my conversations with them could be more open and direct than any I had known in the past decade. Also with these new students I could set aside my family problems for a few hours each day, a respite that during those months of tension I greatly valued.

One day, however, I returned home from my class to find a letter from Tang Dan. One of her regimental leaders, she wrote, would visit Beijing to reassure parents of the young people on her farm about conditions in Heilongjiang and inform them about their children's revolutionary accomplishments. Tang Dan had learned that many parents would prepare gifts and hoped I would also take advantage of this chance to secure her return. It was late in 1975 and the New Year was approaching. I thought at length about what gift would be the most attractive, the most distinctive, knowing that my political status was much lower than that of many other parents, and realizing with a sense of urgency that this might be my only chance to help my daughter.

Subsequent letters notified me when the leader would arrive in Beijing and where he would stay. On the day of his arrival, Lao Tang and I visited his hotel room in Haidian, carrying gifts of spiced meat and expensive wine. He was a very arrogant military man, his attitude condescending, as if he enjoyed making his supplicants struggle for his favors, but I persevered, assuming a humble manner and inviting him to have dinner with us the next day. He appeared pleased, and I hurried home to prepare a suitable banquet. All evening he talked about Tang Dan, praising her work and reporting her many contributions. Acknowledging that he knew of her health problems, he agreed to send her home at the first opportunity.

After returning to Heilongjiang, he told Tang Dan how much he had enjoyed his meal and repeated his assurances that she would be considered first when it came time to send people back to the city. Again we were very hopeful, but after three months I knew that nothing would happen, that I might as well have dropped my gifts into the sea. Frustration and helplessness drove away all of my earlier optimism; I could think of no other way to help Tang Dan.

The solemn announcement in early January of Zhou Enlai's death from the cancer that had confined him to his hospital bed for most of the previous year abruptly refocused my attention on politics. Widely regarded as the person most genuinely and selflessly concerned about the future of China, Premier Zhou was revered as someone apart from the struggle for power, someone who had saved many from persecution during the Cultural Revolution. His death occasioned a national outpouring of profound grief, and like many other families at Beida, we hung his picture, draped with white streamers and rosettes, on the wall across from our door. Inevitably, however, our feelings of loss were compounded by anxiety over who would succeed him.

Relieved to be rid of their most formidable opponent, the Gang of Four tried to control the expressions of mourning by imposing strict limits on who could pay final tribute to the Premier's body in the hospital and by keeping secret the date that he would be moved to Babaoshan for cremation. Nevertheless, word leaked out and a million people lined the streets on January 11, seizing this chance to express their love and respect for their fallen leader. "For ten *li*, such a long street, the people wait to say farewell," recorded one grieving witness among the tearful masses.

339

Aware that they must provide some outlet for the public's emotions, the leaders announced that the Premier's ashes would be placed in the Workers' Cultural Palace, the imposing Ming dynasty structure to the east of the Gate of Heavenly Peace, for three days. Learning of this, my father asked me to accompany him to pay his respects. By then seventy-five, he was still healthy and vigorous, able easily to walk the several blocks from the temporary bus stop through mobs of people to the center of the square. Like everyone else, we wore white paper flowers in our lapels as symbols of bereavement, and after filing past the ashes crossed to the Martyrs' Monument to entwine these simple flowers with those of thousands of other mourners in the surrounding hedge. Already the green needles were almost invisible in a wall of white, a silent testimony to the numbers who had come to honor their beloved Premier.

Everyone jostled to get near enough to see the inscriptions on the wreaths that adorned the monument. Those who were closest would read the dedications aloud, then others would pass the words back through the crowd. Despite the biting wind, we stayed for three hours, listening to the poems and sharing in the outpouring of grief and concern. Some of the boldest in the crowd used loudspeakers to make impromptu speeches, others composed verses on scraps of paper and attached their poems to the wreaths with needles and thread. Emotions long suppressed surged forward as people mourned not only the sufferings of the Premier but of the whole society. It had been years, I reflected, since the people had voiced their sentiments so openly, so fervently.

As we walked toward the bus stop, my father reminded me of the death of another faithful and talented leader. Father had been a student at Beida in 1924 when Sun Yatsen died and had gone to pay his last respects to Sun's ashes when they lay in state in Zhongshan Park, just on the other side of the Gate of Heavenly Peace, later joining the large crowd of students that followed Sun's body to its interim resting place in the Fragrant Hills. More than fifty years earlier, my father remarked fervently, he had felt grave concern about China's future. Now China was unified, warlords no longer threatened the country, but the present moment seemed even more perilous than in 1924.

"The premier we mourn today," he commented tensely, "faced

an even more difficult task than Sun Yatsen, because of the necessity of subordinating himself to a powerful ruler, a situation that undoubtedly contributed to his death." Both of us shared in the prevailing opinion that Premier Zhou's cancer had been exacerbated by the terrible stress of his position. "Jiang Qing," my father continued passionately, "can bring nothing but harm to China." I urged him not to speak of such things on the street, but he would not be still, blaming Jiang Qing for the Cultural Revolution which had brought such disaster to the country, for my mother's death, and for his own humiliating interrogation in 1970 as well.

In Guiyang before Liberation he had occasionally aided students being pursued by the Guomindang, giving them money and once concealing a revolutionary book for them on the rafters of our house. But that was the extent of his political involvement. Nevertheless, he was investigated during the Cultural Revolution. One of his former middle-school students had been arrested as a foreign spy because of connections with the Catholic missionaries in Guiyang, and under torture had finally confessed whatever his interrogators demanded. Later the young man died in jail. Among his forced revelations was the statement that my father had been a high-level advisor to a British intelligence organization. My father, in fact, had always enjoyed speaking English with the missionaries, sometimes hiking with them in the hills where they lived, sharing a meal, or exchanging foreign stamps. Because of these activities, he was now ordered to report to the security office every morning at eight o'clock for questioning.

During the interrogation sessions his investigators shook their fists at him and threatened him with dire punishment if he refused to confess his crimes. Such intimidation only made him angry, however, and he replied that he was an old man, that they could do with him whatever they liked. Each day for two months he sat on a bench with a group of other alleged counter-revolutionaries, being harangued to write his confession. Finally, when the sessions had accomplished nothing, he was told to wait at home for a decision.

After I returned from Liyuzhou and learned from my brother of my father's ordeal, I recalled an earlier instance of his obduracy. In 1942 the Guomindang government decided to build a road across the beautiful garden that my father had carefully designed around our home in Guiyang. When an official came to suggest that the road could be diverted in exchange for a substantial bribe, he became instantly angry, so offending the official that our wall was destroyed, the road built through our courtyard within just a few yards of our house. Admiring my father for his uncompromising adherence to principles, I also realized how fortunate he was not to have been accused as a spy until relatively late in the Cultural Revolution. In the frenzy of the early months, he might well have been beaten to death by the Red Guards for his refusal to cooperate. In 1970, however, the most passionate young revolutionaries were in the countryside, and he had escaped with just verbal abuse. I wanted to have his case resolved, his name formally cleared, but he was tired of the whole proceeding and refused to pursue it.

Almost every week when I visited him in the months after my return from the cadre school, to carry a fresh supply of water to his house, he would present me with a new piece of paper on which he had written a traditional eight-line poem. Those stanzas were always ironic denunciations of Jiang Qing, sometimes condemning her as the worst woman in Chinese history, sometimes predicting that she would die a horrible death. I urged him not to write such blasphemous lines, but he replied vehemently that his anger would suffocate him if it didn't find some outlet. Knowing that any criticism of Jiang Qing was viewed as a direct attack on the Communist Party, my father still rejected my entreaties that he burn his verses, and instead hid them behind a chair cushion in case he wanted them someday to be published.

The poems I had heard at Tiananmen Square eulogizing Zhou Enlai convinced me that my father's sentiments were widely shared. Liang Xiao's articles, I had to admit, could have been directed against Zhou Enlai, as my father had often argued. Filled with concern for Lao Tang, I returned home that night to recount what I had seen and broach again the question of his severing all connections with that group. The struggle had grown too sharp, he replied; to reveal any disloyalty to Jiang Qing and Chairman Mao would be far too dangerous. Any indication of disaffection in such tense times was sure to bring serious reprisals, and besides, no one could foresee the outcome. I knew Lao Tang was right; we could do nothing except remain vigilant and wait.

That evening I wrote a poem, called "White Chrysanthemums in the Pine Hedge," to express my grief at the death of Zhou Enlai and my apprehensions about the future. Many others wrote poems as well in the weeks following the Premier's death. Meanwhile, passions grew after Deng Xiaoping disappeared from view, his eulogy for Zhou Enlai his last public appearance. I knew the Premier's enemies were redoubling their efforts to secure permanently the succession that had so long been in doubt. As Qingming, the traditional day for sweeping the ancestors' graves and mourning the dead, approached, wreaths began to reappear on the Martyrs' Monument, their numbers steadily increasing. News of this challenge to the Gang of Four's authority spread rapidly throughout the city.

Each day my children joined the huge crowds in Tiananmen Square, since Tang Dan was at home to seek a diagnosis of her menstrual problems. They provided dramatic accounts of what they had witnessed, as well as copies of the memorial poems for me to read. Fearful that the testimonials would be removed, my children told me, people were making their displays larger, heavier, and more cumbersome. Workers from two factories had even created enormous wreaths out of steel, removable only with cranes, and these metallic flowers shimmered in the light, visible from long distances. Like the huge banner emblazoned with bold characters expressing not only sorrow at the death of Zhou Enlai but the willingness to "struggle against any evil power," the mountain of wreaths and poems clearly had a twofold purpose.

Obvious to everyone was the determination to fight that underlay the expressions of grief. One couplet epitomized this dual message:

> Premier Zhou, when you look back, you may feel some
>   consolation,
>   You may even smile,
> To know that so many young people have swords to kill the
>   monsters
>   And follow you.

Another poem, titled "To a Certain Woman," amazed me with its daring assault upon Jiang Qing:

You must be mad
To want to be an empress!
Here's a mirror to look at yourself
And see what you really are.
You've got together a little gang
To stir up trouble all the time,
Hoodwinking the people, capering about.
But your days are numbered.*

Another distinctive poem, written in large characters and later taken as a symbol of the counter-revolutionary sentiments being unleashed, frightened me with the boldness of its language. Knowing that thousands of young people had memorized its lines, the authorities began to try every means to capture the young worker who had penned them.

In my grief I hear demons shriek;
I weep while wolves and jackals laugh.
Though tears I shed to mourn a hero,
With head raised high, I draw my sword.†

Such open expressions of opposition to the Gang of Four electrified the city. Never before had the people dared to utter such feelings.

At Beida the Party leaders instructed everyone to stay on campus because of the counter-revolutionary activities occurring in Tiananmen Square. The Liang Xiao members were advised that some people were trying to take advantage of Zhou Enlai's death to foment a movement against Chairman Mao. Fearful for the safety of our children and not knowing whether the leaders would retaliate, Lao Tang warned Tang Dan and Tang Shuang, to no avail, not to go near Tiananmen Square. Each night as I read the poems they had recorded, the proclamations of grief and apprehension mingled with the spirit of resistance, I saw my own feelings reflected so precisely, so bravely, that finally I too decided to ignore Lao Tang's wishes and go to see for myself.

*Trans. in Xiao Lan, ed., *The Tiananmen Poems* (Beijing: Foreign Languages Press, 1979), p. 29.
†*The Tiananmen Poems*, p. 24.

I left early on April 4, squeezing into a bus packed with others bound together in a common purpose. I had never seen such spontaneously formed crowds; two million people, it was later estimated, visited the Square that day. The faces around me were solemn, as if in anticipation of unknown but threatening developments. As in January, people with loudspeakers read out the lines written on the hundreds of commemorative wreaths, but this time the mood was different. Tension, determination, anger filled the air, and I too felt infected by the extraordinary thrill of the moment, by the sense of participation in this mass expression of genuine feeling. Noticing a small vase of roses with a streamer signed "a teacher from Beida," I thought the donor very brave indeed to ignore both the campus leaders' warnings and the prohibition against individual testimonials. Knowing that even to be seen at Tiananmen was dangerous, I walked around for only an hour before returning home.

Next morning the Martyrs' Monument was bare; trucks had hauled away every wreath, every poem, while the city slept. The sense of crisis mounted rapidly on April 5, my cousin told me that night. As more and more people filled the Square, officials with loudspeakers commanded everyone to return home. The crowds remained orderly until that afternoon, when someone shouted out that the people were misled about Zhou Enlai, that he was not perfect and was not a god but was a human being with his own weaknesses. Outraged, the crowd chanted shrilly, "Down with anyone who opposes Zhou Enlai," chasing their enemy into the Great Hall of the People, where the security police protected him, insisting they had seen no one enter. When a propaganda car passed by, its loudspeaker blaring "Everyone must go home, Qingming is over," the irate mob overturned the vehicle, then proceeded to the command post for Tiananmen Square's security and demanded that the person who had so insulted Premier Zhou be handed over. Frustrated again, they set fire to the security headquarters. At eight o'clock that evening Mayor Wu De arrived in another propaganda car to announce that everyone must leave the square immediately, that actions would soon be taken to determine who among the crowds were political enemies, and that anyone who stayed after ten o'clock would be presumed a counter-revolutionary. At this point my cousin, fearing the violence that would follow, left for home.

Two hours later, I learned the following morning from Xiao Pan, the young army journalist who often visited me on his trips to Beijing, the militia, made up of factory workers and people called in from the countryside, moved in. The confrontation was brutal; many fell prostrate before the stout clubs wielded freely by the militiamen. More than a hundred people had remained beside the monument, all of them arrested and taken to the Workers' Palace for the night. My young PLA friend had stayed until ten o'clock, then escaped before the siege reached its peak. Rumors spread rapidly that at daybreak blood stains could be seen in Tiananmen Square.

Like many others, I was shocked and depressed by the brutality of the Tiananmen suppression, conscious that this was the first time since the founding of the New China that violence had been used to oppose a mass demonstration. Even though no evidence of a counter-revolutionary plot had been discovered, people had been arrested and cruelly beaten. I had formerly thought only the Guomindang capable of such indiscriminate attacks, but now Communist leaders were resorting to similar tactics. In the aftermath of this unpardonable violence, I tried to grasp what had gone wrong over the last ten years, struggling to understand how the people's government could have turned against the people.

Initially, I had believed the Cultural Revolution necessary, and had applauded Chairman Mao's intention to root out bureaucracy, but now the irony of the outcome struck me with bitter force. When Chairman Mao had urged the nation's young people to "bombard the headquarters" and overturn the bureaucracy that had, during the seventeen years since Liberation, become increasingly oppressive, his purpose had been the abolition of privileges separating the leaders from the people and the establishment of true economic and political equality. Realizing that in every small unit those in power had become petty tyrants, "emperors in their own domains," he had urged the people to attack their leaders, as in the Hundred Flowers period. If it took violence to end the oppression of this privileged class, if it took another revolution to accomplish what we had fought for at such great cost in 1949, then I felt willing to suffer that ordeal in order to reach Chairman Mao's goal.

I knew that his attempt to eliminate the abuse of power peacefully in the rectification campaign of 1956 had been unsuccessful and that he had launched the Anti-rightist Campaign out of fear that he would lose control of the country. Having seen how many were speaking out about the mistakes of the Party and concerned that his own power might also come under attack, he had moved to suppress the very critics he had previously encouraged. Then a decade later in 1966, bolstered by the fervor and adulation of the Red Guards who massed to see him in Tiananmen Square, he had experimented again, boldly relinquishing control from the top and allowing the people to conduct the revolution themselves. In just a few days he had succeeded in paralyzing the entire Party apparatus, but then he had nowhere to turn except to some inexperienced Red Guard leaders ambitious for power, a group that would soon oppress the people far more ruthlessly than had the Party cadres they replaced.

Chairman Mao's inability to eliminate the contradictions between the officials and the people, either peacefully or through violence, no doubt had many explanations. Important among them, however, were his failure to retain control of what was happening after unleashing the Cultural Revolution's anarchy, and his refusal to give up himself the very kinds of privilege and tyrannical control that he was attacking. Then when the people expressed their anger at the outcome of this decade of disastrous struggle on the occasion of Premier Zhou's death, they were arrested and beaten, victims of precisely the kind of despotic leadership that the Cultural Revolution had been launched to eliminate.

Clearly, the country's problems were a long way from being solved, I reflected wearily. I had known of many examples of vicious cruelty perpetrated by individuals against individuals at the height of the factional violence, when people at Qinghua had had their teeth extracted one by one, at Beida had had nails driven into their knees, to force their confessions. But what the crushing of the Tiananmen demonstrators represented was the brutality of the authorities against the masses. I could not imagine a socialist government clubbing young people's heads and imprisoning demonstrators overnight with no food or water, even beating those in jail to

make them reveal the identities of their accomplices. As the shocking details about the Tiananmen suppression came to light, the
conclusion that the Cultural Revolution had resulted in the total in-
version of its goals was impossible to avoid.

An Unknown Future

FOR CENTURIES people in China have believed that an unusual occurrence in the natural world presages an upheaval of comparable dimensions in human affairs. The historical records bear witness to remarkable affinities between the physical universe and the world of man, testifying that the death of a great leader or a change in dynastic rule is often preceded by some cataclysm of nature. The ominous events of 1976 seemed to confirm this time-honored wisdom. In March a shower of meteorites fell on the Northeast, followed by spring floods on the Yellow River, then in July by the earthquake that devastated Tangshan. Despite newspaper articles urging people to avoid superstition, there was no way to prevent this constellation of natural disasters from being seen as harbingers of further calamity.

An era was ending, and no one knew what the future would hold. Photographs of seven leaders, hierarchically arranged in order of their political standing, remained etched in my memory. They had looked down from the wall upon our every Party branch meeting, Mao Zedong, Liu Shaoqi, Zhou Enlai, Zhu De, Chen Yun, Lin Biao, Deng Xiaoping, and they were disappearing one by one. First, Liu Shaoqi had died in 1969 after more than two years of incarceration, illness, and neglect after his repudiation. Then, Lin Biao had died in an airplane crash in 1971 after plotting to overthrow the government he had helped to form. Next, Zhou Enlai had died early in 1976 after a long battle with cancer, his end no doubt hastened by the enmity of Jiang Qing and her allies. When in early July 1976 Marshall Zhu De died, many people said out of anger at the Gang of Four, we were all conscious that the revered leaders of our revolution were passing away. Chairman Mao, aged and ill, would not long survive. The fate of our country seemed totally in doubt.

My own gnawing sense of foreboding reached alarming proportions when I was jolted from sleep at four o'clock on the morning of July 28 by the earthquake. Lurching from bed, I felt as if I were on board a ship gripped by a tidal wave. There was no time to dress or even grab for shoes in the darkness as I rushed panic-stricken outside with Lao Tang and my niece. When the first shock had subsided, I dashed off to see my father, fearing that his house, which was old and made of mud bricks, could never withstand such a convulsion. On his street many of the adobe walls had crumbled, and I could see immediately that the roof of the small side room he used as a study had collapsed. He was shaken but unhurt.

Two days of steady rainfall had turned the unpaved lanes and alleys of Beijing into rivers of mud. As I headed home, the slippery streets had come alive with activity, and the whole campus was plunged into a state of confusion. Crowds of people were carrying food and supplies, as all buildings had been declared unsafe, and an order issued to construct temporary shelters and prepare a three-day supply of food. The university was providing bamboo poles for use as supports and, like everyone else, I hurried out in search of plastic sheeting, anxious to secure some kind of protection from the rain before nightfall. By the end of the day, every street and courtyard was filled with red, green, and yellow plastic shelters, their bright colors glistening with an incongruous cheerfulness under the threatening skies.

Lao Tang and I were fortunate the second night and could move inside our single-story house to sleep, while those who lived in dormitories and apartment buildings still camped in leaky tents because of the continuing danger of aftershocks. Having passed one uncomfortable night with rain dripping on my bedding and streaming beneath my bed frame, I spent hours in my kitchen cooking for friends still unable to return to their homes. By the third day the rains were even heavier, punctuated with claps of thunder and jagged streaks of lightning. I would see the roses beside my door tremble every two or three hours, and my heart trembled too, uncertain when another quake might follow.

Before a week had passed Jiang Qing, Chi Qun, and Xie Jingyi visited the campus to renew the commitment of the Liang Xiao members, many of whom had curtailed their participation as much as they dared, certain by now that this was not an academic group aimed at criticizing bourgeois theory but something far more political. The official entourage first visited Feng Youlan, the group's advisor, to wish him well, and then moved on to the guest house to greet the other Liang Xiao members and pose for photographs, a gesture they repeated on the Qinghua campus. A few days later the photographs, greatly enlarged, were placed in the glass display case before the dining hall, many showing just the most important leaders, Jiang Qing, Feng Youlan, and Zhou Peiyuan, but one a group shot with Lao Tang in the second row, laughing happily.

After seeing that picture, Tang Dan rushed home very upset. She could not bear to watch her father laughing so merrily in that company; the sight was so disgusting that it made her want to place a caterpillar in her father's open mouth, she declared with great agitation. Lao Tang responded to her anger defensively, explaining that someone had told a joke, after which he could not help laughing with the others, but Tang Dan felt strongly that when the earthquake had killed so many people, when everyone was still sleeping outside in such discomfort, it was unbearable to see her father looking so jovial. Many other people made sarcastic remarks about that photograph to me, for the antipathy to Jiang Qing and her supporters had grown intense. Tang Dan's outrage was symptomatic and I too felt ashamed. From then on, I always avoided the dining hall area, not wanting to see Lao Tang appearing pleased to be a member of that company.

My earlier support for Lao Tang's participation in Liang Xiao was gone. Ruefully I recalled my former pleasure at his many advantages, my sense of honor to our family, my hope that someday Tang Shuang would be a delegate to the People's Congress, following in the footsteps of his father and grandfather. The power and prestige clearly had appealed to my vanity, but now I felt only shame and remorse. I too wished that somehow I could steal that offensive photograph from the display case and erase Lao Tang's connections to the group completely. Such an expression of mirth was indeed unendurable.

Back in 1973, however, Lao Tang's participation in Liang Xiao had seemed to me part of the natural evolution of his career. During the Cultural Revolution he had been attacked as a black gang member and severely criticized, both for following the "white and expert way" and for influencing the students by his example. Determined never to be in such a vulnerable position again, he had decided to eschew any form of expertise, either white or red, and had even stopped reading the newspapers, preferring not to know about political developments, much less participate in them. After being selected as a teacher at the Jiangxi cadre school, however, he had developed a close friendship with one of the propaganda team leaders, a worker from the February 7 Railway Manufacturing Company who urged him not to give up his academic work but instead to follow the "red and expert way," to recommit himself to politics in order to contribute to the future of the country.

Lao Tang had been moved by his friend's entreaties and by Chairman Mao's call for "unity without turmoil." From then on he had tried to make his scholarly work serve the goals of politics. Having reached that decision in 1971, and believing sincerely in the importance of supporting and propagating Chairman Mao's pronouncements, he had seen his membership in the criticism group as an opportunity to serve his country and had participated enthusiastically in the early stages of Liang Xiao, grateful as well to be respected and influential once again.

Later, when Liang Xiao's political role had become obvious, there had been no way to cancel his affiliation. No one, in fact, had ever left the group except at the very outset, after the initial trial period, perhaps out of the same fear that kept Lao Tang a reluctant member. The only way to escape from participation was illness. Lao Tang spent two uncomfortable weeks, having fallen sick with flu at the time of the earthquake, living under plastic sheeting outside the gymnasium where the campus clinic had been evacuated. Later his back pain kept him home. Huang Liming, the husband of Tao Qun, an expert on Hegel, and our neighbor, found a similar excuse. Previously ill with hepatitis, he was able to obtain a doctor's certificate that he also needed to rest at home, and he and Lao Tang took turns handing in those certificates for each other.

To the acute discomfort of many in Liang Xiao, Jiang Qing's policies during the months following the Tiananmen incident became increasingly repressive. Frightened by the recent mass outpouring of anger and resistance, she initiated a movement to "clean and investigate," its goal the identification of anyone who had been involved with the demonstrations, anyone who had written poems or even copied them down. Her primary concern was whether the Tiananmen sympathizers and participants had connections with each other, since always in China the eventuality most threatening to those in power is the development of an organized group. Her hope was that the ringleaders could be identified as Deng Xiaoping's supporters, but never could she find such evidence. A grace period of one week was announced during which any Tiananmen materials could be voluntarily relinquished to a person's unit, but if any were found after this week, the possessor would be "held accountable." Everyone knew that it was a crime to attack Jiang Qing and that concealing such contraband documents was a serious matter. Nevertheless, Tang Dan refused, against her father's wishes, to turn over her two books of poems; and a middle-school friend of Tang Shuang's hid the many photographs that he had developed at his home in a makeshift darkroom.

During this movement to make clear who was an enemy, every unit was ordered to investigate as well which of its members had repeated unflattering comments about Jiang Qing or her associates. To have talked about how she had disagreed with Chairman Mao or about some incident described in her interviews with Roxanne Witke, for example, was now viewed as a crime. We were all supposed to reveal what rumors we had heard and their source so that the real enemies of the Gang of Four could be identified. People were smart, however, and when asked where they had heard some disparaging remark would answer, "on a bus" or "in a shop."

Lao Tang's close friend Lao Li, an assistant professor of philosophy at People's University, known as Renda, had come frequently to our home during those months, had openly expressed his antipathy to Jiang Qing and his certainty that she would bring disaster to our country. From him Lao Tang had learned about Roxanne Witke's book and about Chairman Mao's angry response. So strong was his opposition to Jiang Qing that he ignored the risk of speaking so openly. One night in early September, when the "clean and investigate" movement was at its peak, a knock on our door at about eleven o'clock made us all very nervous, as no one ordinarily would come to call so late. To our relief we found Lao Li outside, but his face looked strained with worry. His critical comments about Jiang Qing had been reported, he explained; Lao Tang might well be questioned also, as many people knew of their friendship.

Lao Li's exemplary background had protected him during the Cultural Revolution, for he had joined the Red Army at the age of fifteen when a middle-school student in Fukien province. Having also joined the Party at an early age, he was one of the few faculty members at Renda, where he became advisor to the Heaven faction Red Guards, who escaped attack. Before the Cultural Revolution he and Lao Tang, who shared the same viewpoint on many academic issues, had joined together in a study group, composed of two faculty members from each university, to write articles about Chinese philosophy under the pseudonym "Four Marxist Essayists," Si Mawen. Together they had published some ten articles in newspapers and journals.

Their friendship had survived the struggles of the past decade, even though they had supported different factions. After Lao Tang was seized as a black gang member, Lao Li had visited me several times to offer encouragement and support. His visits took place before the two factions had become strongly separated, but still such meetings were dangerous, as Lao Tang was well known after the International Hotel conference. All of Lao Tang's other friends had disappeared; no one else even asked about him, but Lao Li would offer sympathy and reassurance, urging me not to worry and counseling me that this time would pass. His three visits were very precious.

But now Lao Li had learned that one of his friends, the undergraduate leader of the Heaven faction at Renda, had betrayed his confidence. That young man, a well-known Red Guard figure, had always depended on Lao Li, but after the Tiananmen affair he was investigated by authorities in his unit in the "clean and investigate" movement. Threatened with severe punishment if he failed to confess everything he knew, he could be held accountable for his crimes as a Red Guard leader when he had ordered people beaten, he was told. Moreover, he was known to be a friend of some counter-revolutionaries arrested at Tiananmen Square. Frightened by this pressure and knowing that he could easily be sent to jail for his past actions and suspected present connections, he had wanted to clear himself; repeating Lao Li's remarks about Jiang Qing helped to prove his own loyalty. Immediately afterward he warned Lao Li of what he had done.

In that hasty late-night conversation, Lao Li vowed that he would never reveal his conversations with Lao Tang, that this would be their mutual pledge, that anything an interrogator told them to the contrary should never be believed. Thinking of what might result from Lao Li's arrest, I grew more frightened than ever, but after three days the whole matter was apparently forgotten, so preoccupied had the authorities become with the event that would determine the course of China's future.

On September 9, a day with gloomy, overcast skies, I was attending a meeting to learn about Chairman Mao's twenty-four instructions when a colleague entered the room sobbing, bringing news that Chairman Mao had passed away. Some of the teachers couldn't hide their tears, but I didn't weep. My thoughts returned to the sorrowful moment in 1953 when the loudspeakers had announced the death of Stalin, the head of our Big Socialist Family. Hearing the mournful music, I had been unable to contain my grief, thinking this event an incalculable loss for the Communist cause. Then I had shut myself in my room, but this time I had no tears. I thought about how intensely I had loved Chairman Mao, about how precious he still was to me, but also about how skeptical and suspicious I had become after Lin Biao's death.

About these issues my mind was still very confused. I believed unshakably that Chairman Mao had made enormous contributions to our country, uniting and strengthening China as no one else could have done. When he took power after 1949, I had genuinely admired him as "honored, right, and great." But during the Cultural Revolution he seemed to have become remote from the common people, more like a god than a leader, and I had begun to doubt whether his actions and policies were correct.

Learning of his death, I wondered how history would evaluate this man who had influenced my own life so profoundly. I remembered the touch of his hand, so warm and large, but then immediately began to worry about the future, so unknown and threatening. I feared that Zhang Chunqiao might take power. Convinced that he and Jiang Qing were responsible for the disasters of the Cultural Revolution, I expected that they would only continue the turmoil and oppression. But I also feared that if Deng Xiaoping took charge, Lao Tang would suffer terrible reprisals.

Lao Tang went twice, along with thousands of others, to bid farewell to the body of our great leader, but I didn't really regret that I was not offered that opportunity. Every day on television I watched the mourners, many from the countryside, crying sadly because they still respected and worshipped Chairman Mao; I could tell that their emotion was genuine. But I felt so uneasy about the future of the country and of my family that I could never share in their grief.

The subject of how to dispose of Chairman Mao's remains aroused great controversy, especially after the decision to construct a huge mausoleum was announced. Some said we had insufficient technical skills for such permanent embalming, that only experts from the Soviet Union were capable of so preserving Lenin's body. Many argued for burial, while others said we could not just bury so great a man in the ground. Yet a third opinion held that elevators should be installed in the mausoleum so that the body could be displayed during the daytime and be removed to subterranean freezer compartments at night. One of my foreign students, a Canadian woman, asked me why, since Marxists were materialists and opposed to the worship of idols, they would want to preserve this body so that it could be forever revered. Unable to think of a satisfactory answer, I replied that perhaps it was because the people felt such strong emotions about Chairman Mao. I joined the Beida contingent for a day's labor digging the foundation for the mausoleum, but even as I worked I felt skeptical about whether the project was a worthy one when our country was in such turmoil and there seemed so many more important tasks to be done.

All this time I worried about who would ultimately gain power over the country. Hua Guofeng, formerly the Minister of Public Security and a vice-premier, had been promoted to First Vice-chairman of the Party and thereby designated as Chairman Mao's successor, but people doubted whether his appointment would be permanent. Nevertheless, the National Day celebrations on October 1 were very lavish, with Hua Guofeng visiting several of the city's parks during the afternoon to show his solidarity with the people and create the impression of unity and stability. Jiang Qing, wanting to enlist popular support, confidently declared that the country's future would be happy and prosperous. Seeing those two so convincingly indicating they would work together as Chairman Mao's successors, no one could guess that Hua Guofeng within days would order the Gang of Four's arrest.

Later that week Lao Li again knocked at our door, this time filled with excitement and optimism, to report that the Gang of Four had been apprehended by the PLA's 8341 unit. Warning Lao Tang that an attack on Liang Xiao was inevitable, he urged us to be careful, advising us that the move against the criticism group would be harsh but only temporary. After he left, we just looked at each other, sick with worry. Again there was nothing we could do but wait.

The next morning a cadre came to the door to order Lao Tang to report immediately to the Liang Xiao headquarters. The man's tone was peremptory, his face stern. I replied nervously that my husband was unwell, that he had a medical certificate, that he must go to the hospital, but the official was unyielding. I stared at the closed door, having no idea what would befall us next.

The outpouring of righteous indignation and anger after the smashing of the Gang of Four plunged me into a deep depression. I wanted to share in the rejoicing, knowing this to be a positive step for our country, for the future, but once again I was cast out from the mainstream, isolated in my private unhappiness. My life seemed to bear witness to the Buddhist proverb "Every ten years will bring a disaster." In the late 1950s I had been labeled a rightist; a decade later the Cultural Revolution had brought us great suffering; and now after another decade had passed, Lao Tang was facing the most serious accusation of his life. During the Cultural Revolution his fate had been shared with many others, but now in the whole country there was only one Liang Xiao, only thirty-two individuals to bear the brunt of the people's wrath and resentment. It was said that this would be the last struggle, and I feared it might be the most terrible of all.

That first week after Lao Tang disappeared with the cadre, I was assaulted by daily rumors of what had befallen the members of Liang Xiao. It was reported accurately that a detachment from 8341 had surrounded the guest house, that the occupants had been guarded outside while the soldiers searched for evidence of a secret plot by the Gang of Four to seize state power, but the rest of the rumors I could never corroborate. A locked file had supposedly been found in Pang Wenjun's room, but when the soldiers had demanded a key, Pang had claimed he could not find one. The rumor spread that he had tried to impede the PLA's mission, hiding the key out of loyalty to the Gang of Four, perhaps to conceal plans for a new government in which the Liang Xiao members would all be important officials. The guest house was even rumored to contain guns for the members' defense. I could not judge whether any of these allegations was true, but when I heard that Lao Tang had supposedly jumped from a third floor window on the night of the arrest, I knew that some of the stories in circulation were wild exaggerations. Tang Dan heard that account as far away as Heilongjiang and wrote an anxious letter the next week asking if her father had been killed and if she should return home immediately.

From Tao Qun, who knew someone on the work team responsible for the Liang Xiao investigation, I had learned that nothing serious had happened to Lao Tang, but I was desperate for precise news. All I had been told was that the group's members had been confined and ordered to write down the details of their affiliation with the Gang of Four. Three days after Lao Tang had been taken away, unable to sit idle any longer, I gathered some of his clothing, bought an expensive bar of chocolate, and headed for the guest house. I didn't dare write a note, but hoped that the clothing and candy would convey my concern and support. The guard promised that my package would be delivered. I walked home slowly around the lake, noting the willow fronds now yellow and drooping, feeling overwhelmed by sadness. The rest of the country felt joyous liberation, while for us the future was utterly black.

During that first week many posters demanded the release of the Liang Xiao members to the masses for questioning, insisting that these villains be made to listen to the people. Other posters declared that no punishment was too harsh for the accomplices of the Gang of Four, or that its members should be made to run through the streets like rats chased by people with clubs. Such threats made my stomach knot with fear; the people sought an outlet for their anger toward the Gang of Four and I dreaded a reenactment of the cruel struggle sessions I had witnessed before. For nearly three years Liang Xiao's articles had been accepted as law; everyone had been obliged to discuss and accept the group's pronouncements and interpretations, stifling any alternative opinions. Liang Xiao had dictated the official viewpoint on every issue connected with literature and philosophy, history and anthropology, making people gleeful at the thought of retribution. How unjust was my fate, I thought; for years we had suffered because of the Gang of Four's cruelty in the Cultural Revolution, and now we were being pilloried along with them.

Walking through the central campus one day later that week and hearing the sound of shouting, I joined the crowd that quickly gathered. To my relief just four people from Liang Xiao were being marched to the dining hall: Li Jiakuan, the leader from 8341; Wang Shimin and Song Bolin, the two vice-leaders; and one other prominent member who had written an important article at the time of Chairman Mao's death, which the whole country had been organized to study and which was now interpreted as an attack on Hua Guofeng and an endorsement of Zhang Chunqiao as premier. In the dining hall these four were vehemently denounced, but after just half an hour the students paraded them around the campus to read the wall posters and learn the people's views. Seeing these enemies for the first time, many in the crowd raised their fists and shouted: "The Liang Xiao members must admit their crimes and reveal their deeds." Believing still that they had been acting in accordance with Chairman Mao's instructions, the four people in the parade remained resolute, their faces betraying neither fear nor humiliation, even though the onlookers shouted angry questions, stopping them to demand, "What kind of privileges did you have?" "What did you do with Jiang Qing at Dazhai?"

Excluded from the public euphoria and indignation, I rarely left my house during those weeks except to go out once a day to read the posters and gather whatever news was available. Some of the posters criticized the articles written by Liang Xiao, some the privileges enjoyed by the group's members. Others focused on the trips made by Liang Xiao members with Jiang Qing to places like Dazhai or Xiaojinzhuang, a model village in Hebei province famous because its peasants could all sing songs from the model operas or compose poems, and because of its luxurious bathroom constructed for Jiang Qing's use. Because both Lao Tang and Pang Wenjun had visited this village, some of the posters demanded that they confess what they had done on their trip with Jiang Qing. One poster even attacked the Liang Xiao cook, accusing him of obtaining special foods, such as fish, fresh fruits, and other luxuries unavailable to the people, and of preparing midnight meals for those who stayed up late to write articles. Disinterested in these petty offenses, the work team pressed the members to reveal what things of consequence they had done, to explain the goals of their leaders and how those objectives were to have been carried out.

For some six weeks the members were required to write their confessions day and night, until the middle of November, when a big struggle meeting against Liang Xiao and the Gang of Four's major accomplices was announced. Rather than holding the meeting in the dining room, the leaders had reserved Capital Sports Arena, where the proceedings could be carefully controlled. This mass criticism session would serve as an example for the whole country to illustrate how the Gang of Four's supporters should be treated. Like everyone else at Beida, I was given a ticket and told to attend, expected to draw a line to separate myself from my husband. Everyone was excited to see how these people, formerly so powerful and arrogant, would be made to account for their actions.

When I arrived, the arena was nearly full. I had been there once before to watch beautifully costumed figure skaters, and as I waited for the proceedings to begin, I stared at the two doors from which the skaters had glided on that far happier occasion. Lao Tang, too, had been to Capital Arena before, I recalled, thinking of the irony of his being publicly denounced in the same place where he had delivered a key address on the Lin Biao documents to the Party's highest leaders in 1949. A traditional proverb flashed across my mind: "In the morning, welcomed as the guest of a high official; in the evening, held as a prisoner under the steps."

Promptly at ten o'clock the doors opened, and Wang Lianlong, the secretary of the Beida Party Committee, and Li Jiakuan, the head of Liang Xiao and a vice-secretary of the Beida committee, walked toward the center of the arena, each of them closely followed by a pair of Red Guards. Aside from Chi Qun and Xie Jingyi, who had already been arrested and were in seclusion, those two people bore the greatest responsibility for supporting the Gang of Four. Two other vice-secretaries of the Beida committee appeared next, joining their predecessors in the center of the hushed arena. It was apparent that, like the figure skaters' performance I had witnessed years before, this meeting had been carefully choreographed.

Watching the silent, solemn faces, I felt unbearable tension, waiting for Lao Tang to appear, wondering what would happen to him in front of these thousands of onlookers. When the doors opened again, sixteen of the most prominent Liang Xiao members filed out, eight from each side, to form a line behind their superiors across the middle of the arena. Knowing that their positions were significant, I noted with relief that Lao Tang was fourth from the center. Now twenty accomplices were arrayed for all to see. From the platform Zhou Peiyuan, in his capacity as president of Beida, announced the start of the meeting.

A member of the special work team handling the investigation recited a formal description of the crimes committed by these people, then a summary of the conclusions that could be drawn from their confessions. The official's face was grave, his tone shrill as he declared Liang Xiao to be a counter-revolutionary organization manipulated by the Gang of Four to be their servants and their workdogs. Still, I took courage from his assertion that the crimes committed by the members of the criticism group were not uniform. The crowd, responding to cues, enthusiastically shouted slogans, "Long live Chairman Mao Zedong," "If the Gang of Four doesn't surrender, we will smash them," "Liang Xiao must reveal all that it has done." Finally a squad of uniformed police marched to the center of the arena and led away the four Beida Party leaders in handcuffs. My stomach clenched, but the other sixteen people were escorted out by the Red guards, a sign that they would not be taken directly to jail. The meeting lasted only an hour, but I was exhausted from the tension.

Following that meeting the members who had not been jailed were permitted to return home on alternate weekends if their attitudes had been cooperative. I was making dinner when Lao Tang returned home the first time; more than a month had passed since I had spoken with him. It was already growing dark, and as I cooked I heard the door close softly. When no one appeared, I turned around and saw him sitting on the sofa in the darkened room, his shirt dirty, his face unshaven, his eyes anxious and forlorn, reminding me of a famous Russian painting, often reproduced, of a man who had returned from Siberia after years in exile. Lao Tang saw me, but didn't speak. When I asked gently what had happened, he replied that there was nothing to tell. After a moment of awkward silence, he spoke in an anguished tone: "It's terrible to think that you have been condemned as an ultra-rightist and now I am supposed to be an ultra-leftist. What will happen to our children? We cannot know, but the question tortures me. Our lives no longer matter, but for the children to share our destiny, to suffer for us, is too sad."

As I sat beside him in the darkness, I could imagine his ordeal, picture him writing page after page of his confessions. It wasn't necessary to ask about details, and the big question looming in our hearts no one could answer. When Tang Shuang came home, hungry for dinner, I went out to finish cooking, but our meal was eaten in silence.

Thinking back to my first date with Lao Tang, I recalled how we had strolled through the Temple of Heaven, how he had explained the special techniques enabling that majestic blue cone-shaped roof to be constructed without nails. He had been so concerned with defining the nature of goodness, with probing the unanswerable questions, while I had been the more pragmatic person, less concerned with abstract conceptualizations. Now he had been condemned as ambitious for power, as an arch conspirator against his country. History sometimes makes people go through a wrong door, I realized, pledging that I would stand beside him, extending all my support and sympathy.

The next morning Lao Li paid us a brief visit, hoping to bring some comfort. As head of a special group investigating Xue Yishan, an assistant to Chi Qun and a supporter of the Gang of Four within the Ministry of Education, Lao Li was in a position to observe how Jiang Qing's accomplices were being treated. He had gone to visit Xue Yishan in jail; speaking from firsthand experience, he tried to reassure Lao Tang that even imprisonment would not be so terrible. The situation in jail might in fact be preferable, Lao Li commented gently, for there you have a room to yourself, the food is not so bad, you can read newspapers and Chairman Mao's works, and you must just answer questions two or three times a day. While I felt somewhat relieved to hear concretely about what we had been conceiving as the worst eventuality, Lao Li's description of prison life seemed to make Lao Tang only more apprehensive. When he returned to his quarters that evening, he took along an extra set of underwear, certain that he might be arrested any day.

After that, whenever Lao Tang came home he was always profoundly depressed. I would try to offer comfort, but my words had little effect. I felt that, like me, he had really became a victim of politics, that even though Liang Xiao had indeed provided much support for the Gang of Four, Lao Tang was really not guilty of all that the posters claimed. I knew he had never been ambitious politically, that he had done what the propaganda team leaders and

Party leaders had asked, that probably anyone else would have acted similarly. Recalling how I had felt upon being condemned as a rightist, how I had believed my humiliation would never end, I urged him to adopt a long-term perspective, not to think just of the present.

Every weekend I would prepare special meals when Lao Tang came home, then pack his favorite green vegetable and some cooked meat in a glass jar for him to share with his roommate. After dinner on Sunday nights, I would accompany him back to his dormitory. Feeling that he had lost face so much, he never wanted to be seen on campus, so we would allow an extra hour to walk by a very circuitous route, across rice fields and along the university wall. At the end of the small bridge near his building, I would stop and watch him head quickly down the path and inside. Alone again, I would take the direct route home, through the center of the campus, trying to turn my thoughts away from Lao Tang's misery.

Always these alternate weekends followed a similar routine, but one Saturday when I had prepared some special meat for Lao Tang I waited until nine o'clock at night and still he did not come. I could think only that he must finally have been arrested and sent to jail. The next morning, unable to stand the uncertainty any longer, I resolved to find out what had happened. In his building I knew there would be no guards, for by then no one wanted to have any contact with these outcasts, so guards were unnecessary. At nine o'clock I simply walked to his room in the basement of the lakeside teachers' canteen.

His roommate, whose family lived far away, leaving him no place to go on the weekends, explained that Lao Tang had refused to admit any intention to oppose Zhou Enlai, insisting that the Liang Xiao Party branch committee had even scheduled a memorial meeting after the Premier's death. Moreover, the investigators felt that Lao Tang had not provided a satisfactory account of the third installment of materials criticizing Lin Biao and Confucius, whose assembly and writing had been his responsibility. The work team claimed that he must have received some special instruction about the true target of those materials. Accusing Lao Tang of refusing to cooperate and being unwilling to confess completely, the leader

364

had cancelled his weekend at home, ordering that he would spend that Saturday night and Sunday being questioned further. I left the jar of preserved vegetables and returned home, my worries partially alleviated. At least he was not yet in jail.

Punctuated only by Lao Tang's fortnightly visits, the first half of 1977 dragged on. Every evening I forced myself to concentrate on preparing the next day's lecture for the foreign students, drained of the enthusiasm that had prompted such excited plans for a new approach to Chinese literature just months before. Tang Dan was far away in Heilongjiang, my father in Guiyang living with his new wife. Alone with Tang Shuang, I didn't dare probe into his thoughts, afraid to know how he must feel now that his father was being held responsible for the Cultural Revolution and the bloody Tiananmen incident. Sadly I watched him pour all of his energy during the spare moments of his last semester at middle school into the construction of a large, intricate warship with remote control, which he periodically tested in our bathtub. Shunned by my neighbors and colleagues, isolated from my family, I felt more alone, more desolate, than even during my own sojourn as an enemy of the people.

Farewell to Spring

THE ANNOUNCEMENT in the summer of 1977 that university entrance examinations would be administered once again fired the aspirations of thousands of young people from intellectual families who for a decade had been denied all access to higher education. The adulation of "blank paper heroes" like Zhang Tiesheng was now totally repudiated, condemned as ultra-leftism along with the policy of holding children accountable for their parents' mistakes. Students were to be selected on the basis of academic merit rather than class background or political reliability. At last Tang Dan and Tang Shuang might have a chance to escape from the shadow of our political past. To provide them with this opportunity became for me a kind of obsession.

An air of vitality replaced the gloom of our household as the earnest voices of young people could be heard discussing their studies in our living room until late into the night. Tang Shuang, who had just graduated from middle school with the highest grades in his class, and Tang Dan, who had taken an extended medical leave from her military farm to prepare for the exams, gathered over their books with their schoolmates, hardly stopping to eat, so intent were they on making the most of this precious opportunity. I helped them whenever I could, offering advice about composition techniques and about Chinese literature, but as the fateful day drew closer, I became more and more apprehensive.

Even when the exams were past and the correct answers announced, confirming Tang Shuang's belief that he had missed very few questions, the children's reassurances could not allay my fears. Unable to stand aside while their destiny was being decided, and worried that Lao Tang's Liang Xiao affiliation would inevitably be held against them, I decided to approach the person responsible for their father's case, a young man who had been for two years a student in my political writing course.

When I arrived at the building where the Liang Xiao members were sequestered, this investigation team leader maintained a cold, formal manner, pretending not to know me. My inquiry about whether Lao Tang's circumstances would affect my children's future received only a stiffly official reply. "According to the policy of the Party, the parents' situation generally does not influence their children," he replied, adding, "but that depends upon Tang Yijie's attitude. If he confesses thoroughly, things will progress more smoothly." While this response was hardly encouraging, it did not totally dash my hopes, for the newspapers had carried many articles asserting that now, when the Gang of Four's policies were all being overturned, a family's political problems would not be used to penalize the children. Still I remained skeptical.

Having been one of the teachers to grade the literary section of the entrance exams, I was familiar with the regulations dictating admissions procedures. Each applicant filled out nine choices for university enrollment and was then ranked according to his score. If his grade was above a basic cutoff point, he was eligible for admission to some institute of higher education, but his grade must be above a higher cutoff point for him to qualify for one of the newly designated key-point universities. In addition to academic achievement, political level and physical condition would also be evaluated. I knew that a separate office had been established to investigate the political background of every applicant, an indication that this criterion would be considered very seriously, and that a written report on the political and moral level of each candidate had already been submitted by the teacher responsible for his middle-school class. My children had filled in the mandatory application forms requesting at the top the parents' names, their employment, and their political classification, by stating that their mother, formerly a rightist, was now reinstated as a teacher, but leaving the space beside their father's name glaringly blank. Their teachers, I knew, would surely have included some mention that their father was under investigation and awaiting a final judgment. Perhaps, I reminded myself calmingly, their recent Youth League memberships, so long denied—Tang Shuang's in his final semester of middle school and Tang Dan's at the age of twenty four and a half, a decade past the customary age of fourteen—were encouraging signs.

The announcement of the examination results ended the first period of suspense, greatly bolstering my children's morale. Both received scores above the higher cutoff line, qualifying them for the coveted key-point universities, fueling their hopes and at the same time my anxieties. Again I approached the Liang Xiao office, this time with a specific request for a letter certifying that Lao Tang's situation should not be held against my children. Although I had summoned all my resolve, I could not hold back my tears as I described how Tang Dan had spent eight years in Heilongjiang, struggling to master all the course material required for a middle-school education, so great was my distress at what my children had endured. Since the policy of the Party was clear, the leader intoned, it was unnecessary for me to request any special explanatory document. At any rate, Lao Tang's case remained undecided; no one could yet say what would be his final verdict.

My apprehension was not unique, of course; many of the Liang Xiao members had children, and I knew that other parents had requested similar guarantees. Tao Qun had gone to plead with the investigation team leaders several times, for example, so I too returned, this time to be told that a letter had been sent to every unit involved declaring that, according to the policy of the Communist Party, the ongoing investigation of a Liang Xiao member should in no way influence the university admission of his children. Such a letter, so clearly stated, I thought, would surely have some effect, but I couldn't leave any approach untried. The physics teacher who had been informally tutoring Tang Shuang for two years, as well as the physics department chairman, both wanted him admitted to Beida because of their confidence in his ability, and they advised me to go directly to Zhang Longxiang, the vice-president of the university, for help.

Zhang was very encouraging as he counseled me to have faith in the Party and its policy. Sounding warm and concerned, he assured me that our country needed talented young people to help build China's future, but I knew that however sincere, such talk alone was meaningless, and asked him to write a letter directing that Tang Shuang's admission not be influenced by his father's investigation. When Zhang agreed, I felt very hopeful and returned the next morning to pick up the letter. It had already been sent to the person responsible for Beida's admissions, I was told curtly, my alarm instantly rearoused. I knew that I must see the letter for myself and hand carry it to someone I really trusted for it to have any effect. I would have to go directly to the person responsible for admissions, a man I had known before I was declared a rightist, even though the admissions committee was billeted in a hotel two hours away by bus, a distance designed to discourage supplicants like myself.

This Lao Ying was busy, I was informed brusquely, so I waited two hours until the committee members emerged from their meeting, then approached him about my children. His insistence that he could not divulge to me the contents of the letter from Zhang Longxiang, that I should not worry but just return home, signaled to me that all was not well.

On the day that admission to the key-point universities was to be announced, I waited anxiously with my children for the mail to arrive. Tang Shuang, knowing that his score was among the top ten in Beijing, stayed behind his closed bedroom door trying to read a novel. Tang Dan, more seasoned about society and politics, wandered in and out of the house nervously until dark, making phone calls and visiting friends to inquire about their results. By six o'clock we knew for sure that no mail would be delivered; even Tang Shuang's score had failed to gain him admission. Since both children were physically fit, we knew the problem was political. Believing that there must be some way for the Party's policy to be enforced, Tang Dan and I could not passively accept this outcome or share Tang Shuang's mood of resignation.

The next morning we visited a contact on the Beijing Admissions Committee to ask whether anything could be done, only to learn that neither of my children's files could even be located. Their papers had apparently not been submitted for consideration; we would have to inquire at the political investigation office. There the clerks were abrupt and dismissive. I should consult my unit for information, they insisted. Besides, they never granted personal interviews, and there was no responsible person available anyway. Refusing to be put off, we returned the next day. I was determined to explain to someone in authority that my children had never wavered in their support of Zhou Enlai, that even when it was very dangerous, they had preserved the verses collected at Tiananmen, that Tang Dan had always opposed her father's membership in Liang Xiao, that Liang Xiao was not supposed to influence the children's situation anyway. I had Tang Dan take the special book into which she had copied the Tiananmen poems, and I took a letter from Tang Shuang's teacher testifying that he was politically trustworthy, that he had always aided his classmates with their political study, that he had been a dedicated Youth League member, that he had several times gone to mourn for Premier Zhou. However, we arrived to find that the office had moved unannounced, no doubt because it had been deluged with complaints similar to mine. A return visit to my friend would be necessary to find out the new location of the political investigation group. Our mission was urgent; the acceptances for ordinary universities would be announced in a few days and it was crucial to act quickly if my children were to be considered. I was so frantic that my hair began to turn gray.

Armed with the necessary address, we set off very early the following day, hoping to catch the leader just when she arrived. The new headquarters was in a large, deserted building still filled with dust and hung with spider webs, located on the outskirts of the city. Two small rooms had been hastily cleaned to accommodate their new occupants. Having found the woman in charge, I poured out to her my concern for my children and with it my tears of frustration and helplessness. Despite her impassive manner, she listened for an hour, then stated that she really could not assist us, since all such decisions were made by a committee. Still, she agreed to relay what we had told her and advised us to go back and wait and hope for good news. In any event, there might be additional university space opening up later, she said, and it would still be possible to get admitted after this second deadline had passed. Initially encouraged, I later realized that such reassurances were only a device to make us go away and wait indefinitely.

I had exhausted every contact. When the second round of acceptances was announced with Tang Dan and Tang Shuang again excluded, I knew there was no hope. All I could advise my children was not to look for jobs but to stay at home and prepare for the 1978 examinations in case the political situation should improve. Seeing my tears of disappointment, Tang Shuang comforted me, observing that he was still young and could have a chance at university admission later. In the meantime he would read more and improve his skill at Chinese composition, for if his score on that section of the exam had been higher, his test paper would have received the highest grade for all of Beijing. "Let's agree not to speak about this again," he urged. "There are many others who have not been admitted, and it is pointless to lament what cannot be helped." By then it was late October.

Later I learned from someone in my department who had sat on the Beijing Admissions Committee that Zhang Longxiang, unable to assume responsibility for the letter I requested, had asked for guidance from the political work group of the Beida Party Committee. The statement they had issued declared that while the parents' situation should not ordinarily influence a child, still they preferred that Tang Shuang not be admitted to Beida. I knew that after this precedent had been set, no other university would dare to admit him either. The opportunity was completely lost; the children's studying and my loathsome begging for favors had all been in vain.

Having come to terms with his disappointment, Tang Shuang had his hopes aroused again that winter when several universities and science academies announced the decision to admit graduate students. The professor with whom he had continued to study math after graduating from middle school wanted to accept him in the Academy of Sciences, provided that he could achieve a passing score on the forthcoming graduate-studies exam. In this first year to admit graduate students, the exam was open to anyone, regardless of educational background. After another frenzied bout of preparation, Tang Shuang left early for the middle-school classroom where the exam was to be held.

So great was my anxiety during those weeks that I became uncommonly worried when later that morning a pouring rain began to fall, fearful that Tang Shuang would get drenched on his walk home, catch a cold, and be unable to sit for the second day of tests. Grabbing my umbrella, I dashed out to search for the middle school where the exams were being administered, finally arriving wet and mud-spattered at the proper building. Through a window I could watch Tang Shuang writing intently, surrounded by people much older than he. Pride in my son mingled with desperation as I waited, hoping so urgently for him to succeed.

When those scores were announced and his was well above the passing mark, his professor wrote a letter accepting him into the Institute for Applied Mathematics. His educational opportunity was finally assured, and we all rejoiced for two days. Then his professor called, his voice tense with anger, to say that the Institute's political certification office had overruled his decision. Tang Shuang would not after all be admitted. The professor tried to reassure me that it might actually be more beneficial for Tang Shuang to receive an undergraduate education first rather than to plunge immediately into graduate work, but I was hardly comforted.

That winter I could find no relief from my depression. During the anti-rightist period, I recalled miserably, at least I had been able to rely on the suport of my family to bolster my spirits and give me some confidence in the future. Even during the Cultural Revolution I had not been without hope, knowing that our problems were shared by many others. All the teachers were oppressed together, and we knew, despite our travail, that so many people could not be classed as enemies indefinitely. We had sometimes even been able to laugh at the absurdity of our treatment, as when my labor team was forced to sing the "howling wolf song," and we had kept alive the conviction that the madness would have to end. Now all such confidence was gone. The years of calamity had indeed ended for everyone except thirty-two families.

By the end of 1977, the investigation of Liang Xiao was supposedly completed. The members, having confessed their every action, had nothing more to write. Allegations about a plot by the Gang of Four to seize state power and about the Liang Xiao members' promised role in that new government had never been substantiated. Gradually, popular sentiments began to change, the campus gossip took on a less condemning tone. The leader of Beida's propaganda team decided that it was time to set the scholars free, but others demanded that they first write self-criticisms explaining why they had worked to support the Gang of Four and why they had attacked Deng Xiaoping. With this last task completed, more than a year after their incarceration, they were sent home. We took two bicycles and a three-wheeled cart to carry back all the bedding and books that Lao Tang had accumulated during his three years in the Liang Xiao guest house.

After his release, I encouraged Lao Tang to read and plunge again into his academic work, but he just lay on the bed, claiming that his back was too painful. He had so often been forced into the jet plane position during the Cultural Revolution that his back injury had indeed been aggravated, intensified by the dampness of the kitchen storeroom where he had lived for fifteen months, never able to dry out his quilt. Often I had to help him walk to the bus for his hospital massage three times a week, and once he had to be pedaled on a three-wheeled cart by Tang Shuang's friend. But it was clear that his pain was also psychological, for he felt that his life was forever ruined, that he would never again be able to engage in teaching or scholarly research, that he had brought irreparable harm to our children. Turning the sequence of events over and over in his mind, he reproached himself harshly for not leaving Liang Xiao, knowing at the same time that such an option had never existed.

Once it had been made clear that Liang Xiao was not part of any secret conspiracy with the Gang of Four, people even began to see the group as victims of the times, as dedicated academics who had acted out of loyalty to Chairman Mao. Nevertheless, we were still

373

isolated; no one would risk coming to our house except Tao Qun and occasionally Lao Li. The latest movement to "clean and investigate," an attempt to identify anyone who had connections with the Gang of Four so that its influence could be eliminated, deterred anyone else from approaching us. Lao Li had even been the target of one wall poster at the Ministry of Education, a demand that he make clear his relationship with Lao Tang. Having previously attacked Jiang Qing so fervently, however, his position was sufficiently strong that he never had to respond.

While on the surface our life during those months of 1978 was quiet, it was filled underneath with terrible uncertainty. We didn't know when a conclusion about Lao Tang's case would be reached, having heard only that it was under discussion at the Beijing Party Committee, and we waited anxiously for news. One day I learned from Tao Qun's friend on the special investigating team that twenty of the Liang Xiao members had been judged to be on the side of the people and would be reinstated as teachers, while ten others would bear the responsibility for all the group's actions. Those ten had apparently been pronounced active counter-revolutionaries, a crime deserving severe punishment, and Lao Tang's name was on that list.

In the late spring I heard that this list of ten had been shortened to six, with four more Liang Xiao members exonerated. It was crucial to find out whether Lao Tang was on the short list of enemies, so I nervously approached first my department, then Lao Li, then Tao Qun's friend for details. My heart sank when I learned finally that Lao Tang was indeed among the six held responsible for the whole group's counter-revolutionary activities. So great was my distress that I could not bear to return home. Even Pang Wenjun had been eliminated, I was told, but Lao Tang had been seated on the platform at the Fourth People's Congress, and had been responsible for the third installment of materials attacking Lin Biao and Confucius. Of the six so indicted, I knew that three were already in jail, the other two the principal authors of inflammatory Liang Xiao articles. I would conceal the news from Lao Tang, I decided, for it would only increase his worry, but my face apparently betrayed my distress. With studied casualness I remarked that even though his name was on the list, it was said that if he maintained a good attitude, he could still be treated as if he were on the side of the people.

Throughout this miserable spring my children were studying hard to prepare for the next entrance exam. Tang Dan now felt far more pressure to succeed because she had a boyfriend, a middle-school classmate who had been assigned to the same military farm in Heilongjiang, where their relationship had deepened even though they had rarely dared to speak together. In 1976 this young man had acquired a doctor's letter certifying some medical infirmity and had then, after the inevitable gift giving, received the necessary Beijing residence card. On the basis of his 1977 test scores, he had been admitted to the Railways University and then three months later to the physics department at Qinghua after taking the graduate-studies exam. His success and Tang Dan's failure had created a difference in status that Tang Dan found intolerable, consigned as she was indefinitely to the border area as an educated youth. She decided to give up the relationship, but when her friend offered to renounce his university position and return with her to Heilongjiang, she reconsidered. Now she wanted desperately to secure a place in a university. I had continued to plead and give gifts in an effort to have her transferred to Beijing, all to no avail, and finally reconsidered the possibility of sending Tang Shuang, now successfully graduated from middle school, to the army.

Joining the PLA had previously been a popular avenue of advancement for young men, but with so many children of high officials and workers aspiring to a university education, it was primarily peasants' children who continued to apply to the army. Perhaps Tang Shuang could be accepted. A few years in the PLA would not make a crucial difference in his life, he agreed, but his sister was twenty-five and would soon be over the age limit for university entrance. I was moved by his generosity, knowing it would not be easy for someone from an intellectual family to spend three years in the army, where the discipline was strict, the conditions spartan. In the spring of 1978, Tang Shuang went to enlist. Wanting to help, I asked his teacher for another political recommendation explaining how thoroughly his views differed from his father's. But when we saw the announcement that ten boys from his middle school had been admitted, he was not among them. His father's situation had also excluded him from the army.

In desperation I decided to try one more time to use Tang Dan's health as grounds for a transfer. The herbal medicines prescribed for her in 1975 had initially helped, but for the past two years these intermittent menstrual periods had stopped altogether. We visited several doctors to request a certificate stating that her illness would be exacerbated by continued exposure to extreme cold, and I even tried to have her transferred elsewhere in Hebei province, all efforts which necessitated the giving of gifts. At last I managed to get an introduction to an important doctor at the Woman's Hospital. Agreeing to examine my daughter, she warned that the procedure might spoil her virginity, a normally important consideration that at the moment we felt must be ignored. This doctor would accept no gifts, announcing that she would do nothing more than the medical facts warranted. After the examination, she concluded that Tang Dan indeed required a change of climate and wrote a strong letter stating that continued exposure to the harsh conditions of the Northeast would be medically harmful.

Tang Dan returned to her farm with this precious document and many gifts, two bottles of the best wine, ten cartons of foreign cigarettes, available only at such places as the Friendship Hotel where Tang Shuang's friend was a waiter, as well as yarn, baby suits for the cadres' children, and candy. After two weeks she wrote to say that the leaders had, for whatever reason, accepted the medical certificate. Knowing that this approval from her company was only the first step, we were afraid to rejoice prematurely and remained cautious. Her company must make a recommendation to the regiment, which must in turn send all the relevant materials to the neighborhood committee in Beijing, which would investigate the case to decide whether the request was warranted. Tang Dan wrote that she would have to wait until a tractor was traveling to the regimental office with food or supplies so that she could personally carry the request for her transfer, to insure that the letter didn't just sit somewhere unattended in a pile of papers. In fact, she stayed at that regimental headquarters for a whole week to make certain that her file had been sent off, then spent a last week with her own company before returning to Beijing. Each day she inquired of the street committee whether her papers had arrived, finally succeeding in making a friend in that office, who notified her after several days that her transfer request had arrived. Still she must wait her turn, and it was mid-July before she received the long awaited permission to return to Beijing. At last she could legally get a job in the city even if she failed in her bid for university entrance.

I was very nervous when the 1978 exam scores were announced, but both of my children did very well. Tang Shuang had filled out the forms differently after his earlier failure, stating Zhejiang University as his first choice, despite the future disadvantage of leaving Beijing, hoping that in another province he might have a better chance. Lao Tang and I had both encouraged him in this choice.

The Beijing Admissions Committee was meeting now in a middle school in Daxing county, its location kept a careful secret to prevent the intrusion of agitated parents, but I managed to find out the location through a friend at the Normal College who knew one of the heads of this group. My friend even agreed to accompany me, since the committee member might otherwise refuse to talk with me. Everyone knew that high officials would routinely send notes to members of this committee requesting that a certain applicant be well taken care of, but such influence was far more difficult for ordinary people to exert. When we arrived, the person we sought was busy, so we found his room and just sat down to wait. It was a hot September day, and the dirt from the streets had coated the buildings and trees with a thick layer of dust. I recalled my two tension-filled months at the Daxing county cadre school, now disbanded, its labor judged too demanding, its isolation from the worker, peasant, soldiers criticized along with its distraction of the students from their studies.

Finally the committee member returned. After hearing my request, he promised to try to help my children, but advised me that a candidate's political investigation was still very important and that the whole issue of admissions was hotly disputed. Some cadres were incensed that the policy once again favored the children of intellectuals, who always presented the best academic records, and discriminated against the children of workers and peasants. "To accept a student whose father is a member of Liang Xiao while at the same time rejecting other students who are from worker or peasant backgrounds will not be easy," the friend warned me. I could of course understand the logic of what he said, for I too believed that our socialist country needed to educate its worker, peasant, soldier young people, while at the same time I naturally wanted my own children to be accepted.

When the group to be admitted to key-point universities was announced after the 1978 exams, again my children's names were missing from the list. I felt so desperate that the next day I went to see my contact on the admissions committee again, pleading for my children to be given a chance, even at a distant or undistinguished institute. I no longer cared that they be admitted to a prestigious university, I just wanted them to have some opportunity to continue their education. Unable to suppress my tears, I told him that their father's situation was not the children's fault, that Tang Dan had not wanted him to remain a member of Liang Xiao. Once again I stressed their devotion to Zhou Enlai, their daily trips to Tiananmen, the reports from the military farm that Tang Dan's political viewpoint and her labor had always been exemplary. The man assured me that he would try his best but that he could offer no guarantee. Like the character in Lu Xun's short story "A New Year's Sacrifice," I thought, I have become a woman without hope, just endlessly relating my sufferings, each time with diminishing effect.

I returned home after dark to find Lao Tang lying on the bed, lost in his own feelings of frustration and hopelessness. I didn't need to speak for him to know that I had no good news to report. His eyes filled with tears as he said softly that perhaps only his death could help our children. Realizing anew how much he was suffering, I felt swept by waves of sympathy and reproached myself for expending all my concern on my children's needs when his were so much greater. Struggling to conceal my own desolation, I assured him that we must not give up hope, pretending that the person on the admissions committee had promised to help and all the while telling myself that I must not cry, that I must summon all my strength to help Lao Tang. At last he suggested that I visit Lao Li, who by then had become very prominent. The next day I explained the whole saga of frustration and disappointment to our old friend, who agreed that our children should not be made victims and promised to help.

My entreaty brought immediate results. A sympathetic friend of Lao Li's suggested writing a letter to Fang Yi, the director of the Academy of Sciences, a vice-premier, and a person known to be open-minded. I should write down all the recommendations of my children's teachers, I was advised, describe their political viewpoints and activities at Tiananmen, and emphasize their insistence upon studying throughout the whole decade of political turmoil. Lao Li also suggested gently that it was probably impossible for two children from a Liang Xiao family to gain university admission and recommended that we try first with Tang Shuang, who was younger and more academically distinguished.

I worked on that letter the whole night, wanting every word to be convincing. Lao Li would give it to Fang Yi's secretary, who would in turn see that it reached Fang Yi's hand. Without this personal connection there would be no hope of such a request reaching the vice-premier, as a secretary would either throw it away or turn it back to the writer's work unit, an action that would likely cause the petitioner to be criticized. In just one week my letter was returned with Fang Yi's brief instructions to his secretary at the bottom. "Children should not be held accountable for their parents' mistakes, however serious, so please consider how to assist this person." Lao Li then suggested that Tang Shuang apply, not to Zhejiang University, where neither he nor the secretary had personal contacts, but to the Science and Technology University, a key-point school run by the Academy of Sciences in Anhui province. We gratefully agreed, and in just five days received word that Tang Shuang had been admitted. The stone that for so long had stuck in my throat was finally dislodged.

It was already late September, the fall semester well under way, so we made hectic preparations, Tang Shuang having never been away from the family before and needing me to sew a new quilt and buy new shirts and underwear. As I said good-bye to him at the bus stop, I traced a Taoist charm in his palm, a symbol of good luck I had used twice before as he left to take the entrance exams. My mother had traced this Taoist talisman in my own palm when I left Guiyang to go north to study, and with a comparable mixture of apprehension and confidence, I bestowed the same talisman upon my son.

When Tang Dan returned from the train station, her eyes red from weeping, I realized how sad she must feel to say farewell to her brother when she herself had no hope of acceptance. Knowing how much more difficult her life had been than her brother's, I wished I could have sent her to university first, for I could feel the misery in her heart. After all, Tang Shuang had always stayed with us and had been admitted to a university just one year after graduating from middle school, while she had missed her middle-school education entirely, spending eight years in the harsh Heilongjiang climate. When the announcement of admissions to ordinary universities appeared, again her name was not on the list. Everyone told me that I must be satisfied, that I had one child at a university and another with a job at the Beida library, work that my sister-in-law had been able to arrange for Tang Dan. I should be practical, I was told; I should not want too much. But if my daughter was academically qualified, I kept thinking, she should not have to remain a political victim.

Following this second announcement of university admissions in 1978, the many young people with passing grades who were denied entrance grew angry and began to protest. The authorities tried to placate them by claiming that many applicants had scored above the cutoff line and not everyone could be accepted. We all knew, however, that admission depended heavily on family connections as well as on political background. The young people mounted a poster campaign to accuse the authorities of unfair practices and protest the handling of university admissions. Slogans and small flags made of pink and green paper declared their demands: "Equal Enrollment," "Down with the Idea of Reactionary Blood." Perhaps a hundred students marched in front of the small office in Daxing that continued to function as an admissions headquarters on the day that Tang Dan and I were there requesting reconsideration of her case. Some of the demonstrators were that year's middle-school graduates, some were educated youths returned from the countryside. I advised Tang Dan not to participate, for she could easily be singled out by the authorities because of her Liang Xiao connections, but we were both excited by the protest.

During this time of the Democracy Wall movement, many other demonstrations were taking place as well, one staged by the association of painters known as the Stars, for example, a group that had been denied space to display their work in the Museum of Fine Arts and had taken to the streets instead. Under pressure from such actions, the authorities needed some way to mollify the young people, some of whom were worker, peasant, soldiers and thus couldn't be indefinitely ignored. Finally the mayor of Beijing, Lin Hujia, deciding that something must be done, established the policy of developing more opportunities for higher education. Every university was consequently requested to set up an affiliated school as a way to accommodate more students and at the same time make use of the large number of teachers who effectively had no work. In my department, for example, there were 108 teachers for 300 students, and I had often said we could staff two or three Beidas given the size of our faculty. Again we were hopeful that the new policy would enable Tang Dan to further her studies. When a new cutoff line was announced in February 1979 for the previous summer's exams, her score was at the very top.

By then attitudes toward Liang Xiao had continued to moderate, and people often said that since its members had been appointed by the Party, they could not be held wholly responsible for what they had done. This new viewpoint created a way for the group to be forgiven. Moreover, that list of six enemy names that had so frightened us had never been officially approved, because no one could accept responsibility for such an important decision. Throughout the country, after all, there were many organizations with connections to the Gang of Four, especially in Shanghai where another criticism group had been very active and where Zhang Chunqiao's support group had even planned an armed rebellion. Not all of these accomplices could be punished.

Deng Xiaoping's policy instead was known as the "cold treatment of steel," an approach that postponed any decision about how to deal with the followers of the Gang of Four until people's minds were no longer heated. As part of a campaign to "ask the masses to make the decision," groups of teachers had been formed in each Beida department to discuss the nature of Liang Xiao and suggest how its members should be treated. In my department the teachers concluded that Liang Xiao had made mistakes, that some of its members were more guilty than others, but that even they were not solely responsible for their actions, since they had been carrying out Chairman Mao's orders. The prevailing viewpoint seemed to be that they should be made to learn from their past mistakes.

As a part of this latest campaign, the Liang Xiao people were returned to their separate departments for criticism. At the several meetings held for the eight members from my department, there were angry attacks on the group's articles, angry denunciations of their special privileges, angry accusations of their support for the Gang of Four, but still the mood had changed. Slogans were shouted at the beginning and end of the meeting, not all the way through as in the Cultural Revolution, and there were no Red Guards on the platform, no twisting of arms. The offenders just stood for two hours accepting the criticism of the masses. Those who tried to defend themselves by saying their Party branch had sent them to Liang Xiao were criticized again until they learned to keep silent and say only that they had made some mistakes, had written some articles that were wrong. Then they were dismissed. No one wanted to see a return to the violence of the earlier years. Besides, these Liang Xiao members had formerly been highly esteemed members of our faculty. I could see from the others' attitudes that much of the animosity towards Liang Xiao had finally dissipated.

Later that spring I learned that a new report on the Liang Xiao case had been issued to the Beijing Party Committee. Desperate to know whether the document contained the long-awaited verdict, I finally found out that now only three people were being held responsible, the same three who were already in jail. At last we realized that Lao Tang would not be labeled an enemy of the people, that his case would not be treated as seriously as we had earlier

feared. Before too long even those three were released and returned to their homes, sometimes asked to do some physical labor
on the campus. Although Lao Tang still had no job and no official
resolution, the danger had passed.

That same spring Tang Dan was admitted to the new Beida affiliated school where she chose to study library science and comput-
ers. I had urged her to select biology, believing this field to afford
many opportunities, but she argued that the most important consideration was achieving a stable life. If she chose library science,
she would not have to worry about being assigned work outside of
a major city. At her age I had been concerned about very different
things, wanting to do something adventurous, to contribute to the
country's future, but her generation had known both adventure
and idealistic effort and had suffered great hardship and disillusionment in the process. I could understand why Tang Dan's goals
would be different from mine.

The worries that had so long preoccupied me were disappearing
one by one. That fall Lao Tang was assigned to teach philosophy
once again, and as he began to recover his earlier relationship with
his colleagues and students, he slowly regained his inner balance
and became less tense and withdrawn. At about the same time it
was formally announced that while the Anti-rightist Campaign had
not been altogether a mistake, it had given rise to excesses and
harmed too many people.

Hearing this news, people even expected that all the money
withheld from the rightists over the years would be returned, just
as it had been for the cadres after the Cultural Revolution, some of
whom had received as much as fifty thousand *yuan* in back pay.
Everyone knew that the amounts owed to the rightists were even
greater because our reduced salaries had been in effect for twenty
years. I discounted the rumors about financial reimbursement, certain that our country was not wealthy enough to repay such large
sums, but I did begin to think seriously about what it would mean
to have the verdict I had lived with so long finally reversed.

One day the vice-secretary of our department's Party committee
called me into her office. As I sat beside her desk in the room where
I had conducted so many meetings, she stated in a flat, unemo-

tional voice that it had been decided the case against me was in error. While I had made some mistakes in seeking individual fame and not identifying sufficiently with the masses, still this had been a problem of personality, not a political matter, and had caused me wrongly to be designated a political enemy. This mistaken judgment would now be corrected. Looking as if she expected me to weep with gratitude, she asked whether I wished to make any response, but I declined, my feelings far too complicated to express. Next she inquired in the same professional tone whether anyone who might have suffered on account of my incorrect verdict should be informed of the reversal. This question gave me pause.

The one most hurt had been my mother, who had looked to me to achieve what her own life had denied. Now that her bones had so long lain cold, no one could inform her that her daughter had been wrongly pronounced an enemy and that the accusation had been rescinded. Also badly injured had been my children, so long discriminated against because of their rightist mother, deprived for years of membership in the Youth League and of any hope of higher education. Now their humiliation was past, and they were safely enrolled in universities, but no one could heal the wounds burned deep in their hearts. Lao Tang had been attacked for having a rightist wife and ordered to separate himself from me, and no one could take away the pain he had suffered.

I also thought of Fei Ming who, after our months together during the land reform, had written me such warm and poetic letters, declaring that he saw in me the hope for our country's future. After I was condemned as a rightist, he had asked one of his students to make inquiries about me at Beida, but the student had been unable to locate Lao Tang, and Fei Ming never knew. He would be soothed to learn that my rightist label was all a mistake, that the person he had seen as representing the hope of the future was in fact not an enemy; but now his ashes lay somewhere in far-off Changchun. In the Cultural Revolution he had been bitterly attacked as a "reactionary academic authority" who had defended traitors like Zhou Zuoren, and he had died alone and neglected—some said of hunger, since he was nearly blind and could not purchase food without assistance.

384

There seemed no point in telling anyone that my case had been dismissed, I realized sadly, especially since no one took rightist matters seriously anymore. Looking up, I told the vice-secretary she need inform no one. Apparently unaware of my pain, she continued routinely to state that the dismissal of my Party membership had also been a mistake and that it was hoped I would return to the Party. With my seniority calculated from 1949, with thirty years of membership, I would be entitled to the honored title of "veteran Party member." The choice was mine to make, she finished in the same disinterested voice.

I looked at her sitting across from me, that woman I had known for so many years, and recalled the time we had spent together in Liyuzhou, where we had even been given the same nickname. She was called Zhou Dali, while I was called Yue Dali, a name meaning "great strength" that was usually bequeathed to a man. Not only were we both strong and able to do strenuous physical labor, but we were also the same height and would often work together to carry buckets of manure to the fields on a pole slung between our shoulders. I also recalled her dejection during the Four Clean-ups Campaign when she had been my roommate in the dormitory, and how I had tried each night to console her after the propaganda team leaders' accusations that she was ambitious for power. Now it seemed that she had forgotten all we had endured together. I was just another person to be dealt with in the course of her work; she spoke to me no differently than to anyone else.

Just after my condemnation as a rightist in 1958, she had arrived to assume her departmental Party post. A young textile worker from Shanghai and the descendant of several generations of workers, she was proud of her proletarian background and very trusted. The first time we met I could see her eyes fill with disdain, since she was a leader of the working class while I was the people's enemy. I wondered what she was thinking now as she announced my right to rejoin the Party, whether she actually believed my verdict to have been a mistake. Her eyes just looked at me calmly and steadily, betraying nothing.

It seemed so easy for her to announce that she would correct the errors made more than two decades before, I thought, but such official reversals could hardly bring people like Zhu Jiayu back to life or restore the youth of those who had spent more than two decades on the margins of society. I knew that this vice-secretary had no personal responsibility for the treatment of rightists, but still I doubted whether she really regretted what had befallen me and so many others.

Having anticipated that like others being rehabilitated I would be offered the choice of rejoining the Party, I had already thought about my decision. Much had changed since that bright, clear July 1 when I had become a Communist. On this late autumn morning thirty years later there was haze in the sky. Gone was the foliage of summer, and the trees wore varying hues, the green of their leaves now largely replaced by red, yellow, and brown. My views of life, I realized, had become similarly variegated; the optimism and idealism of youth were not altogether gone, but the encounters with pain, hardship, and isolation had forced me to acknowledge doubt and disillusionment, at times even despair. In the early 1950s when our goal had been to make China another Soviet Union, almost everyone had been confident, unaware of the pitfalls ahead, but there had been many steps backward during the thirty years since Liberation. The model of the Soviet Union had long been discarded, shattered like many another idol, and after the death of Stalin we had known we must find our own way. In learning the dimensions of this task, we had all aged. I knew that springtime would not come again, either for me or for my country. Ahead were our harvest years.

Now I must decide whether to remain outside of politics, attempting at last to lead a peaceful life, or whether to rejoin the Party, hoping once again to contribute to the goals of the revolution. After the mistakes of people like Lin Biao had been revealed, their corruption and distance from the people unveiled, I had grown discouraged about the Party's policies and skeptical about its leaders. But I still could not forget all those who had died for its cause, sacrificing their lives for the ideals of Liberation.

I thought again about Zhu Jiayu, who had spoken out in 1956, wanting to improve the Party, unable to bear the insult of being labeled an enemy, now lying on the bottom of the ocean. I thought of Lao Shi, who had refused to dissemble, refused to flatter those in authority, first sent to the Yunnan border and then beaten to death by the Red Guards. I thought also about Lin Zhao and Ma Mingzhen, who had dared to query official policy and had voiced their beliefs, both dead from an executioner's bullet. So many had paid with their lives for telling the truth.

But even as I recalled the disappointments of my own life and the tragic loss of my friends, I realized that some flame still burned in my heart. It had flickered at times but had never finally been extinguished. Surely the hardships, the losses suffered together, would not be redeemed unless we strove to keep that flame alive. I would join in the efforts to rebuild the Party, convinced that whatever its past mistakes, it alone could lead China forward. I was far less confident of success than in 1949 and far less certain that I could contribute, but I knew that I had to try.

POSTSCRIPT

In October 1984, Yue Daiyun held a joint appointment as
associate professor of Chinese literature and vice-chairman
of the Center for Comparative Literature at Beida; and as
chairman of the Chinese Literature Department and Director
of the Institute of Comparative Literature at the newly
established Shenzhen University. Tang Yijie was jointly
associate professor of philosophy at Beida and head of the
Philosophy Department's teaching and research group in
Chinese philosophy; and at Shenzhen University, he was
director of the Institute for Chinese Culture. Tang Dan was
pursuing a graduate degree in computer science and living
with her husband in New York City. Tang Shuang was
studying for a Ph.D. degree in physics and living with his
wife in New York State.

GLOSSARY

Persons

Cao Yi'ou	Wife of Kang Sheng
Chen Xianche	See Lao Chen
Chi Qun	Chairman of Qinghua University's revolutionary committee; also responsible for Beida
Daolan	*Ayi* in Yue Daiyun's home
Deng Minghua	Teacher in Beida economics department; in charge of rightists at Zhaitang
Deng Pufang	Son of Deng Xiaoping; injured by Red Guards
Fei Ming	With YDY in land reform and colleague at Beida; exiled to Changchun in 1952
Fourth Aunt	Tang Yongtong's sister
Gao Yuanping	Nie Yuanzi's representative at Beida's Hanzhong campus
Gao Zhongyi	YDY's cousin; exiled to Xinjiang
Guo *ayi*	Additional *ayi* in YDY's expanded household
Guo Yanli	Teacher in Chinese literature department; criticized in Clean the Class Ranks movement
Hu Wenli	Party secretary in Beida physics department; attacked in Cultural Revolution
Huang Liming	Beida professor of philosophy, husband of Tao Qun
Jian Bozan	Veteran Party member and head of Beida history department
Kuai Dafu	Red Guard leader at Qinghua
Lao Chen	Leader of new students going to Beida; later Party secretary of Chinese literature department
Lao Ding	Member of Chinese literature department; cook at cadre school

Lao Gu	YDY's leader in Beida student underground
Lao Hong	Vice-chairman of YDY's group at Prague Student Congress
Lao Li	Philosophy professor at Renda, friend of Lao Tang
Lao Lin	A favorite student of YDY, who attacked "To the Storm"
Lao Lu	YDY's colleague and friend, head of *Contemporary Heroes*
Lao Pan	Fourth person in Chinese literature to be accused as a rightist; later attacked YDY
Lao Shi	Fifth person in Chinese literature accused as rightist; YDY's close friend at Zhaitang
Lao Song	Student in Chinese literature criticized in 1955
Lao Sun	Vice-chairman of Chinese literature department
Lao Tang	YDY's husband; full name, Tang Yijie
Lao Wan	Third person in Chinese literature to be accused as rightist
Lao Wei	Beida teacher of history; fellow rightist at Zhaitang
Lao Wu	Teacher in Chinese literature; neighbor of YDY
Lao Xiang	Teacher in Chinese literature; attacked as a favorite of Lu Ping
Lao Xie	Second person in Chinese literature to be accused as a rightist
Lao Yang	The first person in Chinese literature to be accused as a rightist
Li Jiakuan	A leader of Liang Xiao
Lin Liguo	Lin Biao's son and fellow conspirator
Lin Lihen	Lin Biao's daughter
Lin Zhao	A woman Chinese literature student at Beida; executed in 1975
Lu Ping	President of Beida, 1960–1966; early Cultural Revolution target
Ma Mingzhen	Woman worker in Guiyang; executed for criticizing Lin Biao
Mei Kewen	Teacher in Chinese literature; criticized in Clean the Ranks movement
Meng Kun	YDY's teacher and professor of Chinese literature at Beida
Nie Yuanzi	Woman cadre in Beida philosophy department; leader of New Beida Red Guard group
Niu Huiling	Leader of Beida's Jinggang Mountain Red Guard group

Pang Wenjun	Beida history professor; attacked in Cultural Revolution, later a member of Liang Xiao
Peng Zhen	Mayor of Beijing, 1951–1966; early Cultural Revolution target
Song Bolin	Vice-leader of Liang Xiao
Tang Dan	YDY's daughter, born in 1953
Tang Shuang	YDY's son, born in 1957
Tang Yijie	YDY's husband, usually called Lao Tang
Tang Yongtong	YDY's father-in-law, a scholar of Buddhism and president of Beida, 1949–1952
Tao Qun	YDY's Beida neighbor; friend at cadre school
Wang Lianlong	Vice-commissar of PLA's 8341 Unit; head of army and workers propaganda team at Beida
Wang Ming	YDY's student; criticized for essay about Three Red Banners
Wang Shimin	Vice-leader of Liang Xiao
Wang Yonggan	Student killed in accident at cadre school
Widow Huang	Suspected secret society leader in Xiaohongmen
Xia Zhang	A Jinggang Mountain Red Guard leader; friend of Tang Dan
Xiao Pan	PLA journalism student at Changping
Xie Jingyi	Vice-chairman of Qinghua revolutionary committee
Yang Dama	*Ayi* for YDY's children
Yang Li	Leader of sent-down women cadres in Zhaitang
Ye Qun	Lin Biao's wife
Zhang Chengxian	Leader of second Party work team sent to Beida in June 1966
Zhang Longxiang	Vice-president of Beida in 1977
Zhang Panshi	Leader of first Party work team sent to Beida in 1964
Zhang Tiesheng	Student famous for submitting a blank exam paper
Zhou Peiyuan	President of Beida, 1977–1980
Zhu Jiayu	YDY's fellow student and closest friend

Terms

Anti-rightist Campaign	The Communist Party's repressive reaction, starting in June 1957, to the criticisms in the Hundred Flowers movement

ayi	A woman who helps with housework and child care
Babaoshan	The principal cemetery and crematorium in the southwest suburb of Beijing
Beida	Beijing National University, China's leading university of humanities and social sciences
Clean the Class Ranks Movement	A movement started in late 1968 to purge officials attacked in the Cultural Revolution
Clean and Investigate Campaign	A movement started in the spring of 1976 to purge persons suspected of supporting the Tiananmen Incident
dazibao	Wall posters, big-character posters; the common mode of expression in the Cultural Revolution
Earth faction	A major Red Guard group, including Beida's Jinggang Mountain, opposed to Nie Yuanzi and the Heaven faction
Five black types	Landlords, rich peasants, counterrevolutionaries, bad elements, rightists
Five same-thing teachers	Teachers who eat, live, labor, study, and reform their thoughts together with students: a Cultural Revolution goal
Four Clean-ups	A phase of the Socialist Education Movement in 1964: intended to rectify politics, the economy, organization, and ideology
Four olds	Old ideas, culture, customs, and habits: a Cultural Revolution slogan, 1966
Gang of Four	Jiang Qing, Zhang Chunqiao, Yao Wenyuan, and Wang Hongwen: blamed for the radical excesses of the Cultural Revolution
Great Leap Forward	A wildly extravagant production drive in 1958, which established the communes and ended in famine
Heaven faction	A major Red Guard group, including Xin Beida, that supported Nie Yuanzi
Hundred Flowers	A period in the spring of 1957 when intellectuals responded to Mao's call to express freely their opinions about the Party
Jet airplane ride	A humiliating and painful posture imposed on Red Guard victims
jin	In old China, a *catty*: about 1⅓ pounds; in today's China, half a kilo: 1.1 pounds
Jinggang Mountain	An important Red Guard group, affiliated with the Earth faction, generally less radical and opposed to Nie Yuanzi

kang	A heated platform in North China houses for sleeping and sitting
Liang Xiao	A group of scholars from Qinghua and Beida originally formed to prepare analytical criticism of Lin Biao
mao	Ten cents (roughly five American cents)
mou	Approximately one-sixth of an acre
Occupied and Anti-Occupied Struggle	A 1964 debate over educational policy which foreshadowed the Cultural Revolution
Qinghua	China's leading science and engineering university, close to Beida
Qingming	A second lunar month festival to honor ancestors and sweep their graves; popular attempts to honor Zhou Enlai on that day in 1976 were suppressed
Red Guards	A self-description coined by students in the Cultural Revolution
Renda	People's University, Beijing
Socialist Education Movement	The attempt, 1962–1966, to deal with problems, chiefly rural, caused by the Great Leap Forward; disagreements in implementation led into the Cultural Revolution
Three points in a straight line	The university library, dining hall, and dormitory: a Cultural Revolution accusation used to emphasize the need for a new educational policy
Three Red Banners	The Great Leap Forward, the people's communes, and the general line for socialist construction
Three Separations	The separation of the university from practice, politics, and manual labor
Tiananmen Incident	On April 5, 1976, large crowds protested the removal of wreaths honoring Zhou Enlai from the Martyrs Cenotaph in Tiananmen Square
The Triple Evils	Subjectivism, sectarianism, and bureaucratism: targets of a rectification campaign in April 1957
Two Erroneous Viewpoints	That knowledge is a private possession, and that education can disregard politics
wok	The shallow, round-bottomed Chinese cooking vessel
Yiguandao	A secret society in North China
yuan	The Chinese "dollar" (roughly 50 American cents)

INDEX

Compositor: G&S Typesetters, Inc.
Text: 10/13 Palatino
Display: Palatino
Printer: Edwards Brothers, Inc.
Binder: Edwards Brothers, Inc.